Movies and American Society

Wiley Blackwell Readers in American Social and Cultural History

Series Editor: Jacqueline Jones, Brandeis University

The Wiley Blackwell Readers in American Social and Cultural History series introduces students to well-defined topics in American history from a sociocultural perspective. Using primary and secondary sources, the volumes present the most important works available on a particular topic in a succinct and accessible format designed to fit easily into courses offered in American history or American studies.

Published:

American Indians
edited by Nancy Shoemaker

The Civil Rights Movement
edited by Jack E. Davis

The Old South
edited by Mark M. Smith

American Radicalism
edited by Daniel Pope

American Technology
edited by Carroll Pursell

American Religious History
edited by Amanda Porterfield

Colonial American History
edited by Kirsten Fischer and Eric Hinderaker

Movies and American Society, Second Edition
edited by Steven J. Ross

Slavery and Emancipation
edited by Rick Halpern and Enrico Dal Lago

American Environmental History
edited by Louis Warren

American Sexual Histories, Second Edition
edited by Elizabeth Reis

Popular Culture in American History, Second Edition
edited by Jim Cullen

Movies and American Society

Second Edition

Edited by Steven J. Ross

WILEY Blackwell

This edition first published 2014
© 2014 John Wiley & Sons, Inc.

Registered Office
John Wiley & Sons, Ltd, The Atrium, Southern Gate, Chichester, West Sussex,
PO19 8SQ, UK

Editorial Offices
350 Main Street, Malden, MA 02148–5020, USA
9600 Garsington Road, Oxford, OX4 2DQ, UK
The Atrium, Southern Gate, Chichester, West Sussex, PO19 8SQ, UK

For details of our global editorial offices, for customer services, and for information
about how to apply for permission to reuse the copyright material in this book
please see our website at www.wiley.com/wiley-blackwell.

The right of Steven J. Ross to be identified as the author(s) of the editorial material
in this work has been asserted in accordance with the UK Copyright, Designs and
Patents Act 1988.

Library of Congress Cataloging-in-Publication Data is available for this title

ISBN (pb): 9780470673645

A catalogue record for this book is available from the British Library

Cover image: First-nighters posing for the camera outside the Warners' Theater before
the premiere of *Don Juan* with John Barrymore, New York City, August 6, 1926. The Art
Archive/National Archives Washington DC
Cover design by Simon Levy

Set in 10/12.5pt Plantin by SPi Publisher Services, Pondicherry, India
Printed in Malaysia by Ho Printing (M) Sdn Bhd

1   2014

Contents

Preface

The past may always remain the same, but the ways in which we understand and look at it changes over time. The recent wars in Afghanistan and Iraq have generated an unprecedented array of filmic representations of the conflict: films taken by combat soldiers, those produced by documentarians, and feature films made by commercial studios. Consequently, I have added a new chapter to this volume, "American Film in the Age of Terror: The Wars in Afghanistan and Iraq," that features an essay by Susan Carruthers, a number of pertinent documents, and suggested readings and screenings. I have also selected new essays for Chapter 9, now retitled "Race, Violence, and Film: From the Blaxploitation Era of the 1960s to the 'Hood-Homeboy' Movies of the 1990s," and for Chapter 13, "Hollywood Goes Global: The Internationalization of American Cinema."

The second edition's biggest change comes in the Readings and Screenings sections. I have updated the suggested readings in every chapter with an eye toward providing students with fully current bibliographies they can use for writing essays or term papers, or simply learning more about a subject they find interesting. As for screenings, videos are now a thing of the past. Consequently, the films I recommend can be seen on DVD or downloaded from popular websites such as Netflix, Voodo, Hulu, and YouTube. Many older films can also be viewed on Turner Classic Movies (TCM). *VideoHound's Golden Movie Retriever 2013* (Farmington Hills, MI: Gale, 2012) offers an excellent guide to movies "on all home entertainment formats." For websites that can help you locate more obscure silent era productions, see www.silentera.com and http://www.welcometosilent movies.com (both last accessed August 2013).

Steven J. Ross

Preface to the First Edition

Most of us go to the movies to have fun: to laugh, cry, boo, cheer, be scared, thrilled, or simply to be amused for a few hours. But movies are something more than just an evening's entertainment. They are also historical documents that help us see – and perhaps more fully understand – the world in which they were made. *Movies and American Society* is designed to introduce students and general readers to recent scholarship in film history and to expose them to new ways of thinking about the relationship between movies and American society. In assembling this volume, my goal was to use film as a prism into the beliefs, values, stereotypes, prejudices, and aspirations of the past. I was less concerned with discussing the aesthetics or inner workings of movies – something others have done quite well – than with seeing them as historical agents. I wanted to show how movies addressed, or failed to address, the critical problems of the age.

The volume's 12 chapters survey the landscape of American film and American history from the early twentieth century to the present. The collection explores ideas and problems relating to the Progressive era, the Roaring Twenties, the Depression and New Deal, World War II, the Cold War, domestic life in the 1950s, Civil Rights, the Vietnam War, the Reagan revolution, and the internationalization of Hollywood. This is a volume of social and cultural history without the politics taken out. Essays and documents illuminate the ways in which a wide array of problems – as well as contemporaneous ideas about class, race, gender, ethnicity, and politics – were portrayed on the screen during each era. Taken collectively, they also reveal how those portrayals changed over time. Although there are many different kinds of films, the material in this volume focuses largely on narrative fiction films and, to a lesser degree, on newsreels and documentaries.

Each chapter contains five basic parts: a brief set of introductory remarks that place the subsequent essay and documents in their historical context and highlight the key issues raised by the author; an essay that explores how movies made during a specific period dealt with problems of the time; a series of discussion points that students might keep in mind while reading the essay; a number of primary documents (many of which have never appeared in any previous collection); and a readings and screening section that lists books and films for those interested in pursuing a particular topic in greater depth. In selecting the main essays, I looked for two key qualities: articles or book chapters that explicitly addressed the relationship between film and society during a particular era, and were written in a clear, jargon-free prose that could be understood on the first reading. The essays have all been edited down to about 20 pages. I generally eliminated all endnotes except for direct quotations.

Reading about movies should be fun, as well as instructive. To that end, I have included documents that offer a glimpse into some of the social practices and controversies surrounding movies. In addition to more serious discussions of the positive and negative impact of film, documents also reveal how havoc occasionally broke out in theaters when early audiences mistook a fly that flew into a projection lens for a monster, or how parents worried about teenagers making out at the movies, or gossip columnist Hedda Hopper's amazement at discovering that teen idol James Dean was quite a smart and perceptive young man (who showed up for his interview on time!). Above all, I wanted to present documents that offer us a sense of how audiences responded to movies and moviegoing – something that historians and cinema scholars acknowledge as crucial but difficult to determine.

The Readings and Screening section contains a list of recommended books that place films within their historical context. Since this volume stresses the importance of using films as historical documents, I only recommend movies made *at the time* about the problems of the time. That means I do not list a film like *Hester Street* (made in 1975) to talk about immigrant life in the early twentieth century. Rather, I suggest that those interested in learning more about life on New York's Lower East Side watch D. W. Griffith's *The Musketeers of Pig Alley* (made in 1912). One last caveat: because it is important to *see* the movies you read about, almost all the films I recommend can be rented or purchased on video or DVD. One of the best places to find them is the Internet Movie Database (us.imdb.com) which, in addition to providing movie credits, lists whether a film is available on video or DVD in the United States and Europe. Outlets for purchasing films include Kino Video, 333 West 39th Street, Suite 503, New York, NY 10018 (www.kino.com); Video

Yesteryear, Box C, Sandy Hook, CT 06482–0847 (www.videoyesteryear. com); and Facets Multimedia, 1517 West Fullerton Ave, Chicago, IL 60614 (www.facets.org). Copies of more obscure films can also be ordered from the Library of Congress (lcweb.loc.gov/rr/mopic/), but be warned that their duplication fees are much higher than the cost of most video purchases.

There are a number of excellent studies of movies and the movie industry that cover several decades of film – if not the entire twentieth century. Rather than list them over and over again, let me recommend them right here. The best single volume history of the relationship between film and American society is Robert Sklar, *Movie-Made America: A Cultural History of American Film* (New York: Vintage Books, 1975, revised 1994). I also recommend Garth Jowett's film *The Democratic Art: A Social History of American Film* (Boston: Little, Brown and Company, 1976). For works that offer a century-long look at movies, politics, and society, see Brian Neve, *Film and Politics in America: A Social Tradition* (London and New York: Routledge, 1992); Terry Christensen, *Reel Politics: American Political Movies from* Birth of a Nation *to* Platoon (New York and Oxford: Basil Blackwell, 1987); and James Combs, *American Political Movies: An Annotated Filmography of Feature Films* (New York and London: Garland Publishers, 1990).

No scholar ever works in total isolation. A number of people offered helpful suggestions about articles and book chapters to include in the collection: Benjamin Alpers, John Bodnar, Robert Lindsey, and Thomas Wartenberg. Several friends looked over early drafts of the table of contents and suggested readings that made this a better collection. Thanks to Ron Gottesman, Sumiko Higashi, James Kraft, Lynn Luciano, Lary May, George Potamianos, and Lynn Spigel. I am especially grateful to several other friends who read and commented on the volume's introduction: Bill Deverell, Phil Ethington, Nancy Fitch, Dana Polan, Michael Renov, Vanessa Schwartz, Robert Slayton, and Leila Zenderland.

On the production end, my editors at Blackwells, Susan Rabinowitz and Ken Provencher, were incredibly gracious and patient with me. Jackie Newman was enormously helpful and resourceful in securing the rights for the various essays and documents. I want to thank Susan Faludi for helping me get permission to reprint her wonderful book chapter. Finally, my last and most heartfelt acknowledgment goes to my family. My children, Lydia and Gaby, are always ready to go to the movies with daddy. My wife, Linda Kent, who makes movies rather than just writing about them, has been my best friend, toughest editor, and loving companion for almost two decades.

Source Acknowledgments

The editor and publisher gratefully acknowledge the permission granted to reproduce the copyright material in this book.

Chapter 1 article: Richard Butsch, "The Celluloid Stage: Nickelodeon Audiences," in *The Making of American Audiences: From Stage to Television, 1750–1990* (New York and Cambridge, UK: Cambridge University Press, 2000), 139–157, 339–45. © Richard Butsch 2000. Reprinted with permission of Cambridge University Press.

Chapter 2 article: Kay Sloan, "Front Page Movies" in *The Loud Silents: Origins of the Social Problem Film* (Urbana and Chicago: University of Illinois Press, 1988), 1–16, 130–32. Reprinted with permission.

Chapter 3 article: Steven J. Ross, "Fantasy and Politics: Movies and Moviegoing in the 1920s" in *Working-Class Hollywood: Silent Film and the Shaping of Class in America* (Princeton, NJ: Princeton University Press, 1998), 173–211, 327–38. Reprinted with permission.

Chapter 4 article: Gregory D. Black, "Hollywood Censored: The Production Code Administration and the Hollywood Film Industry, 1930–1940." *Film History*, 3 (1989), 167–89. © 1989 University of Indiana Press. Reprinted with permission of University of Indiana Press.

Chapter 5 article: Lary May, "The Recreation of America: Hybrid Moviemakers and the Multicultural Republic," in *The Big Tomorrow: Hollywood and the Politics of the American Way* (Chicago and London: University of Chicago Press, 2000), 55–99. Reprinted with permission of University of Chicago Press.

Chapter 6 article: Thomas Cripps, "Others' Movies," in *Hollywood's High Noon: Moviemaking and Society Before Television* (Baltimore and

London: Johns Hopkins University Press, 1997), 118–39. © 1997 The Johns Hopkins University Press. Reprinted with permission of Johns Hopkins University Press.

Chapter 6 document 3: John H. Winge, "Some New American Documentaries in Defense of Liberty." *Sight and Sound*, Spring 1939. Reprinted with kind permission of Sight and Sound, British Film Institute.

Chapter 7 article: John Belton, "Hollywood and the Cold War," in *American Cinema/American Culture* (New York: McGraw-Hill, Inc., 1994), 233–54. Reprinted with permission of McGraw-Hill Education.

Chapter 8 article: Leonard Quart and Albert Auster, "The Fifties," in *American Film and Society Since 1945* (New York and Westport: Praeger, 1991), 41–70. Reprinted with permission of ABC CLIO LLC.

Chapter 8 document 1: "Teen Idol: Hedda Hopper Interviews James Dean." *Chicago Tribune-New York News*, March 27, 1955. Reprinted with permission.

Chapter 8 document 2: Reviews of *Rebel Without a Cause. Cue*, October 29, 1955; Bosley Crowther, *New York Times*, October 30, 1955. © 1955 The New York Times. All rights reserved. Used by permission and protected by the Copyright Laws of the United States. The printing, copying, redistribution, or retransmission of this Content without express written permission is prohibited. Reprinted with permission of *The New York Times* via Pars International.

Chapter 9 article: Ed Guerrero, "Black Violence as Cinema: From Cheap Thrills to Historical Agonies," in J. David Slocum, ed., *Violence and American Cinema* (New York and London: Routledge, 2001), 211–25. Reprinted with permission of Taylor and Francis USA.

Chapter 9 document 1: *Variety* Reports Audience Reactions to *Guess Who's Coming to Dinner?* Issues of *Variety*, February 28 to October 16, 1968. Reprinted with permission of *Variety*.

Chapter 9 document 2: Alvin F. Poussaint, "Blaxploitation Movies: Cheap Thrills That Degrade Blacks," *Psychology Today*, 7(9) (February 1974), 22, 26–27, 30, 32, 98. Reprinted with permission of the author.

Chapter 10 article: Michael Ryan and Douglas Kellner, "Vietnam and the New Militarism," in *Camera Politica: The Politics and Ideology of Contemporary Hollywood Film* (Bloomington and Indianapolis, IN; Indiana University Press, 1988), 194–216, 316–17. © 1988 University of Indiana Press. Reprinted with permission.

Chapter 10 document 3: Jay Sharbutt, "Reunion: Men of a Real Platoon." *Los Angeles Times*, February 7, 1987. Reprinted with permission.

Chapter 11 article: Susan Faludi, "Fatal and Fetal Visions: The Backlash in the Movies," in *Backlash: The Undeclared War Against American Women* (New York: Anchor Books, 1991), 112–39. Copyright © 1991 by Susan Faludi. Used by permission of Crown Books, an imprint of the Crown Publishing Group, a division of Random House LLC. All rights reserved. Any third party use of this material, outside of this publication, is prohibited. Interested parties to apply directly to Random House for permission.

Chapter 11 document 2: Phyllis Schlafly, "A Backlash Manifesto," in *The Power of the Positive Woman* (New Rochell, NY: Arlington House Publishers, 1977), 9–20. Copyright © Phyllis Schlafly. Reprinted with kind permission of the author.

Chapter 11 document 3: Richard Cohen, "A New Stereotype: The Crazy Career Woman." *Washington Post*, October 6, 1987. Reprinted with permission. © 1987 Washington Post Company. All rights reserved. Used by permission and protected by the Copyright Laws of the United States. The printing, copying, redistribution, or retransmission of this Content without express written permission is prohibited.

Chapter 12 article: Susan L. Carruthers, "Limited Engagement: The Iraq War on Film," in Cynthia Lucia, Roy Grundmann, and Art Simon, eds, *The Wiley-Blackwell History of American Film*, vol. IV (Malden, MA and Oxford: Wiley-Blackwell, 2012), 472–94. Reprinted with permission of John Wiley and Sons Ltd.

Chapter 12 document 1: Tom Streithorst, "Why Iraq War Films Fail." *Prospect*, March 17, 2010. www.prospectmagazine.co.uk/magazine/why-iraq-war-films-fail/ (last accessed July 2013). Reprinted with permission of Prospect Publishing Limited.

Chapter 12 document 2: John Markert, "Total Receipts and Production Costs for for Films About Afghanistan and Iraq." Chart taken from www.the-numbers.com (last accessed August 2013). Reprinted with permission.

Chapter 13 article: Tyler Cowen, "Why Hollywood Rules the World, and Whether We Should Care," in *Creative Destruction: How Globalization is Changing the World's Cultures* (Princeton, NJ: Princeton University Press, 2004), 73–101. Reprinted with permission of Princeton University Press.

Chapter 13 document 2: Motion Picture Association of America, Inc., "Global Box Office Climb Continues in 2011," report released March 22, 2012, www.mpaa.org/resources/9308dcf8-c857-4fbe-89e0-0255d193288b.pdf (last accessed August 2013). Reprinted with permission of MPAA (Motion Picture Association of America, Inc.).

Every effort has been made to trace copyright holders and to obtain their permission for the use of copyright material. The publisher apologizes for any errors or omissions in the above list and would be grateful if notified of any corrections that should be incorporated in future reprints or editions of this book.

Introduction:
Why Movies Matter

From the appearance of the first films in the 1890s until the present, movies were never just a medium of entertainment. They have simultaneously reflected *and* shaped changes in American society. What audiences see, a *New York Times* reporter observed in 1923, "is partly a reflection of what they are. And what they are is no less influenced by what they see." Several years later, movie industry leader and former US Postmaster General Will Hays spoke glowingly of the medium's ability to influence popular fashions and consumer habits. "No longer does the girl in Sullivan, Indiana, guess what the styles are going to be in three months. She knows, because she sees them on the screen." Likewise, the "head of the house sees a new kind of golf suit in the movies and he wants one. . . . Perhaps the whole family gets a new idea for redecorating and refurnishing the parlor – and down they go to the dealers to ask for the new goods."[1]

Movies do more than simply show us how to dress, how to look, or what to buy. They teach us how to think about race, gender, class, ethnicity, and politics. And they do so in a way that penetrates our consciousness far more effectively than most things we read or hear in the classroom. Unlike a book, longtime Pennsylvania movie censor Ellis Paxson Oberholtzer remarked in 1922, a movie "sinks into the consciousness without turning the page. It is presented in a vivid, impressive form, a form which all but the smallest child can unmistakably understand." For better or worse, many Americans pay far closer attention to the politics they see on the screen than to the pronouncements of politicians or civic leaders. As Republican Senator Arlen Specter recently noted: "Quite candidly, when Hollywood speaks, the world listens. Sometimes when Washington speaks, the world snoozes."[2]

Movies are also more than just images on the screen. They are part of the social glue of American life. Going to the movies and watching films quickly emerged as a common cultural denominator that provided a wide variety of Americans with similar social rituals. By 1914, every American town with a population over 5,000 had at least one movie theater; six years later, 50 million Americans – nearly one-half the population – regularly flocked to one of the nation's 15,000 theaters each week or to one of the 22,000 churches, union halls, school, or voluntary associations that screened movies. By 1930, weekly admission figures approached 100 percent of the nation's population.[3]

For over 100 years, movies have served as a powerful means of disseminating ideas to millions of people who would eagerly watch on the screen things they might hesitate to read about. In shaping our vision of the promises and problems of American life, movies matter the most about the things which we know the least. People who had little daily contact with unionists, radicals, feminists, gays and lesbians, African Americans, Latinos, Asians, and various other minority groups were most likely to be influenced by what they saw on the screen – especially if they were exposed to the same kinds of images over and over again until they came to assume the appearance of "reality." Movies, suggests psychiatrist Alvin F. Poussaint, are "at least partially responsible for teaching blacks and whites that Africans were savages, and that their Afro-American descendants were lazy, happy-go-lucky, thieving, sexually promiscuous, and mentally inferior."[4]

The battle among filmmakers to create and perpetuate a dominant set of images about class, race, gender, ethnicity, and political life was nothing less than a battle to control the mind's eye of millions of citizens. Take for example the question of class. During the first three decades of the twentieth century, when dramatic changes in production created great confusion over class identities (particularly among the rapidly expanding ranks of white-collar and service-sector workers), many Americans gained their understanding of what it meant to be working class, middle class, or upper class by watching movies. Filmmakers translated abstract ideas about class identity and class conflict into vivid images that people could *see* and understand. Many Americans got their first glimpse of what a capitalist, socialist, or union organizer looked liked by watching movies. Whether white-collar men and women would think of themselves as working class or middle class, and whether public opinion would support unions or big business might well be decided by what people saw on the screen. The same also held true for competing images of women: Was it "better" to be a working woman or a housewife? A sexually fast flapper or a sexually modest "good" girl? A heterosexual or a lesbian?

As the first great medium of mass culture and mass persuasion, movies have played an important role in the civic, as well as the social, life of the nation. The motion picture industry emerged at a time when businesses were busily developing new techniques of mass persuasion. Advertising agencies and attitudinal studies were being used by a wide variety of organizations to measure and shape public consciousness. Movies were a logical extension of these developments. People in all walks of life spoke of film's remarkable potential for reaching unprecedented numbers of Americans with all kinds of ideas. Newspapers were certainly the main medium of political information at the turn of the century, but their ability to reach a mass audience was limited by the fact that some people preferred to read papers that were closely tied to a political party, while others preferred to read a native-language periodical.

Movies offered filmmakers a new way to reach a mass citizenry, a cinematic public sphere that could be used to communicate ideas and shape public opinion. "By 'public sphere'," political theorist Jürgen Habermas explained, "we mean first of all a domain of our social life in which such a thing as public opinion can be formed. Access to the public sphere is open in principle to all citizens." Movies fit this definition in two key ways: they convey a variety of ideas to a vast array of people, and, they could be made – at least until the late 1910s – by anyone with access to several thousand dollars. Unlike newspapers, movies reached a genuinely mass audience that cut across class, ethnicity, gender, race, religion, age, geography, and political affiliation. "The tremendous propaganda power of the hundred thousand projectors," radical filmmaker William Kruse proclaimed in October 1924, "outshines all the newspapers, magazines, pulpits, lecture platforms, and public libraries put together."[5]

When most people hear the word "Hollywood" they think of multi-million dollar productions made by wealthy studios that feature famous movie stars, dazzling special effects, and plots that generally avoid political controversy. But the movie industry was not always this way. In 1910, Hollywood, California, was a sleepy town of fewer than 4,000 residents with no movie studios. The movie industry began as a relatively small-scale, highly decentralized business with hundreds of producers, distributors, and exhibitors scattered throughout the country. During the first two decades of the twentieth century – and especially before the rise of the powerful studio system that came to be known as "Hollywood" – the relatively low costs of making films ($400–1,000 a reel in many instances) allowed diverse groups we would not usually associate with filmmaking to participate in this fledgling industry. Quickly grasping the medium's potential for "political, social, religious propaganda, for muckraking ... [and] for revolutionary ideas," organizations as politically diverse as the Women's Political Union, the Ford Motor Company, the Socialist Party, the National Association of Manufacturers, the American Federation of Labor, the Russell Sage Foundation, and various religious groups and government agencies produced films that presented their causes to a mass public. Exhibitors' constant need for fare to fill their daily bill meant that these movies would be shown in hundreds or thousands of movie theaters.[6]

While primarily devoted to entertaining millions of Americans, movies also served as a new kind of political communication, a medium that combined entertainment and politics in a highly accessible form. Many filmmakers did not see a separation between entertainment and the obligations of citizenship. "The camera is the agent of Democracy," famed director D. W. Griffith wrote in 1921. "It levels the barriers between classes and races." Emerging in the midst of the Progressive era, a time of unbridled optimism when many Americans believed they could solve the problems of society, motion pictures quickly became part of an expanding public sphere in which competing political ideas were discussed and public opinion molded. Movies succeeded in bringing the problems of the age to life in a way no other medium could rival. Ideas previously confined to the written or spoken word now moved across the screen in marvelously realistic and compelling fashion. And because movies were mass produced, copies of the same film could be shown simultaneously in large cities and small towns across the country. Comparing the impact of movies to newspapers, one reporter noted in 1908: "Far more people are today reached by the moving picture than by the daily press, [and] while we read the newspaper only in parts, the moving picture we see complete."[7]

From the start, filmmakers understood that what people saw at the movies could – and often did – affect their decisions as voters. Filmmakers continually entered into the most controversial national debates of the age. Movies depicting the evils of child labor, the demand for women's suffrage, the financial hardships of the elderly, the tragedy of racism, and the problems of sexual discrimination helped raise public consciousness and in so doing helped ease passage of bills aimed at remedying these problems.[8]

The outbreak of World War I precipitated dramatic changes in the evolution of the American movie industry and the politics of American film. In 1914, the United States produced approximately half the world's movies; by 1919, with European film production in shambles, that figure rose to 90 percent. During the 1920s, Hollywood – the place and the way of doing business – came to assume its modern identity. The geographically scattered array of small and medium-sized producers, distributors, and exhibitors of the early years was supplanted by an increasingly oligarchic, vertically integrated studio system with production centered in Los Angeles and business offices in New York. Movies became a multimillion dollar industry and as in other industries, the most successful companies increased their profits by securing greater control over the market and expanding into new areas. By the end of the 1920s, eight major studios controlled over 90 percent of the films made and distributed in the United States: Paramount, Fox, Metro-Goldwyn-Mayer, Warner Brothers, Universal, United Artists, Columbia, and RKO.[9]

The devastating economic impact of the Great Depression and the increased expenses of making "talking" pictures in the early 1930s drove many smaller companies out of business. Yet studios and independent filmmakers continued to make movies about the most vexing problems of the times. As cinematic tough guy Edward G. Robinson explained in 1938: "While all pictures have to be made from the primary standpoint of entertainment, every now and then there is an opportunity to combine entertainment and larger implications that 'point up' social aspects and encourage social awareness." The Hollywood studio system dominated the world market until the late 1940s and early 1950s, when challenges from television and court decisions ordering the separation of production and exhibition wings weakened its near monopolistic hold on the industry – at least until 1985, when the Department of Justice overruled the 1948 antitrust decision. This sparked a new round of mergers and corporate takeovers that once again placed Hollywood studios at the forefront of the world market.[10]

The essays and documents in this collection reveal many of the themes and ideas discussed by filmmakers and audiences from the silent era to the present. Progressive-era cinema, as our readings suggest, dealt with issues of concern to a broad range of reformers and often presented solutions to those problems. The renewed prosperity of the 1920s led to movies that stressed new ideas about the promises of consumption and the end of old ideas about the conflictual nature of class relations. Cross-class fantasy films with plots involving a rich boy/girl who marries a poor girl/boy set a pattern of romantic fantasies that would be replicated in more recent times by extravagant features like *Titanic* (1997). During the 1930s, audiences regularly watched films about "Sexual liaisons unsanctified by the laws of God or man . . . ethnic lines crossed and racial barriers ignored . . . economic injustice exposed and political corruption assumed . . . vice unpunished and virtue unrewarded . . . in sum, pretty much the raw stuff of American culture, unvarnished and unveiled."[11] With the outbreak of war in Europe in 1939 and America's entry into the conflict in December 1941, studios produced films stressing themes of national unity, harmony, patriotism, and the heroic struggles of our men and women fighting abroad. Once the war ended, filmmakers grappled with an array of issues ranging from the difficulties of postwar readjustment to the threat of Communist invaders to the problems of anti-Semitism, the Korean War, juvenile delinquency, racial discrimination, and drug and alcohol abuse. Updated versions of these themes continued to fill the screen into the twenty-first century. During the 1960s, 1970s, and 1980s, audiences were also exposed to new cinematic debates about black militancy, the Vietnam War, the role of the American military after Vietnam, the problems of being a man or woman in an age of sexual revolution – and then in an era of conservative backlash – and the pleasures and dangers of the new world of Yuppie (young urban professional) prosperity. Finally, the globalization of the movie industry in the second half of the twentieth century created a new set of questions concerning the extent to which big-budget Hollywood films with foreign financing, foreign directors, foreign writers, and foreign stars – and aimed at a world audience – reflected American values and culture.

Audiences and the Impact of Movies

Filmmakers have repeatedly confronted the most controversial issues of their day. But did anyone pay attention? What happened when the lights went on and people left the theater? What impact did movies have on audiences? These are difficult questions to answer with any certainty for audience reactions to movies were as varied and complicated as the people who watched them. Film scholars often analyze reception in terms of movie patrons' reactions to a particular film. This approach to reception is too narrow, for the impact of film often extended far beyond the movie theater and affected more than just the immediate audience. To assess the collective power of movies, we need to expand our notion of the "audience" and the arenas in which reception occurs. Audiences included not just ticketholders sitting in movie houses, but people outside the theater who reacted strongly to what was shown on the screen: censors, government officials, police, religious and civic leaders, capitalists, union officials, and a wide range of organizations that represented special interest groups. We might refer to these varied groups as reactive audiences.

Movies can change the ways in which people think about themselves and their world, but how they do so is a subject of heated debate among scholars. Initial scholarship about audience reception focused on what is known as the "hypodermic needle" approach: that is, scholars and critics assumed that audiences interpreted films in the way filmmakers intended them to do. In short, they assumed that audiences were blank slates upon whom producers could easily impose their message. This approach was adopted by intellectuals who emphasized the allegedly manipulative powers of mass culture. Neo-Marxist theorists (from Frankfurt School writers of the 1930s and 1940s to New Left radicals of the 1960s and 1970s) and conservative "mass society" critics of the Cold War era tended to portray movies, radio, and television as activities imposed from above upon gullible audiences. Movies, they argued, were designed to preserve the status quo rather than to make people question the fundamental tenets of their society.[12]

During the past few decades, a new generation of scholars has rejected the idea that people must be "cultural dopes" and documented the ways in which audiences interpreted films. European and American scholars showed how movies and other forms of mass culture served as contested terrains of resistance and accommodation to the dominant and alternative ideas and values of society. Rejecting the concept that audiences were blank slates, they demonstrated that moviegoers did not passively accept everything that was shown on the screen. Movie theaters were fluid social centers in which many messages could be seen and heard. People's responses to films were shaped by the environment in which they viewed movies and by their class, race, gender, ethnicity, religion, and political beliefs.[13]

These general views about reception were complemented by studies that detailed how audiences protested against films which they believed reflected badly on their lives or the life of the nation. African Americans launched massive demonstrations to halt the exhibition of D. W. Griffith's *The Birth of a Nation* (1915); Catholic groups such as the National Legion of Decency threatened boycotts of all Hollywood films during the 1930s unless filmmakers curbed excessive displays of sex, violence, and crime; anti-Communist conservatives effectively stopped screenings of the radical film *Salt of the Earth* (1954); Italian Americans protested against *The Godfather* (1972), Asian Americans against *Year of the Dragon* (1988), and gay and lesbians against *Basic Instinct* (1992) on the grounds that these films presented negative stereotypes of particular ethnic, racial, and sexual groups.[14]

Throughout the twentieth and twenty-first centuries, people in positions of power – reactive audiences – were deeply concerned about how moviegoers would respond to the images and ideas they saw on the screen. Federal Bureau of Investigation (FBI) director J. Edgar Hoover considered movies about class conflict so dangerous that as early as 1918 he assigned secret agents to monitor the activities of radical filmmakers and send him extensive summaries of their films. Hoover was not being paranoid. Union records and labor newspapers contain repeated reports of how certain movies inspired viewers to launch strikes or to join unions and radical movements. Two decades later, Hoover's agents sent him a report declaring the motion picture industry "as one of the greatest, if not the very greatest, influence upon the minds and cultures, not only of the people of the United States, but the entire world."[15]

Hoover was not the only government official who worried about the impact movies had on audiences. In August 1941, the Senate Subcommittee investigating Moving-Picture and Radio Propaganda, led by isolationist Senators Gerald Nye and Bennett Clark, concluded that movies such as *Confessions of a Nazi Spy* (1939) and *Sergeant York* (1941) had been "used extensively for propaganda purposes designed to influence the public mind in the direction of participation in the European war." Six years later, in his opening remarks before the House Committee on Un-American Activities (HUAC as it was popularly known), conservative Congressman and committee chairman J. Parnell Thomas spoke of "the tremendous effect which moving pictures have on their mass audiences" and observed that "what the citizen sees and hears in his neighborhood movie house carries a powerful impact on his thoughts and behavior."[16]

The persistence of censorship throughout much of the twentieth century further testifies to the perceived power of film. If movies did not really matter, then why have so many people been so determined for so long to prevent audiences from seeing certain kinds of images? Concerned about the potential impact of a medium that bypassed traditional authorities and spoke directly to millions of men, women, and especially children, a wide array of politicians, clergy, reformers, and civic leaders struggled to censor or at least limit what the public could see. They were worried that actions seen on the screen might prompt similar actions off the screen. Censorship began shortly after the appearance of the first nickelodeons in 1905, and by 1926 censorship boards operated in 100 cities and nearly a dozen states. From July 1, 1934 until 1968 external censorship was replaced by internal self-censorship as besieged movie industry leaders agreed to follow a code of "General Principles" that listed what could and could not be shown: no positive portrayals of adultery, no plots siding with evil rather than good, no lurid sex, no nudity, no obscene language, no glorification of criminals, and no ridiculing of religion. The Code, as it was known, survived until 1968 when competition from television and foreign films forced Hollywood to become more daring. That year, the Motion Picture Producers and Distributors Association adopted its current alphabet ratings system.[17]

The concern over film's impact on audiences is no less pronounced today. Civic, religious, and political leaders in both main parties continue to blame movies for fostering violence, criminal behavior, drug addiction, and sexual promiscuity among the nation's youth. "Washington Again Taking on Hollywood" is a newspaper headline that appeared frequently after the tragedy at Columbine High School in 1999, during the presidential campaign in 2000, and most recently during Senate hearings "to restrain Hollywood's pitch to minors – at least when it comes to sexual and violent material." On the other hand, Hollywood leaders staunchly defend movies as agents of world democracy. "The power of film cannot be underestimated," Walt Disney Studio president Richard Frank told Congress in July 1989. "I won't be so bold as to say that American movies are responsible for the popular uprising in China. But I am willing to bet that for more than a few Chinese citizens our films served as an inspiration to strike for something better."[18]

Watching and Talking About Movies

In addition to entertaining people, films can often provide a mechanism for discussing some of the most important ideas of the day. One of the key goals of this collection is to show how films visualized a variety of social, cultural, political, sexual, and economic problems and how these earlier understandings helped shape our own world. To do that, we need ways to talk about the importance of film that go beyond simply saying "I liked it" or "I hated it." We need a language that allows us to discuss how a large body of films dealt with particular issues – and often did so in conflicting ways. The constant repetition of similar images in dozens of films until they become embedded in our minds as "reality" can affect the way we think about the world. As cinema scholar Robert Sklar suggests, the "meaning of American movies lay in the multiple and cumulative messages of the more than ten thousand good, bad, and indifferent films that played selectively across the vision and consciousness of their viewers."[19]

The concepts of ideology and, most especially, discourse offer us fruitful approaches to discussing the collective meaning of film. The distinction between the two is subtle. I propose that we use the term ideology to talk about individual films and the term discourse to describe the cumulative impact of a large group of films that express a similar world view. Ideology is generally defined as a systematic body of ideas about the way the world is or ought to be. Discourse can be thought of as a collection of works (films in this instance) that share a common ideology – be it conservative, liberal, or radical. Discourse is not meant to imply an absolute truth; whether a particular cinematic discourse is true or false is less important than its ability to create a dominant sense of reality. To put this in plain English: it did not matter whether a particular discourse about "proper" gender roles or class relations or what blacks were "really" like was ultimately true or false. What mattered was that viewers would believe one discourse more than another and use it as a way to understand something about gender or class or race.[20]

Discourse teaches us how to think about the normal progression of reality. For example, seeing union workers depicted over and over again as stupid rather than intelligent and as violent rather than peaceful (i.e. a conservative versus a liberal discourse) undoubtedly affects the ways in which those unfamiliar with labor organizations are bound to think about them. Likewise, competing discourses about gender tell us how men and women should act and what happens when individuals follow or deviate from proscribed roles. For example, conservative anti-feminist discourses of the 1920s and the 1980s repeatedly portrayed women who pursued careers over marriage as unhappy, unfulfilled, and ultimately unwomanly. Given this set of logical consequences, who would want to be a career woman?

So how do we use the idea of discourse while watching movies? As former baseball star and one-time movie critic Yogi Berra allegedly said: "You can see a lot just by looking." Students of cinema can begin to understand a particular discourse (or competing discourses) by watching a number of films about a specific topic and seeing the ways in which filmmakers conveyed their ideas through the repeated uses of similar story lines, stock images (are characters being stereotyped? how so?), casting decisions (what does the hero/heroine look like? the villain?), costuming (are characters dressed in appealing or unappealing attire – and what kind of message does each form of attire convey?), and choreography (e.g. conservative films about class conflict choreographed scenes of large groups of workers as a mob, while liberal films depicted them as a crowd). While it is important not to ascribe too much significance to any one film, when seen as part of the collective discourse about a particular phenomenon, a close examination of plots and other cinematic devices can reveal a great deal about the ways in which audiences are taught to understand the "normal" progression of reality.

The images and ideologies we see on the screen can affect our views of the past, the present, and the possibilities for the future. The challenge facing us today, as students and citizens, is to understand how movies have affected and continue to affect our visions of Americans and American society. My hope is that the articles and documents in this collection will provide readers with a modest starting point.

Notes

1　*NewYork Times*, July 1, 1923; Will Hays, "Supervision from Within," in Joseph P. Kennedy, ed., *The Story of Films* (Chicago and New York: A.W. Shaw Company, 1927: reprinted by Jerome S. Ozer Publisher, 1971), 38.

2　Ellis Paxson Oberholtzer, *The Morals of the Movie* (Philadelphia: Penn Publishing Company, 1922), 70; Specter quoted in *Los Angeles Times*, May 30, 1997.

3　For attendance figures, see Russell Merritt, "Nickelodeon Theaters 1905–1914: Building an Audience," in Tino Balio, ed., *The American Film Industry* (Madison, WI: University of Wisconsin Press, 1976), 63; *New York Daily Worker*, April 14, 1924; US Department of Commerce, *Historical Statistics of the United States: Colonial Times to 1970*, 2 vols (Washington, DC: Government Printing Office, 1975), I, 400.

4　Alvin F. Poussaint, "Blaxploitation Movies: Cheap Thrills that Degrade Blacks," *Psychology Today*, 7 (February 1974), 26.

5　Jürgen Habermas, "The Public Sphere," in Chandra Mukerji and Michael Schudson, eds, *Rethinking Popular Culture: Contemporary Perspectives in Cultural Studies* (Berkeley, CA: University of California Press, 1991), 398; *Chicago Daily Worker*, October 6, 1924.

6　"Definition of Censorship Prepared by the National Board of Review of Motion Pictures. 1913," Subject Papers, Box 166, Papers of the National Board of Review of Motion Pictures, Special Collections, New York Public Library.

7　D.W. Griffith, "Innovations and Expectations," in Harry M. Geduld, ed., *Focus On D. W. Griffith* (Englewood Cliffs, NJ: Prentice-Hall, 1971), 56; *Moving Picture World*, October 30, 1908.

8　For discussions of early social problem films as well as films made by various groups outside the movie industry, see Kay Sloan, *The Loud Silents: Origins of the Social Problem Film* (Urbana, IL: University of Illinois Press, 1988); Kevin Brownlow, *Behind the Mask of Innocence: Sex, Violence, Prejudice, Crime: Films of Social Conscience in the Silent Era* (New York: Alfred A. Knopf, 1990); Steven J. Ross, "Cinema and Class Conflict: Labor, Capital, the State, and American Silent Film," in Robert Sklar and Charles Musser, eds, *Resisting Images: Essays on Cinema and History* (Philadelphia: Penn Publishing Company, 1990), 68–107; Steven J. Ross, *Working-Class Hollywood: Silent Film and the Shaping of Class in America* (Princeton, NJ: Princeton University Press, 1998); Shelly Stamp, *Movie-Struck Girls: Women and Motion Picture Culture After the Nickelodeon* (Princeton, NJ: Princeton University Press, 2000).

9   Production figures for 1914 and 1919 are taken from Lewis Jacobs, *The Rise of the American Film* (New York: Teachers College Press, 1968), 159, 287. The rise of Hollywood and the studio system have been described in hundreds of books and articles. The most useful recent works include David Bordwell, Janet Staiger, and Kristin Thompson, *The Classical Hollywood Cinema: Film Style and the Mode of Production to 1960* (New York: Columbia University Press, 1985); Douglas Gomery, *The Hollywood Studio System* (New York: St. Martin's Press, 1986); Thomas Schatz, *The Genius of the System: Hollywood Filmmaking in the Studio Era* (New York: Pantheon, 1988); Ethan Mordden, *The Hollywood Studio System: House Style in the Golden Age of the Movies* (New York: Simon and Schuster, 1988).

10   Edward G. Robinson to Professor Taft, December 22, 1939, Box 29, folder 9, Edward G. Robinson Papers, Special Collections, University of Southern California, Los Angeles, CA. For a look at Hollywood and the studio system in more recent years, see David A. Cook, *Lost Illusions: American Cinema in the Shadow of Watergate and Vietnam, 1970–1979* (New York: Charles Scribner's Sons, 2000); Stephen Prince, *A New Pot of Gold: Hollywood Under the Electronic Rainbow, 1980–1989* (New York: Charles Scribner's Sons, 2000); and Tyler Cowen's essay, "Why Hollywood Rules the World, and Whether We Should Care," in Chapter 13 of this volume.

11   Thomas Doherty, *Pre-Code Hollywood: Pre-Code Hollywood: Sex, Immorality, and Insurrection in American Cinema, 1930–1934* (New York: Columbia University Press, 1999), 2–3.

12   For an overview of various theories about audiences, popular culture, and mass culture, see John Storey, *An Introduction to Cultural Theory and Popular Culture* (Athens, GA: University of Georgia Press, 1998); Dominic Strinati, *An Introduction to Theories of Popular Culture* (London and New York: Routledge, 1995); Donald Lazere, "Introduction: Entertainment as Social Control," in Lazere, ed., *American Media and Mass Culture: Left Perspectives* (Berkeley, CA: University of California Press, 1987), 1–26.

13   Quote from Stuart Hall, "Notes on Deconstructing 'the Popular'," in Raphael Samuel, ed., *People's History and Socialist Theory* (London: Routledge and Kegan Paul, 1981), 232. For a sampling of European and American writing on movies and audiences, see ibid.; Raymond Williams, *Problems in Materialism and Culture* (London: Verso, 1980); Tony Bennett, Colin Mercer, and Janet Woollacott, eds, *Popular Culture and Social Relations* (Milton Keynes, UK: Open University Press, 1986); John Fiske, *Understanding Popular Culture* (Boston, MA: Unwin Hyman, 1989); Roy Rosenzweig, *Eight Hours For What We Will: Workers and Leisure in an Industrial City, 1870–1920* (New York: Cambridge University Press, 1983); Kathy Peiss, *Cheap Amusements: Working Women and Leisure in Turn-of-the-Century New York* (Philadelphia: Temple University Press, 1986); Lizabeth Cohen, *Making a New Deal: Industrial Workers in Chicago, 1919–1939* (New York: Cambridge University Press, 1990); Richard Butsch, *The Making of American Audiences: From Stage to Television, 1750–1990* (New York and

Cambridge, UK: Cambridge University Press, 2000); also see the sources cited in the previous note.

14 For a brief overview of audience protests, see Charles Lyons, "The Paradox of Protest: American Film, 1980–1982," in Francis G. Couvares, ed., *Movie Censorship and American Culture* (Washington and London: Smithsonian Institution Press, 1996), 277–318.

15 Report of Special Agent, "Communist Infiltration of the Motion Picture Industries," October 11, 1943; for further excerpts from this report, see the FBI document in Chapter 7 of this collection. Hoover's surveillance of radical filmmakers and audience responses to their movies are discussed in Steven J. Ross, *Working-Class Hollywood*.

16 1941 Committee hearings quoted in Gerald Mast, ed., *The Movies in Our Midst* (Chicago: University of Chicago Press, 1982), 477; Thomas quoted in John Howard Lawson, *Film in the Battle of Ideas* (New York: Masses and Mainstream, 1953), 12.

17 A series of self-censorship codes were adopted by industry leaders as early as 1924. However, it was not until 1934 that the more stringent Production Code Administration was put into effect. For an overview of censorship and its impact, see Francis G. Couvares, *Movie Censorship and American Culture*, and Chapter 4 of this volume.

18 *Los Angeles Times*, June 21, 2001; Hearings Before the Subcommittee on Telecommunications and Finance of the Committee on Energy and Commerce, House of Representatives on Television Broadcasting and the European Community (Washington, DC: US Government Printing Office, 1990), 51. Richard Frank's testimony is excerpted in Chapter 13 of this volume.

19 Robert Sklar, *Movie-Made America*, 87.

20 For further discussions of ideology and discourse, see Raymond William, *Keywords: A Vocabulary of Culture and Society* (London: Fontana, 1976); Michel Foucault, *Power/Knowledge: Selected Interviews and Other Writings 1972–1979* (New York: Pantheon Books, 1980); Terry Eagleton, *Ideology: An Introduction* (London and New York: Verso, 1991); John Storey, *An Introduction to Cultural Theory and Popular Culture*; Dominic Strinati, *An Introduction to Theories of Popular Culture*.

1

Going to the Movies: Early Audiences

Introduction to Article

Movies were a new form of entertainment for a new century of leisure-hungry Americans. As the average work week decreased and wages rose, men and women sought new ways to spend their increased time and money – and entrepreneurs were happy to accommodate them, for a price. In large cities and small towns, the thirst for fun sparked the rise of a wide range of commercial recreations: amusement parks, dance halls, billiard parlors, vaudeville and burlesque houses, and professional sports. But none of these activities was as popular or widespread as the movies. The first nickelodeon – a term that combined the price of admission with the Greek word for theater – was opened in Pittsburgh on June 19, 1905. The low cost of attending this new institution made it accessible to all but the poorest Americans. By 1910, nearly one-third of the nation flocked to the movies each week; by 1920, weekly attendance equaled 50 percent of the nation's population. People loved the movies.

Richard Butsch looks at nickelodeon audiences and describes what it was like to go to the movies during the early years of silent film. He discusses who went to the movies, what they saw, and what they did. Butsch shows how movie theaters served as community centers for many poor urban residents. Yet, while millions of Americans eagerly

Movies and American Society, Second Edition. Edited by Steven J. Ross.
© 2014 John Wiley & Sons, Inc. Published 2014 by John Wiley & Sons, Inc.

embraced them, numerous civic leaders denounced movies and movie theaters as dangerous entities that posed grave physical, moral, and sexual risks to audiences – especially the nation's children. These moral leaders fought to censor and control what audiences could see and do at the movies. Moviegoing, then, was not a simple activity but one filled with controversy. No new amusement caused greater pleasure and fear than the movies.

Discussion Points

How did various people and groups respond to the promises and problems of the movies? Who opposed the movies and why they did judge them as dangerous? Who supported them? Consider what would happen today if a new form of popular entertainment emerged that was aimed largely at immigrants and poor workers and was located in "bad" or "dangerous" sections of a city. How would various groups – youths, parents, city leaders – respond to such an activity?

The Celluloid Stage: Nickelodeon Audiences

Richard Butsch

Source: Richard Butsch, *The Making of American Audiences: From Stage to Television, 1750–1990* (New York and Cambridge, UK: Cambridge University Press, 2000), 139–57, 339–45

A decade after their first commercial exhibition, millions of people made movies a weekly habit. But who went to the movies in the early days and what was the character of the early movie theaters were matters of debate. Multiple images of movie theaters and audiences vied for acceptance. Reformers and *flâneurs* described movies as immigrant entertainment, yet small-town entrepreneurs promoted it as an entertainment for the middle class. The working-class nickelodeon was described on the one hand as community center and conqueror of the saloon, and on the other as a school for scandal teaching adolescent boys to steal and girls to be promiscuous. The latter image of endangered children represented a shift from the nineteenth-century concern about women's respectability to a twentieth-century fixation on children's welfare, and from the place to the performance as the cause of the problem. This would give rise in the 1920s to research on the effects on children and the beginnings of a mass communication research tradition. In this chapter I will explore how some characterizations were contradicted by the growth of middle-class attendance, but nevertheless continued to fuel popular worries about and eventual research interest in the effects of the media on children.

From Kinetoscope to Nickelodeon

Movies were first shown commercially as a technological novelty, *moving* pictures. It did not much matter *what* was filmed, just that it *moved*. People were intrigued by films of such simple things as smoke puffing from a chimney or waves breaking on a beach. The earliest commercial exhibition was by kinetoscope, a machine through which one person at a time could view the film. For a penny one could view a film lasting about a minute. By the end of 1895 kinetoscopes were operating in most major cities and even small towns like Portage, Wisconsin and Butte, Montana. While kinetoscopes were installed in department stores, hotel lobbies, barrooms, drug stores, and so on, they became identified with penny arcades. The arcade patrons were primarily men and boys, who came to peep through the kinetoscope, often at sexually suggestive films. Movie historian Benjamin Hampton said patrons of arcades, parlors, and dime museums had an insatiable appetite for these movies and went from place to place in search of films they had not seen.

But the kinetoscope fad was brief; by 1900 projector and screen displaced it. Movie projection was commercially demonstrated first in April 1896 at Koster and Bial's Music Hall, the sporting vaudeville theater near Herald Square in New York. A newspaper lithograph shows an audience of men in tails and top hats engrossed in watching the novel demonstration. That same summer movies were included as a novelty in programs of vaudeville houses, amusement parks, traveling exhibitors and lecturers, legitimate theaters, phonograph and kinetoscope parlors, and church groups around the country.

Soon, the Keith vaudeville circuit began to feature movies and other big-time houses followed suit. Movies became the featured "act" and created a boom in "refined" vaudeville between 1898–1900, during which time vaudeville provided the main exhibition outlet for movies. But this novelty also wore off, and until films with more sustaining interest than waves on beaches were produced, it could not hold an audience. By 1900 continuous vaudeville managers began to use the short films as "chasers" to clear the house before the next performance.

Nickelodeons became the next dominant exhibition form. As early as 1895, a few storefronts were converted into motion picture showrooms. They held from 200 to 500 people – the number often limited by theater licensing laws or building codes – who were seated on ordinary kitchen chairs not fastened to the floor. Enterprising arcade owners bought screens and projectors, and opened back rooms to audiences. *Variety* claimed it was "the natural outcome of the Penny Arcade." In 1905, nickelodeons in converted storefronts spread across the country so rapidly that *Billboard* called them the "jack-rabbits of public entertainment" and the *Moving Picture World* said they were "multiplying faster than guinea pigs." By 1910 there were reputedly over 10,000. Even smaller cities had several: Grand Rapids had fifteen in 1908, Youngstown twenty.[1]

Shows ran from morning to night. The films changed each day, encouraging daily attendance. The films were short, about fifteen minutes, and movie projection was erratic. The picture flickered on the screen, and the projector was hand-operated. Nevertheless, the realism was a dramatic change from the sets of cheap melodrama.

Nickelodeon Demographics

Film history tradition has characterized nickelodeon audiences as urban immigrant workers who found in the nickelodeon a place to socialize, and in the movies ideas to negotiate the transition between the old country and their new home. This image derived from a turn-of-the-century fascination with the Lower East Side of New York City by intellectuals who created vivid public images of every aspect of the lives of these poor immigrants, including their attraction to nickelodeons.

Ample evidence does indicate the presence of a substantial working-class audience and of many nickelodeons in immigrant neighborhoods. Nickelodeon was one of very few entertainments affordable to working-class immigrants, and the silent films proved no barrier to their lack of English. In 1910, nickelodeons in Manhattan were concentrated in or on the periphery of tenement neighborhoods filled with immigrants. Progressive reformer Annie MacLean in 1910 found that foreigners preferred nickelodeons over theaters in Johnstown, Pennsylvania. A study of the steel-mill town of Homestead, Pennsylvania, home of many Hungarian and Polish immigrants, describes their situation.

... five cents for a show consisting of songs, moving pictures, etc., which lasts fifteen minutes or so. ... Men on their way home from work stop for a few minutes to see something of life outside the alternation of mill and home; the shopper rests while she enjoys the music, poor though it be, and the children are always begging for five cents to go the nickelodeon.[2] ...

The image of the urban nickelodeon as an immigrant refuge made it inappropriate for middle-class clientele. Lights, posters, and a barker with megaphone outside gave the theater a circus atmosphere and inside it was dark and odorous. The *Moving Picture World* editor said "any person of refinement looked around to see if [he were] likely to be recognized by anyone before entering the doors."[3] The movie exhibition industry and trade press strove to distinguish movie houses from this disreputable nickelodeon image. *Moving Picture World* in 1909 cited the neighborhood Audubon Theater of the Washington Heights neighborhood of Manhattan as a family theater attracting children of the "better classes" and the Parkway Theater at 110th and Central Park West as having "high class character of the patrons ... quite a family aspect."[4]

Recent research looking beyond immigrant working-class neighborhoods finds other sites with other audiences. Movies were popular in cities with few immigrants and small working-class populations, such as Kansas City in 1912. In big cities there were a variety of opportunities for the middle class to go to movies, in better theaters, in vaudeville, or in amusement parks. Middle-class shoppers dropped into nickelodeons along Fourteenth Street and Sixth Avenue in New York – although they attended vaudeville or theater at night.

That the audiences were middle class has been inferred from the geographic location of many nickelodeons on retail streets served by mass transportation within major cities. In Boston before 1910 several movie houses had opened in the central shopping district amid the major department stores, vaudeville houses, and legitimate theaters. The Stanley theater chain began in Philadelphia in the city center, next to the largest department stores. Similarly, Milwaukee movie houses were located near transit lines and shopping streets. In New York in 1908, many were located on main thoroughfares or along transit lines. Seven were located around Union Square, near the refined vaudeville houses of Proctor and Keith. Many others were located in other entertainment streets of the city such as 125th Street and along the Second and Third Avenue streetcar lines, near lower-middle- and middle-class ethnic neighborhoods whose residents were somewhat better off than the new immigrants of the Lower East Side. Many of the earlier movie houses in Chicago were located in business districts rather than working-class neighborhoods. The *Chicago Sunday Tribune* said in 1906 that "there is hardly a section of the city that is without this class of show house ... from three theaters in the heart of the shopping district on State Street ... to the more modest establishments well up North Clark Street."⁵ ...

English professor Edward Wagenknecht reminisced that middle-class children attended with glee. The storefronts he described were on commercial streets in the lower-middle-class neighborhood of Lawndale around 1907. It was a German–Irish neighborhood of Chicago with a growing number of Jewish families. The nickelodeons were rather humble places with posters pasted in the windows, no wider than an ordinary city lot, and with ceilings so low that the top of the picture sometimes was cut off. He mentions his favorite nickelodeon doing badly. The owner remedied the problem by opening a saloon in the front and continuing to show movies in the rear. The remaining movie patrons deserted at once and the theater closed. Apparently the saloon was not an acceptable solution, as it might have been in a working-class neighborhood.

Small-town movie houses, which accounted for a substantial part of the audience, also contradicted this shoddy immigrant image. Small-town patterns of moviegoing varied not only from those of big cities but also from region to region. In general, however, the small-town movie house was more dependent on the middle class, as it needed broad approval not only for sufficient attendance but also to prevent attacks from moral crusaders. Here, perhaps sooner and more consistently than in cities, we find efforts to ensure the respectable nature of the movie house. One producer touring the small towns of the Northwest reassured readers of *Moving Picture World* that exhibitors were respected members of their communities and that the best class of people attended. An exhibitor of Pennsylvania in 1910 noted that small-town houses catered to the "best people" because they needed everyone's patronage to survive.⁶

All of this indicates an early differentiation of houses: the small, dark, and crowded neighborhood nickelodeon seating only a couple hundred people; the larger houses on commercial blocks, some formerly vaudeville or drama theaters; and the spare but respectable small-town movie theater. The larger houses in downtown shopping districts were more profitable, but the neighborhood storefront dominated public imagery of movie houses.

The equating of the nickelodeon with the immigrant working class has been largely a matter of nomenclature. The term "nickelodeon" was and continues to be used synonymously with a cheap movie house with a low-income patronage, producing a tautological argument about patronage. Other movie outlets received little description in the press, making the nickelodeon by default *the* representative of movie exhibition in public discourse. Film history research continued this reduction of exhibition to that of cheap houses full of immigrants, perhaps due to the plentiful descriptions of nickelodeons and the obscurity of others. Only recently have film historians begun to pay attention to the wide variety of other exhibition venues with similarly varied audiences.

A more complete description includes movie houses ranging from frugal to fancy and the clientele likewise. The frugal ones, in poorer neighborhoods, were called nickelodeons; the fancier ones were called theaters. Moviegoing included a variety of audiences distributed across these venues: the middle class, who had not previously patronized stage entertainments because of religious beliefs; more prosperous working-class patrons of melodrama or vaudeville, who abandoned stage entertainment for movies; and the urban working class, who seldom spent anything on entertainment until the movies.

The debate about the class of movie audiences has left in the shadows the consideration of other groups. Blacks, Indians, Mexicans, and Asians were segregated to galleries or excluded altogether. Such exclusion constituted a minimal measure of respectability for any public place in this era. However, a few black-owned theaters offered an alternative and advertised that blacks were free to sit anywhere. According to the black weekly newspaper, the Indianapolis *Freeman*, in 1909 there were 112 "colored theaters" of all types in the United States, most of them outside major cities and being combination vaudeville and movie houses. From the first, black-owned theaters in Chicago's South Side and in the small city of Lexington, Kentucky combined live entertainment, particularly by black musicians, with movies. In both cities they advertised the "high-class" nature of their clientele, distinguishing them from the rougher patrons of black saloons and dance halls.[7]

Women were an important part of the audiences, even in immigrant nickelodeons. Low costs and convenient location made the nickelodeons accessible to women workers and shoppers. Their informality meant mothers did not have to "dress up" to attend them. A trade journal in 1907 attributed the growth of nickelodeon to women and children. A photograph of an audience in a Troy, New York movie house shows mostly women and children. Several sources noted baby carriages lining the sidewalk or cluttering the entrances to movie houses. Social reformer Mary Heaton Vorse commented, "Prayers finished, you may see a mother sorting out her own babies and moving on serenely to the picture show down the road" after evening church services.[8]

As with theater sixty years earlier, the image of mother and child in attendance would help to certify the safety and propriety of the nickelodeon. Some exhibitors and producers fostered this image by encouraging women to bring the children. Theaters in Lewiston, Maine in 1907 offered teddy-bear souvenirs, checked baby carriages, and encouraged parents to send their children unattended. Some mothers apparently agreed and let their boys go unattended.

A large percentage of the regular audience were children. Estimates of children in the audience ranged from 20 percent in Detroit and Madison, Wisconsin to two-thirds in Pittsburgh and Portland, Oregon. Reports from New York and Cleveland complained that large numbers of these children were unescorted by adults. The thought of unchaperoned teenage girls in particular raised fears of sexual promiscuity. A *Chicago Tribune* reporter in 1907 observed a downtown nickelodeon at 6 p.m. "composed largely of girls from the big department stores who came in with bundles under their arms." The reporter's concern was that they made "undesirable acquaintances [men] of mature age."[9]

Young single immigrant working women enjoyed the freedom of going to the nickelodeon on their own. An Italian garment worker from New York's Lower East Side reminisced:

> The one place I was allowed to go by myself was the movies. I went for fun. My parents wouldn't let me go anywhere else ... I used to enjoy going to the movies two or three times a week. But I would always be home by 9 o'clock.

An Italian girl met her boyfriend on the sly at the movies in the afternoon.[10]

Recreational surveys by reformers found that location and hours made great differences in audience profiles. Men predominated in downtown houses while women and children were more common in neighborhood houses, especially on Saturday and Sunday afternoons. A survey in Cincinnati characterized the daytime audience as being predominantly men, with an occasional woman, sometimes with children, and a few truant boys and girls; a noon audience was composed of young people from stores and factories and a downtown high school. In evenings, downtown theaters were "evenly mixed," while the residential theaters were attended by mostly women and children. A study of Madison in 1915 reported a similar pattern. Whether movies were a male or female, children or adult pastime, depended on the time and place.[11]

A Mass Medium

Some film historians have claimed that immigrant working-class movie-goers represented a new market for commercial entertainment. Yet, through the late nineteenth century and into the movie era, immigrants supported their own ethnic theaters. ... Lower East Side Jews were avid supporters of Yiddish theater and Sicilians were supporters of puppet shows. Descriptions of their behavior are interchangable with those of ethnic movie audiences. The movies benefited from the entertainment habits nurtured by the stage: avid theatergoers became avid moviegoers.

What distinguished movies from previous stage entertainments was *not* the creation of a new market of immigrants or working-class people. Rather it was the *depth* of saturation of these markets that was new. Actual data on saturation rates do not exist. But commentary and overall attendance suggest that higher proportions of all groups must have been attending movies to achieve such high numbers of admissions and receipts. Clearly more people, especially children, went regularly to nickelodeons than ever went to previous stage entertainments. Places of exhibition were numerous and admission cheap, even compared to cheap vaudeville, so that accessibility was increased dramatically for those with low incomes and those living in remote places. ...

Many went. The *Independent* claimed in 1908 that the movies attracted "thousands who never go to the theater, and particularly [were] appealing to the children." Surveys in the prewar period indicate that weekly attendance was approximately equal to the city's population in most cities. More people went and more went more frequently than they had to other theater entertainments. Most movie shows in the nickelodeon era were cheap, half the price of the gallery for drama theaters or vaudeville, making frequent attendance feasible for lower-income groups and even children. Frequent moviegoers always represented a large portion of the movie audience. Many adults and children went more than once per week.[12]

Working-Class Audiences, Autonomous Publics

In contrast to the extensive literature on the *demographics* of the nickelodeon audience, there is relatively little about their *behavior*. But these descriptions, mostly of working-class immigrants, are intriguing for their resemblance to that of nineteenth-century working-class audiences, in their sociability and appropriation of nickelodeons as an alternative public space. Contemporary writers described the nickelodeons as family and community centers, contradicting the fears about unchaperoned children in the audiences. Lewis Palmer noted in 1909, "Certain houses have become genuine social centers where neighborhood groups may be found any evening of the week ... where the regulars stroll up and down the aisles between acts and visit friends." A 1914 Portland, Oregon study claimed, "Many of them are family resorts. Community pictures are shown, the people chat in a friendly manner, children move freely about the house and the manager knows his patrons personally ... these houses already take in many a nickel and dime that would otherwise go over the bar [of saloons] ... people attending all kinds of theaters are orderly, quiet and courteous."[13]

For temperance reformers the nickelodeon was a happy contrast to the "workingman's club," the saloon, because it was free of alcohol and re-united men with their families. According to the *Willamantic* (Connecticut) *Journal*, "Men not often seen in the company of their wives on the street were now taking whole families to the motion pictures night after night." Many surveys noted a diminished attendance at saloons attributed to men going to movies with their families. In 1914, Presbyterian minister Charles Stelzle asserted that movies were cutting into the profits of saloons; in a 1916 article in the *Independent* he favored the movies as a substitute for the saloon. The motion picture house, he claimed, was democratic just as the saloon, where the working man could feel comfortable and at home. He could come just as he is, without dressing up. But in addition he could take his family there, where he could not to the saloon. A few years later a saloonkeeper of Middletown told sociologists Robert and Helen Lynds, "The movies killed the saloon. They cut our business in half overnight."[14]

Observers described audiences, to a significant degree, as determining their own use of the space in the nickelodeon and even in the small theaters of the silent era of the 1920s. Even though film had displaced live actors, the performance was not yet standardized. Managers edited movies to fit their audiences' tastes. Sometimes projectionists would change the speed of the film and even run the film backward for the amusement of the audience. There was a notable interaction between audiences and projectionists and managers.

Live musical accompaniment to the film also provided a rich source of interaction, akin to that for stage performers. Piano players, mostly women, took pride in their improvisational skills, through which they responded to the audience, especially in neighborhood theaters. When movie producers began in about 1910 to distribute cue sheets for musicians to accompany their movies, many musicians rejected these and continued to play according to their own tastes and that of their audiences. Musicians and audiences could thus entirely alter the mood and intent of a scene. A serious drama could be made into a farce.

Managers of small theaters attempted a delicate balance between acquiescing to their audiences' wishes and "managing" the audience. They were generally supportive of musicians' efforts to please the audience, regardless of the impact on the dramatic effects of the movie, and despite objections of movie producers. Managers also used sing-alongs and sometimes giveaways to modulate and manipulate their audiences. Illustrated songs were often advertised to the less-inhibited working-class and small-town audiences. Almost all nickelodeons had a singer who led the audience, who were guided by song slides. Sing-alongs were familiar from cheap vaudeville. Almost every house used illustrated songs while the projector was loaded with a new reel of film. Reformer Michael Davis said about audience participation in sing-alongs, "no warm-blooded person can watch the rapt attention of an audience during the song, and hear the voices swell as children and adults join spontaneously in the chorus, without feeling how deeply human is the appeal of the music, and how clearly it meets a sound popular need."[15]

But nickelodeons were rarely sites of political activism. A few held benefits for strikers, much as other local merchants would often advance credit to strikers. In 1911, some theaters screened an announcement supporting a campaign against a local gas company. But there is no record of the kinds of crowd actions that had been common in early nineteenth-century theaters, in which working-class audiences often orchestrated the political messages on-stage, objecting to some, demanding others. Working-class audiences exercised some autonomy in controlling the space and defining its purpose to suit their own needs. In doing so they collectively shaped the reading of both the situation and the movies to fit their own working-class experience, and thus used the nickelodeon as a site for producing an alternative culture. But they rarely expressed overt political consciousness or purpose, unlike the saloon that often had been the meeting place for unions and strikers. This perhaps made it reassuring to middle- and upper-class reformers worried about social control.

Changing Habits, for Better or Worse

If people were frequently going to the movies, what had they stopped doing, what had they previously done with this time? The citizens of Middletown told the Lynds that "movies have cut into lodge attendance" and probably the patronage of saloons and attendance at union meetings as well. Saloonkeepers' concern over loss of business was a reason for middle- and upper-class rejoicing. But theater owners worried that people were leaving drama theater for the movies. The galleries were empty, they said, because the boys who had formerly sat there now frequented the movies. Hard times favored the nickelodeon over other entertainments. When people could not afford a theater or vaudeville ticket they could still muster a nickel for the movies. In the 1907–8 recession many theaters closed but nickelodeons were booming. *Lippincott's* magazine said that the movies caused decreases in box office at legitimate and vaudeville theaters and disbanding of theater companies. It claimed the nickelodeon attracted "nearly every class of those we term theater-goers" and that "it is a common occurrence to enjoy amusement by machinery in what was a regulation playhouse." In 1910, *World's Work* cited nine New York theaters from which "the Biograph manager has driven vaudeville and the old-fashioned first-class drama." In 1911 the same magazine claimed movies had replaced theatrical performances in 1,400 former playhouses. Robert Grau claimed that seventy traveling theatrical companies had to fold because of the movies and that movies had "contributed principally" to the decline of melodrama. The *Jewish Daily Forward* commented on the impact of movies on Yiddish performances in 1906. "A year ago there were about ten Jewish music halls in New York and Brooklyn. Now there are only two [while at movies] hundreds of people wait in line."[16] ...

As movies moved out of storefronts into regular theaters, they demonstrated their greater profitability even in drama's own home. Movies provided a greater profit even on Saturdays, the traditional theater night. Drama theaters that traditionally closed for the summer began to show movies instead. Movie companies began aggressively buying and closing theaters or pressuring local governments to tax or restrict licensing for drama productions. The result was a greater difficulty for touring companies to find a theater at an affordable rent. By 1914, movie palaces were being built in Times Square that were equal in comfort and luxury to those of drama theaters, with admission of 25 cents instead of 2 dollars ...

Children, Movies, and Reformers

The movies stirred new concerns among moral reformers. Even though children attended theaters in the nineteenth century, reformers directed their concerns toward the dangers to young men and women and to the general moral climate of the community as a whole. The central issue about nineteenth-century audiences had been respectability, which applied to adult behavior and especially to women. The primary focus of criticism was the behavior in the audience, the rowdiness, drinking, and prostitution. Even in the concert saloons the primary concern was not the entertainment, but the alleged licentious behavior of the waiter girls with the clientele.

By the turn of the century, women's respectability was no longer the issue. This older fear was overshadowed by concerns about the safety and socialization of children. Children were being redefined sympathetically as innocent and impressionable, a departure from earlier Calvinist conceptions of children as evil barbarians in need of discipline. Adolescence was being defined as a distinct developmental period, subject to many pitfalls. Charitable organizations began to direct attention to lower-class child abuse and neglect; juvenile delinquency was distinguished from adult crime, and states instituted the first juvenile courts. Children were defined as endangered creatures.

Accompanying the shift in focus from women to children was a shift in attention to class. The primary concern in the era of respectability was its certification of the class credentials of the middle and upper classes. The new concern about children was centered on the lower classes. Society women's charities as well as middle-class professionals focused on socializing lower-class children, especially the growing numbers of urban-dwelling immigrants, who they believed lacked adequate parenting.

Almost from the first, what drew the attention of movie crusaders were the large numbers of unchaperoned adolescents and children in nickelodeon audiences. Reformers feared that moviegoing led to delinquency among boys and sexual immorality among girls. For the first time, reformers concentrated their attention on the effect of the show rather than on the behavior in the audience as the primary concern, although audience behavior continued to be part of the discussion. Previous New York state laws focused on theaters (1839) and concert saloons (1862) as *places* of delinquency, but not on the performance. But in the nickelodeon era the movie itself became a central focus and censorship the means to control its dangers.

Jane Addams, settlement house founder and reformer, in a series of essays published in 1909 as *Spirit of Youth*, worried about the many children who seemed addicted to the motion pictures. She cited a group of young girls who refused a day's outing in the country because they would miss their evening at the nickelodeon; and four daughters of a shopkeeper who would steal movie admission from his till. Addams identified movie *content* as the root cause of the children's misbehavior. She called the nickelodeon the "house of dreams" to indicate movies' inducement of fantasies in children's minds.[17] She told a tale of boys nine to thirteen years old who saw a movie of a stagecoach holdup and mimicked it themselves. They bought a lariat and a gun and, one morning, lay in ambush for the milkman, nearly killing him. Addams was only one among many writers at the time who publicized stories of children imitating movie crimes.

As a result, censorship became an early instrument of reform. Chicago enacted the first movie censorship ordinance in 1907, followed by dozens of other cities. By 1913 several states and cities had laws prohibiting children's attendance without an adult after a certain hour. In a cover letter to a report on movies, the mayor of Cleveland in 1913 cited movies of crime as the major evil of movie exhibition and urged censorship in that city. *American Magazine*, citing the Cleveland report, urged industry self-censorship over government censorship. To protect themselves from government regulation the Motion Picture Patent Company, an organization of movie producers, formed a censorship board for New York and enlisted the cooperation of the People's Institute. This soon became the voluntary National Board of Censorship. Producers hoped to counter criticism that might threaten their efforts to capture a middle-class market.

Reformers claimed censorship markedly improved the moral quality of movies. Louise de Koven Bowen, wealthy friend and patron of Jane Addams, claimed the Chicago ordinance of 1911 which her Juvenile Protection Association of Chicago advocated, had made a difference. Similarly, Michael Davis credited the Board of Censorship, with which he was involved, for much improvement from 1908 to 1910.

Censorship blunted but did not stop criticism. Many continued to object to movie content, whether or not censorship had been instituted in their city. In a 1914 debate in the *Outlook*, some letter-writers still worried that girls might be led into prostitution by what they called "white slave" films, which they said did not depict the awful consequences for girls. Another article expressed fear that movies would give immigrant children unrealistic expectations of what they could have and accomplish in America, leading to their disillusion and dissolution: "The version of life presented to him in the majority of moving pictures is false in fact, sickly in sentiment, and utterly foreign to the Anglo-Saxon ideals of our nation. In them we usually find this formula for a hero: He must commit a crime, repent of it, and be exonerated on the ground that he 'never had a mother' or 'never had a chance' – or perhaps that he was born poor."[18]

Fears of the effects of movies were accompanied by a belief that movies were unusually effective in "implanting" – a word often used at the time – ideas in children's minds. In an address to the People's Institute in New York, Reverend. A. Jump in 1911 expressed the theory that movies operated through "psychologic suggestion" to put ideas in the viewer's head without his knowing it. He therefore wanted to make sure, through censorship, that these ideas were what he considered good. The same sentiments were expressed at the Conference of the National Child Labor Committee by a Birmingham Alabama Boy's Club superintendent. Making the same claim in more "scientific" garb, Harvard professor Hugo Munsterberg concluded in *The Photoplay: A Psychological Study*, "The intensity with which the plays take hold of the audience cannot remain without social effects ... the mind is so completely given up to the moving pictures."[19] These were the first expressions of what would later be called "hypodermic" theories of media effects.

Critics did not entirely ignore the atmosphere within the storefront theater itself. The two concerns were sometimes intermingled in the same article. They related many "horrors" perpetrated therein, some reading like a tabloid front page. Censorship was no guarantee of the conditions within the theater. Theater ownership was not centralized, leaving each to compete in the market as he chose. Critics were dismayed at the darkness in the storefront theaters, which they saw as encouraging and enabling sexual encounters. Louise de Koven Bowen cited as an example of the dangers a case in which a Chicago proprietor had enticed young girls into his theater and molested them. She claimed that "boys and men in such crowds [outside nickelodeons] often speak to the girls and invite them to see the show, and there is an unwritten code that such courtesies shall be paid for later by the girls," and that "darkness afforded a cover for familiarity and sometimes even for immorality." *American Magazine* reiterated to its nationwide readership the dangers of darkness, "indiscriminate acquaintance," and foul air in the theaters.[20] ...

Nevertheless, after censorship, reformers often preferred movies to other entertainments, particularly cheap vaudeville. As a neighborhood and family institution, the nickelodeon was much less threatening than more anonymous entertainments farther from the reach of family and neighborhoods. By contrast, reformers sometimes condemned cheap vaudeville's sexual immorality, in terms reminiscent of the criticisms of concert saloons in the 1860s, except now the attention was on stage acts. The Cleveland study referred to cheap vaudeville acts as "positively degrading," and in describing an audience of one indecent dancer stated, "the ladies in the audience hid their faces ... many of the older men turned their heads while the young men and boys stamped their feet, clapped their hands, many of them rising out of their seats, waving their hats, at the same time shouting vulgar suggestions to the performer." A few simply condemned its very low intellectual level and deadening effects educationally.[21]

Reverend H. A. Jump, in his address to the People's Institute, the home of the National Board of Censorship, praised the movies as "the cleanest form of popular entertainment being given indoors today" and thanked the Board for this. He claimed those who thought movies immoral did so on the prejudice that cheap admission implied immorality. Yet movies had a high standard which "would never be allowed to apply to the drama patronized by the well-to-do." He considered movies to have a good educational and moral effect upon the "common people."[22]

A Madison, Wisconsin report in 1915 expressed a definite change in attitude since censorship – "of course there is nothing alarming in children going to movies in the afternoon unattended by elders" – and accepted the claims that movies have "substituted good recreation for many less desirable forms" and "tended to draw families together by giving them a common interest." It too complained of the worst types of vaudeville, the mixed bill of vaudeville acts and movies. A recreation survey of Cincinnati 1913 described the movies as "unobjectionable and provided clean recreation ... films of distinctly educational and high recreational value are frequently shown. ... There can be no doubt that the quality of recreation offered by the moving picture show has vastly improved in the last few years and is still improving."[23]

Later in the 1910s women's groups began to pressure local exhibitors to offer special showings for children in neighborhood theaters. Local civic groups in several cities organized Saturday matinee movies for children in the mid-1910s. While these often were located in movie houses, the theater managers were not the initiators but simply cooperators. The Women's Press Club of New York sponsored Saturday morning movies in two commercial theaters in 1916–17. The Club selected the films for moral education. They excluded films that depicted crimes, convicts, fighting, saloons, gambling, and sex. They also chose films with an eye to their entertainment value to ensure the theater owners of some profit. A women's club of Chicago organized a Better Films Committee to advise local groups on how to organize children's or family programs and what films to show. If local exhibitors would not cooperate they advised groups to buy a projector and show films in schools. Such programs were not commercial but reform efforts, often directed at working-class children. Organizations and businesses sometimes bought blocks of tickets to distribute free to poor children or to their employees. Programs were "planned for clean entertainment, making education secondary." However, the results were mixed, as some children still preferred to see the more exciting adult movies.[24]

The thrust of almost all of the discussion, although ostensibly about children, when examined more closely, is about class. Middle- and upper-class reformers worried about the lower classes absorbing dangerous ideas from movies, many made by immigrants themselves. Lists of topics to be avoided in movies included workers' strikes. The recreational surveys quoted above were sponsored by private elite groups and directed primarily at gathering data on working-class neighborhoods and working-class children. Michael Davis looked in depth at three tenement districts in Manhattan, and the Cincinnati study targeted similar districts for closer examination. Cover letters, introductions, conclusions, and recommendations typically reveal a fear of working-class juvenile delinquency. They proposed funding public recreation facilities for these working-class neighborhoods, since such neighborhoods could not afford private clubs. There is almost complete absence of comment about middle- and upper-class youths' recreation. Such attention might have raised questions about the surveyors' own child-rearing practices.

Magazine articles also reveal the same concerns. In one expression of this attitude, some reformers equated uneducated adults with children, claiming they could not discern reality from fiction and were more susceptible to movies than the better educated. One reformer in 1909 claimed "the constant picturing of crime ... is a harmful and degrading thing, especially when a large percentage of the patrons of such theaters is made up of minors, or adults without education." The *Outlook* stated, "Undeveloped people, people in transitional stages [i.e., immigrants] and children are deeply affected [by movies]." The quote reveals what lay behind these fears of the movies, that these immigrants would not learn to behave like the middle- and upper-class "Anglo-Saxon" reformers. It considered sympathy for the circumstances of the poor to be misplaced and not a suitable explanation for crime.[25]

More optimistic reformers saw movies as potentially being a great educator for adult poor and immigrants. Mrs. W. I. Thomas considered movies not inherently bad but "an educational medium that is historic" in its potential, which had been "turned over to these mere 'promoters of pleasure.' " The *Outlook* similarly contended that movies "could be made as effective a means of instruction in such social problems [as white slavery] as either fiction or the stage." They hoped to harness this great resource and use it as a tool of social control.[26]

But whether pessimists or optimists, their concerns were often rooted in class-based fears of lower-class disorder, the underlying concern of much Progressive reform and the overt fear of conservatives in efforts such as the eugenics movement. While the subject was ostensibly children, this discourse was part of the larger concern about the huge wave of lower-class immigration into the nation in this era.

Notes

1   "Nickel Vaudeville," *Variety* (March 17, 1906), 4; "Moving Pictures," *Billboard* 18: 41 (October 13, 1906), 21; "The Nickelodeon," *Moving Picture World and View Photographer* 1: 9 (May 7, 1907), 140; Kenneth MacGowan, *Behind the Screen: The History and Technique of the Motion Picture* (New York: Dell, 1965), 129, on number of nickelodeons.

2 Annie Marion MacLean, *Wage-Earning Women* (New York: MacMillan, 1910), 143–53, on Pennsylvania mining towns; Margaret Byington, *Homestead: The Households of a Mill Town* (New York: Charities Publication Committee, 1909), 40.

3 Elaine Bowser, *The Transformation of the Cinema, 1907–1915* (Berkeley: University of California Press, 1990), 1, for quote from *Moving Picture World*.

4 Bowser, 122–3, on Audubon Theater.

5 Musser, 421–4, on Chicago.

6 Bowser, 37.

7 Bowser, 9–10, for estimated numbers.

8 Peiss, 150, on Mary eaton Vorse quote.

9 Lauren Rabinovitz, 73, on Chicago; also Peiss, 151–3, on unchaperoned girls.

10 Elizabeth Ewen, "City Lights," 55.

11 "Recreation Survey of Cincinnati", (1913), 26–7.

12 Robert E. Davis, "Response to Innovation; A Study of Popular Argument About New Mass Media" (Ph.D., University of Iowa, 1965), 55, on *Independent* quote.

13 Lewis Palmer, "The World in Motion," *Survey* 22 (June 5, 1909), 356; Foster, "Vaudeville and Motion Picture Shows," 27–8.

14 Bowser, 2, on *Willamantic Journal*; Lynd, *Middletown*, 265; also Bartholomew, 7.

15 Michael Davis, 24.

16 Lynd (1929), 265; Day Allen Willie, "The Theatre's New Rival," *Lippincott's* 84 (October 1909), 458; *World's Work* (1910 and 1911), on closings cited by Robert E. Davis, "Response to Innovation," 467–8; Grau (1910), 172; Lary May, *Screening Out the Past: The Birth of Mass Culture and the Motion Picture Industry* (New York: Oxford University Press, 1980), 35, on *Daily Forward* quote.

17 Addams, 92.

18 "'Movie' Manners and Morals," *Outlook* (July 26, 1916), 695.

19 Reverend H. A. Jump , "The Social Influence of the Moving Picture" (New York: Playground and Recreation Association of America, 1911); quote of Munsterberg in Garth Jowett, "Social Science as a Weapon: The Origins of the Payne Fund Studies, 1926–1929," *Communication* 13: 3 (December 1992), 213.

20 Bowen, 2, 4–5, 9.

21 Bartholomew, 13–15.

22 Reverend H. A. Jump, 8.

23 "Madison Recreational Survey," 52, 54, 59; "Recreation Survey of Cincinnati," 27–9.

24 Richard DeCordova, "Ethnography and Exhibition: The Child Audience, The Hays Office and Saturday Matinees," *Camera Obscura* 23 (May 1990), 91–106.

25 R. E. Davis, 234, for 1909 quote; "'Movie' Manners and Morals" (July 26, 1916), 694.

26 Mrs. W. I. Thomas, 147; "The White Slave Films: A Review," *Outlook* (February 1914), 345.

Documents

Introduction to Documents

The rise of the movies spurred intense debates over their character: Did these new forms of entertainment exert a positive or negative influence on audiences? Were they to be feared or embraced? Much of the early public debate over these questions was conducted by elites. However, the following sources offer us insights into how people of the time felt about these new moving images and the moviegoing experience. Barton W. Currie describes the appeal and attraction that nickelodeons held for ordinary Americans in 1907 and offers a sense of what it was like to go to one of these new "movie" theaters and experience the wondrous sights of a world most audience members would never get to see in person. Social surveyor Robert Bartholomew takes us outside of New York City and describes the pleasures and perils of moviegoing in Cleveland, Ohio. The last document from the *New York Call*, a popular working-class newspaper, tells how inexperienced – and sometimes even experienced – early moviegoers could get so caught up in the action on the screen that they lost all sense of reality.

The Nickel Madness

Barton W. Carrie

Source: *Harper's Weekly*, August 24, 1907

The Amazing Spread of a New Kind of Amusement Enterprise Which is Making Fortunes for its Projectors

The very fact that we derive pleasure from certain amusements, wrote Lecky, creates a kind of humiliation. Anthony Comstock and Police-Commissioner Bingham have spoken eloquently on the moral aspect of the five-cent theatre, drawing far more strenuous conclusions than that of the great historian. But both the general and the purity commissioner generalized too freely from particulars. They saw only the harsher aspects of the nickel madness, whereas it has many innocent and harmless phases.

Crusades have been organized against these low-priced moving-picture theatres, and many conservators of the public morals have denounced them as vicious and demoralizing. Yet have they flourished amazingly, and carpenters are busy hammering them up in every big and little community in the country.

The first "nickelodeon," or "nickelet," or whatever it was originally called was merely an experiment, and the first experiment was made a little more than a year ago. There was nothing singularly novel in the idea, only the individualizing of the moving-picture machine. Before it had served merely as a "turn" in vaudeville. For a very modest sum the outfit could be housed in a narrow store or in a shack in the rear yard of a tenement, provided there was an available hallway and the space for a "front." These shacks and shops are packed with as many chairs as they will hold and the populace welcomed, or rather hailed, by a huge megaphone-horn and lurid placards. The price of admission and entertainment for from fifteen to twenty minutes is a coin of the smallest denomination in circulation west of the Rockies. ...

An eloquent plea was made for these humble resorts by many "friends of the peepul." They offered harmless diversion for the poor. They were edifying, educational, and amusing. They were broadening. They revealed the universe to the unsophisticated. The variety of the skipping, dancing, flashing, and marching pictures was without limit. For five cents you were admitted to the realms of the prize ring; you might witness the celebration of a Pontifical mass in St. Peter's; Kaiser Wilhelm would prance before you, reviewing his Uhlans. Yes, and even more surprising, you were offered a modern conception of Washington crossing the Delaware "acted out by a trained group of actors." Under the persuasive force of such arguments, was it strange that the Aldermen befriended the nickelodeon man and gave impetus to the craze? ...

Already statisticians have been estimating how many men, women, and children in the metropolis are being thrilled daily by them. A conservative figure puts it at 200,000, though if I were to accept the total of the showmen the estimate would be nearer half a million. But like all statisticians, who reckon human beings with the same unemotional placidity with which they total beans and potatoes, the statistician I have quoted left out the babies. In a visit to a dozen of these moving-picture hutches I counted an average of ten babies to each theatre-et. Of course they were in their mothers' or the nurse-girls' arms. But they were there and you heard them. They did not disturb the show, as there were no counter-sounds, and many of them seemed profoundly absorbed in the moving pictures.

As a matter of fact, some mothers – and all nurse-girls – will tell you that the cinematograph has a peculiarly hypnotic or narcotic effect upon an infant predisposed to disturb the welkin. You will visit few of these places in Harlem where the doorways are not encumbered with go-carts and perambulators. Likewise they are prodigiously popular with the rising generation in frock and knickerbocker. For this reason they have been condemned by the morality crusaders.

The chief argument against them was that they corrupted the young. Children of any size who could transport a nickel to the cashier's booth were welcomed. Furthermore, undesirables of many kinds haunted them. Pickpockets found them splendidly convenient, for the lights were always cut off when the picture-machine was focused on the canvas. There is no doubt about the fact that many rogues and miscreants obtained licenses and set up these little show-places merely as snares and traps. There were many who thought they had sufficient pull to defy decency in the choice of their slides. Proprietors were said to work hand in glove with lawbreakers. Some were accused of wanton designs to corrupt young girls. Police-Commissioner Bingham denounced the nickel madness as pernicious, demoralizing, and a direct menace to the young. ...

But if you happen to be an outlaw you may learn many moral lessons from these brief moving-picture performances, for most of the slides offer you a quick flash of melodrama in which the villain and criminal are always getting the worst of it. Pursuits of malefactors are by far the most popular of all nickel deliriums. You may see snatch-purses, burglars, and an infinite variety of criminals hunted by the police and the mob in almost any nickelet you have the curiosity to visit. The scenes of these thrilling chases occur in every quarter of the globe, from Cape Town to Medicine Hat.

The speed with which pursuer and pursued run is marvellous. Never are you cheated by a mere sprint or straightway flight of a few blocks. The men who "fake" these moving pictures seem impelled by a moral obligation to give their patrons their full nickel's worth. I have seen a dozen of these kinetoscope fugitives run at least forty miles before they collided with a fat woman carrying an umbrella, who promptly sat on them and held them for the puffing constabulary.

It is in such climaxes as these that the nickel delirium rises to its full height. Young and old follow the spectacular course of the fleeing culprit breathlessly. They have seen him strike a pretty young woman and tear her chain-purse from her hand. Of course it is in broad daylight and in full view of the populace. Then in about one-eighth of a second he is off like the wind, the mob is at his heels. In a quarter of a second a half-dozen policemen have joined in the precipitate rush. Is it any wonder that the lovers of melodrama are delighted? And is it not possible that the pickpockets in the audience are laughing in their sleeves and getting a prodigious amount of fun out of it?

The hunted man travels the first hundred yards in less than six seconds, so he must be an unusually well-trained athlete. A stout uniformed officer covers the distance in eight seconds. Reckon the handicap he would have to give Wefers and other famous sprinters. But it is in going over fences and stone walls, swimming rivers and climbing mountains, that you mount the heights of realism. You are taken over every sort of jump and obstacle, led out into tangled underbrush, through a dense forest, up the face of a jagged cliff – evidently traversing an entire country – whirled through a maze of wild scenery, and then brought back to the city. Again you are rushed through the same streets, accompanying the same tireless pack of pursuers, until finally looms the stout woman with the umbrella.

A clerk in a Harlem cigar-store who is an intense patron of the nickel-odeon told me that he had witnessed thief chases in almost every large city in the world, not to mention a vast number of suburban towns, mining-camps, and prairie villages.

"I enjoy these shows," he said, "for they continually introduce me to new places and new people. If I ever go to Berlin or Paris I will know what the places look like. I have seen runaways in the Boys de Boulong and a kidnapping in the Unter der Linden. I know what a fight in an alley in Stamboul looks like; have seen a paper-mill in full operation, from the cutting of the timber to the stamping of the pulp; have seen gold mined by hydraulic sprays in Alaska, and diamonds dug in South Africa. I know a lot of the pictures are fakes, but what of that? It costs only five cents."

The popularity of these cheap amusement-places with the new population of New York is not to be wondered at. The newly arrived immigrant from Transylvania can get as much enjoyment out of them as the native. The imagination is appealed to directly and without any circumlocution. The child whose intelligence has just awakened and the doddering old man seem to be on an equal footing of enjoyment in the stuffy little box-like theatres. The passer-by with an idle quarter of an hour on his hands has an opportunity to kill the time swiftly, if he is not above mingling with the *hoi polloi*. Likewise the student of sociology may get a few points that he could not obtain in a day's journey through the thronged streets of the East Side.

Of course the proprietors of the nickelets and nickelodeons make as much capital out of suggestiveness as possible, but it rarely goes beyond a hint or a lure. For instance, you will come to a little hole in the wall before which there is an ornate sign bearing the legend:

FRESH FROM PARIS
Very Naughty

Should this catch the eye of a Comstock he would immediately enter the place to gather evidence. But he would never apply for a warrant. He would find a "very naughty" boy playing pranks on a Paris street – annoying blind men, tripping up gendarmes, and amusing himself by every antic the ingenuity of the Paris street gamin can conceive.

This fraud on the prurient, as it might be called, is very common, and it has led a great many people, who derive their impressions from a glance at externals, to conclude that these resorts are really a menace to morals. You will hear and see much worse in some high-priced theatres than in these moving-picture show-places.

In some of the crowded quarters of the city the nickelet is cropping up almost as thickly as the saloons, and if the nickel delirium continues to maintain its hold there will be, in a few years, more of these cheap amusement-places than saloons. Even now some of the saloon-keepers are complaining that they injure their trade. On one street in Harlem there are as many as five to a block, each one capable of showing to one thousand people an hour. That is, they have a seating capacity for about two hundred and fifty, and give four shows an hour. Others are so tiny that only fifty can be jammed into the narrow area. They run from early morning until midnight, and their megaphones are barking their lure before the milkman has made his rounds.

You hear in some neighborhoods of nickelodeon theatre-parties. A party will set out on what might be called a moving-picture debauch, making the round of all the tawdry little show-places in the region between the hours of eight and eleven o'clock at night, at a total cost of, say, thirty cents each. They will tell you afterwards that they were not bored for an instant. Everything they saw had plenty of action in it. Melodrama is served hot and at a pace the Bowery theatres can never follow. In one place I visited, a band of pirates were whirled through a maze of hair-raising adventures that could not have occurred in a Third Avenue home of melodrama in less than two hours. Within the span of fifteen minutes the buccaneers scuttled a merchantman, made its crew walk the plank, captured a fair-haired maiden, bound her with what appeared to be two-inch Manila rope, and cast her into the hold.

The ruthless pirate captain put his captive on a bread-and-water diet, loaded her with chains, and paced up and down before her with arms folded, *à la Bonaparte*. The hapless young woman cowered in a corner and shook her clankless fetters. Meanwhile from the poop-deck other pirates scanned the offing. A sail dashed over the horizon and bore down on the buccaneers under full wing, making about ninety knots, though there was scarcely a ripple on the sea. In a few seconds the two vessels were hurling broadsides at each other. The *Jolly Roger* was shot away. Then the jolly sea-wolfs were shot away. It was a French man-of-war to the rescue, and French men-of-war's men boarded the outlaw craft. There were cutlass duels all over the deck, from "figgerhead" to taffrail, until the freebooters were booted overboard to a man. Then the *fiancé* of the fair captive leaped down into the hold and cut off her chains with a jack-knife.

Is it any wonder, when you can see all this for five cents and in fifteen minutes, that the country is being swept by a nickel delirium? An agent for a moving-picture concern informed the writer that the craze for these cheap show-places was sweeping the country from coast to coast. The makers of the pictures employ great troops of actors and take them all over the world to perform. The sets of pictures have to be changed every other day. Men with vivid imaginations are employed to think up new acts. Their minds must be as fertile as the mental soil of a dime-novelist.

The French seem to be the masters in this new field. The writers of *feuilletons* have evidently branched into the business, for the continued-story moving-picture has come into existence. You get the same characters again and again, battling on the edges of precipitous cliffs, struggling in a lighthouse tower, sleuthing criminals in Parisian suburbs, tracking kidnapped children through dense forests, and pouncing upon would-be assassins with the dagger poised. Also you are introduced to the grotesque and the *comique*. Thousands of dwellers along the Bowery are learning to roar at French buffoonery, and the gendarme is growing as familiar to them as "the copper on the beat."

And after all it is an innocent amusement and a rather wholesome delirium.

Report of Censorship of Motion Pictures and of Investigation of Motion Picture Theatres of Cleveland

Robert O. Bartholomew

Source: Robert O. Bartholomew, *Report of Censorship of Motion Pictures and of Investigation of Motion Picture Theatres of Cleveland* (Cleveland, 1913), 6, 10, 11–12, 13, 17, 18, 28

Fifteen down-town theaters open at 10 o'clock in the morning in which continuous programs are exhibited until late in the evening. All other theaters are open in the evening beginning at 6:30. ... Small neighborhood theaters close between the hours of 9 and 10 and all other theaters are closed by 11 p.m. The very nature of the entertainment in all theaters excepting those presenting vaudeville performances, tends to relax the muscles of the hard-working person and to prepare him for complete rest so that he is glad to leave early. ...

At one theater in the city three cents is charged for admission; at 111 theaters five cents is charged during the week with a ten-cent charge for Sundays, holidays and occasions when special feature pictures are shown. The other [19] theaters charge ten cents or more. For the above fee one can have from one to three hours entertainment consisting of four or five photoplays, good music, and in a few instances, the added vaudeville acts.

Motion picture theaters form neighborhood social centers. They are very generally scattered among all nationalities represented in the city and in all neighborhoods. They do in a real sense provide a means of reasonably priced, wholesome recreation for the man of small or average means without the necessity of his going from the neighborhood for necessary relaxation.

One hundred and one Motion Picture theaters are located adjoining or within one-half block of one or more saloons. ... As one daily attends theaters scattered hither and thither in the city and sees the thousands of young people who would, but for the motion picture theaters probably be spending their recreational hours in saloons, he is tremendously impressed with the good that the motion picture theaters are doing by saving young lives from the degrading companionships formed when innocent young people and those trained in unscrupulous practices gather in questionable places without other attractions for thought than the vile inventions of their silly minds. ... [T]he Motion Picture theater is today the greatest competitor and one of the strongest enemies of the saloon with its degrading companionships. ...

[I]t would seem that about 115,000 men, women, and children attend motion picture theaters [daily], while the average for Sundays is about 200,000, or in other words, one in every six of our citizens attends a motion picture theater each week day and one in every three when such leisure time as Saturdays, Sundays, and holidays is granted. ...

The opinion has prevailed among the managers of Motion Picture theaters during the past that it was necessary to have the theater dark in order that the motion picture might appear clear and distinct. This belief has been responsible for conditions in the theaters that have justified criticism. There in the darkness of the rooms young people, many of them mere children, are thrown close together where uncontrolled affections soon lead to serious excesses. These young people begin by slight familiarities and are soon embracing each other in the dark during the progress of the entertainment. This condition can be best illustrated by a case taken from the records of our juvenile court. A young girl, 16 years of age, frequented a certain very poorly lighted motion picture theater in this city. A flirtation with a strange man considerably her senior soon sprang up. Soon they were daily attending the theater sitting in the dark recesses of the room and embracing each other. Later an illegitimate child resulting from this association was thrown over the back fence by the irate mother and the case became a court record. The girl who had always been known as decent up to the time she started on her downward path, became incorrigible and is now detained in one of our public institutions because of her gross immorality which she claims she cannot live without. ... The numerous cases found where young people were unduly familiar with those of the opposite sex indicates the necessity of requiring adequate lighting of theaters. In one instance three young men were handling one girl in a most vulgar manner. The manager's attention was called to the case but he failed to correct the performance.

The condition of the air in the theaters is best described in the words of a little fifth grader when he says: "Some moving picture shows are unhealth [*sic*] to go in because it smell bad and they need funigating [*sic*]." The matter of proper ventilation has been greatly overlooked. ... [In many theaters] the air is changed only as patrons come to or leave the theater. It was found that attendants in one or two instances, by the use of large atomizers, squirted a solution around the room to ally the odor of the foul air. ... In ten theaters the air was found to be so foul that the investigators could not stay more than a few moments and even this short stay resulted in sneezing, coughing and the contraction of serious colds. ...

Good music is to be heard in most Motion Picture theaters. ... At eighty of the Motion Picture theaters there is first-class piano music. There are first-class orchestras in thirty-five and organola music in twelve theaters while only four do not have music. At only a few of the theaters can one hear cheap and trashy tunes.

In passing upon the moral tone of the Motion Picture theaters principal emphasis has been laid upon the attitude of the managers in their endeavor to eliminate objectionable conduct. ...

The investigation shows that in fifty-eight of the theaters the moral tone is most excellent; in forty-six the moral tone is good and in twenty-seven theaters the moral tone is bad. ...

Tables compiled covering investigations at twenty-two theaters visited show that two-thirds of the young children attending motion picture theaters in the evening are unaccompanied. The largest period of attendance of unaccompanied children is from 7:30 to 8:15 in the evening. The facts show that practically all of the children leave the theater before 9 o'clock. ... The chief objection to children going to the Motion Picture theaters in the evening comes from the school teachers who complain that the children are dull and sleepy in school the following day if allowed to remain out late in the evening. It must be remembered in this connection that there are thousands of fathers and mothers who pay little if any attention to their children during the evening hours, it would seem that children should not be prohibited from attending Motion Picture theaters unaccompanied after a certain given hour in the evening, rather should the theaters be made wholesome places of recreation and the children be encouraged to attend, for only in this way will thousands of children, living in the congested sections of the city, be kept from the streets.

House Fly Panics Pittsburgh Movie Audience

Source: *New York Call*, February 7, 1914

A common house fly, magnified several hundred times, which had in some manner made its way onto the lens of a moving picture machine in a [Pittsburgh] North Side nickelodeon, was the cause of a panic among the audience last night which, but for the prompt action on the part of a few cool heads, would have turned into a tragedy greater than was being depicted on the screen.

The machine operator had barely begun to run off the "thriller" of the night when there appeared on the screen a monster with legs like the limbs of a big tree, eyes as big as saucers, a huge body covered with hair that looked like standing wheat. At the first appearance of the monster women and children screamed in terror, and a rush was made for the door by the panic-stricken audience.

Suddenly some one, guffawed and yelled, "It's only a flying machine." This brought the panic stricken people to their senses and quiet was quickly restored. Several people, however, were severely bruised during the rush.

Readings and Screenings

There has been a great deal of innovative work on movie audiences since the first edition of this volume. For a sweeping look at the cultural and political history of theater, movie, and television audiences from the nineteenth century to the present, see Richard Butsch, *The Citizen Audience: Crowds, Publics, and Individuals* (New York: Routledge, 2007). For overviews of nickelodeons, movie theaters, and early movie audiences, see Melvyn Stokes and Richard Maltby, eds, *American Movie Audiences: From the Turn of the Century to the Early Sound Era* (London: British Film Institute, 1999); Melvyn Stokes and Richard Maltby, eds, *Hollywood Spectatorship: Changing Perceptions of Cinema Audiences* (London: British Film Institute, 2001); Melvyn Stokes and Richard Maltby, eds, *Identifying Hollywood's Audiences: Cultural Identity and the Movies* (London: British Film Institute, 2008); Richard Maltby, Melvyn Stokes, and Robert C. Allen, eds, *Going to the Movies: Hollywood and the Social Experience of the Cinema* (Exeter, UK: University of Exeter Press, 2008). Older works that are still useful include, Douglas Gomery, *Shared Pleasures: A History of Movie Presentation in the United States* (Madison, WI: University of Wisconsin Press, 1992); Charles Musser, *The Emergence of Cinema: The American Screen to 1907* (New York: Charles Scribner's Sons, 1990); Eileen Bowser, *The Transformation of Cinema: 1907–1915* (New York: Charles Scribner's Sons, 1990); Richard Kozarski, *An Evening's Entertainment: The Age of the Silent Feature Picture, 1915–1928* (New York: Charles Scribner's Sons, 1990). Moviegoing experiences outside large urban centers are explored in Gregory Waller, *Main Street Amusements: Movies and Commercial Entertainment in a Southern City, 1896–1930* (Washington, DC: Smithsonian Institution Press, 1995); Kathryn Fuller,

At the Picture Show: Small Town Audiences and the Creation of the Movie Fan (Washington, DC: Smithsonian Institution Press, 1996); Kathryn H. Fuller-Seeley, ed., *Hollywood in the Neighborhood: Historical Case Studies of Local Moviegoing* (Berkeley and Los Angeles, CA: University of California Press, 2008). For a close look at ethnic, racial, gender, and working-class moviegoing habits, see Jacqueline Stewart, *Migrating to the Movies: Cinema and Black Urban Modernity* (Berkeley and Los Angeles, CA: University of California Press, 2005); Shelley Stamp, *Movie-Struck Girls: Women and Motion Picture Culture After the Nickelodeon* (Princeton, NJ: Princeton University Press, 2000); Kathy Peiss, *Cheap Amusements: Working Women and Leisure in Turn-of-the-Century New York* (Philadelphia, PA: Temple University Press, 1986); Lauren Rabinovitz, *For the Love of Pleasure: Women, Movies, and Culture in Turn-of-the-Century Chicago* (New Brunswick, NJ: Rutgers University Press, 1998); Roy Rosenzweig, *Eight Hours For What We Will: Workers in an Industrial City, 1870–1920* (Cambridge and New York: Cambridge University Press, 1983); Steven J. Ross, *Working-Class Hollywood: Silent Film and the Shaping of Class in America* (Princeton, NJ: Princeton University Press, 1998). For collections of essays and documents that survey filmgoing patterns from the silent era to the 1990s, see Richard Abel, *Americanizing the Movies and Movie-Mad Audiences 1910–1914* (Berkeley and Los Angeles, CA: University of California Press, 2006) and Gregory A. Waller, ed., *Moviegoing in America: A Sourcebook in the History of Film Exhibition* (Malden, MA and Oxford: Wiley-Blackwell, 2001).

Although films such as *The Crowd* (1928) feature scenes of audiences at the movies, there are no silent films about going to the movies that I would recommend.

2

Heroes and Heroines of Their Own Entertainment: Progressive-Era Cinema

Introduction to Article

Most people associate movies with Hollywood and escapist entertainment. However, that was not always the case. In the years before World War I, movies were made by dozens of companies scattered throughout the United States. Early filmmakers did not necessarily believe that politics and entertainment were incompatible. Social problem films dramatized many of the controversial issues raised by Progressive-era reformers and were made by a wide variety of groups we would not usually associate with the movie industry. These activist filmmakers were determined to help people understand their world and change it for the better.

Kay Sloan looks at the early years of silent film, before Hollywood became Hollywood – that is, before a highly organized studio system, located in Los Angeles, changed both the content of film and the way movies were made. She shows how early movies became vehicles "for overtly presenting social problems to the public." Movies about suffragists, poverty, birth control, socialism, labor-capital conflict, and the like challenged the dominant political, social, economic, and gender ideas of the time. Sloan explores the diverse messages of these films and the ways in which filmmakers set out to depict and offer solutions to the most

Movies and American Society, Second Edition. Edited by Steven J. Ross.
© 2014 John Wiley & Sons, Inc. Published 2014 by John Wiley & Sons, Inc.

vexing problems of their age. Much to their surprise and delight, working-class and immigrant moviegoers found their lives sympathetically depicted on the screen in a manner that often turned them into the heroes and heroines of their own entertainment.

Discussion Points

After reading about what silent films tried to accomplish, do you think that movies today should aspire to educate us about the problems of everyday life or should they just concentrate on entertaining us? Is it possible or desirable to do both? If you were a filmmaker, what kinds of problems would you want to portray?

Front Page Movies

Kay Sloan

Source: Kay Sloane, *The Loud Silents: Origins of the Social Problem Film* (Urbana and Chicago: University of Illinois Press, 1988), 1–16, 130–2

Sheiks, flappers, comic tramps, and vamps: silent film has left a legacy of bizarrely colorful images preserved in the popular mind by nostalgia. Yet in the early days of the primitive film industry, the cinema treated social problems in a way that was, ironically, as fantastic as the glamorous stars and tinsel world of Hollywood's later silver screen. The earliest audiences pushed their coins across box office windows to watch melodramas and comedies that often celebrated characters who literally animated the social and political dilemmas of the Progressive Era. The cinema turned these dilemmas into fairy tales of the day. Greedy corporate tycoons, villainous landlords, corrupt politicians, flamboyant suffragettes, and striking workers flickered across the bedsheets that sometimes sufficed for screens in hastily created moviehouses just after the turn of the century.

This is the story of that early silent cinema, a largely precorporate, inconsistently censored film industry that had its roots not in Hollywood but in the nation's inner cities. It is an important story both for the vision it provides of how entertainment can deliver social problems to the public, and for the historical portrait it paints of America just after the turn of the century. In the era before World War I, moviegoing often involved paying a nickel or a dime to watch a series of short one or two reelers in the cramped quarters of storefront theaters that populated the urban ghettos. The elaborate movie "palace" was, for the most part, an anomaly; so was the feature film. Film companies were small business operations that might shoot several one-reel films every week in a make-shift studio. This was a time when the traditions of the cinema were in the process of formation, when both the subject matter and the form of film were in flux. Inventions rapidly became conventions that helped shore up a sense of social order, as a new art form began to link human desire with the needs of society.

In New York, Chicago, Boston, and in an obscure community called Hollywood out in California, small film companies often turned to the literary and political milieu of the muckrakers and the Progressives for storylines. The "muckraking" cinema cranked out stories that enter-tained primarily working-class audiences who could afford the five- or ten-cent price of admission to the nickelodeons. There, seated on wooden folding chairs, moviegoers watched graphic portrayals of America's social problems, some of which were part of their everyday lives.

In 1910, Walter Fitch, a film critic for the *Moving Picture World*, one of the film industry's first trade journals, stepped back from the immediacy of the new medium – it was, indeed, a cinema in search of itself – to take a long look at its potential and its possibilities. Filmmakers, mused Fitch, "may play on every pipe in the great organ of humanity."[1] The early cin-ema did indeed attempt to compose euphonious sounds from the cacoph-ony of the era. With titles such as *Capital Versus Labor, The Suffragettes' Revenge, A Corner in Wheat, The Usurer's Grip, The Girl Strike Leader*, or *The Reform Candidate*, all released in the first fifteen years of the twentieth century, the cinema championed the cause of labor, lobbied against polit-ical "bosses," and often gave dignity to the struggles of the urban poor. Conversely, other films satirized suffragists, ridiculed labor organizers, and celebrated America's corporate leaders in antilabor melodramas that the American Federation of Labor denounced and boycotted.

The period itself encompassed vast contradictions. While socialists such as Eugene Debs and Mother Jones fought for drastic changes in the nation's economic system, the new industrial leaders attempted pater-nalistic, philanthropic solutions to labor activism. At the same time that radicals pushed for fundamental changes in American life, middle-class reformers lobbied for legislation on labor and women's rights that would offer moderate change within the existing structure. Progressive thinkers such as the economist Richard T. Ely and the sociologists Edward A. Ross and Thorstein Veblen condemned what they saw as the dynamics of inequality in America; their voices became part of the milieu of protest in which the movies were born. Others like Louis D. Brandeis, later a Supreme Court justice, indicated the banking system he analyzed in *Other People's Money*, and successfully challenged corporate America in the courts. Muckraking journalists exposed the horrors of child labor and the corruption of political machinery in the nation's magazines and newspapers. Articles by such investigative journalists decried "the shame of the cities" and their failure to adequately meet the needs of their citizens. Upton Sinclair created a national furor by exposing unsanitary meat-packing conditions in his novel *The Jungle*; Frank Norris took on railroad tycoons in *The Octopus*. Lincoln Steffens's articles for *Everybody's Magazine*, with their prostitutes, gamblers, policemen "on the take," corporate tycoons, and greedy landlords, provided an array of stories that pointed to the need for social change.

It was a volatile, exciting world for the new lively entertainment form of the motion picture to enter. Conflicts that challenged the foundations of society found their way into the cinema as film companies seized on the news in the headlines for rich melodramatic and comic material. They also documented contemporary events in early newsreels. In an era long before the advent of television, motion pictures served as news reportage and propaganda at the same time that they revolutionized entertainment. Savvy political figures quickly learned to use the new medium to advertise themselves. In 1906, William Randolph Hearst made talking films of his campaign speeches to circulate in areas in which his personal travel was difficult. Performing a function similar to that of a modern television reporter, the filmmaker Siegmund Lubin released films in 1908 reporting the campaigns of the political rivals William Jennings Bryan and John W. Kern. But, though the films showing news events or national political campaigns served as important justifications for the existence of the often-criticized new medium of the motion picture, the fictions of those actual conflicts told a richer story about the climate of the period. The fictionalization of conflicts allowed an injection of fantasy and ideology into the stories. Films interpreted the nation's headlines in dramatic visual images that at once persuaded and entertained. The comedies, melodramas, and occasional westerns about labor conflict, tenement poverty, or political corruption reveal through fantasy an America torn with ideological conflict.

Often, special interest groups made their own motion pictures in collaboration with film industrialists. An important part of the process of translating the news involved opening the channels of filmmaking to groups advocating change. The earliest film audiences watched motion pictures made or sponsored by groups like the National Child Labor Committee, the National American Woman Suffrage Association, and even by individuals such as Upton Sinclair and the Progressive New York Governor, William Sulzer, who produced and starred in his own melodrama in 1914. Other Progressive activists joined them. For instance, the birth control activist Margaret Sanger made a melodrama to promote the basic civil liberties that she was repeatedly denied during the Progressive Era.

Conservatives as well as Progressives seized on the new medium as a way to dramatize their ideas. Organizations such as the National Association of Manufacturers and the Russell Sage Foundation made film melodramas to promote corporate paternalism. Such films circulated through the nation's moviehouses as if they were no different from slapstick comedies, westerns, and historical dramas. Distributors offered such politically oriented films to exhibitors along with material produced solely for entertainment. Often, a film reviewer would suggest to exhibitors that a motion picture with a prolabor message, for instance, or a plea for women's rights would be popular in areas where such ideas were already accepted. Essentially, the early audiences paid their nickels and dimes to see the political tracts of special interest groups on the same program as less controversial material.

Regardless of the ideological message, however, the vision that commercial film could serve as a vehicle for overt political causes seems startling – even revolutionary – today. For instance, Progressive Era woman suffragists made melodramas in collaboration with Hollywood film companies. Certainly it is difficult to imagine a modern-day equivalent: the National Organization of Women collaborating with Twentieth Century Fox in the early 1980s to make a melodrama starring Meryl Streep or Jane Fonda promoting the Equal Rights Amendment might be such an event. By contemporary standards, such a film would be an utter aberration from Hollywood practices. Yet in the early twentieth century, such was the notion of what film might – and even should – be. Film became a vehicle for overtly presenting social problems to the public.

The rise of the feature length film during the World War I years contributed to the decline of the numerous early social problem films. Since demand for motion pictures dictated that the companies turn out films rapidly, it was crucial that story ideas be readily found. It was easier for filmmakers to take risks about controversial issues in an era when the companies were releasing, as one Hollywood veteran remembers, at least "one reel a week."[2] When film companies turned out several short films a month, the production of a potentially controversial film was far less of an economic risk than it would be in the later age of the blockbuster. Even without the encouragement and participation of special interest groups, the young film companies made melodramas and comedies that exploited the issues splashed across the nation's headlines.

One of the most notorious of these films bore the innocent title of *Why?* Released in 1913, *Why?* shocked critics with its tale of corrupt elites and its vision of workers revolting against capitalism in America. The film's hero, a fiery-eyed immigrant with wild hair, dreamed of revenge against the wealthy classes who feasted while enslaved workers starved. The three parts of *Why?* contained episodes of capitalists and workers shooting it out with revolvers over child labor, corporate greed, and class inequality. In a scene that could have been scripted by Marx himself, the capitalists turn into sacks of gold when shot. Released by the American arm of the independent French company Eclair Films, *Why?* culminated with workers burning down Manhattan. The blazes, ironically, had been handpainted red by workers for the capitalist film company. The film ended with the Woolworth building still burning, violating one of the ideological tenets of the bourgeois narrative closure that flames, like western bad guys or melodramatic villains, have to die in the end. Instead of restoring responsibility and order, the film simply left its audience in a liminal world that granted power and legitimacy to unleashed desire. "Socialist doctrine!" cried one outraged reviewer.[3]

Why?'s virtual celebration of anarchy frightened censors as well as critics. Early censors feared the political content of films as much as their occasional sexual content. The potential of the cinema to champion such organized violence disturbed Frederic C. Howe, the chairman of the National Board of Censorship of Motion Pictures. That organization had been formed by the filmmakers themselves in 1909 to discourage "immoral" or "lurid" material that had roused criticism from more traditional sectors of society. Howe feared the mounting success of radical, politically oriented moving pictures. He was a liberal reformer, but hardly a radical. Despite local outcries over the supposed "immorality" of the movies, Howe suggested that the political role of film was potentially as threatening to society as were its challenges to a Victorian moral code.

Particularly since the early films touched the sentiments of masses of people, including the millions of newly arrived immigrants to whom the English printed word was still a mystery, they elicited condemnation from those, like Howe, who feared the power of the motion picture over those in the ghetto. Motion pictures, noted one journalist in 1908, had become "both a clubhouse and an academy for the workingman."[4] The class of people attending motion pictures, stated another observer delicately, "are not of the rich."[5] At their outset, motion pictures found audiences primarily among the many Americans whose lives were dominated by the uncertainties of poverty and the cultural ruptures of immigration.

Thus Frederic Howe worried about the content of films in 1914. The films that "tended to excite class feeling or ... tend to bring discredit upon the agencies of the government," wrote Howe, could lead to a time "when the movie ... becomes the daily press of industrial groups, of classes, of Socialism, syndicalism, and radical opinion."[6]

Howe's fears, of course, remained unfounded. The revolutionary content of *Why?* was an anomaly among the early social problem films. The young film companies themselves attempted to make their business more "respectable," and broaden the appeal of motion pictures to the middle classes. They made the social problem films as part of that process, with the notion that such films might be seen as "educational" and "uplifting."

It was a cinematic role encouraged by critics. In 1913, one film journalist suggested that the cinema might be a weapon "in the battle against child labor, white-slavery, labor-conflicts, and vice development."[7] He suggested that film should take up the subjects headlined on the front pages of the nation's newspapers and "expose injustice, cruelty, and suffering in all their naked ugliness."[8] This critic suggested that both the film industry's need for stories and America's pressing social problems might be settled if only the filmmakers would turn their attention to social issues. But the solution to such issues, he emphasized, must be calm, reasoned change, not the revolutionary message of a film like *Why?*

Such liberal film critics played an important role in channeling film into a vehicle for middle-class reforms. They pointed out causes that might be taken up in melodrama and applauded those films that did crusade. The *Moving Picture World*'s Louis Reeves Harrison promoted the role that film could play in pointing out the need for social reform, and he denounced what he called "the desire for power on the part of the ruling classes." Filmmakers, he urged, should pay attention to such inequities in corporate society.[9] The cinema might act as a cultural watchdog, appealing for responsibility from all levels of society. One issue demanding treatment by the moving pictures, suggested Harrison, was child labor – another was what he applauded as women's "broadening knowledge and experience." The expression of those issues could not only strengthen the nation, but the role of film in it.

In 1912, Harrison reminded filmmakers that the often-denigrated cinema might serve as a tool for "uplifting" the masses. He offered a virtual litany of themes for the melodrama that expressed the interests of both the era's reformers and some early filmmakers:

> the social battle for justice to those who do the world's work, the adjustment of compensation to labor, the right of common people to liberty and the pursuit of happiness, the betterment of humanity through the prevention

of crime rather than its cure, the prevention of infant mortality, and the prevention of hoggishness wherever theatrical trusts will permit, the self-conflict between material tendency and spiritual clarification, all these furnish subjects of widespread interest which the dramatist may handle with or without gloves.[10]

The film industry increasingly addressed the issues suggested by Harrison. In 1914, one film director boasted that he got the "best points for [his] work from the newspapers," turning the turmoil of the era into comedy and melodrama.[11]

Concerned that the cinema raised subversive questions, Howe neglected the important role it played in laying them to rest. *Why?*'s radical solution to class conflict was, not surprisingly, rare in the cinema. It represented the starkest challenge to the nation's economic powers – the wheat speculators, tenement owners, loan sharks, or captains of industry. More typically, the films dealt with social problems in a way that muted their critiques of economic or social injustice. They called for careful reforms or fatalistic surrenders to uncontrollable "natural" forces that doled out troubles and misfortunes. Such films proved that the radically new entertainment form of the cinema could act as a conservative force in the emerging industrial society.

For instance, the Thomas Edison Company's *The Usurer's Grip* was a modern-day fairy tale set in the tenements. Funded by the Russell Sage Foundation in 1912, the film warned audiences about unscrupulous money lenders who thrived on the poverty stricken, hounding them further and further into financial desperation. The film's hero and heroine found themselves in mounting debt to a usurer, but they were saved at last by an understanding businessman who directed them to the loan division of the Russell Sage Foundation. There they were rescued by the paternalism promoted by Sage's vision of benevolent capitalism. *The Usurer's Grip* was a self-serving advertisement for the Sage Foundation. Such early films precursed modern television advertising by blending entertainment with commercial messages. Through melodrama, the Edison Company and the Russell Sage Foundation advertised direct social reform and suggested that philanthropic measures might remedy urban poverty.

Increasingly, the early films moved from primitive one or two reelers exploiting class conflict to more sophisticated films with complicated plots. At times, they advocated specific reforms. Film began to shift from the sensationalism of muckraking issues into serious calls for reform through "enlightenment" – whether it be better management to assuage striking workers, calls for woman suffrage, the abolition of child labor, poor tenement conditions, and the illegality of birth control. Film industrialists tried to establish the middle-class nature of the cinema by allowing reform groups or special interest groups access to the medium. In 1912, the National Association of Manufacturers (NAM) collaborated with Thomas Edison's Company to make a propagandistic melodrama on factory safety called *The Crime of Carelessness*. It was written by the Progressive writer James Oppenheim, who was quickly earning a reputation as a writer of what the *New York Times* called "social films."[12] His first film for the Edison Company, titled *Hope*, had dealt with the problem of tuberculosis. With *The Crime of Carelessness*, he turned to the more controversial issue of problems in the workplace. The film laid equal blame for hazardous working conditions on workers and negligent owners – but insidiously punished a careless worker for a factory fire. The problems of the workplace, then, might be resolved merely by responsibility on the part of individual employees. It was, wrote the *New York Times* critic, a "long and stirring drama," one of a line of Oppenheim's "social films."[13] NAM's film, of course, did more than link industrial problems with careless workers. It also linked the interests of the film industry with those of the larger corporate interests represented by NAM.

A similar theme emerged in the Vitagraph Company's *Capital Versus Labor*, an exposé of labor problems made in 1910. Punctuated by bloody scenes of rioting workers battling company-hired thugs, the film suggested that the strikers had legitimate grievances to air. But the workers alone were powerless to change their situation. The eventual "happy ending" came not through the organized protests or negotiations of labor unions, but through the intervention of the church. The violence in *Capital Versus Labor* continued until a minister finally calmed the mobs and convinced the greedy capitalist to compromise with his workers. The film thus revealed the futility of rioting in the streets while it still acknowledged the validity of the strikers' complaints. From such plots came a dual statement about workers in America: while the films granted them dignity and self-worth as individuals, it also rendered them and their organizations powerless. *The Crime of Carelessness* and *Capital Versus Labor* serve as examples of how workers might be portrayed as irresponsible individuals who are ultimately dependent on the good graces of their generous bosses.

Such films relied on the "happy ending," which provided audiences with continuity and faith in "the system." Even actual historical events were rewritten to accommodate that expectation. A 1915 melodrama on political corruption in New York City provides a telling example of how important the happy ending had become. *The Governor's Boss* took a political tragedy and transformed it into victory for the democratic process. The film was one of the most unusual melodramas made about political corruption for another reason: it actually starred an impeached governor of New York, William Sulzer.

Sulzer publicized his case against the Tammany Hall machine in 1915 with a melodrama written by James S. Barcus, a friend and political crony. He first took it to Broadway, where the play had a brief run of sixteen performances at the Garrick Theatre. Following the play's unsuccessful Broadway run, he turned to the cinema with the script. To heighten the realism of the film, Sulzer played himself in the starring role, but he took the unique opportunity that film provided to rewrite his own history with a happy ending. *The Governor's Boss* ended not with Sulzer's impeachment, but with the defeat of his opponents in court. Sulzer restored justice and democracy to New York City through the power of the cinema rather than the power of political office. Imagine Richard Nixon producing and starring in a cinematic version of Watergate in 1975 – with an ending in which he retained his grip on the presidency. Despite the vast differences between Sulzer and Nixon, the preposterous nature of the contemporary example is nevertheless a striking indication of just how unique this Progressive Era vision of film as political propaganda was.

Like the many previous melodramas calling for social change, *The Governor's Boss* restored democracy in such a way that rendered the film a less powerful statement against Tammany Hall. The *New York Times* critic found the ending so absurd that he sarcastically observed that "the Governor, his secretary, his daughter, and Virtue in general triumph."[14] Even real occurrences took on fantastic proportions to assure a society in distress that its institutions worked for the good of all, despite the news broadcast in the nation's headlines.

The headlines were powerful material in a time when muckraking journalists and novelists like Ida Tarbell and Upton Sinclair constantly probed the underside of the "American Dream." Both Sinclair and Tarbell were among the era's crusaders who made their own films. Their cinematic efforts reflected a period in film history when the motion pictures were seen as a medium that might be open to the public, particularly to those with a cause. Tarbell, who had condemned John D. Rockefeller when she exposed the ruthless practices of the Standard Oil Company in 1902, collaborated with Vitagraph Studios in 1914 as part of their series of photoplays scripted by "famous authors."[15] Interestingly, she chose not a political subject but a historical play to dramatize, as part of a broader effort by the membership of the Authors' League of America to help less recognized writers. In 1913, Upton Sinclair ambitiously put his powerful exposé of the meat-packing industry, *The Jungle*, into five reels of a motion picture. At the same time, however, the issues that Tarbell and Sinclair were publicizing with their news articles and novels found their way into the cinema in ways that were less overtly political than *The Jungle*. Motion pictures took on the preoccupations of muckraking journalists and absorbed them into the ethos of individualism and the "virtue" that mended society in *The Governor's Boss*. In that process, they helped establish film as a respectable entertainment form, as they mediated the problems of society.

Many security-minded reformers from the educated middle class saw that new function of film and moved from their early position of unrelenting condemnation of the newly emerged entertainment form to an attempt to "re-form" it. These reformers realized that film had the capacity to solve problems, to suggest solutions that would contain disorder and push forward moderate change. Their motion pictures raised issues among masses of people that the printed word might not reach, as Walter Fitch had commented in 1910. Film critics such as Louis Reeves Harrison and his colleagues at the *Moving Picture World*, W. Stephen Bush and the Reverend E. Boudinot Stockton, all had long stressed the use of film to "uplift." Jane Addams turned from her call for censorship of the moving pictures ("debased" and "primitive" she had called them in 1909)[16] to actually starring in a melodrama in 1913 titled *Votes for Women*. Filmmaking seemed to have become fashionable among liberal reformers.

In their collaboration with professional filmmakers, the reformers used some of the conventions rapidly developing in the film to serve their own purposes. Through the "happy ending," the films presented the possibility that change could take place without massive upheaval or disruption. Such purposes led reformers such as Jane Addams to move from initial condemnation of the motion picture to praise for its capacity to "uplift" or "educate." Film could serve the interests of the middle class and of the film industry by appealing to a broader audience by using virtuous calls for reform.

The reformist dramas provided a respectable mission for a cinema in search of itself. By 1915, the poet and film critic Vachel Lindsay could observe that "the motion picture goes almost as far as journalism into the social fabric in some ways, further in others."[17] Whatever their political message, however, films penetrated the social fabric even further than did muckraking journalists by tapping fantasy as well as reality, animating and heightening the stories told in print. The cinema offered fantastic solutions that appealed to unconscious human desire at the same time that it raised problems of everyday life.

Some of this process had been observed as early as 1915 during the height of the early silent film era. In the summer of that year, a portly, balding psychologist from Harvard discovered a diversion from Boston's humid afternoons. Professor Hugo Munsterberg became one of the cinema's most ardent devotees. Munsterberg's first movie experience, a somewhat risqué film called *Neptune's Daughter,* had been, by his own daughter's account, one of the most startling adventures of the professor's life. Settled in the anonymous darkness of a theater, he had watched a fascinating phenomenon unfold. On the movie screen before him, the actress Annette Kellerman danced in a costume that left little to the imagination. But what fascinated the professor even more than Kellerman were the actual illustrations of the nuances of human perception that he had studied and taught for years in the university. Munsterberg was captivated by the manner in which the camera appeared to virtually become the human eye, and in which it might also create a new vision of the world controlled by moral forces. He spent the rest of the summer of 1915 carefully studying the new art form, even securing for himself a personal tour of the Vitagraph Studios.

Part of Munsterberg's interest lay in interpreting how the cinema dwelled on human needs and how it could direct the emotions of audiences. In a treatise on the motion picture, *The Photoplay,* published by the psychologist shortly before he died in 1916, he laid the foundation for a sophisticated theory of film. One of the greatest attractions of the cinema, he suggested, was its "stirring up of desires together with their constant fulfillment."[18]

More than a simple mirroring of visual perception, motion pictures became immensely popular with the masses in those formative years because, in part, they captured the enduring subtleties of human desire, with their tales of wistful longing for a better life. "The work of art," explained Munsterberg, "aims to keep both the demand and its fulfillment forever awake."[19] The theater thus roused longing while it also left audiences with the "constant fulfillment" recognized by the psychologist. The popular culture emerging at the turn of the century acted as an agent of both social cohesion and the desire for change. That process emerges as the protest films addressed political and social subjects that held the capacity to rupture society.

Entertainment in itself involves a certain rupturing – a temporary suspension of belief in the outside world takes place along with a suspension of disbelief in the inner world constructed through entertainment. The melodrama of social protest suspended audiences between what they escaped *from* (their everyday lives) and what they escaped *to* (a more romantic version of the situation that structured those daily lives). By often resolving those situations in "happily ever after" endings, movies released their audiences from the grim cinematic creations of shabby tenement life, or sweatshop lines, into a world transformed, however briefly, into a realm where fantasy entered the tenement or sweatshop on the wings of romance or sudden wealth. If the melodramas refused to allow such interventions, they at least endowed their heroes and heroines with dignity.

A whole host of archetypal villains and victims danced in the flickering lights of the nickelodeons in a melodramatic exorcism of social wrongs. Such archetypes have never really left the motion picture – nor has the "happy ending," which restored faith in the enduring individual. In its early era of inventions, the cinema also set conventions. The primitive social problem films were the beginning of a long psychological trip into the present with which they are intimately joined. Like any pioneers, the early movies were original, but the trail they blazed into the American psyche became a familiar path marked with desires and frustrations – and so timeworn that we have taken its twists and turns for granted.

By the eve of World War I, most of the small film companies were gone, and with them the storefront nickelodeons and those primitive short films that raised social problems, much as the muckrakers did. Those formative years of the cinema, unique as they were, established the manner in which films continue to raise social issues while at the same time containing them in satisfactory bourgeois resolutions. America's dilemmas are in many ways similar to those faced by the country just after the turn of the century – overcrowding, sexual inequalities, political corruption, and corporate irresponsibility still find their way into a cinema that solves those problems in a private fashion, just as the early films did. But never again will the process be quite so blatant as in the silent social problem films.

Something was forgotten in the following decades, or lost in sentimentalized versions of the early period. In 1915, Vachel Lindsay expressed a thought that is poignant in retrospect. He dramatically claimed that film is a "new weapon of men, and the face of the whole earth changes."[20] Lindsay, regrettably, was wrong. Much still remains to be explored and "remembered" from that era when "the whole earth changed" because of a new entertainment form.

In those one or two reelers are more than the origins of the social problem film. The films contain cultural signposts of paramount importance about how entertainment shapes the political issues affecting the lives of moviegoers. They are a reminder of the capacity of film to explore the problems of society and lessen their threat while still suggesting the need for change. When Stephen Crane's fictional Maggie attended her turn-of-the-century melodramas, she would leave "with raised spirits" after watching people like herself defeat those with power over them. Though such triumphs in the cinema were measured in terms of religious redemptions or acts of fate, they were still significant glimpses into class conflict in America. Within that complex role is buried an even deeper significance.

The films also reveal a society struggling to maintain order in a period of terrific unrest – an order that allowed inequality and the essential power-lessness of the average American to continue.

Those days when the film industry was young reveal that the cinema reverberates through time itself. It goes beyond its specific era to illuminate the ongoing power of the motion picture to dramatize the needs and desires of its viewers through generations of archetypal characters and situations. Like H. G. Wells's heroes, one can travel into the past with the flick of a switch on a projection machine and discover America at the turn of the century. Unfortunately, however, such a cinematic "journey" can be as difficult as a ride on Wells's time machine: many of the films simply no longer exist, and can be known only through reviews or synopses. When silent films lost their commercial viability within several years after release, the film companies, eager for fast production and quick profits, carelessly discarded them. Often the companies themselves were too short-lived to maintain their films. The perishable silver nitrate stock on which the motion pictures were printed further reduced their chance for survival. As early as 1906, one critic recognized the danger of losing such valuable cultural artifacts as the new motion picture. "We often wonder where all the films that are made and used a few times go to," he wrote, "and the questions come up in our minds, again and again: Are the manufacturers aware that they are making history? Do they realize that in fifty or one hundred years the films now being made will be curiosities?"[21] Now, some eighty years later, one only wishes that filmmakers had listened to his admonition. The films that exist today are rare cultural documents.

Though the preserved film footage offers valuable insight into the climate of American cultural and political tensions, an understanding of their full impact must, ironically, rely heavily on original printed material. Controversy over the issues of social protest spilled over into the pages of early trade magazines such as the *Moving Picture World*, *Motography*, *Variety*, and *Photoplay*. Their reviews testify to the lively arguments over workers' rights, class conflict, political graft, and sexual politics that the films once delivered.

Such themes that the films repeatedly explored illustrate the larger dilemmas of society in dealing with injustices and inequalities. ... [Movies examined] the class-bound nature of early melodrama and what the sociologist Edward A. Ross called "criminaloids" – those who grew wealthy by exploiting the poor. Such characters made ideal villains in films that ventured into the inner circles of the nation's corrupt elites. ... [They also explored] the "cinema of the submerged," particularly as D. W. Griffith defined it. There, a cinema made heroes and heroines out of those "submerged" in powerlessness. Tenement dwellers attempted to flee the ghetto, and escaped prisoners tried to elude their captors in plots that pointed out the plight of the victims of economic or legal injustice.

In the labor union films … working-class heroes fought back against their employers. But the problem of "Capital Versus Labor," as the film of that title designated it, varied from visions of unruly "ferret-eyed workers" to cruel "fat cat" factory owners who exploited children and honest working people. White slavery, a subject of … sexual politics, was one of the most controversial topics ever sensationalized by the cinema. Taken alone, it was a euphemism for forced prostitution. The central concern of the explosive white slavery films and the melodramas on alcoholism and birth control was the preservation of the private sphere of the family.

The films about the woman suffrage movement … brought together a wide spectrum of propaganda for and against the movement. Caricatures of man-hating suffragettes paraded across movie screens as comedies ridiculed the notion of women voting. Suffragists themselves fought back with movie cameras, countering the comic attack with persuasive melodramas starring beautiful suffragist heroines. They elevated film into a significant political tool for their cause. The suffrage films, with their span of satire, newsreels, and melodramas, offer an opportunity to look at the tremendous range of political positions that the cinema took on a single subject.

The early risk-taking silent filmmakers saw their new medium as one that could both entertain and, in due course, instruct. They catered to the masses with a gamut of social commentary that reflected the traditional American belief that once social wrongs were exposed to the people, the people would see to it that they were righted. More importantly, the companies catered to the masses to build their own business empires. Thus they were reformers who also sought a profit; with their sermons on social injustice and their faith in the individual, they became, quite unintentionally, America's newest street preachers, making movies that became indeed "loud silents."

Notes

1   Walter M. Fitch, "The Motion Picture Story Considered As A New Literary Form," *Moving Picture World* 6, 19 February 1910, 248.
2   Fred J. Balshofer and Arthur C. Miller, *One Reel A Week* (Berkeley and Los Angeles: University of California Press, 1967).
3   "Why?" *Moving Picture World* 16, 14 June 1913, 1138.
4   Lucy France Pierce, "The Nickelodeon," *Views and Film Index*, 24 October 1908, 4.
5   "Moving Pictures Shows in Manhattan," *Views and Film Index*, 9 June 1906, 8.

6   Frederic C. Howe, "What To Do With the Motion Picture Show: Shall It Be Censored?" *The Outlook* 107, 20 June 1914, 412–16.

7   Carl Holliday, "The Motion Picture and the Church," *The Independent* 74, 13 February 1913, 353.

8   Ibid.

9   Louis Reeves Harrison, *Screencraft* (New York: Chalmers Publishing Company, 1916), pp. 34–9.

10   Louis Reeves Harrison, "Wake Up! It's 1912!" *Moving Picture World* 12, 6 January 1912, 21.

11   Quoted in Robert Grau, *The Theatre of Science* (New York: Benjamin Blom, 1914), p. 106.

12   "Writing the Movies: A New and Well-Paid Business," *New York Times*, 3 August 1913, in Gene Brown, ed., *New York Times Encyclopedia of Film, 1896–1928* (New York: New York Times Books, 1984).

13   "Writing the Movies: A New and Well-Paid Business," *New York Times*, 3 August 1913.

14   "Sulzer Hero of Weak Play," *New York Times*, 15 April 1914, 13; "The Governor's Boss," *Variety*, 18 June 1915, 17.

15   "Well-Known Authors Act Their Own Plays in 'Movies,'" (February 1914) in Gene Brown, ed., *New York Times Encyclopedia of Film, 1896–1928* (New York: New York Times Books, 1984).

16   Jane Addams, *The Spirit of Youth and the City Streets* (New York: Macmillan Company, 1909 and 1913), p. 87.

17   Vachel Lindsay, *The Art of the Moving Picture* (New York: Macmillan Company, 1915 and 1922), p. 225.

18   Hugo Munsterberg, *The Photoplay* (New York: D. Appleton and Company, 1916), p. 157.

19   Ibid.

20   Lindsay, *The Art of the Moving Picture*, p. 289.

21   "History and the Motion Picture," *Views and Film Index*, 1 December 1906, 1.

Documents

Introduction to Documents

Although early films were attacked by many civic and religious leaders, they were also staunchly defended by people who, like *Moving Picture World* reporter W. Stephen Bush, spoke eloquently about the new medium's value as a "means of agitating for the betterment of social conditions." Social problem films, as Bush goes on to argue, served as powerful tools for educating the public about the ills of society and urging moviegoers to use the ballot box to remedy those ills. Our first document focuses on films that dealt with the problems of child labor and the role they played in promoting passage of legislation aimed at protecting minors working in factories and stores. Our second document suggests that Richard Butsch's claim that "nickelodeons were rarely sites of political activism" was not entirely true. The owners of the Los Angeles Socialist Movie Theater sought to combine politics and entertainment in a palatable form. Socialist audiences in Los Angeles got so fed up with the anti-labor, anti-radical images they saw on the screen that they opened their own theater and vowed to show only films that presented positive images of working people. The theater owners also invited speakers to engage audiences in discussions of strikes and ongoing political work.

The Social Uses of the Moving Picture

W. Stephen Bush

Source: *Moving Picture World*, 12(4), April 27, 1912, 305–6

The value of the moving picture as a means of agitating for the betterment of social conditions is self-evident. Nothing affects us more powerfully than the truth when it is preached in pictures. Less than a hundred years ago our social system was full of grave wrongs and abuses, which were eventually remedied and destroyed by pictures, cartoons and descriptions. The pen-picture, even when drawn by a masterhand, can never be as quickly and as universally convincing as the picture which derives its realism from the fact that it moves.

Abuses and wrongs cannot live except in darkness. The moment we throw a strong enough light on a real social wrong half the battle is won. A striking illustration of this fact was afforded recently during the last session of the New York Legislature. It appears that several efforts had been made to obtain an appropriation for shelter for poor blind children. The legislators who, no doubt, possessed the same sympathy for suffering that every human being feels, neglected to act in the matter; not out of callous indifference but because the rush of business and their own individual affairs claimed their attention. One day a little blind child suffering from the want of such a shelter was placed beside the presiding officer of the Senate. The sight so affected the legislators that the appropriation was voted at once without a dissenting voice.

Any motion picture portraying deplorable social conditions is therefore an agent for good. Some of the best known film makers of our country have given us pictures dealing with social evils and making a strong appeal for redress and reform. The Biograph, Selig, Vitagraph and notably the Edison studios deserve credit for their efforts along these lines.

The boldest, most timely and most effective appeal for the stamping out of the cruelest of all social abuses has been made in a two-reel production by the Thanhouser Company. The pictures are based on the touching poem of Elizabeth Barrett Browning entitled, "The Cry of the Children." More than two generations have passed away since the noble poetess told of the "children weeping ere the sorrow comes with years."

Since that time great efforts have been made by many good men and women to stop this evil. We are ashamed to say that the agitation against child labor has been far more successful in other civilized countries than in our own. For more than half a century all attempts to remedy the evil in the cotton mills of the South, where it appears in its most hideous shape, have been unavailing.

After an agitation lasting from the period of reconstruction to the present day, the best that has been accomplished was done by the present Congress. A law has now been passed, establishing a Federal Bureau, which, however, can do nothing but investigate conditions. It has no authority to change hours of labor or order any other restrictions. It cannot even recommend legislation, because Congress, under the Constitution, lacks authority to pass such laws. The best that can be hoped for is the creating of public sentiment through the publication of the results of its inquiries. There was evidence before Congress that boys and girls as young as six and seven years were put into the mills and compelled to work ten and eleven hours a day. The results of such a state of affairs in degrading and debasing humanity, need not be described in detail here.

We are glad to say that the Thanhouser picture will accomplish the same results that are expected from the work of the Federal Bureau, to wit: the arousing of public indignation. The pictures are admirably conceived, do not at any time go beyond the line of probability and bring home their lesson in a forceful, but perfectly natural and convincing way. No dramatic derrick has been used to drag in a counterfeit love story. The makers of the film have kept before their eyes the one idea: the enlightening of the public as to the conditions and effects of child labor. While the picture skilfully paints the extremes of our modern social life, it has steered clear of the fatal error of the old time melodrama in which, instead of human beings, the spectator was compelled to see a set of angels and a set of devils. THE CRY OF THE CHILDREN as rendered by the Thanhouser Company, makes it plain that the mill-owner is as much a creature of circumstances and surroundings and economic conditions as the laborer. The picture shows the common bond of humanity between them and how the touch that makes all the world akin does not lose its magic in the wretched tenement of the laborer or in the mansion of the mill-owner or in the whirr of the factory.

A laborer and his family consisting of a wife and some half-grown children try to live in peace with the world and with themselves in spite of the awful conditions which surround them. They cannot, however, fight off the inevitable. The awful strain begins to tell on the mother who bears the heaviest burden. When she breaks down, the youngest child in the family who had been kept at home and treated as the favorite was compelled to go to work. She could not stand up to her cruel task and live. Nature had not made her little limbs for bearing the burdens of hard toil and the little girl dies a victim of overwork. The mill-owner's wife had offered to adopt the little child, but her offer had been rejected by the child herself. Later when the child began to realize the odds against the laborer in the struggle of life she went to the mill-owner's wife and asked to be adopted, thinking in that way to lighten the burdens of her parents and sisters. But the grime of toil had replaced the child-like grace and sacrifice of former days. The bitter hours in the factory had changed the happy laughing child into a haggard looking waif. In her altered appearance she found no longer favor in the eyes of her employer's wife and necessity drove her back into the house of torture. The end of the picture shows the grief of the parents and sisters of the dead child and the bitter and cutting remorse of the mill-owner and his wife. As we look at the latter we feel the awful weight of the poem's words:

> But the child's sob in the silence curses deeper
> Than the strong man in his wrath.

Wherever these pictures are shown, converts to the necessity of thorough child labor reforms will be made by thousands. Owing to the determined opposition of Southern members of Congress the Federal Bureau entrusted with the investigation of child labor has had its powers narrowed and limited in many ways. In order to hamper the work of the Bureau as much as possible an amendment was tacked on to the law, which prohibits an investigator from entering the laborer's home, if the householder objects. This amendment was not dictated by any tender regard for the privacy of the home, but is to be a weapon in the hands of the mill-owner, who by threats and intimidation will seek to influence his employee against the investigators. Right here the power of the motion picture asserts itself. They may be able to bar the investigator, but they cannot bar the man with the camera. The camera must create the demand for remedial legislation and second the labors of the Federal Bureau.

The remedy, of course, lies entirely with the legislatures of the individual states. The report of the Federal Bureau will be read by hundreds at best, while the picture will be seen by millions. It seems to us that in the near future this fact will be recognized by the people most concerned in the matter, we mean organized labor. It was the labor element which forced the establishment of the Bureau from an unwilling Congress. The labor element ought to realize the advantages of the motion picture as a means of agitation and be swift in making use of them. The protection of the minors working in store and factory is one of the live issues of the coming campaign for the election of a president. The pictures here mentioned are therefore very timely and ought to be welcome to every intelligent and progressive exhibitor. We will confess ourselves much mistaken if THE CRY OF THE CHILDREN in motion pictures will not serve as a valuable campaign argument long before the votes will be counted in November.

Los Angeles Socialist Movie Theater

Source: *Appeal to Reason,* October 7, 1911; *Los Angeles Citizen,* September 15, 22, 1911

Socialists in Los Angeles have opened a moving picture theater where moving pictures depicting the real life and ideals of the working class will be shown. It has now been in operation for several weeks and is a pronounced success. A competent manufacturer of films is making the pictures and the plant will soon be in readiness to suppress reels to other cities. ...

[Frank Hillyard, owner of theater, talks about his goals] "The worker, hat in hand, in front of the forging boss, has at last worked on our nerves; and we want a theater that will portray working-class life without insulting us. Most people, perhaps, do not know there is a moving picture trust and that it now controls fully 30 percent of the business; within the next year it will control most of it, so if the laboring people are to have any truthful pictures of their life it is necessary to have a theater devoted exclusively to such films."

"Where will you get your themes?" I inquired of the young man.

"From life," he replied. "You must know the old pictures were not at all true to life. They were often so untrue as to be almost slanderous. Our theater is the result of the rebellion of the audiences against what was given to them. Take for example a recent picture run here pretending to portray a coal miners' strike. It was made to appear that the men struck without justice or reason and came back hat in hand in the spirit of bad children who had been punished into submission. We propose to reply to such pictures as that by running films showing the truth of labor disputes. We are weary to the soul of films that always represent us looking up to the magnate as the star of hope. They are not only an insult to the working man but out of harmony with the spirit of American institutions: besides being a poor education for growing children."

The Socialists' picture house on 5th Street is a flattering success from the start and from the first week's business it is indicated that it will become a good source of revenue to the party. All organized labor is back of the enterprise. ... The hit of the week is the Labor Day parade film manufactured in Los Angeles for this house and by union labor. ... The picture is an excellent one and gives many familiar faces in the great labor movement of this city.

During the week a specially prepared film will be shown depicting the Socialist activity in the present [election] campaign, showing the activity in each department, from speech-making to mailing the countless pieces of literature that is being sent out from headquarters in the Canadian building. Following this a special film will be shown of the activity of the women in the suffrage campaign. The picture will be given under the auspices of the Wage Earners' Votes for Women League.

The hoodoo that has been hovering over this house ever since it opened has been broken. Last Sunday afternoon and evening recorded over a thousand paid admissions. At one time the line of eager patrons extended into the street, the first time in the history of Fifth Street picture houses. The theater has been crowded every evening during the week and the demand to see the great Labor Day film is as keen as at the opening day.

All pictures that are to be shown at this house are to be the product of union labor and posed by union labor, depicting labor scenes. The demand for the Labor Day parade picture that is being made by other houses only shows what can be accomplished when the Socialist picture has its films ready for the trade. ...

Last Wednesday evening the women of the Wage Earners' Suffrage League had charge of the theater and slides depicting the activity of the women workers were shown upon the canvas. Mrs. Joe Cannon made interesting talks during the exhibition of the slides. This unique contribution to the cause of woman's suffrage made a decided hit with the patrons of the house, judging from the very good receipts at the box office. ... The house is well ventilated and the character of the pictures shown make it an inviting place to spend an hour in a quiet and wholesome rest.

Readings and Screenings

Social problem films of the silent era are most thoroughly explored in Sloan, *Loud Silents*; Kevin Brownlow, *Behind the Mask of Innocence* (New York: Alfred A. Knopf, 1990); Lewis Jacobs, *The Rise of the American Film: A Critical History* (New York: Teachers College Press, 1968); Lary May, *Screening Out the Past: The Birth of Mass Culture and the Motion Picture Industry* (New York: Oxford University Press, 1980). Useful works that focus on how silent films dealt with various social issues include Charlie Keil and Ben Singer, eds, *American Cinema of the 1910s: Themes and Variations* (New Brunswick, NJ: Rutgers University Press, 2009); Robert L. Hilliard, *Hollywood Speaks Out: Pictures that Dared to Protest Real World Issues* (Malden, MA and Oxford: Wiley-Blackwell, 2009); Miriam Hansen, *Babel and Babylon: Spectatorship in American Silent Film* (Cambridge, MA: Harvard University Press, 1991); Michael Slade Shull, *Radicalism in American Silent Films, 1909–1929: A Filmography and History* (Jefferson, NC: McFarland and Company, 2000); Steven Ross, *Working-Class Hollywood*; Thomas Cripps, *Slow Fade to Black: The Negro in American Film, 1940–1942* (New York: Oxford University Press, 1977); Donald Bogle, *Bright Boulevards, Bold Dreams: The Story of Black Hollywood* (New York: Ballantine Books, 2005); Gerald R. Butters, Jr., *Black Manhood on the Silent Screen* (Lawrence, KA: University Press of Kansas, 2002); Daniel Bernardi, ed., *The Birth of Whiteness: Race and the Emergence of U.S. Cinema* (New Brunswick: Rutgers University Press, 1996). Robert Sklar's *Movie-Made America: A Cultural History of American Movies* (New York: Vintage Books, revised edition 1994) remains the best single volume overview of the history of film and its relationship to American society.

There are quite a few silent films – many available either separately or as part of DVD collections or on Youtube – that illuminate themes raised in the article and documents. The best starting place for surveying social issue films is the National Film Preservation Foundation's multi-volume "Treasure" series. Each volume includes several DVDs that feature optional voice-over narration and a volume of film notes. In particular, see *Treasures from American Film Archives: 50 Preserved Films*, *More Treasures from American Film Archives 1894–1931*, *Treasures III: Social Issues in American Film, 1900–1934*, and *Treasures 5: The West, 1898–1938*. Poverty and social injustice are explored in *The Kleptomaniac* (1905), *A Corner in Wheat* (1908), *From the Submerged* (1912), *One Is Business, The Other Crime* (1912). For crime and gangs, see *The Musketeers of Pig Alley* (1912). The exploitation of children, women, and the elderly are dramatized in *The Song of the Shirt* (1908), *What Shall We Do With Our Old?* (1911), *Children Who Labor* (1912), and *The Cry of the Children* (1912). *Traffic in Souls* (1913) and *The Wages of Sin* (1914) tell how poor women were often forced into prostitution. Labor-Capital conflict is portrayed in *The Iconoclast* (1910), *The Crime of Carelessness* (1912), *A Poor Relation* (1914), and *Intolerance* (1916). Although nearly a century old, Charlie Chaplin's films remain popular with undergraduates. His more amusing early send-ups of authority figures include *Work* (1915) and *The Floorwalker* (1916). My favorite silent film, *The Italian* (1915), offers a moving portrait of the American Dream gone bad for one immigrant family. It is a must see. Finally, though not considered a social problem film, D. W. Griffith's *The Birth of a Nation* (1915) is a landmark movie for anyone interested in the ways in which early film represented – or misrepresented – the Civil War, Reconstruction, and race relations.

3

The Rise of Hollywood: Movies, Ideology, and Audiences in the Roaring Twenties

Introduction to Article

The years after World War I witnessed dramatic changes in the structure of the movie industry, the class composition of audiences, and the political content of silent films. During the late 19teens and 1920s, movies played an important role in reshaping the ways in which Americans looked at and thought about concepts of class and class identity. While Progressive-era cinema focused heavily on the problems of immigrants and working people, movies of the 1920s shifted their attention to the rapidly expanding world of that diverse and amorphous group known as the middle class. Abandoning the more serious social problem films described by Kay Sloan, postwar filmmakers increasingly turned out features that emphasized fantasies of love, consumption, and harmony among the classes.

Politicians have long accused Hollywood of being a bastion of liberalism. But Steven Ross argues that the rise of the studio system that came to be known as "Hollywood" was accompanied by a conservative shift in the class politics of American films. Ross explores the factors that contributed to this change. He reveals how during the 1920s, studios (many financed by Wall Street investors) sought to increase their profits by attracting greater numbers of prosperous patrons while retaining their loyal working-class fans. They did so by building exotic movie palaces

Movies and American Society, Second Edition. Edited by Steven J. Ross.
© 2014 John Wiley & Sons, Inc. Published 2014 by John Wiley & Sons, Inc.

and making lavish films aimed at turning the moviegoing experience in one that reshaped traditional ideas about class. These seemingly harmless fantasies, Ross suggests, entailed political costs that altered the way in which people thought about the problems of daily life and their possible solutions.

Discussion Points

How did movie palaces and cross-class fantasy films change the ways in which Americans thought about class? If an alien were to arrive on Earth and its only knowledge of American life was gained by watching films, how might that visitor describe contemporary ideas about class in the United States? Would the alien see class as a good or bad thing? Why?

Fantasy and Politics: Moviegoing and Movies in the 1920s

Steven J. Ross

Source: Steven J. Ross, *Working-Class Hollywood: Silent Film and the Shaping of Class in America* (Princeton, NJ: Princeton University Press, 1998), 173–211, 327–38

The cold March winds could not stop thousands of determined men and women from being part of movie history. They began gathering early in the day, and by 7 p.m. over 10,000 excited people stood at the corner of 7th Avenue and 50th Street. Housewives wrapped in their warmest winter coats, blue-collar workers in sturdy galoshes and long underwear, and young lovers cuddled in each other's arms all hoped to catch a glimpse of the rich and famous. It was March 11, 1927, opening night at the world's largest and most expensive movie palace, New York's $12 million Roxy Theater. Twenty years earlier, police were busily closing down seedy nickelodeons frequented by the city's immigrant and working-class population. But that night, 125 cops stood outside the theater to protect the arriving guests, including Mayor Jimmy Walker, movie stars Charlie Chaplin, Norma Talmadge, and Harold Lloyd, and "6,200 leaders in [the] city's commercial, professional, and artistic life." As they entered what the neon-emblazoned marquee announced to be "THE CATHEDRAL OF THE MOTION PICTURE," the most privileged guests flashed their engraved invitations to the ticket takers, while lesser luminaries clutched the special green tickets that cost $11 each (about $83 in 1990 dollars).[1] ...

Opening night at the Roxy, like opening nights at movie palaces around the country, was confined largely to the rich and famous. But the next morning, and for 365 mornings and evenings each year, the doors were thrown open to anyone willing to buy a ticket. Clerks, lawyers, waitresses, teachers, stenographers, plumbers, doctors, and factory workers enjoyed the same opulence and grand treatment accorded to movie stars, politicians, and aristocrats. Neighborhood theaters still continued to serve their largely working-class clientele. But the exhibitors who built luxury movie palaces during the 1920s expanded the class composition of the audience and ushered in what many heralded as a new age of democratic fantasy. "What greater democratic institution exists than the movie theater?" New York Socialist Assemblyman Samuel Orr asked in 1921. "It is there where rich and poor, young and old, men, women and children gather by the millions everyday throughout the land to laugh together and cry together."[2]

By the time the Roxy opened, movies and movie theaters were respected forms of mass culture that drew perhaps as many as 100 million people a week, a figure that nearly equaled the entire national population. Movies had long attracted the "masses," but in the 1920s they also attracted the "classes." Although some wealthy and middle-class folk frequented movies before the war, it was only in the postwar era that moviegoing became a *regular* part of their lives, especially for the latter. In the decade following the end of World War I, major studios and exhibitors set out to increase their profits and establish greater control over the industry by creating a cross-class entertainment experience designed to attract greater numbers of prosperous middle-class patrons, while retaining their steady working-class following. To that end, they erected exotic movie palaces and produced lavish films aimed at turning moviegoing into an experience that both transcended and reshaped traditional class boundaries.

The creation of these seemingly democratic centers of entertainment, as the exuberant Samuel Orr failed to note, exacted political costs that went far beyond the price of a ticket. At the same time that worker filmmakers were trying to heighten class consciousness, movie industry leaders were merging fantasy and politics in a manner that eschewed class hostilities in favor of appealing to cross-class fantasies of luxury, comfort, and consumption. These fantasies took two distinct forms: movie palaces that brought different classes together to bask in the same opulent surroundings for several hours, and cross-class fantasy films that promoted glamorous but ultimately conservative visions of consumption and class interaction. The goal of these cross-class fantasies was not to integrate the classes in any lasting way, but to increase movie attendance and revenues by drawing them into the same theaters.

The 1920s marked a turning point in the history of the movie industry and in the formation of modern understandings of class and class relations. The proliferation of white-collar employees and the widespread participation of wage earners in a flourishing consumer economy created great confusion over modern class identities. Were white-collar employees middle class or working class? Should class status be based on one's work or one's ability to consume? Did class even matter anymore? Capitalists and socialists alike spoke about the blurred "lines of demarcation" between social classes and of the "powerful agencies that consciously and unconsciously aid in blurring the group lines of American society." Movies and movie theaters were among the most powerful of those agencies.[3]

Scholars such as Lary May see the 1920s and the rise of Hollywood as signaling the triumph of an emancipatory consumer culture over the highly restrictive Victorian culture that dominated American life at the turn of the century. Yet in emphasizing the "liberating" aspects of cultural change, scholars often overlook the more problematic political consequences of change. Although consumer goods certainly eased the lives of many citizens, Hollywood's emphasis on consumer fantasies marked a conservative retreat from the far more serious and ideologically diverse treatments of class conflict that characterized prewar filmmaking. As major studios shifted their attention toward building a broader audience, labor–capital films that highlighted struggles between the classes were supplanted by cross-class fantasy films that focused on harmony among the classes. I use the term "cross-class fantasy" to describe a broad category of films that stressed messages of class harmony and explored the interactions and romantic involvements between an upper-class and either working-class or middle-class protagonist. In emphasizing these themes, movie industry leaders reinforced a growing capitalist discourse that promoted a new perception of class identity – one rooted in the more alluring world of consumption than in the conflictual world of production. Taken collectively, cross-class fantasy films stressed individualism rather than collective action; acceptance rather than change; and contentment with one's class position rather than aspiring to something more. ...

Although movies had attracted great numbers of people since 1905, it was not until the 1920s that they became a genuine institution of mass culture – one that reached *all* Americans regardless of their class, race, gender, ethnicity, or geographical location. Consequently, movies grew even more important as vehicles of propaganda and political suasion. Never before had so many people from so many different backgrounds seen the same films at roughly the same time; and never before could so many people be influenced by what they saw and experienced at the movies. Whether Americans perceived class conflict as a continuing problem or as a past concern that was now resolved might well depend upon the images that dominated the screen.

It was during the 1920s that Hollywood and the studio system that created it came to dominate the movie industry. For better or for worse, corporate ownership of studios and movie theaters meant that leading Hollywood studios exerted tremendous control over the fantasy lives and political consciousness of millions of Americans. Understanding how this came about requires us to look at the complex interaction of several interconnected forces: how changing attitudes toward work, leisure, and consumption affected people during the 1920s; how exhibitors capitalized on these changes to expand their audience base; how studios orchestrated the political messages viewers saw on the screen; and how these developments affected the various groups struggling to challenge Hollywood's visions of fantasy and politics.

Leisure, Consumption, and Class

In the nation's dominant political circles, the 1920s were known as the "Age of Normalcy." The progressive spirit that marked the Wilson era waned in the postwar decade as three successive Republican presidents – Warren Harding, Calvin Coolidge, and Herbert Hoover – steered the nation on a more conservative, business-oriented course. But life in the social arena was anything but "normal" as new attitudes toward leisure and consumption "revolutionized the habits of the people." A leisure revolution that began in modest fashion at the turn of the century now swept the entire nation as millions of men and women of all classes spent their time and money on a wide array of goods and amusements. Commercial recreations achieved a new patina of respectability in the 1920s as civic leaders in Cleveland, Buffalo, Salt Lake City, Indianapolis, and elsewhere insisted that movies and other previously suspect amusements for the masses now occupied "a large and legitimate place" in the life of the nation's citizenry.[4] ...

The leisure revolution that supporters hailed and critics condemned was part of a broader set of changes wrought by the rapid development of industrialization – changes that altered the nature of work, consumption, leisure, and class identity. The adoption of mass production techniques pioneered by Henry Ford and the heightened emphasis on division of labor proved successful beyond the average employer's wildest dreams. Dramatic increases in productivity led to lower prices and made consumer goods more affordable to tens of millions of grateful Americans. ...

As the desire for goods and entertainment permeated all groups during the 1920s, consumption emerged as an important arena in which battles over competing visions of class identity were fought. Consumer goods certainly existed well before this decade and some historians trace the origins of the nation's consumer economy back to the eighteenth century. Yet it was not until the 1920s that the concept of a "consumer society" became part of the national lexicon. Although capitalists and labor leaders alike welcomed this development, they spoke about its significance in markedly different ways. Business leaders, advertisers, and politicians promoted a new discourse of class identity based on one's ability to consume rather than on one's occupation. Anyone who could afford a vaguely defined middle-class style of consumption was considered middle class – regardless of what collar they wore. Advertisers heralded the power of consumption to end class inequalities by creating a new cross-class democracy in which all Americans had equal access to goods. ...

Although capitalists used appeals to consumption to blur class divisions, labor leaders used them to reinforce the importance of united class actions. The steady decline in union membership and the wage earners' heightened cry for more goods and leisure time led American Federation of Labor stalwarts to place obtaining what was popularly known as the "American Standard of Living" at the forefront of union demands. This standard, explained Bureau of Labor Statistics head Royal Meeker, would provide workers "with all the necessaries, many of the comforts, and a goodly supply of the luxuries of life."[5] ...

Despite the ever-growing number of leisure possibilities in the 1920s, movies remained the nation's most frequented commercial entertainment. Movie box-office receipts soared from $301 million in 1921 to $720 million in 1929, a figure nearly four times greater than the combined receipts for all spectator sports and live theatrical entertainments. Movies remained so wildly popular because they remained so eminently affordable. With admission to most neighborhood theaters still a modest 10c to 50c, most Americans could afford to go to the movies. Movies were cheap enough that any working woman could take herself to a show without waiting for a man to ask. And women often did. ...

Selling entertainment was now very big business. But theater owners were no longer content with the nickels, dimes, and quarters of their long-time working-class patrons. Ambitious exhibitors wanted to devise a higher-priced entertainment experience so fantastic it would attract people from all classes. But how was this to be done? How could they lure people away from the neighborhood houses that so carefully catered to the class, ethnic, and gender needs of their patrons? Would people really pay $1 ($7.50 in 1990 dollars) to go to a *movie* theater? Although efforts to create a new movie experience were begun in the prewar years, it was not until the postwar era that exhibitors turned moviegoing into a genuinely cross-class entertainment. And few did so more creatively or successfully than two Jewish boys from Chicago.

Palaces for the People

For twenty years, Abraham Joseph Balaban and Sam Katz took the pulse of the people and made it beat faster. At a time when most theater owners were content to provide customers with a good movie, Balaban and Katz offered them an experience that indulged their fantasies and desires. No one, not even the celebrated Roxy, was more responsible for opening movies to a wider audience than these two sons of immigrants. In 1917 the partners owned only one theater. In 1925, when they sold their business to Paramount, they were making more money than any other chain and their methods were adopted by theaters across the nation. Their career reveals the rapid transformation of movie theaters from humble nickelodeons that served immigrant and working-class patrons to luxurious palaces that appealed to a broad array of Americans and in which movies were only a small part of an evening's entertainment.

Born in Chicago in 1889 to Russian Jews who ran a small grocery store, Abe Balaban entered the movie business in 1907 when he took a night job singing songs at the Kedzie, a 103-seat storefront theater in the city's west-side Jewish ghetto. In January 1908 he used his family's savings of $178 to buy the Kedzie, and several months later, with more audacity than money, began building the 700-seat Circle Theater on Sawyer and 12th Street. Aided by his brother Barney, Abe attracted large crowds by supplementing his films with a four-piece orchestra and popular vaudeville acts such as Sophie Tucker and the Four Marx Brothers. This formula proved so successful that the brothers soon opened a film exchange and purchased an interest in three more theaters.

Running the Circle taught the Balabans that to stay ahead of the competition they needed to offer audiences more show for the money and keep expanding into neighborhoods where people were hungry for entertainment and willing to pay for it. To carry this concept out on a grander scale, the financially strapped pair entered into partnership with Sam Katz in 1916. Also the son of Russian Jews, Katz grew up in a dreary west-side tenement and supported himself by, among other things, playing piano in a nickelodeon owned by Carl Laemmle. In 1912, he bought a small movie theater next to his dad's barber shop and by 1915 the twenty-one-year-old Katz owned three theaters. But Sam wanted to run a theatrical empire, not just several neighborhood houses. Together, the partners realized that dream by fashioning a theater chain built, as film scholar Douglas Gomery observes, on five key factors: "location, the theater building, service, stage shows, and air conditioning."[6]

Balaban and Katz developed an innovative strategy aimed at attracting a broad array of collars and classes. Instead of remaining in the crowded downtown entertainment district, they erected several luxury theaters in outlying areas that were being rapidly populated by middle-class and upwardly mobile working-class families. The Central Park, the partners' first theater, was built in suburban North Lawndale, "where immigrant Jewish families like the Balabans and Katzs moved in order to prove they had 'made it.'" A year later, on October 2, 1918, they opened the Riviera Theater on Chicago's fashionable North Side. That opening was followed in February 1921 by an even bigger luxury palace, the Tivoli, built on the South Side. The steady profits from these ventures soon allowed them to build several more suburban palaces and a massive theater in the downtown entertainment district. Not content with remaining a Chicago institution, B&K also acquired regional theater chains in the surrounding Midwestern states.[7]

Choosing the right location was critical to their success, but it was less important than the partners' ability to know what patrons wanted. Having seen the hardships endured by parents, relatives, and neighbors, Balaban and Katz understood that watching films was only a small part of the reason people went to the movies. People wanted fantasy, and the more fantastic the experience, the more willing they were to pay for it. The goal of B&K theaters, Abe explained, was to "make people live in a fairyland and to make them forget their troubles." Fantasy, as Balaban and Katz conceived it, was less an escape *from* something than an adventure *into* a wonderfully different world. Luxury, service, and entertainment at affordable prices became the dominant features of the B&K theater chain. They hired the best architects to design their theaters, the best musicians to play in them, the best art directors to create their stage shows, the most talented people to perform in them, the hottest jazz bands to set the place on fire, and the latest air-conditioning systems to cool it off.[8]

The key to their success, however, lay in persuading audiences to spend $1 to go to the Tivoli, Riviera, or Chicago rather than twenty-five cents to attend a more modest neighborhood theater. To that end, the partners tried to make their patrons feel that walking into a B&K theater was like entering another world – the world of the rich and pampered. Ornate outside facades dazzled people with exotic images and styles drawn from Spain, France, Italy, and the Orient, while inside, boasted Balaban, paintings, sculptures, "furnishings and fountains fit for museums and king's palaces were familiarly seen and used by our patrons." Customers were also offered a variety of comforts to make their visit more pleasant: spacious lounges near ladies' and men's rooms; nurseries and playrooms where parents could leave their children; air-conditioning systems that provided welcome relief from hot, muggy summer nights; and a small army of uniformed ushers trained to attend to the moviegoers' every need and to treat even the rudest patron with a deferential "yes, sir" or "no, ma'am."[9]

Audiences enjoyed being surrounded by elegance and impeccable service, but it was the fabulous stage show that kept luring them back week after week. A typical show lasted two and a half hours and it hardly mattered that B&K (because they were not part of a studio) had "little access to Hollywood's top films." It was the stage show and not the film that drew the crowds. Weekly shows, the equal of many Broadway productions, cost $3,000 to $5,000 to mount; special holiday extravaganzas ran upward of $50,000. Whereas the former usually drew on local talent, holiday shows included the likes of Fannie Brice, Bill "Mr. Bojangles" Robinson, Sophie Tucker, John Philip Sousa, Paul Whiteman, Eddie Cantor, and the Marx Brothers.[10]

This mixture of elegance, style, and fun, observed the *Chicago Herald-Examiner*, turned the B&K theaters into the "meeting place of the aristocrat and humble worker." Yet although aristocratic pretensions graced the theaters' walls and interiors, democracy ruled the box office. Unlike legitimate theaters that charged a variety of prices depending on location, Balaban and Katz "established one price to make all men feel equal in the pocketbook." The partners refused "to establish financial class distinctions, or to divide our auditoriums by means of reserved sections which seem to be more desirable and exclusive [because] *the American people don't like this distinction*."[11]

Success at the box office proved they were right. By 1925, B&K was the chain store of the movie business, dominating Chicago's luxury trade and controlling theaters throughout Illinois, Iowa, and Nebraska. The B&K "style," observed one-time associate Arthur Mayer, was "widely copied all over the country with even greater pomp, less taste – and similar profits." Adolph Zukor was so impressed by their operation that he merged Famous Players' Theaters with B&K in November 1925 and sent Sam Katz to New York to head up the new Publix Theater chain. By 1930–1, Publix, using B&K methods, reigned as the largest exhibition circuit in the industry's history, drawing in 2 million people a day and grossing $113 million for the year.[12]

Balaban and Katz may have been the best at what they did, but they were certainly not unique. The age of the movie palace began in 1914 with the opening of the Strand Theater in New York. Yet it was not until the early 1920s that picture palaces, to quote the renowned king of malaprops Samuel Goldwyn, spread like "wildflowers." The battle for control of exhibition and its lucrative earnings began in earnest in 1919, when Adolph Zukor used the proceeds from Paramount's $10 million stock issue to fund his expansionist ambitions. It continued throughout the decade as First National, Fox, Loew's, Universal, Warner Brothers, and a number of smaller but powerful regional theater chains joined the fray. The number of movie theaters soon rose from about 15,000 in 1919 to 20,500 in 1928. ...

In retrospect it is clear that movie palaces proved extraordinarily successful. Yet it was not so clear during the late teens and early twenties. Exhibitors knew what *they* wanted: a larger audience willing to pay higher ticket prices. But simply buying established theaters or building new ones was no guarantee of future success. Entrepreneurial ambitions, not democratic instincts, fueled the movement toward building a cross-class audience. Like Balaban and Katz, palace owners around the nation discovered they could do this by combining location, architecture, interior comfort, service, stage shows, and movies in a way that would satisfy their customers' taste for luxury and fantasy and make them come back for more. Silent movies may well have been a universal medium that required no English-language skills, but it was palace exhibitors who turned the movie theater into a universal gathering place where all classes could enjoy an evening together. ...

To attract a cross-class audience exhibitors had to convince people that class did not matter, at least not in the movie theater. Though the ownership and control of palaces grew increasingly oligopolistic during the twenties, the theaters themselves maintained a steadfast atmosphere of democracy – at least for their white patrons. Unlike opera houses or symphonic halls, declared William Fox, in movie theaters "there are no separations of classes. Everyone enters the same way. There is no side door thrust upon those who sit in the less expensive seats. ... In the movies the rich rub elbows with the poor and that's the way it should be." Though certainly self-serving, Fox was correct to a point. Any white man or woman who could afford the cost of admission was free to enjoy the same comforts, luxuries, and services as the palace's wealthiest patron. At New York's luxurious Rialto and Rivoli theaters, Roxy explained in 1918, "the man who comes to the theater on foot rubs elbows with the man who arrives in a limousine, and no favoritism is shown to either one or the other."[13]

Movie-theater democracy did have its limits. Like most arenas of American life, segregation was the rule and people of color were shunted off into distant balconies, inconspicuous orchestra seats, or excluded from the theater altogether. Those gaining admission were carefully watched by the armies of ushers who patrolled the aisles. Exhibitors considered such discrimination necessary in order to make middle-class customers, perhaps already nervous about potential lower-class seat mates, more comfortable. Racism also extended to theater employees. African-Americans and Mexican-Americans were rarely hired as uniformed ushers or ticket takers, but were relegated to less- visible and low-paying jobs such as messengers, maids, porters, or page boys.

For audiences, however, the appeal of moviegoing transcended the prejudices of theater owners. Limited in their ability to join the festivities at white palaces, African-Americans, Asians, and Hispanics eagerly flocked to theaters that welcomed their trade. In Washington, DC, African-Americans could choose from among fifteen movie houses (though only two were considered Class A theaters); in Chicago, the South State area between 26th and 39th Streets, popularly known as the "Stroll," served as the central entertainment district for black residents and featured a number of first-run houses. Movies remained equally popular among other people of color. The Japanese community of Los Angeles found a welcome respite at the Fuji-kan Theater on East First Street. The city's Hispanic residents congregated at downtown houses near the river, while Chicago's Mexican-American population patronized neighborhood theaters in the Back of the Yards area.

Whatever the color of the audience, deluxe theaters provided men and women with a rare opportunity to forget their worries and indulge their fantasies. For a few hours, working-class and middle-class audiences could live like the rich and receive the respect and care they rarely saw at work or at home. Indeed, the very purpose of the palace was to allow fantasy and desire to run rampant; to create a magical place where, as one Balaban and Katz associate remarked, "men who worked hard all day in subordinate capacities and women escaping for a few hours from the bondage of stoves and diapers ... might for a change be subordinated to."[14] ...

Through a combination of fantasy, luxury and comfort, movie palace owners built an audience that crossed political, class, ethnic, gender, and, in some cases, racial lines. By the middle of the decade, deluxe houses throughout the country were attracting a mix of what one DeQueen, Arkansas, theater manager called the "masses and classes." The investment bankers at Halsey, Stuart and Company, who preferred not to speak in class terms, observed that palaces were "drawing largely from new groups – the music lovers, the church people, 'society' – bringing new throngs to the theaters and creating an irresistible demand for more seating capacity."[15] ...

The success of new exhibition strategies presented studios and producers with a number of new questions: What kinds of films should they offer this new cross-class audience? Should they produce movies that catered to specific ethnic, political, class, and gender interests? Or should they make films less likely to offend the industry's increasingly heterogeneous clientele? In particular, how would filmmakers deal with the thorny issue of class conflict? Movies may not have been the most important reason people went to luxury palaces, but without movies the industry would surely collapse. Exhibitors could still earn profits if they showed several bad films; producers could not. Too many box-office disasters would lead to ruin for even the largest studio. Thus the decision of what to offer the public was not just a matter of catering to audience desires. It was a life-and-death proposition for the rapidly growing studio system and even more so for the independent production companies that hoped to survive long enough to challenge it.

Fantasy on the Screen

At the same time that luxury palaces were expanding the class composition of audiences, filmmakers were refashioning the ways Americans looked at class relations. In the 1920s, as in the 1910s, the industry's first priority was to make movies that would entertain audiences and earn money for their producers. Filmmakers turned out comedies, melodramas, mysteries, westerns, and adventure stories that played to the fantasies of the widest possible audience. Fantasy, of course, took many forms: the child who imagined himself or herself as a hero or heroine in the time of Robin Hood or Cleopatra; the young man who dreamed he was more sheikish than Rudolph Valentino; the young woman who saw herself dancing till dawn in Parisian night clubs. Yet when it came to the subject of class, the fantasies seen in 1920s films were markedly different from their predecessors. Labor–capital films that focused on conflict between the classes were superseded by cross-class fantasy films that emphasized love and harmony among the classes – a point of view seemingly more in tune with the mingling of classes that was occurring in the movie palaces themselves. Labor–capital films did not disappear from the screen, but by the mid-1920s they grew fewer in number and were rarely shown in the first-run theaters that gave films their greatest visibility and profits. Audiences may have still wanted to see these kinds of movies, but Hollywood producers were reluctant to make them.

In trying to reverse earlier depictions of audiences as passive receivers of mass culture, scholars have recently stressed the power movie patrons had in shaping the social environment of neighborhood theaters and interpreting the meaning of the films they saw. It is important, however, not to overemphasize the power of audiences; audiences were certainly free to accept or reject the messages on film, but in the end their power was limited to choosing among the films that producers wanted to make.

The question of whether audiences get the films they want is as old as the movie industry itself. Speaking before an International Sales Convention in May 1930, veteran movie mogul Carl Laemmle bluntly declared, "I don't care what you want or what I want, it is what the public wants that counts, because in the end they have to pay and they have the say." But unlike countless others who invoked similar platitudes, Laemmle quickly admitted that when it came to deciding *what* the public wants, "Nobody knows."[16]

Laemmle was right. There was no way of knowing what audiences really wanted because audiences may not have known themselves. Moviegoers wanted to be entertained, but entertainment could take many different forms. Producers tried shaping audience tastes by accustoming them to certain kinds of films. Movie industry head Will Hays frequently spoke about the filmmakers' ability to shape popular fashions and consumer habits. "No longer does the girl in Sullivan, Indiana, guess what the styles are going to be in three months," he explained in 1927. "She knows, because she sees them on the screen." Likewise, the "head of the house sees a new kind of golf suit in the movies and he wants one. ... Perhaps the whole family gets a new idea for redecorating and refurnishing the parlor – and down they go to the dealers to ask for the new goods."[17]

If audiences could get their ideas about fashion from the screen, why not their understanding of class relations? During the 1920s, producers both responded to and helped accelerate changes in the dominant class discourse by producing cross-class fantasy films that shifted attention away from the deadening world of production and toward the pleasures of consumption. Taken collectively, these films suggested that old ideas about class no longer mattered; that participation in a modern consumer society made class differences irrelevant. Filmmakers also shaped audience tastes and consciousness through the films they did not make. During the 1920s, they made fewer and fewer labor–capital films. Although many factors contributed to this shift in the class politics of American cinema, two were especially important: first, industry leaders' belief that films stressing class harmony and consumer fantasies would help build a cross-class audience and increase attendance at the highly profitable movie palaces that showed them; and, second, their knowledge that opposition by censors made production of politically volatile labor–capital films a financially risky proposition. Filmmakers, then, found themselves caught up in a complex effort to respond to audience tastes, while also accustoming them to new, less problematic, kinds of productions.

During the late teens and early 1920s, producers, like exhibitors, catered to the rapidly expanding, if somewhat amorphous, ranks of the middle class and assumed that working-class fans would continue going to movies regardless of what was shown. Postwar audiences, they insisted, wanted to forget about war and social problems and instead celebrate the flowering of peace and prosperity. Wartime service, industry leaders argued, acted as a temporary equalizer of classes and led many Americans to believe that they now deserved a taste of the good life. "Class distinctions had broken down," observed producer Benjamin Hampton. "The way of the rich was becoming the way of the land, and the people were suddenly interested in etiquette, in social forms, in behavior, in the standards and clothes and beauty lotions and habits that would help them to be like the people they admired." Although Hampton had an exaggerated sense of the breakdown of class distinctions, it was one shared by many of his peers.[18]

As postwar politicians, business leaders, studios, and voters succeeded in supplanting the idealism of prewar Progressivism with a new emphasis on materialism, producers and exhibitors shied away from making or showing hard-hitting social-problem films. "Picture palaces were designed to take people out of their mundane lives," observed silent-era scholar Kevin Brownlow, "not push them back in." It was the Cecil B. DeMilles and James Cruzes, not the Lois Webers or D. W. Griffiths, who best understood the changing needs of the industry. Money, sex, beauty, and luxury was the DeMille formula, and his films, in brother William's words, were "hailed with loud hosannas by the public of that day. ... This was what the people as a whole wanted to see; a sumptuous and spectacular dramatization of the age of jazz, prohibition, and flaming youth." Studios quickly turned out features with such provocative titles as *Sex, Flapper Wives, Ladies of Ease, Gigolo, Reckless Youth, Jazzamania, Daughters of Pleasure, A Slave of Fashion, Extravagance, Success,* and *Money, Money, Money.*[19]

These flights of fantasy did not entirely monopolize the efforts of producers and studios. Postwar strikes and the fear of Red invaders kept class conflict fresh on the minds of Americans and kept labor–capital films on movie-theater screens. Yet as labor and radical activism declined after 1922, films about Reds, radicals, and unions no longer appeared quite as salient to Hollywood studios. Filmmakers also hesitated to make labor–capital films because censors threatened to ban them. By 1926, film censorship boards were operating in 100 cities and nearly a dozen states, each with different standards. Censors repeatedly acted against any producer – labor film company or Hollywood studio – who made features or newsreels that criticized capitalists or offered sympathetic depictions of working-class life and struggles. Pennsylvania censors demanded substantial changes in William S. Hart's *The Whistle* (Famous Players-Lasky 1921), a liberal film that exposed unsafe working conditions in textile mills. State censors also ordered Pathé, Hearst, Gaumont, and Fox to cut scenes of newsreels showing ongoing strikes and labor agitation on the grounds that "they tend to incite riot and disorder." Sympathetic footage of coal miners' strikes in Ohio, Pennsylvania, Illinois, and West Virginia never reached the screen.[20]

Studios could, of course, refuse to comply with censors' demands. But doing so would mean delaying, perhaps even canceling, a film's release in any number of states. With the cost of an average feature film spiraling from $12–18,000 in 1918 to $40–80,000 in 1919, and to $300,000 in 1924 (plus tens of thousands more for advertising, publicity, and the like), producers took a much harder look at the kinds of politics they wanted to put on the screen. "The advance commitments of a company on its pictures are so heavy," Laemmle explained, "that one or two box-office failures may make serious inroads on the reserves built up during periods of success." This was especially true for struggling smaller companies to which, as Jack Warner emphasized, "every nickel counted." Potential losses were heightened for powerful moguls such as Zukor and Fox, for whom the delay of a film meant less product and less profit for their distribution and exhibition wings.[21]

The scandals that rocked the nation following the manslaughter trials of popular comedian Roscoe "Fatty" Arbuckle (who was accused of killing actress Virginia Rappe at an allegedly decadent party) and the suspicious murder of director William Desmond Taylor in 1921 drew closer attention to the values seen on the screen and prompted outraged cries for even greater censorship of motion pictures. Producers moved to avert more government censorship by organizing the Motion Picture Producers and Distributors Association (MPPDA) in 1922, hiring squeaky-clean Postmaster General Will Hays as its president, and agreeing to follow a voluntary censorship code in 1924 that Hays promised would maintain "the highest possible moral and artistic standards in motion picture production." With Hays's office rejecting scripts deemed "too provocative" and "anesthetizing anything political," and with "Wall Street watchdogs" (who handled shares for eleven movie corporations by 1925) constantly offering what Jesse Lasky and others felt was "much unappreciated advice," industry leaders grew even more conservative in their choice of productions.[22]

Given the enormous financial risks involved, producers decided to cut back on labor–capital productions. After all, studios were in the movie business and not, like worker film companies, in the consciousness-raising business. ...

Hollywood continued to deal with class issues throughout the 1920s, but it presented its class visions in the form of cross-class fantasies rather than riskier labor–capital features. Like working-class films of the prewar era, cross-class fantasy films cut across established genres and included comedies, dramas, and melodramas. Yet unlike working-class films, they also included a group of movies that cinema scholars refer to as society films. These films, explained Richard Koszarski, "typically dealt with tribulations in the lives of the rich and famous and served as showcases for glamorous costumes and settings. Often a working-class character, usually female, would be introduced into upper-class society by some twist of fate. This allowed the filmmakers to demonstrate the moral superiority of the working class while lavishing attention on the glamorous life-styles of the wealthy."[23]

When it came to dealing with the "problems and possibilities of interclass and intercultural relationships," the range of characters in cross-class fantasies was far greater than Koszarski's brief quotation suggests. Changes in the class composition of postwar audiences and the occupational structure of the workplace precipitated changes in the class composition and occupations of the protagonists seen on the screen. Whereas society films generally depicted upper-class and blue-collar interactions, and labor–capital films the conflicts between male factory workers and their employers, cross-class fantasy filmmakers expanded their scope to include the rapidly growing ranks of middle-class professionals, white-collar workers, and sales and service employees – people who were among the industry's most sought-after patrons.[24]

Filmmakers also recognized the growing presence of women in the work force and eagerly catered to their dreams and desires. Cross-class fantasies were generally less paternalistic than prewar working-class films, in which sweatshop and factory women were seen as helpless objects in need of protection. Instead, these films explored the experiences and fantasies of seemingly more independent women who worked as clerks, secretaries, stenographers, telephone operators, department store sales people, and owners of businesses who sometimes did better than the men they loved. ...

The blue-collar screen of the nickelodeon era grew increasingly white in the 1920s as "new" and "old" middle-class and upper-class protagonists came to dominate Hollywood films. Studio heads often assumed that white-collar workers wanted to see themselves living a middle-class life. A close examination of subject headings in one film catalog reveals that between 1921 and 1929 "society" films outnumbered labor–capital films 308 to 67. Fantasies about cross-class relations now proved more important and profitable than discourses about class conflict – at least in the minds of filmmakers.

These films proved so popular because of the tremendous variety of fantasies they offered male and female audiences. Film critic Welford Beaton was struck by how many of these fantasies were geared to a new generation of white-collar workers: "the discouraged stenographer is inspired by the fact that the stenographer in the picture marries the boss, and the traveling salesman is given fresh hope when he sees Dick Dix or Bill Haines playing a salesman cop the millionaire's daughter in the final reel." Producers also offered fantasies for those who dreamed of getting lots of money without having to earn it. In *The Millionaire* (1921), Herbert Rawlinson plays a $25-a-week bookkeeper who suddenly inherits $80 million, and in *A Daughter of Luxury* (1922) Agnes Ayres is a homeless girl who discovers she is really a wealthy heiress.[25]

Dreams of wealth, mobility, respect, and luxury could all be found on the screen, but love between the classes remained the cornerstone of these films. All problems, both personal and societal, could be solved through love; and true love was strong enough to break down any class barriers. After all, class was an artifical construct, love was real. Cross-class fantasies offered viewers almost as many varieties of love as Heinz made condiments. Modern versions of Cinderella and Cinderfellar stories could be seen almost every week. But instead of love between a peasant and handsome prince or beautiful princess, love permutations in these films included mixes of urban-based blue collars, white collars, professionals, business owners, servants, the working wealthy, and the idle rich.

In the movies, if not in life, wealthy women showed a particular affinity for marrying white- or blue-collar men. In *Taking Chances* (1921) a wealthy capitalist's daughter spurns a rich financier in favor of her father's secretary, a former book salesman. More traditional Cinderella tales saw rich men marrying department-store clerks, chorus girls, and typists.

Sometimes Prince Charming assumed the more modest guise of a successful professional (architect, doctor, lawyer) who weds a waitress or factory operative. ...

Whatever the combination, cross-class romances invariably offered audiences glimpses of the extravagant life styles and luxurious possessions of the American aristocracy. DeMille and directors like him, argues Lewis Jacobs, thought "every shopgirl longed to be accepted as the heroine of the film, into the social circles of the rich, and sought a knowledge of table etiquette, how to dress, how to be introduced, how to order, and how to conduct oneself in general."[26] Most, if not all of these desires, could be satisfied in a good cross-class fantasy. Factory and tenement settings, so popular in earlier social-problem films, now gave way to films set in lavish hotels, magnificent mansions, fashionable clothing boutiques, and costly night spots where the rich liked to amuse themselves.

In telling their story of love between the classes, cross-class fantasies removed the overtly contentious political edge that accompanied most labor–capital films and offered a point of view that fit well into the conservative Republican politics of the decade. Individualism and personal fulfillment were the dominant ideological undercurrents of these films – a sharp contrast to the sense of collectivism and cooperation advocated by labor filmmakers of the 1920s. Although acknowledging inequities of wealth and power in society, cross-class fantasies suggested that there was no need for unions or any kind of collective activity to achieve one's dreams. Love and moral superiority would lead the way to happiness.

These often subtle political themes were presented within seemingly liberal calls for cross-class tolerance and mutual respect: whatever the barriers and distance separating them, working class, middle class, and upper class could learn from one another. Yet in looking more closely at the values characters actually taught each other, these films reveal an extremely conservative and patronizing attitude toward class relations. Working people, whether blue collar or white, were inevitably portrayed as salt-of-the-earth types who taught the wealthy the value of hard work. The rich, in turn, instructed these good-hearted but socially inept folk in manners, grace, and the proper way to consume luxury. The most conservative films offered their working-class characters – and viewers – a taste of the good life, but in the end suggested they were ultimately happier loving and consuming within their own class. Thus, while movie palaces brought the classes together, cross-class fantasy films pulled them back apart.

No one brought these conservative messages to the screen with greater success than Cecil B. DeMille. In his skillful hands, working hard, wanting a taste of luxury, and remaining content within one's class seemed the natural thing to do. His movies helped justify the dominant class system by suggesting that its openness lay in the realm of consumption rather than in movement across class boundaries. The son of a minister, DeMille was born in August 1881 to a prominent family in Ashfield, Massachusetts. DeMille entered the movie business in 1913 when he assumed the position of director-general of the Jesse L. Lasky Feature Play Company. A successful filmmaker before the war, he grew even more prominent afterward. DeMille gained his postwar reputation as an innovative director of society comedies and dramas. One film critic praised him for opening up "a whole new world for the films, a world that middle-class audiences, newly won to the movies by the luxurious theaters then springing up, wanted to see."[27]

DeMille imbued his productions with a conservative political edge that reflected his personal politics. Dubbed by Kevin Brownlow as "perhaps the most conservative figure in Hollywood," DeMille (unlike his liberal brother William) remained a rabidly anti-union, anti-Communist Republican most of his life. He rejected films that focused on mass movements in favor of making movies that concentrated on individuals. "The audience is interested in people," he wrote in his autobiography, "not masses of anonymous people, but individuals whom they can love or hate, in whose fortunes they can feel personally involved." Working people craved entertainment, not political sermons. "Your poor person," he declared in 1925, "wants to see wealth, colorful, interesting, exotic." Yet whatever his professions, the poor people watching the minister son's films also had to sit through his sermons.[28]

Saturday Night (Famous Players-Lasky 1922) offers us a glimpse into the political mindset of DeMille and his many imitators. The movie opens by focusing on four discontented protagonists who fantasize about leading a better life. Pretty Irish laundress Shamrock O'Day (played by Edith Roberts) "is a modern Cinderella who is tied to Drudgery and Cotton Stockings and longs for French Perfume and a French Maid." Her handsome next-door neighbor Tom McGuire (Jack Mower) is "a Chauffeur, who is so fed up on the Corned Beef and Cabbage of Life, that he longs for a little of the Caviar." On the more upscale side of town live the equally discontented Iris Van Suydam (Leatrice Joy), "one of the Lilies in Life's Hot-House – who 'Toils Not, Neither does she Spin,'" and her wealthy fiancé Richard Prentiss (Conrad Nagel), "who is just as tired of the Silken Women of her class, as she is bored with the Men of his." Cross-class love quickly blossoms when Shamrock delivers laundry to Richard's magnificent mansion and winds up clumsily falling down his staircase and sprawling clothing in every direction. Richard immediately falls in love and drives her home. When Iris sees the two leave, she flies into a jealous rage and decides that if Richard can drive a laundress, she can picnic with a chauffeur. Of course, she turns out to be a reckless driver and Tom winds up saving her life and falling in love. After passing out, Iris awakens in Tom's arms and declares: "Tom, I have just learned how much more important Red Blood is – than Blue!" Tom, swell guy that he is, responds: "I don't blame you, you poor kid! You just haven't been brought up right."[29]

Meanwhile, back at the mansion, a lavish ball is in progress and audiences could delight in watching tuxedoed men and expensively gowned, diamond-bedecked women gracefully dancing to the sounds of a large orchestra. Richard spots Shamrock, who has returned with his laundry, and leads her out to the dance floor. Mom is aghast, his sister ashamed, and the guests amused. But Richard does not care one fig. Likewise, the besmitten Iris asks Tom to take her away "where I can cook for you, and sew for you, and just be your Wife!" An intertitle quickly warns: "Romance laughs at the heavy Chains of Tradition. But Society metes out swift punishment to those who Break the Chains." Both couples defy the strictures of their class and get married. Shamrock moves into a luxurious bedroom in the mansion (which we see in great detail), while Iris gets to live in a small, noisy apartment next to the elevated line.

The rest of the film dwells on the seemingly humorous situations that arise from these class-crossed marriages. Each character continually lives up to the class stereotypes drawn by DeMille. When a maid prepares a midweek bath, the startled Shamrock tells her in ungrammatical English that "it ain't Saturday night." Lacking proper table manners, she embarrasses everyone at a fancy dinner party. Iris has an equally tough time being a working-class housewife. She is unable to cook or clean, and when she lights up a cigarette at a disastrous dinner party Tom angrily barks: "Cut the smokin'! Do you want my Friends to think you're fast?" Both husbands are constantly embarrassed by their wives' inability to adjust to their new situations. Whatever their class prior to marriage, women in this film are clearly expected to adopt the class characteristics of their husbands after marriage.

Through a combination of misadventures, Tom and Shamrock wind up spending a happy evening together stuck atop a Coney Island ferris wheel, where they manage to fall in love. Richard goes looking for her at Tom's apartment and when the errant couple finally arrive, Shamrock tells him of her new love. "Dick, dear, it ain't our fault! I like Tom because he likes Gum, and Hot-Dogs, and Jazz! Just as you, and Iris, like High-Brow Operas, and Olives – and such." All conversation is halted when a fire breaks out in the building. During the ensuing confusion, Tom rushes off with Shamrock and when Richard comes back to rescue Iris she confesses, "In the end, Dick – it's always – Kind to Kind." The film cuts to seven years later, and, in two consecutive scenes, we see Tom and Shamrock having fun with their three kids at Coney Island, while Iris is dressed in a gorgeous black gown, surrounded by wealth, servants, and an admiring Richard.

The conservative undertones of *Saturday Night* and its patronizing attitudes toward working-class life are apparent throughout the film. Wealth and luxury, DeMille argues, do not bring contentment; whatever people think they might want, they will be happier marrying and consuming within their own class. Different classes may come to love one another, but they cannot live together in an intimate setting. ...

DeMille's brand of conservatism was only one of many varieties seen in cross-class fantasies. Be satisfied and content with your lives was the message that accompanied the frequent salt-of-the-earth portrayals of working-class protagonists. Many of these films advanced a nostalgic reverence for the dignity of work and the work ethic that workers either rejected or found hard to achieve off the screen. It was precisely because work had lost so much of its meaning that people wanted shorter work days and more leisure. Working-class men and women preferred the allures of the new consumer ethos to the old Protestant work ethic that stressed the importance of frugality, self-denial, and deferred gratification. Yet in Hollywood movies, work and the work ethic were portrayed as powerful forces that could redeem and transform the idle rich. In the course of promoting these twin values, producers conceded a sense of moral superiority to hard-working blue- and white-collar audiences, while also offering them a voyeuristic look at the decadent but fascinating lives of the filthy rich.

Upward mobility was another area where film fantasies outpaced the realities of work life. Since the nation's beginnings, rising up to own a business served as a benchmark of independence and success. Yet as massive factories and highly capitalized corporations replaced artisan shops and small manufactories during the nineteenth and twentieth centuries, the percentage of self-employed Americans steadily declined. In the movies, however, success and independence were easily attained if one worked hard and persevered. *Sure Fire Flint* (1922) typified capitalist fantasies of upward mobility. A poor soldier who comes home and labors at a number of unskilled jobs gets a big break when he returns a coat filled with money to a steel mill owner. Flint's honesty earns him a job in the mills and "almost overnight," notes one reviewer, he rises to the position of manager, foils a robbery, and then marries the boss's daughter.[30] Plumbers, blacksmiths, factory workers, and superintendents were all featured in similar rags-to-riches films.

Women figured prominently in these films as passionate upholders of the work ethic. Gender stereotypes crossed class lines as wealthy and poor women alike insisted that their men work. An artist's model in *The Woman He Married* (1923) refuses to marry a young millionaire until he is able to do something other than spend money and smoke gold-tipped cigarettes. In *Wealth* (1921), a young illustrator marries an idle rich man and begs him to work and accomplish something with his life. When he ignores her, she leaves him; but he wins her back when he follows her advice. According to this film, remarked one labor reviewer, the "trouble with wealth is … it gives you no chance to develop character, it leaves you a spineless creature and worst of all, it does not allow you to perform what is known as 'a man's work.'" The daring reviewer quickly added that he "would risk the danger and accept any number of millions of dollars which might be willed to us by kind uncles."[31]

The work ethic was meant to apply to men of all classes, but not to all women. Poor women were expected to help support their families. This was made abundantly clear in films about ghetto life, like *Humoresque* (Cosmopolitan 1920) and *His People* (Universal 1925). But gender, class, and the work ethic created an uncomfortable mix when it came to looking at middle-class career women. Cross-class fantasies took a decidedly anti-careerist perspective and showed the misfortunes that befell women who preferred careers to raising families. They may have become successes in business, but they were failures as women. This was especially true for women who proved more driven than their husbands. As the advertisement for *This Freedom* (1924), a film about a successful female banker, warned: "The story of home or a career and the resulting chaos caused by a woman too ambitious for her own welfare."[32]

Not all cross-class fantasy filmmakers assumed such reactionary positions. Even by the late 1920s, Hollywood movies did not present a monolithic view of class relations. Like labor–capital films, a number of cross-class fantasies contained a biting anti-authoritarian edge that poked fun at the values and aspirations of various classes. Few actors were better at skewering the arrogant pretensions often found among the rising cadre of white-collar supervisory personnel than Harold Lloyd. The Charlie Chaplin of the middle class, Lloyd was especially popular with blue-collar and low-level white-collar audiences. Chicago trade unionists praised his films for offering "wholesome fun with a punch" and starting "the beholder thinking in the right instead of the wrong direction." In *Safety Last* (Roach 1925), the bespectacled Lloyd plays a bumbling sales clerk who always runs afoul of – but ultimately bests – the store's extraordinarily pompous head floorwalker, Mr. Stubbs, a man who has grown "Muscle-bound," as an intertitle tells us, "From patting himself on the back." The film not only mocks the autocratic floorwalker, but also the overbearingly ambitious young men who are confident they will rise quickly through the white-collar ranks to become great successes.[33]

Comedian Buster Keaton lampooned middle-class norms in a somewhat different fashion. "Where Lloyd accepted middle-class order and made comedy from the foolish antics of the man on the make," observes film historian Robert Sklar, "Keaton's existence within the same social setting was predicated on a recognition of not his but *its* absurdities." The ethos of upward mobility and limits of cross-class love are wonderfully parodied in *Cops* (1922), *The Navigator* (1924), *Sherlock Jr.* (Keaton 1924), and *The General* (Schenck 1927).[34]

Moviegoers who wanted to see hard-hitting portrayals of class relations were not likely to find them in the cross-class fantasies that played to the cross-class audiences who flocked to the nation's movie palaces each week. When it came to dealing with class tensions these films were notable for what audiences did not see: strikes, radicals, union organizing, and mass movements. Love and inner happiness, not conflict and class struggle, were the preferred themes of these films. Working-class and white-collar audiences were repeatedly told how superior they were to the upper classes; yet these movies also advised them to do nothing to remedy the situation in which the so-called superior class was being oppressed by the inferior class. Look and desire, but be satisfied with your lot was their collective message. Working-class viewers, remarked one labor weekly, were constantly being told "that you must be content to be poor and not kick about it."[35] By portraying class interactions in such a way, cross-class fantasies helped legitimize the class hierarchies and inequalities that dominated American society.

Watching films in the same environment did not mean that different classes accepted and assimilated the same ideas. Producers may have homogenized the politics of their movies, but not the political perspectives of all moviegoers. The nation's labor press blasted Cecil B. DeMille as a "subtle propagandist for the enemies of the workers." The *Chicago New Majority* bitterly complained how in *Saturday Night* "all working men and girls eat with knives and are brutish, selfish boors," while "all finer feelings are monopolized by those of gentle birth ... Workers stink and bathe only on Saturday night. Only the gentle-born are sweet and clean." The paper's editor conceded that DeMille's movies were technically beautiful, but he accused the director of being "one of the most dangerous propagandists against the public welfare, connected with any established publicity channel. He slides across continual arguments for things as they are, in his elaborately staged photoplays." Working-class movie critics were equally critical of the conservative view of gender roles that permeated many cross-class fantasy films. One labor reviewer denounced *The Famous Mrs. Fair* (1923) for preaching the "reactionary doctrine that a woman has no business trying to have a career, that her place is to slave in the home and take orders from her husband."[36]

Audiences enjoyed the fantasies of the movie palace but not necessarily those of the films that played there. Although producers insisted that people preferred escapist cross-class fantasies to more serious films, movie patrons often expressed a very different point of view. When audiences at New York's Rialto, Rivoli, and Criterion Theaters were asked in June 1923 what kinds of films they wanted to see, they responded in a four-to-one ratio that they preferred "simple true-to-life stories rather than spectacular and fantastic ones and pictures that instruct and provoke thought rather than pictures whose sole purpose is amusement." Specific comments included "More natural stories – less 'hokum,'" "Omit the false impressions of life," and "Less concentration on wealthy class and their aristocratically spectacular life, simple stories of actual people with intelligent direction." Likewise, when the *Saturday Evening Post* asked readers in 1928 whether they preferred "Pictures That Have Lavish Settings, Costumes, Fashions ... [or] A Simple Story Well Told?" a majority of respondents favored the latter.[37]

These limited surveys suggest that producers did not always respond to audience demands. Many patrons still enjoyed seeing serious films about workplace life such as King Vidor's *The Crowd* (MGM 1928), which offered a bleak portrait of the faceless, routinized world of the white-collar worker. Yet although moviegoers may have wanted to see more labor–capital films, producers were hesitant to make them. The opposition of external censors, in-house censorship by studios and the Hays office, and the prospect of losing one's job if a producer failed to make money on a film, proved far more influential than audience surveys in deciding what films would be made. "Seventy-five percent of the motion pictures shown today are a brazen insult to human intelligence," actor Rudolph Valentino, the heartthrob of millions, complained in 1923. "This is because the trusts play the cash register, and that is all that they worry about."[38]

Patrons wanting to see more serious stories about class relations were most likely to fulfill their desires at neighborhood theaters that continued to screen old and new labor–capital films. Yet these theaters held less and less appeal for the millions of moviegoers who grew accustomed to watching films in an atmosphere of luxury, comfort, and fantasy. Although many people went to the movies simply to be entertained and cared little about the ideological content of films, class-conscious fans who read unfavorable reviews in the labor press found themselves having to decide what was more important, fantasy or politics?

Notes

1 New York *Evening Graphic*, March 12, 1927, quoted in Ben M. Hall, *The Best Remaining Seats: The Golden Age of the Movie Palace* (New York, 1975, reprinted 1988), 6.

2 *NY Call*, April 25, 1921.

3 Walter Thompson [Advertising] Company newsletter, no. 139 (1 July 1926), quoted in Lizabeth Cohen, *Making a New Deal: Industrial Workers in Chicago, 1919–1939* (Cambridge and New York, 1990), 100; Nathan Malyn, "Mass Psychology and Socialism," *NY Call*, November 12, 1922.

4 Jesse Frederick Steiner, *Americans at Play: Recent Trends in Recreation and Leisure Time Activities* (New York, 1933, reprinted 1970), 191–2; Cleveland Recreation Survey, *Commercial Recreation* (Cleveland, 1920), 11.

5 Meeker quoted in Horowitz, *Morality of Spending*, 123.

6 Gomery, *Shared Pleasures*, 43.

7 Ibid, 44.

8 Balaban, *Continuous Performance*, 33.

9 Ibid, 159.

10 Gomery, *Shared Pleasures*, 43.

11 *Chicago Herald-Examiner*, October 1917, quoted in Balaban, *Continuous Performance*, 51; second quote, ibid, 173; "The Reason Balaban and Katz Theatres Do Not Reserve Seats," *Balaban and Katz Magazine*, 1 (July 25, 1925), 10, quoted in Nasaw, *Going Out*, 232.

12 Mayer, *Merely Colossal*, 71.

13 Fox quoted in May, *Screening out the Past*, 152–3; *NY Call*, May 18, 1918.

14 Mayer, *Merely Colossal*, 70–1.

15 Arkansas theater manager quoted in Peter Stead, *Film and the Working Class: The Feature Film in British and American Society* (London and New York, 1989), 38–9; Halsey, Stuart and Co., "Motion Picture Industry," 184.

16 John Drinkwater, *The Life and Adventures of Carl Laemmle* (New York, 1931), 235.

17 Will Hays, "Supervision from Within," in Kennedy, *Story of Films*, 38.

18 Hampton, *History of the Movies*, 221.

19 Kevin Brownlow, *Behind the Mask of Innocence* (New York, 1990), 290; William C. de Mille, *Hollywood Saga* (New York, 1939), 239–40.

20 Chicago *Daily Worker*, March 18, 1925.

21 Drinkwater, *Life of Laemmle*, 225; Jack L. Warner with Dean Jennings, *My First Hundred Years in Hollywood* (New York, 1965), 125.

22 Hays quoted in Anthony Slide, *The American Film Industry* (Westport, CT, 1986), 219; Brownlow, *Behind the Mask*, 17; Jesse L. Lasky with Don Weldon, *I Blow My Own Horn* (London, 1957), 144.

23 Koszarski, *Evening's Entertainment*, 184.

24 Rosenzweig, *Eight Hours*, 217.

25 Welford Beaton, *Film Spectator*, May 26, 1928, quoted in Stead, *Film and the Working Class*, 38.

26 Jacobs, *Rise of American Film*, 407.

27 Arthur Knight, *The Liveliest Art* (New York, 1957), 118.

28 Brownlow, *Behind the Mask*, 459; DeMille, *Autobiography*, 169.

29 All quotations are from film's intertitles.

30 *Variety*, January 5, 1923.

31 *NY Call*, June 27, 1921.

32 *Seattle Union Record*, July 12, 1924.

33 *Chicago New Majority*, May 12, 1923.

34 Sklar, *Movie-Made America*, 117–19.

35 From review of *Poor Men's Wives*, see *Chicago New Majority*, April 2, 1923.

36 *Chicago New Majority*, September 9, April 8, December 2, 1922, and May 1 1923.

37 *NY Call*, June 25, 1923; results of *Saturday Evening Post* survey are reprinted in Lewis, *Cases on the Motion Picture Industry*, 134–6.

38 *NY Call*, January 26, 1923.

Documents

Introduction to Documents

By the 1920s, nickelodeons and small theaters of the pre-war era were replaced by movie palaces that were more exotic and fantastic than many of the films they played. Lloyd Lewis describes what it was like for men and women of modest means to attend luxurious movies palaces where for a few hours they were treated like kings and queens. Palaces and less luxurious movie theaters were also popular with the nation's teenage population. Our second document, taken from the *Seattle Union Record*, reveals how young men and women who lacked their own apartments, dormitories, or cars found the dark confines of the movie theater – much to their parents' consternation – a great place for a little kissy-facey. In the last piece, movie star Milton Sills explains to a group of Harvard University Business School students why audiences found movies and movie stars so compelling.

The Deluxe Picture Palace

Lloyd Lewis

Source: The New Republic, March 27, 1929, 175

The legitimate theater, usually known as "Broadway," is in a panic today, with many of its temples dark and many of its priests and vestals rushing about the streets of the walled city, crying out that the movie vandals are at the gates of the citadel at last.

To hear them wail, one would suppose that the old battle between the drama and the films is about to result in the extinction of art, culture and the revered British accent. The movies, armed now with new electrical catapults and strange talking devices, have all but taken the modern Rome. Years ago, out in the provinces, the films conquered the legitimate theaters of "the road." Not only that: the barbarians clubbed and chased those pious missionaries, the Chautauquans. Next they captured Broadway's strolling half-brothers, the vaudevillians, enslaving them to work four and five times a day in the pagan temples which the vandals have erected everywhere. And now, as the Visigoths prepare to take the capital, it sickens the priests and vestals to discover that the cold-blooded bankers of the citadel itself are financing the invasion.

Superficially, it is the advent of talking pictures, backed by enormous capital, that has caused the panic. In reality it is the success in New York of that provincial institution, the big moving-picture theater, that is responsible.

Only in the past year has Broadway awakened to the fact that the colossal film house, known to the trade as the "de luxe" theater, has been as successful in New York as it was for a decade previous in the "sticks." Ten years ago, when the Capitol Theater, itself immense in size, opened on Broadway, the legitimate drama viewed it as a sort of amiable behemoth, likely to attract little more than the chronic moviegoing public. Which was about what happened. But the Capitol was not a typical "de luxe" film house, as that institution has since become standardized over the country. Two years before the Capitol opened, the progenitor of the now accepted type was built in Chicago, a 2,200-seat theater, the Central Park, which some determined and imaginative boys from the nearby Ghetto – the Balaban brothers and Sam Katz – had started, as an experiment upon which they were willing to risk their combined savings. As though inspired by the spirit of audacity which seems contagious in Chicago, they planned their new theater on an unprecedented scale, lined its interior with crimson velvet and marble, adorned the walls with paintings, and filled the lobbies with uniformed and bowing ushers. In a swirl of color and splendor, they experimented with prologues, singers, dancers in diaphanous robes, and "presentations" – in fact, almost everything that the most gorgeous of the 6,000-seat "de luxe" houses offer, on a still vaster scale, today.

As it turned out, magnificence paid well, and, by 1921, the Balabans and Katz had added three other, similar theaters to their list. Presently the clink of money dropping into their box-offices had become such a siren song that moving-picture exhibitors over the country were deserting the old-time "nickelodeons," to make round eyes at the finer and bigger things themselves. By 1926, almost every large city had its "deluxe" house, seating from 2,500 to 4,500 people. Small picture houses died around them like flies. In cities of less than 200,000 inhabitants, the legitimate theaters wilted; vaudeville houses closed or added pictures; Chautauqua circuits shrank.

But each year the "de luxe" houses were more thronged. That pioneer, the Central Park, played to 750,000 patrons in its first year. In 1928, the circuit of Chicago theaters, to which it still belongs, had expanded to include twelve, the other eleven all larger than their progenitor, and had checked over 30,000,000 admissions in the year.

Most of these 30,000,000, of course, were women and children; perhaps not more than 25 percent of all the patrons were men, and many of these were there chiefly in the role of escort. What had the Chicago pioneers put into their temple that was so seductive to American women?

In the dim auditorium which seems to float in a world of dream and where the people brushing her elbows on either side are safely remote, an American woman may spend her afternoon alone. Romantic music, usually played with a high degree of mechanical excellence, gives her a pleasant sensation of tingling. Her husband is busy elsewhere; and on this music, as on a mildly erotic bridge, she can let her fancies slip through the darkened atmosphere to the screen, where they drift in rhapsodic amours with handsome stars. In the isolation of this twilit palace, she abandons herself to these adventures with a freedom that is impossible in the legitimate theater, where the lights are brighter and the neighboring seat-holders always on the edge of her vision: the blue dusk of the "de luxe" house has dissolved the Puritan strictures she had absorbed as a child.

All of this splendor has been planned for her delight, and with a luxuriance that she had imagined was enjoyed only in Cleopatra's court, oriental harems, or Parisian and Viennese society. She strolls voluptuously through lobbies and foyers that open into one another like chambers in a maze; her feet sink in soft rugs, she is surrounded by heavy Renaissance tables, oil paintings, and statues of nudes. She enjoys the sense of leading a sophisticated, continental life, with none of the practical risks. For she sees church members and respectable householders savoring the same delights about her.

When she goes home that evening, she will perhaps clean spinach and peel onions, but for a few hours, attendants bow to her, doormen tip their hats, and a maid curtsies to her in the ladies' washroom. She bathes in elegance and dignity; she satisfies her yearning for a "cultured" atmosphere. Even the hush that hangs over the lobbies means refinement to her: voices that have been raucous on the street drop, as they drop on entering a church. ...

The royal favor of democracy it is: for in the "de luxe" house every man is a king and every woman a queen. Most of these cinema palaces sell all their seats at the same price, – and get it; the rich man stands in line with the poor; and usually tipping is forbidden. In this suave atmosphere, the differences of cunning, charm, and wealth, that determine our lives outside, are forgotten. All men enter these portals equal, and thus the movies are perhaps a symbol of democracy. Let us take heart from this, and not be downcast because our democratic nation prudently reserves its democracy for the temple of daydreams.

Petting at the Movies

E. J. Mitchell

Source: *Seattle Union Record*, March 24, 1927

When movie theaters were established, it marked a boon for lovers – especially those of the petting variety. What could be nicer for lovers than a movie palace – nice comfortable loges, lights soft and low, and romantic pictures, enhanced by the entrancing musical score of "Kiss Me Again," "The Sweetest Story Ever Told," and the like.

Petters have found the automobile not as popular during this month, when the raw winds blow and cold rains sweep down. So they are taking to the picture theaters, there to sit through two hours or more of heavenly bliss, unaware of anything around them but that which spells love.

A lady – one of the dignified type, who considers loving merely a matter of words, the family album and a selection on the organ – protested most vigorously as she came out of a downtown theater recently, against the lovers. "Why," she exclaimed in shocked tones, "there was a couple right in front of me, and the most brazen things, they actually kissed each other several times. Why in my day. ... "

At any rate it goes to show that the movies have a place in the world, at least in the opinion of the lovers if not those of the censors. Watch for the last flicker of the film, when hero and heroine are shown in fond embrace, then watch a pair of lovers. The general result is – soft sighs from two hearts that beat as one; tender gazing into each other's eyes, and then ofttimes a gentle kiss.

The Actor's Part

Milton Sills

Source: Joseph P. Kennedy, ed., *The Story of Films* (Chicago and New York: A.W. Shaw Company, 1927), 188–94

Theirs a Dignified Art

Just as fifteen years ago the actor entering a studio endeavored to conceal the shameful fact, so, until recently, the industry has assumed a defensive, even timorous attitude, in the face of criticism. Today its stand is no longer apologetic. Millions of people all over the world do not pay incredible largess into the pockets of the industry, and of the actor in particular, without receiving a commensurate value in return. What is this value?

Purveyors of Entertainment

We may say all we like about the educative quality of the film, its indirect influence among nations toward the promoting of mutual understanding and world peace, its teaching of the manners and customs, the clothing and interior decoration that we find desirable, its function in advertising our commercial products. Fundamentally, while highly important, these seem to me secondary matters. The one thing the public pays for, without stint, is entertainment. If entertainment performs a distinct service, then the industry, and incidentally the actor, need no further justification, much less apology.

It may be that some vestige of old New England Puritanism persists in us, but until recently the business of amusement has been to some extent regarded as unessential, frivolous, and unworthy. The stage, indeed, the arts in general, were not looked upon as meriting serious consideration. During the war, for the first time, our Federal government put the seal of its approval on the motion picture as an indispensable industry.

What brought about this change? Why do we no longer have to assume a negative attitude of defense?

They Satisfy a Deep Human Craving

Because we are beginning to recognize that amusement satisfies a fundamental human appetite, that it is a commodity as essential to the physical and mental health and well-being of the human animal as lumber, wheat, oil, steel, or textiles, that, in short, it is a staple product in constant demand.

Particularly is this so today. Never before in the history of civilization has there been felt such a need for what is known as entertainment. It is a disquieting fact in modern life that very few of the men and women who carry the burden of the world's work find a compensating joy in that work. Sadly enough, the bulk of it lacks intrinsic interest. It has become overspecialized and standardized.

Drab Lives Illuminated

The jobs of the factory hand, the shop girl, the clerk, and the miner are routine jobs; they represent so much inevitable drudgery, and for the most part in the drabbest surroundings. Little wonder that voices of dissatisfaction are heard, that the menace of revolt against our economic system raises its head. At best, life is hard and dull and tragic for most of us. Some compensation for the miseries and boredom of existence is necessary. If our present industrial and social status is to be maintained, that compensation must be supplied. The problem is how to supply it to 130,000,000 people and at a moderate cost. Answers to problems such as these are met in modern times by the research of the scientist and the ingenuity of the inventor. Just as McCormick solved the problem of wholesale farming by the invention of the harvester machine, so Edison and Eastman solved the problem of the wholesale manufacture of amusement by the motion picture and its retailing at prices within the reach of all.

Vicarious Adventure

But just how does this form of amusement function as compensation to the drudging millions? By providing a means of escape from the intolerable pressure and incidence of reality. The motion picture enables the spectators to live vicariously the more brilliant, interesting, adventurous, romantic, successful, or comic lives of the shadow figures before them on the screen. Here are careers more vivid, saturated, full-blooded. Here there is no suppression, no frustration. Here are men and women of the kind they would like to be; here is the kind of conduct they would elect to make theirs if they could. Here is the Land of Heart's Desire. The film offers them a Freudian journey into made-to-order reverie, reverie by experts. Now reverie may be unwholesome – our psychological studies are still too immature to decide this question – but in our present form of culture it seems to be necessary. In any case, reverie engendered by motion pictures is certainly more wholesome than that engendered by the corner saloon or the drab walls of a tenement house. For an hour or two the spectator identifies himself with the hero or heroine; potential adventurer at heart, he becomes for the moment an actual imaginative adventurer in a splendid world where things seem to go right.

Now the heart of this form of amusement, of this method of vicarious living, happens to be the actor. It is in him and his fictive career upon the screen that the spectator is submerged. It is in him that the public finds escape and compensation. Small wonder that he is popular, that he becomes a beloved idol, a world hero. Small wonder that he is paid accordingly. The people clamor for him, the producers compete for him. The product of careful selection and long training, he is a scarce commodity, and the law of supply and demand operates in his favor.

Meantime, he performs an important public service, ameliorating the dreary lives of countless millions, bringing them charm, romance, laughter, grace, and high adventure. From a hundred to two hundred prints of his contribution are struck off and distributed to every corner of the globe. The technical machinery of the camera, the laboratory, and the projection machine have multiplied him and his wares infinitely and the public buys him in quantity. Taking into account his numerous different roles, he may play before five or six hundred audiences simultaneously and in as many centers. Theatres are, of course, necessary; studios with their elaborate staffs, directors and cameramen, executive and managerial departments, sales and distributing forces, expert financing, are all essential to the industry, but paramount to its existence are two things. The public goes to see stories and it goes to see actors in them. The story and the actor are the hub of the industry, the nucleus of this characteristic entertainment of democracy.

He Becomes the Friend of Millions

The actor belongs to the common people. He is their most intimate and yet mysterious friend, his face and feelings brought almost microscopically close by the miracle of the screen and yet intangibly remote and veiled with the glamor of a romance lent him by the astounding and entrancing fictions he seems to live through. The drama he embodies is not for the intellectual, but for the common mind and heart. The race as a whole cares little about the problems of an Ibsen or an O'Neill, it has never heard of the square root of minus one or the Bohr theory of the atom. The things it is interested in are love, courtship, marriage, divorce, motherhood, crime, gambling, sports, the disastrous forces of nature in fire and flood and earthquakes, the strength of men and women's beauty, the loyalty of friends and the treachery of enemies, all the clash and clangor of human lives in stress. These are the things that are near to them. Their heroes have been Odysseus, Siegfried, Robinson Crusoe, Launcelot, Hamlet, Faust, Napoleon, Joan of Arc, and Cinderella. These figures have become idealizations of themselves, life-enhancing to the world-imagination, redolent of tang and flavor, appealing to the midriff, not the mind. Our modern heroes are Bill Hart, with a brace of guns routing a hundred miscreants; Chaplin, inimitable clown with the tragic heart; Fairbanks, invincible romantic adventurer, the Prince Charming of the fairy books; and Mary Pickford, immortal sweetheart, in whom every Cinderella discovers herself as a fairy princess. These and a few more have become the classic figures of our screen. The public loves to love.

In this brief sketch I have tried to outline the motion picture actor's business status for you and the human demand on which it rests. Along with and through the industry of which he is a part, he seems to me to constitute a formidable and novel development in modern affairs.

Readings and Screenings

For an examination of the ways in which filmmakers recast ideas about class and gender in the 1920s to promote new visions of middle-class life, see Lary May *Screening Out the Past*, Sumiko Higashi, *Cecile B. DeMille and American Culture* (Berkeley, CA: University of California Press, 1994), and Lucy Fischer, ed., *American Cinema of the 1920s: Themes and Variations* (New Brunswick, NJ: Rutgers University Press, 2009). Changing class images of the 1920s are also discussed in Sumiko Higashi, *Virgins, Vamps, and Flappers: The American Silent Movie Heroine* (St. Albans, VT: Eden Press Women's Publications, 1978); Richard Koszarski, *An Evening's Entertainment*. For changing depictions of working-class life and radicalism during this era, see Peter Stead, *Film and the Working Class: The Feature Film in British and American Society* (London and New York: Routledge, 1989); Kevin Brownlow, *Behind the Mask of Innocence*; Lewis

Jacobs, *Rise of American Film*; Steven Ross, *Working-Class Hollywood; Shull, Radicalism in American Silent Films*. For the men who forged Hollywood, see Neal Gabler, *An Empire of Their Own: How the Jews Invented Hollywood* (New York: Anchor Books, 1989); for the women who built early Hollywood, see Karen Ward Mahar, *Women Filmmakers in Early Hollywood* (Baltimore, MD: Johns Hopkins University Press, 2008); Mark Garrett Cooper, *Universal Women: Filmmaking and Institutional Change in Early Hollywood* (Urbana, IL: University of Illinois Press, 2010); Cari Beauchamp, *Without Lying Down: Frances Marion and the Powerful Women of Early Hollywood* (Berkeley and Los Angeles, CA: University of California Press, 1997). Ben M. Hall's *The Best Remaining Seats: The Golden Age of the Movie Palace* (New York: DaCapo Press, 1988) offers a brief history and wonderful photographs of the nation's most luxurious movie palaces. The ingenious strategies that guided Chicago movie palace builders Balaban and Katz are described in Carrie Balaban, *Continuous Performance: The Story of A. J. Balaban* (New York: Putnams, 1942). Audiences did not necessarily interpret films in the way producers may have intended. Lizabeth Cohen's *Making a New Deal: Industrial Workers in Chicago, 1919–1939* (New York: Cambridge University Press, 1990) argues that Chicago moviegoers drew on class, racial, ethnic, gender, and political experiences to give meaning to the images they saw on the screen.

Long before the appearance of *Titanic* (1997), Cecil B. DeMille was making cross-class fantasies about love between the classes. *Male and Female* (1919) and *Saturday Night* (1922) are two of his best examples. Other entertaining films of the 1920s that offered audiences new visions of the interconnections among sex, consumption, class, gender, and the fast life include *Sex* (1920), *The Sheik* (1921), *It* (1927); *Orchids and Ermine* (1927), and *Our Dancing Daughters* (1928). *Smouldering Fires* (1925) is a cautionary tale of what happens when businesswomen become too successful. The Red Scare of the late teens sparked an array of films that vilified unions and radicals and helped pave the way for many workers to think of themselves as middle class. The more interesting films of this genre include *Bolshevism on Trial* (1919) and *Dangerous Hours* (1920). For worker responses, see *The Passaic Textile Strike* (1926) – which can be rented from the Museum of Modern Art, New York. *Labor's Reward* (1925), a previously "lost" film made by the American Federation of Labor, is now available on DVD. Those interested in exploring how silent filmmakers put politics on the screen without using words can consult my website essay (which includes photos and films clips) "Visualizing Ideology: Labor vs. Capital in the Age of Silent Film" at dornsife.usc.edu/hist225g/pages/home/index.html (last accessed August 2013).

4

Who Controls What We See? Censorship and the Attack on Hollywood "Immorality"

Introduction to Article

One of the oldest clichés in the movie business is that audiences always get the films they want. But is that true? Do audiences really get to see what *they* want to see or are their choices limited by outside forces? What are those outside forces? Who controls what we see? Producers? Government agencies? Lobbying groups? Audiences?

Pick up any newspaper today and you are bound to read about some politician or religious or civic leader accusing Hollywood of promoting violence, crime, and sex, and demanding some form of censorship. Such cries are not new. Since the appearance of the first nickelodeons in 1905, authorities in all walks of life have repeatedly blamed movies and the industry that produced them for all that is wrong in America. Gregory Black explores the forces responsible for determining what audiences of the 1930s and 1940s were allowed to see and what they were not allowed to see. He explains how studio heads responded to threats of boycotts and federal censorship by instituting various self-censorship plans. From 1934 until its abolition in 1968, the censors who ran the Production Code Administration, the most powerful of these plans, influenced the social, political, sexual, and racial content of every American film. Designed by Catholic lay leaders, the Code was intended to pressure filmmakers into

Movies and American Society, Second Edition. Edited by Steven J. Ross.
© 2014 John Wiley & Sons, Inc. Published 2014 by John Wiley & Sons, Inc.

upholding "traditional" American values – as defined by Christian civic leaders, politicians, and clergy. But, as Black reveals, clever filmmakers always found ways to subvert the Code and the will of censors.

Discussion Points

Should an institution that reaches millions of viewers each year, many of them children, be subject to some form of censorship? Who should decide what should or should not be seen? Does censorship challenge the constitutional right to free speech? What responsibility should Hollywood take, if any, for governing public morality?

Hollywood Censored: The Production Code Administration and the Hollywood Film Industry, 1930–1940

Gregory D. Black

Source: *Film History*, 3, 1989, 167–89

In July 1934 an editorial in *The Commonweal*, a semi-official organ of the Catholic church, declared that the "muck merchants" of Hollywood, that "fortress of filth" that had been destroying the moral fiber of the American people, had finally been brought to its knees by the Catholic church and its Legion of Decency. In less than a year the church had recruited millions of Americans of all religious denominations to pledge not to attend "immoral" movies. With a national depression already threatening Hollywood's financial stability, movie czar Will Hays, head of the Motion Picture Producers and Distributors of America (MPPDA), accepted the terms of surrender dictated by the church and its legions.

The truce struck between Hays and the Most Reverend John T. McNicholas, Archbishop of Cincinnati, and written and negotiated by Martin Quigley, publisher of *The Motion Picture Herald*, signaled a turning point in a 30-year battle among religious leaders, women's groups, civic organizations, municipal and state censorship boards, and the motion picture industry over the content of Hollywood films. The victory took the form of a new agency inside the MPPDA, the industry's trade association. The Catholics demanded that Hays create a Production Code Administration (PCA) to enforce the censorship code adopted by the industry in 1930. The code, written by a Catholic priest, had not, in the opinion of the church, been enforced. The church demanded, and Hays agreed, that a staunch lay Catholic, namely Joseph I. Breen, would head the PCA and interpret the code.

To guarantee that Breen would have enforcement powers, the agreement forced every studio to submit scripts to the PCA before production. The studios agreed that no production would begin without script approval and that no film would be distributed without a PCA seal of approval. The MPPDA was given power to levy a $25,000 fine against any violator.

But that was not all. The church demanded that Hollywood permanently withdraw from circulation films it viewed as "immoral" and that local theater owners be empowered to cancel any film currently in circulation if they judged it to be "immoral." The industry promptly withdrew a score of films, including Mae West's *She Done Him Wrong* (Paramount, 1933), *The Story of Temple Drake* (Paramount, 1933) (adapted from William Faulkner's *Sanctuary*), and Frank Borzage's filmed version of Ernest Hemingway's *A Farewell to Arms* (Paramount, 1932). Finally, the church demanded that any appeal of PCA decisions be resolved not by a jury of Hollywood producers, as in the past, but by Will Hays in New York.

The PCA, created to mollify religious critics and to disarm proponents of federal censorship, exercised a strong, often dominating influence on movie content for more than two decades. From 1934 until the mid-1950s Breen and his staff closely scrutinized every Hollywood script for offensive social, political, and sexual themes. Although the initial intent was to protect the public from sexual improprieties, Breen was determined to eliminate controversial subjects from the screen to maximize the worldwide appeal of Hollywood films. In the process he imposed on film producers and filmgoers a rigidly conservative view of politics and morality. As film historian Robert Sklar has observed, Breen and the code virtually "cut the movies off from many of the most important moral and social themes of the contemporary world."[1]

Unfortunately most film history is written as if the code and the PCA did not exist. An understanding of Hollywood requires an appreciation of how self-censorship functioned in the studio production system. The fate of two productions from early 1934, Mae West's *Belle of the Nineties* (Paramount, 1934) and Ernst Lubitsch's *The Merry Widow* (MGM, 1934) illustrate the PCA's moral strictures. Two films that contained no moral violations, Walter Wanger's *The President Vanishes* (Paramount, 1934) and Warner Bros. production of *Black Fury* (Warner Bros., 1935), were nevertheless considered "dangerous" by Breen and Hays and show how the PCA prevented films from making serious social or political comment.

By 1934 films had become a collaborative, corporate art form. The industry had come a long way from its beginning as a provider of cheap entertainment for urban immigrants at the turn of the century. Films quickly evolved into a form of mass entertainment that attracted viewers from every segment of American society. Box office success, it turned out, frequently resulted from sexually titillating themes and from stories that seemed to glorify gangsters and social deviants. This in turn brought increasing demands for regulation. Pennsylvania established the first state board for film censorship in 1911, and Ohio and Kansas followed in 1913. By 1915 a host of municipal and state censorship boards had been created to impose local community standards of morality on films by censoring films before their exhibition. The film industry challenged the legality of "prior censorship" in 1915. In a landmark decision that was to influence the content of films until the 1950s, the Supreme Court upheld the right of prior censorship by local communities when it ruled in *Mutual Film Corporation v. Ohio* that movies were not protected under freedom of speech provisions of either the state or federal constitutions.

By the mid-1920s eight states and more than 200 municipalities had enacted censorship boards. There was no real consistency: Pennsylvania was the most strict, Kansas the most pristine (the latter limiting screen kissing to a few seconds and banning scenes of smoking and drinking). The common denominator was that all the censorship boards were committed to eliminating portraits of changing moral standards, limiting scenes of crime (which they believed to be responsible for an increase in juvenile delinquency), and avoiding as much as possible any screen portrayal of civil strife, labor–management discord, or government corruption and injustice. The screen, these moral guardians held, was not a proper forum for discussing delicate sexual issues or for social or political commentary. ...

In the early 1920s the industry was rocked by a series of sensational scandals about the private lives of its stars, the most famous being the scandal involving Fatty Arbuckle. The dual forces of scandal and censorship forced the industry to unite under a common banner, the MPPDA. In 1922 industry leaders chose as their first president Will H. Hays, a prominent Republican politician and architect of Warren Harding's presidential victory. He symbolized the veritable puritan in Babylon. Teetotaler and elder in the Presbyterian church, Hays saw it as his mission to bring a Jewish-dominated film industry the respectability of mainstream middle America. ...

A front man for the industry, Hays served as the lightning rod for public complaints. Promoted by press agents as the movie czar, Hays was in fact no more than an employee of the moguls. As a public relations agent, he was an unqualified success; as a censor or regulator of movie content during the 1920s, he was a failure. Rejecting the notion of censorship by government, Hays embraced a system of industry self-regulation. In 1924 he introduced "The Formula," a series of rules designed to prevent "objectionable" plays and novels from being produced as films. Hays' formula did manage to keep some material off the screen, but he was dependent on voluntary compliance by the studios. A steady stream of "modern" films increased criticism of the industry. In 1927, the year in which sound first accompanied images on the silver screen, Hays created the Studio Relations Committee (SRC). Under the direction of Colonel Jason Joy, the SRC codified the most common demands of the municipal and state censorship boards into a single working document informally known as the "Don'ts and Be Carefuls." This document prohibited, among other things, profanity, nudity, drug trafficking, and white slavery in films and urged producers to exercise good taste in presenting such adult themes as criminal behavior, sexual relations, and violence. Still the studios interpreted these guidelines according to their own taste, however, and still the antimovie lobby fulminated and grew ever larger and more threatening.

Although reformers had favored cooperation with Hays in 1922, by the end of the decade they were convinced that Hays was ineffective and that federal intervention was necessary to control Hollywood. Until the early 1930s the opponents of Hollywood had been primarily an alliance of Protestant ministers and women's organizations. As traditional guardians of public morality, they claimed that Hollywood was directly responsible for the dramatic changes that had taken place in American society in the past three decades. Alarmed at an increasing divorce rate, a rise in juvenile delinquency, and a general flaunting of traditional values by young men and women, the ministers held the movies directly responsible for what they saw as America's moral collapse. ...

If these moral guardians were upset by silent cinema, they were infuriated when films began to talk. The talkies opened up new dramatic possibilities, and the movies became more popular than ever. Now sexy starlets could rationalize their immoral behavior; criminals using hip slang could brag about flaunting law and order; and politicians could talk about bribery and corruption. Film dialogue could and did challenge conventional norms. In 1928 the New York censorship board cut more than 4,000 scenes from the more than 600 films submitted, and Chicago censors sliced more than 6,000 scenes. But even as the censors were snipping away at a furious pace, audiences were flocking to the theaters.

In 1922 the average weekly attendance at movie theaters in the United States stood at 40 million. By 1928 it had leaped to 65 million and by 1930 had reached the staggering figure of 90 million. ...

The Catholic church, before 1930, played no part in the controversy over film content. Church leaders and lay activists consistently lobbied against Protestant efforts to pass censorship laws. Accepting entertainment as a feature of modern life, the church neither banned members from attendance nor restricted Sunday viewing. By 1930, however, a small group of Catholic laymen and priests was becoming more and more uncomfortable with what it perceived as the declining moral quality of films. Martin Quigley, a staunch lay Catholic and owner and publisher of the industry trade journal *The Motion Picture Herald*, took the first steps toward Catholic involvement. An advocate for theater owners, Quigley opposed government censorship and argued that block-booking was in the financial interests of small theater owners because it reduced the overall price they had to pay for individual films. Yet he shared the conviction of other reformers that movies were becoming "immoral" and was further convinced that movies had to avoid social, political, and economic subjects or face strict government censorship. To Quigley, movies had to be "harmless entertainment."

Convinced that the industry could regulate itself through the Hays office, Quigley began to think about a new code of behavior for the movie industry in the summer of 1929. Acting on the advice of his priest Father FitzGeorge Dinneen, who was a friend and confidant of Cardinal George W. Mundelein of Chicago, Quigley invited Father Daniel Lord, a Jesuit from St. Louis, to work with them.

Lord was a professor of dramatics at St. Louis University and editor of the widely read *The Queen's Work*, which preached morality and ethics to Catholic youth. As a boy, Lord wrote in his autobiography, he had been overwhelmed by D. W. Griffith's *The Birth of a Nation* (Epoch, 1915). He left the theater convinced that he had seen a new medium of communication powerful enough to "change our whole attitude toward life, civilization, and established customs." As a young priest he was selected to work as technical adviser to Cecil B. DeMille in *The King of Kings* (Pathé, 1927). When Quigley invited him to think about a new moral code for the industry, he leapt at the opportunity.[2]

Joseph I. Breen was another major figure in this small group of aroused Catholics. An active lay Catholic, Breen had been the press relations chief for the 1926 Eucharistic Congress in Chicago, where he was also public relations director of the Peabody Coal Company. Invited by Quigley to work with the group, Breen was to emerge in 1934 as the director of the PCA.

For several months Quigley, Breen, Lord, Father Dinneen, and Father Wilfred Parsons, editor of the influential Catholic publication *America*, exchanged ideas about a code of behavior for the movies. ... After studying the various state and municipal censorship codes, the Hays office's "Don'ts and Be Carefuls," and the objections of Protestant reformers, Daniel Lord took on the task of writing a new movie code. What emerged is a fascinating combination of Catholic theology, conservative politics, and pop psychology that was to control the content of Hollywood films for the next two decades.

Although the code is most often discussed as a document that prohibited nudity, required married couples to sleep in twin beds, and effectively ruined the movie career of that saucy favorite Mae West, its authors intended it to control much more. Lord and his colleagues shared a common objective with Protestant film reformers: They all wanted entertainment films to emphasize that the church, the government, and the family were the cornerstones of an orderly society and that success and happiness resulted from respecting and working in this system. They believed that entertainment films should reinforce religious teachings that deviant behavior, whether criminal or sexual, costs violators the love and comforts of home, the intimacy of family, the solace of religion, and the protection of law. In short, they believed films should be twentieth century morality plays that illustrated proper behavior to the masses.

As Lord put it, Hollywood films were first and foremost "entertainment for the multitudes" and as such carried a "special *Moral Responsibility*" requisite of no other medium of entertainment or communication. Their universal popularity, cutting across social, political, and economic classes and penetrating communities from the most sophisticated to the most remote, meant that filmmakers could not be permitted the same freedom of expression allowed to producers of legitimate theater, authors of books, or even editors of newspapers. ...

In the late 1920s, when sound was combined with visually striking images, a sensation was created that Lord believed would be irresistible to the impressionable minds of children, the uneducated, the immature, and the unsophisticated. These very groups, Lord believed, represented a large majority of the national film audience. It was because this massive film audience was incapable of distinguishing between fantasy and reality – or so Lord and the film reformers believed – that self-regulation or control was necessary.

Therefore, the basic premise behind the code was that "no picture should lower the moral standards of those who see it." Recognizing that evil and sin were a legitimate part of drama, the code stressed that no film should create a feeling of "sympathy" for the criminal, the adulterer, the immoralist, or the corrupter. No film should be so constructed as to "leave the question of right or wrong in doubt." Films must uphold, not question or challenge, the basic values of society. The sanctity of the home and marriage must be upheld. The concept of basic law must not be "belittled or ridiculed." Courts must be shown as just and fair, police as honest and efficient, and government as protective of all people. If corruption were a necessary part of any plot, it had to be restricted: a judge could be corrupt but not the court system; a policeman could be brutal but not the police force. Interestingly, Lord's code stated that "crime *need not always be punished, as long as the audience is made to know that it is wrong.*" What Lord wanted films to do was to illustrate clearly to audiences that "evil is wrong" and that "good is right."[3]

Quigley immediately took Lord's draft to Hays and began agitating for industry adoption. Quigley's strategy was to combine economic threat and moral pressure. He and Father Dinneen convinced Cardinal George Mundelein of Chicago to "sponsor" the code and to use his influence with the investment firm of Halsey-Stuart, a major industry investor, to pressure the industry to accept it. In a series of meetings in December 1929 and January 1930 with Cardinal Mundelein, Harold S. Stuart, Quigley, Lord, industry leaders, and members of the Hays office, the basic tenets of the code were accepted.

With the dramatic stock market crash only a few weeks behind them film corporation heads in New York were jittery, and Hays convinced them that the code would be good for business. It might quiet demands for federal censorship and undercut the campaign to eliminate block-booking. It remained for Hays to convince Hollywood producers that the code made good sense from an entertainment, as well as an economic, point of view. With the full support of the corporate offices in New York, Hays set off for Los Angeles to "peddle a script" for movie behavior.[4]

Hays found the producers less than enthusiastic over the tone and content of Lord's code. A small group of producers, MGM's head of production Irving Thalberg, studio boss Jack Warner of Warner Bros., production head B. P. Schulberg of Paramount, and Sol Wurtzel of Fox, offered a counterproposal. The producers rejected Lord's basic argument that the movies had to be more restrictive in presenting material than other art forms. They maintained that films were simply "one vast reflection of every image in the stream of contemporary life." In their view, audiences supported movies that they liked and stayed away from those that they did not. No other guidelines were needed, it seemed to them, to determine what audiences would accept. The advent of sound, in their view, brought a wider, not more restrictive, latitude in subject matter to the movies. The addition of screen dialogue, they held, would allow actors and actresses to "speak delicately and exactly" on sensitive subjects that could not be portrayed in silent films. Therefore, the producers countered, the talkies should be able to use "any book, play or title which had gained wide attention."[5]

The two documents could not have been any farther apart. From the producer's perspective Lord's code, representing reformers of all ilks, asked them to present a utopian view of life that denied reality. But Daniel Lord, convinced that the screen was undermining church teachings and destroying family life, wanted a partnership of the industry, church, and state that would advocate a fair, moral, and orderly society. Lord admitted that the world's imperfections were the stuff of good drama, but he saw no reason why films should not show simple and direct solutions to complex moral, political, economic, and philosophical issues. The producers countered that film was no different from any other means of entertainment and required no special restrictions. The American people, they argued, were the real censors, and the box office was their ballot box.

The fascinating aspect of this conflict is that Lord's position, backed by Hays, the Catholic church, and the financial backers of the industry, was adopted almost without a whimper. Why the industry would adopt a code that, if interpreted literally, would cut out important social, political, and economic themes and turn movies into defenders of the status quo remains a question. Why would the industry, enjoying an all-time high of 90 million paid admissions per week, agree to such severe restrictions on content and form?

There are several possibilities. One is that Will Hays wanted to extend his influence from New York to Hollywood. Since his appointment in 1922, Hays had little control over the Hollywood studios. This lack of control kept him in continual hot water with the reformers. When Quigley first approached Hays with Lord's code, Hays was supportive. He recognized immediately that this Catholic plan did not ask for federal intervention, demand outside censorship, or attach the financial cornerstone of the industry, block-booking. It placed movie regulation squarely in the Hays office, just where Will Hays believed it belonged. Furthermore, acceptance of the code by the industry might actually undercut the various religious reform groups. By accepting the Catholic code, Hays prevented, at least temporarily, a Catholic–Protestant antifilm coalition.

Adopting the code also made good economic sense. Although the industry was booming at the box office, the financial structure of the industry was always fragile. Any major interruption in the cash flow from the box office or from the bankers could bring the movie house of cards tumbling down.

With American Catholics making up around 20 percent of the population, and with that population being heavily concentrated in America's largest cities, the industry was especially sensitive to Catholic opinion. The industry likewise needed a steady flow of loans to finance its more than 500 features a year. Catholic threats to pressure bankers, combined with their implied threat of box office pressure, were not lost on Hays or the corporate headquarters in New York.

From the producer's point of view, the industry had lived and prospered with codes since 1911. The various efforts of Hays and the municipal and state censorship boards had been irritating but not destructive. Further, it should be noted that many also believed that Lord was basically right. Perhaps there was too much sex, too much crime, too much drinking, too much corruption, too much violence, and too little good taste in films. Furthermore, few people in Hollywood believed that the code meant exactly what it said. Even if it did, the producers insisted on one provision that gave them, not Hays, the final say over film content: If any studio felt that the Hays office interpreted the code improperly, a "jury" of producers, not MPPDA officials, would decide whether or not the offending scene would be cut. With that understanding, the code was formally adopted by the industry on March 31, 1930.

Hays gave the task of enforcing the code to Jason Joy and the SRC in Hollywood. Producers submitted scripts to Joy, who served as chief censor until 1932, and then to Dr. James Wingate, who served until the Legion of Decency crisis in 1934. Both men attempted to alter films to make them consistent with the code, but both experienced major problems.

Although industry leaders gloated in 1930 that the movies were "depression proof," a serious box office downturn started in 1931. Within a year theater attendance plunged from 90 million to 60 million per week in 1930. The studios responded in typical fashion: They tried to lure fans back into the theater with sensational movies. The crisis was so severe that by 1932 several studios faced bankruptcy, and as a frustrated Joy told Hays " ... with box-office figures down, with high pressure being employed back home [New York corporate offices] to spur the studios to get more cash, it was almost inevitable that sex ... should be seized upon."[6]

Thus despite the code themes of sex, crime, and politics appeared in the movies with increasing frankness. Marlene Dietrich seduced an aging professor in *Der Blaue Engel* (UFA, 1930) and bedded a gangster in *Blonde Venus* (Paramount, 1932). Greta Garbo, rejected by her lover, turned openly to prostitution in *Susan Lenox, Her Fall and Rise* (MGM, 1931). In *Possessed* (MGM, 1931) Joan Crawford rose from a poor factory worker to a life of luxury as the mistress of an ambitious politician. Joy challenged MGM producer Irving Thalberg over this last production, but Thalberg argued that because there was no nudity in the film and because the subject was handled in "good taste" there was no violation of the code. Joy admitted to Hays that there was little he could do to force Thalberg to make changes because, in his view, a jury would most certainly rule for Thalberg.

In 1932 Mae West emerged in Hollywood as the woman who best epitomized the sexual revolution of the past decade. West was kept by no man, did not need nudity to suggest sexuality, and both delighted and infuriated moviegoers with the way in which she flaunted tradition. As a stage performer in 1926, her Broadway production of *Sex* brought notoriety and a ten-day jail sentence for obscenity. Undeterred by what she considered bluenose repression, she followed with another smash hit, *Diamond Lil.* Hays immediately branded it unsuitable as a subject for a film. Nevertheless, in 1932 Paramount Studios, fighting off bankruptcy and desperate for a hit, brought West to Hollywood. In a special ruling the MPPDA Board of Directors gave Paramount permission to film *Diamond Lil* as a story that the studio released under the title *She Done Him Wrong.* Audiences loved West's humor, and within months she was starring again in *I'm No Angel* (Paramount, 1933). By 1934 more than 46 million people had seen the two films. ...

Although West received approval from industry censors, accolades from the critics, and adoration from millions, moral guardians contended that she represented a total collapse of moral standards. When Lord saw *She Done Him Wrong*, he was horrified. He wrote to Hays that he had written the code to prevent just such films. When Hays responded that fans and critics alike had praised the film, Lord demanded that Catholic youth boycott it. While a Mae West craze swept the nation, a groundswell among women's clubs and civic and religious organizations protested the screening of her films. *She Done Him Wrong* was banned in Atlanta; in Haverhill, Massachusetts the town clergy denounced West as "demoralizing, disgusting, suggestive and indecent."[7]

Along with West the popularity of the gangster films illustrated the problems of enforcing the code. In the early 1930s a series of flashy gangsters – Edward G. Robinson in *Little Caesar* (Warner Bros., 1930), James Cagney in *The Public Enemy* (Warner Bros., 1931), and Paul Muni in *Scarface* (UA, 1932) – murdered their way to the top of the gang world. Penetrating the dangerous, but seductive, urban underworld, movie gangsters spoke colorfully, their guns barked out their own form of law, and their cars, squealing around corners at breathtaking speed, epitomized life in the fast lane. In an era of depression, their reward was money, admiring friends, fancy clothes, and even fancier women. They flaunted the traditions of hard work, sacrifice, and respect for institutions of authority. Robinson, Cagney, and Muni dominated each of these films, and despite the fact that their characters were killed in the last reel reformers believed that each film violated the code by creating "sympathy" for the criminal or taught the methods of successful crime to impressionable youth.

The films cut to the center of the controversy over what was acceptable on the screen. ... To be sure, Joy found the gangster films to be violent but, in their overall tone, anticrime and infused with the strong moral lesson that the criminal was the enemy of society and always paid for his crimes in the end. Wingate, fully realizing that Mae West made any attempt at censorship look foolish and being quite aware that she could turn the most innocent-sounding dialogue in a script into blatant sexual innuendo, took her for what she was: a comic, a satirist poking fun at, in Joy's terms, the small, narrow, and picayunish. Although Joy and Wingate each fought with producers to eliminate violence, to cut overt sexuality, and to tame critical views of American life, neither believed that films had to be so restrictive as to eliminate the gangster, the adulterer, or the comic from the screen.

Others did, however. Lord, invited to Los Angeles to evaluate the effectiveness of the code after one year of operation, praised Joy's efforts but condemned the industry for drifting into subject areas that were "fundamentally dangerous" no matter "how delicate or clean the treatment." He urged the industry to move away from stories of "degenerates" and instead to fill the silver screen with uplifting stories of "business, industry, and commerce." He urged Hays to replace stories of gangsters and kept women with the biographies of American heroes such as Lindbergh, sports figures such as Babe Ruth or Bobby Jones, or political leaders such as Al Smith. The code that he had written in 1930, he told Hays, was not a document open to liberal interpretation. Unlike Jason Joy, Lord found no moral lessons in films about gangsters and kept women and, by 1933, was appalled by the sexual humor of Mae West.[8]

From his position in Los Angeles, Joseph Breen confirmed what many already felt: that "nobody out here cares a damn for the Code or any of its provisions." In frustration he wrote Father Wilfred Parsons that, in his opinion, Hays had sold them all "a first class bill of goods when he put over the Code on us." It may be that Hays thought "these lousy Jews out here would abide by the Code's provisions but if he did he should be censured for his lack of proper knowledge of the breed." The only standard of ethics understood in Hollywood was the box office, Breen told Parsons. Breen was convinced that if they were to be successful in reforming the industry it would have to be through box office pressure.[9] ...

By the beginning of 1933 all three men conceded that the code was not working. ... To make matters worse, in the spring a sensational book published by Henry James Forman, *Our Movie-Made Children*, openly accused movies of corrupting the nation's youth. Forman's book was a summary of nine other publications, each written by respected academics under the sponsorship of the Payne Fund. Although the academics had been careful to avoid making sweeping generalizations and stressed that films influenced individuals on different levels, Forman boldly charged that 72 percent of all movies were unfit for children and were "helping to shape a race of criminals." *Our Movie-Made Children* was a sensational indictment of the movie industry and became a national best seller.[10] ...

Sensing that Hays and the industry were now vulnerable to outside pressure, Quigley lobbied for increased Catholic involvement. His opening came with the announcement that the newly appointed apostolic delegate, Monsignor Amleto Giovanni Cicognani, would deliver a speech to the Catholic charities in New York. Meeting with Quigley only days before his speech, Cicognani agreed to incorporate into his speech a draft statement that Quigley had written calling for Catholic action against the movies. "What a massacre of innocence of youth is taking place hour by hour," said Cicognani. "Catholics are called by God, the Pope, the Bishops, and the priests to a united and vigorous campaign for the purification of the cinema, which has become a deadly menace to morals."[11]

The speech kicked off the Legion of Decency campaign, which succeeded beyond Quigley's wildest dreams. Taking the speech as a papal directive, the American bishops ... adopted a three-part plan to (1) create a pressure group; (2) boycott offensive films; and (3) support self-regulation and conformity with the production code. ...

In a matter of a few months the legion counted more than 3 million pledges, and by the end of the year more than 7 million people of all religious denominations had joined the movement.

Although Quigley was delighted with the reaction to the campaign, he was concerned about the direction. ... He was fearful that local boycotts would undercut support for reform among theater owners. He was even more fearful that a new Mae West movie would be released at the height of the decency campaign (*It Ain't No Sin* was in production) and, in part because of the campaign, become a smash hit. If all or any of those things happened, Quigley feared that the opportunity to clean up the movies would be lost.

Quigley and Joseph Breen went to McNicholas with an alternative plan: to allow Joseph Breen to enforce the code by incorporating a "voice for morality" in each film that dealt with sin, to allow theater owners to cancel 10 percent of each block on moral grounds to pacify the anti-block-booking groups, to eliminate the "jury" system, to remove certain offensive films from circulation, and to attach a PCA seal to every film released after July 1934.

The alternative offered by Quigley and Breen was attractive to McNicholas because it took him out of the movie business. ... Will Hays also endorsed Quigley's ideas. He recognized that Quigley offered a formula to mute criticism from the community and yet retain internal control over production and issues that appealed to the mass audience. Quigley's alternative to ad hoc "black lists" and boycotts was the subject of the letters exchanged by Hays and McNicholas in August 1934. After the exchange, Hays announced that the PCA would be under the direction of Joseph Breen.

Breen had been working for Hays in Los Angeles since 1931. In late 1933, Hays appointed Breen to the staff of the SRC. Although he was technically an assistant to James Wingate, Breen was effectively placed in control of Hollywood operations. When Breen was announced as the new director of the PCA he was well known to the Hollywood studios. In appearance Breen was a moral reformer placed in power by the Catholic church, a man with a mission determined to clean up what he saw as "filth" in the industry. But he was also an employee of the industry, a vital part of the studio production system. His job was not to prevent films from being made but to infuse entertainment films with a strong sense of moral value. He fully realized that the very studios that paid his salary were determined to challenge his authority, and he also knew that his power base – the Catholic church – was badly split. ...

Could Breen succeed in enforcing the code with enough strictness to keep the antimovie lobby under control without reducing Hollywood's multimillion dollar fantasy world to pabulum? Would the producers accept the opinions of a journalist and public relations man turned moral reformer? Most important, would the public accept its entertainment infused with a strong dose of Catholic morality?

One of Breen's first actions as head of the PCA was to write a new definition of "moral compensating values" for the movies. This document is vital to understanding Breen's overlordship of the PCA. Breen went further than even Daniel Lord in advocating film as a vehicle to promote proper social and political behavior. Every film, according to Breen, must now contain "sufficient good" to compensate for any evil that might be depicted. Films that had crime or sin as a major part of the plot must contain "compensating moral value" to justify the subject matter. To Breen this meant that these films must have a good character who spoke as a voice for morality, a character who clearly told the criminals or sinner that he or she was wrong. Each film must contain a stern moral lesson: regeneration, suffering, and punishment. He urged that whenever possible stars, not stringers, should play the characters who represented good. In building respect for the law, Breen held that the existing code was a "full mandate to enforce respect for all *law* and all *lawful* authority. Nothing "subversive of the fundamental law of the land" could be shown in a movie. "Communistic propaganda is banned from the screen," he said. The screen was to promote "social spirit" and "patriotism" and not confuse audiences with a "cynical contempt for conventions" nor too vivid a recreation of the "realism of problems" encountered in life.[12]

Breen and his staff looked at each script with an eye toward its impact on "industry policy." This category was reserved for those films that, although technically within the code, were judged by Breen or Hays to be "dangerous" to the well-being of the industry. Undefined to allow as much latitude as possible, "industry policy" was invoked on those scripts that touched on social or political themes. Fearing loss of valuable markets, both domestic and international, the PCA used the code to limit studios in their selection and presentation of social criticism.

Moral guardians believed that no one was more in need of "compensating moral values" than Mae West. Martin Quigley was embarrassed when his *Motion Picture Herald* declared West one of the box office champions of 1933. Her popularity was as strong in small-town rural America as it was in the so-called sophisticated urban areas. The experience of D. W. Fiske, owner–manager of the Fiske Theater in Oak Grove, Louisiana, best summed up the uniqueness of West: "Did the best business of the year" (with *I'm No Angel*). "Whether they like her or not they all come out to see her. The church people clamor for clean pictures, but they all come out to see Mae West and stay away from the clean, sweet pictures. ... "[13]

While Quigley and Breen worked toward strengthening the enforcement of the production code, and while the Legion of Decency's boycott movement steam-rolled across the nation during the spring of 1934, Paramount studios was producing a new Mae West vehicle. *It Ain't No Sin* became a test case for Breen, Hays, and the PCA.

The basic plot was vintage West. The film is set in the 1890s, and West plays the role of Ruby Carter, a St. Louis riverboat queen. Her boyfriend is Tiger Kid, an ex-con and up-and-coming prize fighter. Ruby is hired by New Orleans gambler Ace Lamont as the headline act in his establishment, The Sensation House, and is soon the toast of New Orleans. When one of her many admirers asks her whether she is in New Orleans for good Ruby replies "I expect to be here, but not for good."[14]

When the first script arrived from Paramount, Breen pulled his entire staff into a day-long conference to pore over the material line by line. Unlike his predecessor James Wingate, he was shocked by the script and told Paramount that he was "compelled to reject in toto" the project. His objections were not a matter of cleaning up some bits of dialogue, Breen wrote, because in his view the script was a "vulgar and highly offensive yarn" and was "a glorification of prostitution and violent crime without any compensating moral values of any kind." The character West was to play, Breen wrote, "displays all the habits and practices of a prostitute, aids in the operation of a dishonest gambling house, drugs a prize-fighter, robs her employer, deliberately sets fire to his premises, and, in the end, goes off scot free in the company with her illicit lover who is a self-confessed criminal, a thief, and a murderer." He declared the script to be in total violation of the code.[15]

Breen's letter sent officials at Paramount, where production had already begun, into a panic. They assured Breen that he was "unnecessarily alarmed" over "a harmless comedy." Breen refused to budge and rejected revised scripts submitted in February and March. Paramount chose to ignore Breen and went forward with production. They submitted a completed film to Breen in June 1934, and he rejected it. He informed Paramount president Adolph Zukor that the "low moral tone" of the film was especially "dangerous when viewed in light of the industry's present position with the public."[16] ...

The battle lines were drawn. In Hollywood the studios were determined to make films without interference. In New York the corporate heads were not so sure. The real power in the film industry was in New York, not Hollywood. The corporate offices allowed studio heads a great deal of freedom as long as box office revenues produced a steady stream of profits. But these were trying times, and corporate leaders were uneasy. ... New York officials ordered the studios to tone down publicity on the film to avoid problems with "women's clubs" and "hinterland censors."[17] Hays continued to pressure Zukor and finally convinced the mogul that the studio could have West, but only in a tightly restricted format. New York instructed Hollywood to cooperate with Breen. Mae West would be given an infusion of "compensating moral value." Breen demanded that the studio delete all references to Ruby's past as a prostitute, remove all references to her boyfriend Tiger Kid as an ex-con, remove scenes detailing a "five day affair" between Ruby and Tiger Kid, remove scenes of Ruby stealing jewels from her employer, remove any suggestion that Ruby and her employer were having an affair, and end the film with Ruby and Tiger Kid getting married.[18] ...

Breen believed that these changes infused a sense of compensating moral value into the film. He did not attempt to remove every sexual innuendo from the script, although he insisted that West appear as a "good character" and Tiger Kid as a bit of a dupe and that all criminal activity center on Ace Lamont. With this accomplished, he issued PCA Seal Number 136 to *It Ain't No Sin*. ...

Although these changes did not please everyone, Breen worked quietly behind the scenes to let Catholic leaders know what he had done. Paramount did its part by having West grant a rare interview in which she stated her willingness to clean up her act. "I'm trying to do my best to comply with their wishes," she said. "If they thought I was a little too frank, I want to do as they suggest." And she did. Her next film, *Goin' To Town* (Paramount, 1935) was endorsed by the Legion of Decency, and Breen found the film to be devoid of "fundamentally questionable material" and "highly amusing." Predictably, perhaps, it was a box office bust.[19] ...

Films dealing with social and political topics were subjected to similar restructuring. Falling under the guidelines of "industry policy," Breen and Hays watched with great alarm for scripts that dealt with contemporary issues. Fearing critical reaction from state censorship boards, which were as sensitive to political commentary as they were to expressions of sexual immorality, both men were determined not to allow "social issues" films to damage foreign or domestic markets. Citing "industry policy," they used the code and the threat of external censorship to force producers into providing "harmless entertainment."

A major test came in September 1934, when independent producer Walter Wanger submitted a script for *The President Vanishes*. Wanger and Hays had clashed over another political film a year earlier. In 1933 Wanger had combined forces with newspaper magnate and Cosmopolitan Productions boss William Randolph Hearst to produce one of the most bizarre films in Hollywood history, *Gabriel Over The White House* (MGM, 1933). The film, intended by Hearst as a tribute to newly elected Franklin D. Roosevelt, called for the establishment of a benevolent dictatorship to solve the economic crisis facing America. When Hays saw the film he was dumbfounded. He called an emergency meeting of the MPPDA Board of Directors and forced them to watch the film. Why, he demanded to know, with the nation seemingly ready for radical solutions to the economic crisis, with the Republican Party humiliated in a national election, with Wall Street in shambles, and with the film industry sinking into a sea of red ink, would the industry produce a film calling for martial law and fascism? The next day Hays ordered *Gabriel Over The White House* back to the studio for a political reorientation. Despite the fact that more than $30,000 was spent on retakes, *Gabriel Over The White House* played to American audiences with most of its original message intact. "Fascism Over Hollywood," screamed the *Nation* in its review. A disgruntled Hays warned each studio that he would no longer tolerate code violations. If the studios refused to cooperate, Hays vowed to begin enforcing the code from New York.[20]

In the midst of the legion crisis Wanger proposed *The President Vanishes*, a melodrama that featured a group of greedy American businessmen who conspire to lure America into a world war. Although the industrial "fat cats" publicly speak of patriotism, they speak with scorn for the principles of democratic government. The traditional political parties are befuddled. Only the American Communist Party urges workers not to be fooled into dying for capitalist profits, but the public is easily duped into demanding war. The president views this as folly but is helpless to stop the hysterical demands of the public. As Congress is about to pass a declaration of war, the president arranges for his own kidnapping. With attention being switched to finding the president, the conspirators begin bickering among themselves. Given time to come to its senses the public changes its view, and the president emerges from hiding and promises "Not one American boy will be sent to foreign soil to leave his blood there as a security for loans." The plot is uncovered, and democracy is restored.

Wanger envisioned an antiwar film that clearly took advantage of the public perception that munitionmakers and bankers had tricked Americans into World War I. As an antiwar film *The President Vanishes* paled in comparison to *All Quiet on the Western Front* (Universal, 1930), yet Breen was concerned about the script from the moment it arrived at the PCA. In a series of meetings and letters, he warned the producer not to characterize the vice president as a "drunkard" or a tool of a "gluttonous group of capitalists." He also worried about Wanger's descriptions of the conspirators: Andrew Cullen, a steel magnate; Martin Drew, a banker who supports the Grey Shirts; Hartley Grinnell, a newspaper owner who controls public opinion; George Milton, an oil man; and United States Senator Joseph Corcoran, a pawn in the hands of the conspirators.

From the standpoint of "industry policy," Breen wrote "I ... question the advisability of your designating the heavies" as representatives of American industry. He suggested that Wanger could resolve the problem by making the "heavies" represent "a combination representing international munitions men with an international viewpoint." In his view this "should cut down on the criticism." Perhaps Breen believed the conspiracy thesis of America's entry into World War I. For whatever reason, he approved Wanger's script with only a few changes and gave a seal of approval to the film.[21]

When Hays saw the film in New York he was furious. He told Breen to withdraw the seal of approval because in his view the film was "communist propaganda, subversive in its portrait of American government, contrary to the accepted principles of established law and order, and perhaps treasonable." Hays specifically wanted the following lines of a communist during a street rally removed: "Fellow workers ... it's the workers' blood they are after ... so that the capitalistic bloodsuckers can grow rich ... join the Communist Party." He ordered Breen to renew negotiations with Wanger and arranged an emergency meeting with the Board of Trustees and Paramount's Adolph Zukor.[22]

Hays made his position clear. First he established who was in charge. He told Breen that Breen was to act "as programmed"; that is, he would tell Wanger what had to be done to the film. He was not to negotiate with the producer but to instruct him on the exact nature of the changes required. He pressured Zukor not to distribute the film until the required changes were made and told him "the screen has no right ... to present a distorted picture which condemns the banking industry per se as warmongers, which presents the Communist Party as the leading protagonist ... and which indicated such banality and corruption in our government and political machinery, that even the Secret Service of the nation cannot be trusted to protect the President of the United States." His suspicions were confirmed when *Newsweek* reported that "preview audiences noticed that certain characters resembled Andrew Mellon, John D. Rockefeller, and William Randolph Hearst."[23]

Although Hays was often accused of never going to the movies, he saw *The President Vanishes* in his office several times. He disliked the film and insisted that no amount of editing could eliminate all his objections. Yet Hays was in a difficult position because Breen had given Wanger a seal, and the producer was threatening a legal action if the film were withdrawn. Therefore, Hays agreed to allow the film to play if the line about "capitalistic bloodsuckers" was removed and if several other cuts were made to tone down the film. Wanger agreed, and the film was released. ...

The President Vanishes, with its antiwar, anti-big business tone, was precisely the type of film that Hays, and the Catholic bishops, did not want the industry to make. Determined to be more strict with the studios, Breen and Hays did not have to wait long for another sensitive political topic to be proposed. Warner Bros. submitted a script for *Black Fury*, which dealt with labor problems in the coal industry, in the fall of 1934. Violence, poverty, and despair were the prevailing characteristics of the coalfields of America. Led by John L. Lewis, workers fought for basic rights and dignity in the most conservative industry in America. The subject matter, often front page news, was ripe for dramatization on the screen. But any view of America's coal industry would have to be presented in the strict constraints set by the PCA.

When the script arrived at the PCA, Breen and his staff were disturbed. Although *Black Fury* contained no violations of the code dealing with sexual immorality, it did raise controversial political issues. The first script clearly blamed the mine owner for the miserable working conditions that forced the workers into a strike. The owner reacted typically: He hired scabs and a private police force of thugs to protect his property. The police ruled with terror. Breen worried that this portrait, no matter how close to reality, would cause problems for Hollywood.

Citing "industry policy," Breen asked Warner Bros. to alter the film. He offered the studio a solution: to eliminate the critique of the mine owners and the idea of class struggle in the coal fields by presenting a humane mine owner and a conservative, legitimate union tricked into an unwanted and unnecessary strike by evil labor agitators. Breen suggested that the studio insert several lines of dialogue into the film that would state the conditions in the industry, although not perfect, were constantly improving. The legitimate union representative should state clearly that conditions are "reasonable ... and acceptable."[24]

It was also vital to present the company president in a more positive manner. Breen suggested that several speeches be inserted into the script that would indicate to the audience that the owner was forced to hire strike breakers "very much against his will" to protect the investments of stockholders. He was further to state clearly to the private police force that under no circumstances were they to use violence against his workers. This would allow all the violence necessary for dramatic purposes to be the responsibility of the private police force. By virtue of these changes, *Black Fury* could dramatize a violent strike and workers being dispossessed. The responsibility for these conditions would not be placed on American business or American labor but rather on a police force of "thugs" run by a dishonest owner.[25] ...

Hays was delighted with the rewriting, which he told Breen was "progressing in exactly the proper way." The film that emerged on the screen was not the film that Warner Bros. had originally proposed. Yet Warner Bros. did manage, within the restrictions imposed, to illustrate many of the hardships of life in the mines. Although the mineshafts in the film look big enough for a good game of basketball, it is clear that the miners work hard for little pay. They live in neat little houses, but those houses are owned by the company, not the workers. Nevertheless, the point for Breen and Hays was that *Black Fury* did not place blame on industry or labor for the strike. *Black Fury* was not a social critique of American management or labor. The proof of that was that Breen's version of life in America's coalfields was endorsed by both the National Coal Association and John L. Lewis's United Mine Workers.[26]

Throughout the rest of the decade Breen and Hays worked together to reconstruct political and social films. When MGM submitted a script based on Sinclair Lewis's *It Can't Happen Here*, Breen branded the script "inflammatory" and demanded so many changes that MGM backed out of the project. The studio ran into similar problems with Fritz Lang's *Fury* (MGM, 1936). Lang, who fled Nazi Germany in 1933, soon discovered that censorship existed in America. Lang proposed a powerful antilynching film. When Breen read the first script he informed MGM that *Fury* could not deal with racial prejudice, criticize Southern law enforcement officials, or be "a travesty of justice" story. After several rewrites, Breen accepted the script. The results were obvious to film critic Otis Ferguson, who wrote in the *New Republic* that *Fury* was "a desperate attempt to make love, lynching and the Hays office come out even." The movie code was at work, Ferguson noted, when the movie had the Southern sheriff stand "like Jesus Christ with a rifle" in front of his jail while the mob pelts him with stones.[27]

Breen was unconcerned with the view of movie critics. He wrote to Hays in early 1937 that there was a "definite trend away from serious drama." He told his boss that he saw "no indication, anywhere, of any plans to produce pictures dealing with ... social or sociological questions."[28] ... By the end of the decade Breen's power was so entrenched that John Steinbeck's powerful critique of the American system, *The Grapes of Wrath*, could be brought to the screen without a whimper. With the politics having been written out in the script, Breen told Hays that the film was a modern day "covered wagon" epic. Like the pioneers, Breen saw the Joads going west in search of a better life, and although conditions depicted in the film were "shocking" they were all counterbalanced by "good images" and, most important, by an "uplifting ending."[29]

As long as the industry was determined to reach the largest possible market it was susceptible to economic blackmail, whether it came in the form of a Legion of Decency, state censorship boards, American businessmen, or foreign governments. The goal of Hays, Breen, Lord, the Catholic church, and the entire movie reform movement was to eliminate controversial subjects and ideas from the screen. Yet as the *Nation* complained, if the movies were not allowed to "interpret morals, manners, economics, or politics," what was left? The lowest common denominator was the answer.[30]

Worth M. Tippy, director of the Federal Council of Churches, who had been active in the film reform movement for years and had favored the Legion of Decency movement, was convinced by 1935 that Hays and the PCA were being too restrictive. PCA regulations would not allow a "notable and wholesome film" such as Fritz Lang's *M* (Nero Films, 1931) or *I Am A Fugitive From a Chain Gang* (Warner Bros., 1932) to come to the screen. Was that the purpose of self-regulation, he asked? Further, he believed that the current enforcement of the code was "too preoccupied with sex." There was no room under the current administration to allow the cinema its rightful place in portraying the "moral standards which are emerging out of the present social ferment, and especially of the new concept of industrial and political responsibility." Hollywood had the right, Tippy wrote, to "portray vested evils and entrenched privileges in their true light" but could not do so under the current code.[31]

To do so would have required the industry to challenge various anti-movie groups and perhaps to sacrifice some markets, domestic and international, or to limit attendance at certain films to adults to make serious films dealing with serious topics. The industry chose instead to bow to the censors, to cooperate with the Legion of Decency movement, and to restrict films to the limiting formula established by the PCA. The formula was established and enforced not to protect the public from the industry but to protect the industry from the public. Although the studios sometimes fought for greater freedom of expression on the screen, the PCA remained the dominating force in determining screen content until the late 1940s and early 1950s, when a combination of factors – the rise of television with a parallel box office collapse, the effective deregulation of the industry by the federal government, a Supreme Court ruling granting freedom of expression to films, a determination by independent producers to challenge the authority of the PCA, and the impact of foreign films produced without PCA guidance – eliminated the PCA formula from the screen.

While it existed, the PCA formula was applied to some 20,000 films. Each script that came to the PCA office was different, and Breen and his staff negotiated each film with the studio that offered it. Although there are exceptions, and although sweeping generalizations blur the complexities, it seems clear that the goal of the PCA was to have each film clearly identify evil, make sin and crime appear as deviant behavior, have strong character "stars" play roles representing good, and dilute political and social comment. Convinced that films could educate, the purpose of the code and the PCA was to use popular entertainment films to reinforce conservative moral and political values.

Notes

1   Robert Sklar, *Movie Made America: A Cultural History of American Movies* (New York: Vintage, 1975), 173–4.
2   Daniel Lord, *Played By Ear* (Chicago, 1955), 273–6; 285–91.
3   "Suggested Code To Govern the Production of Motion Pictures," n.d., Lord Papers.

4 Will Hays, *The Memoirs of Will H. Hays* (Garden City, NY: Doubleday, 1955), 440.

5 "General Principles To Govern the Preparation of a Revised Code of Ethics for Talking Pictures," n.d., Lord Papers.

6 Joy to Hays, December 15, 1931, *Possessed*, PCA Files.

7 K.L. Russell to Hays, November 17, 1933, box 33, Hays Papers; Hays to Lord, February 28, 1933, Lord Papers.

8 Daniel Lord, "The Code – One Year Later," April 23, 1981, box 42, Hays Papers.

9 Breen to Parsons, October 10, 1932, box C-9, Parsons Papers.

10 Henry James Forman, *Our Movie-Made Children* (New York: Macmillan, 1933).

11 Parsons to Maguire, June 22, 1934 and Parsons to M. J. Ahern, August 10, 1934, box D-202/203, Parsons Papers.

12 "Compensating Moral Values," June 13, 1934, box 47, Hays Papers.

13 See *Motion Picture Herald*, July 29, 1933, January 20, 1934, February 24, 1934, March 17, 1934.

14 James Rorty, "It Ain't No Sin," *Nation*, August 1, 1934, 124–7.

15 Breen to Botsford, February 23, 1934, Breen to Files, March 6, 1934, and Breen to Botsford, March 7, 1934, *Belle of the Nineties*, PCA Files.

16 Breen to Hays, June 2, 1934, Breen to John Hammond, June 2, 1934, and Breen to Zukor, June 4, 1934, *Belle of the Nineties*, PCA Files.

17 *Variety*, October 3, 1933.

18 "Memo Conference at Paramount," *Variety*, June 6, 1934.

19 *Los Angeles Herald*, June 29, 1934; Breen to Hammell, December 19, 1934, January 16, 1935, January 25, 1935, April 1, 1935, *Goin' to Town*, PCA Files.

20 Wingate to Thalberg, 8 February 1933, Hays to Files, March 6 and 7, 1933, Hays to Wingate, March 11, 1933, *Gabriel Over The White House*, PCA Files; "Facism Over Hollywood," *Nation*, April 26, 1933, 482–3.

21 Breen to The General (Hays), September 14, 1934, Breen to Wanger, September 19, 1934, and September 20, 1934, and Breen to Hays, November 9, 1934, *The President Vanishes*, PCA Files.

22 Hays to Maurice McKenzie, November 21, 1934 and Breen to Wanger, November 21, 1934, *The President Vanishes*, PCA Files.

23 *Newsweek*, December 15, 1934; Hays to Zukor, November 23, 1934, *The President Vanishes*, PCA Files.

24 Breen to Jack Warner, September 12, 1934, *Black Fury*, PCA Files.

25 Ibid.

26 Hays to Breen, September 12, 1934, *Black Fury*, PCA Files.

27 Breen to Warner, June 18, 1936, *Black Fury*, PCA Files; Breen to Mayer, January 27, 1936, *BLACK FURY*, PCA Files; "Hollywood's Half a Loaf," *New Republic*, June 10, 1936, 130.

28 Elizabeth Yetman, "The Catholic Movie Censorship," *New Republic*, October 5, 1938, 234.

29 Breen to Hays, February 27, 1937, *Black Legion*, PCA Files.

30 "The Movie Boycott," *Nation*, July 11, 1934, 34.

31 Tippy to Quigley, March 20, 1935, box C-77, Parsons Papers.

Documents

Introduction to Documents

At the heart of the battle over censorship are two critical questions: What impact do movies have on viewers? Can audiences be trusted to decide for themselves – or their children – what they should or should not see? Americans have been debating these issues since at least 1907. The rapid growth of a new medium that bypassed traditional authorities – church, school, family, politicians – and spoke directly to millions of Americans generated anxiety and hope among national leaders. While some denounced movies as vicious and debasing, others believed they would revolutionize knowledge by making the entire world accessible to the average man, woman, and child. The following quotes offer us a brief glimpse into what early opponents and defenders of the movies thought about the power of the new medium and whether or not it should be censored.

Quotes from Censorship of the Theater and Moving Pictures

Lamar T. Beman (ed.)

Source: Most quotes are from Lamar T. Beman, ed., *Censorship of the Theater and Moving Pictures* (New York: H. W. Wilson, 1931). Sources other than from Beman are marked with *

The Power of the Movies

Much is being said about the "nickel show evil," so much, in fact, that the nickel show good is often forgotten. Like all new mechanical inventions, the moving picture must be gradually fitted into its place and its social value determined. Its possibilities are limitless. It is destined to revolutionize educational methods and to take its place in art and science. The great value of the moving picture is beyond argument. The people want it. It is here to stay.

Editorial, *Chicago Daily Socialist*, June 8, 1912*

The motion picture newspaper – the screen news weekly [i.e., newsreels], while it does not promise to supplant the newspaper, will at least supplement it to so great a degree that it is bound to become a tremendous factor in the molding of public opinion. With its ability to present a living image to the audiences, to recreate happenings that the newspaper, even with its illustrations, can only suggest, it can affect the public more quickly than the press. Also it can reach the emotions more readily, for vision is the most direct route to them.

Hugo Riesenfeld, *New York Call*, May 9, 1920*

The motion picture has come to be recognized by people who are familiar with the industry as one of the greatest agencies for good and evil that exists today. The statistics show that one million people, or one-tenth of the population, see motion pictures each day of the year in the state of New York and about fifteen million in the United States. There is no avenue of communication equal to it. No method is known by which a message can be conveyed to so many people in so short a period of time. The power of the motion picture is understood by but few people. Its appeal is so direct and so easily understood by all people that its influence is incalculable. It attracts the attention of the children and of the illiterate and carries its own interpretation. The industry is young and has had a remarkable growth. Today, the motion picture is the principal amusement of the great majority of our people and the sole amusement of millions.

Annual Report, New York Motion Picture Commission, 1992, pp. 7–8

Thomas A. Edison declared before the Federal Trade Commission that the motion picture is the most perfect instrument for teaching. We get, he said, 80 or 90 percent of our knowledge through the eye. His statements are proved by actual tests on children in his laboratory. Similar statements were made by John J. Tigert, United States Commissioner of Education, and others.

Dearborn Independent, 26: 4, February 20, 1926

Through the movies the whole standards and ideals of a people can be changed. Through them can be spread foulmindedness as easily as cleanmindedness, obscenities as well as decencies. If we want to perpetuate fair play, orderliness, honesty, modesty, and humane attitudes, we can do it readily by this means. Apparently we have not yet realized the power of this instrument which science has placed in our hands for good or evil.

Joyce O. Hertzler, *Social Progress*, pp. 256–7

The clergy, educators, judges, and welfare workers of all kinds might as well lock up the churches, shut the books, close the courts, if they are going to permit the filthy motion pictures to continue. Juvenile delinquency has increased in the past eight or nine years, and I know it is owing to those pictures. I am in a position to know, as I have the confidence of the young people who fall into our hands.

Ellen A. O'Grady, Deputy Police Commissioner of New York City,
National Humane Review, 7: 106–7, June 1919

The motion picture is a great invention, and it has become a powerful factor for good or bad in our civilization. It has great educational power for good or bad. The business has been conducted, generally speaking, upon a low plane and in a decidedly sordid manner. Those who own and control the industry seem to have been of the opinion that the sensual, the sordid, the prurient, the phases of fast life, the ways of extravagance, the risqué, the paths of shady life, drew the greatest audiences and coined for them the most money, and apparently they have been out to get the coin, no matter what the effect upon the public, young or old. When thoughtful people have suggested or advocated official censorship, in the interest of good citizenship and wholesome morals, the owners of the industry have resented it.

Senator Henry L. Myers, *Congressional Record*,
62: 9656–7, June 29, 1922

Another evil which is becoming apparent upon the screen is the dissemination of propaganda which is inimical to American institutions. It is a well recognized fact of which the Department of Justice of the United States has taken cognizance, that there is a persistent effort upon the part of foreign producers and some producers in our own country, to produce films which teach lessons which are destructive of the fundamentals of our government. These films are encouraged by undesirable foreigners who gain admission to our shores and seek to undermine and revolutionize our form of government through insidious propaganda. The legitimate producers of films do not approve films of this character. Nevertheless, they are without power to prevent their being manufactured and exhibited here, and there is no way by which they can be suppressed except thru governmental agencies.

Annual Report, New York Motion Picture Commission, 1922, pp. 9–10

In speaking before the International Boys Work Conference, called by the Rotary International, Prof. Edward A. Ross of the University of Wisconsin, said, "Never has there been a generation so much in revolt against their elders as this. In my judgment this psychic revolt springs chiefly from the motion films, with some aid from the automobile. We have a generation of youth sex-excited, self-assertive, self-confident, and parent-critical. There can be no doubt that the arrival of over-mastering sex desire in the boy's life has been antedated by at least two or three years, thanks to stimulation from the films."

Educational Screen, 5: 35, January 1926

The following statistical tabulation, made by the secretary of the Pennsylvania Board of Censors, is indicative of the character of the pictures viewed by school children: "Fifty percent of the moving pictures are cheap melodrama or have to do with crime; 25 percent are comedy and are often vulgar; and about 5 percent are wholly good. Another authority holds that 25 percent show murders and suicides; 10 percent intemperate drinking and drunkenness; and 27 to 30 percent show robberies, gambling, poisoning, blackmailing, or crimes of the underworld." One need not reiterate facts so generally known. It is conceded that the moving picture depends for its sale upon its appeal to basic human motives. One need only examine a few representative titles to discern the motives appealed to. The following titles are illustrative: *Sinners in Silk, Unguarded Women, A Perfect Flapper, The Gilded Butterfly*, and *The Untamed Lady*. Box office success is the producer's criterion of the picture's merit. The bulk of moving pictures are neither artistic nor instructive.

Harvey C. Lehman and Paul A. Witty, *Education*,
47: 43, September 1926

Any person brought up on the psychology of the movie world is unfit for life. The lower minds go to the movies, and the longer they go, the lower they will be.

Earl Barnes, *Educational Screen*, 5: 36, January 1926

We know now of instances where boys, after seeing moving pictures where murders are committed, have gone out from those places and later committed murders themselves. The purpose to murder was traced to the harmful moving picture.

J. Thomas Hefflin, *Congressional Record*,
71: 4469, October 11, 1929

I come to my main objection to the cinema. I regard it as standardizing the imagination of the white world, and standardizing it downwards; and as debauching the imagination of the brown, yellow, and black worlds.

C. C. Martindale, *Studies*, 18: 446, September 1929

Opponents of Censorship

A federal board of censors will mean nothing further than a central bureau which can uphold all the viciousness of the present system and stifle any movement which may bring a better day. Censorship in itself is vicious. It is but the weapon of the reaction and for the powerful groups which benefit by the vices and exploitation of modern times.

Louis Gardy, New York Call, July 12, 1914*

It is an anomaly in a free country to guarantee freedom to speak, to publish, or to put anything upon the stage and to single out the moving pictures as subject for censorship.

Clarence Darrow, City Club Bulletin, 11: 188, June 3, 1918

Censorship costs more in surrendered intellectual freedom than it can possibly save in any theoretic check upon "temptation" – and, meantime, it may actually whet an interest in the very evils it struggles to suppress.

Charles Merz, New Republic, 33: 179, January 10, 1923

Our civilization rests on virtues which rise from the home, not on virtues imposed from above by authority. A censorship is at best a negative protection. Boys and girls brought up decently are not made into criminals by looking at a motion picture. We can by censorship eliminate some of the experiments in indecency which are put on the screen, but only a positive public opinion will demand and get good movies or good schools or good newspapers. The censorship idea can be overdone. If we assume that Americans are pallid degenerates who must be protected by authority from every temptation, we can logically proceed to censor everything and destroy self-reliance and character.

Independent, 114: 114, January 31, 1925

Stupid and vulgar as our motion pictures are today, they do not need the censorship of a committee of clerics. When public opinion, expressed at the box offices, convinces producers that shoddy is no longer in demand, they may decide to sell honest goods.

Editorial, Independent, 116: 408, April 10, 1926

I do not agree with those who claim that crime among youth is so largely due to what is shown in motion pictures. Of course, some of the weakminded and the vicious have doubtless been stimulated to crime by something good or bad that they have seen in the movies. This may also be said of what they have read in the Bible, the newspapers, magazines, and all kinds of literature, or thru the misuse of automobiles, dancing, or music. But we must always keep in mind that far more good than evil has come out of all these things. Now I am here to say, after talking it over with court officers, who have worked with me for years, that we have yet to find one case of crime among youth that could fairly be traced just to the movies. I do not recall more than two or three cases in my experience of over a quarter of a century on the bench, where there was even reasonable ground to believe that the cause of crime was due just to what the offender had seen in the movies. But I do know of thousands of children who have been elevated, inspired, and made happier because of the movies; who have been kept off the streets, out of the alleys, the vulgar story-telling of the barnyards, and a multitude of idle, evil associates by the wholesome appeals and opportunities of the movies. I also know that other agencies – against which no censorship, local or national, has ever been proposed – have done far more toward producing crime than the movies. If we did not have any motion pictures at all, we would have far more crime than we have. Nothing in the last 50 years of the most eventful history of all time has done more to reduce sin and crime and add to the happiness, education, and progress of the human race than motion pictures. And it is going to do more and more in this regard in the years to come.

Judge Ben B. Lindsey, House Hearings, 1926, pp. 255–6

One cannot legislate morality into people. Education, boycotting of the bad, encouragement of the fine in all things in life create a standard to which producers of all kinds must conform. Legislation to limit in any way art, education, or religion is never constructive and in the end defeats the very purpose it sets out to achieve.

Florence P. Kahn, *New York Times*, January 29, 1928

The National Board of Review, formerly the National Board of Censors, believes that the public is the best censor, and that the public alone can and will command production of good pictures. The Board believes that the instinct of people for that which is right is stronger than the instinct for evil things. And that thru freedom a far higher form of art can be produced than by censorship thru a self-appointed few who at heart hate that which they are censoring.

Frederic C. Howe, *New York Times*, January 26, 1929

Dr. Frederic C. Howe, the first chairman of the National Board of Review, said the Board was constantly pressed to fight the efforts of certain moralistic and evangelical groups that do not like anything related to the theatre and disliked anything that gave pleasure to any one other than themselves. The conflict that exists today, he said, is between the right to be happy in one's own way and that prescribed by law.

New York Times, January 26, 1929

Readings and Screenings

The most entertaining study of early film censorship is Thomas Doherty, *Pre-Code Hollywood: Sex, Immorality, and Insurrection in American Cinema, 1930–1934* (New York: Columbia University Press, 1999). Other books that examine censorship before and after the Code include Frances G. Couvares, ed., *Movie Censorship and American Culture* (Amherst, MA: University of Massachusetts Press, 2nd edition, 2006); Stephen Vaughn, *Freedom and Entertainment: Rating the Movies in an Age of New Media* (New York: Cambridge University Press, 2005); Lee Grieveson, *Policing Cinema: Movies and Censorship in Early-Twentieth-Century America* (Berkeley and Los Angeles, CA: University of California Press, 2004); Matthew Bernstein, ed., *Controlling Hollywood: Censorship and Regulation in the Studio Era* (New Brunswick, NJ: Rutgers University Press, 1999); Leonard J. Leff and Jerold L. Simmonds, *The Dame in the Kimono: Hollywood, Censorship, and the Production Code from the 1920s to the 1960s* (New York: Anchor Books, 1991); Mick LaSalle, *Complicated Women: Sex and Power in Pre-Code Hollywood* (New York: St. Martin's Press, 2001); Gregory D. Black, *Hollywood Censored: Morality Codes, Catholics, and the Movies* (New York: Cambridge University Press, 1994); Frank Walsh, *Sin and Censorship: The Catholic Church and the Motion Picture Industry* (New Haven, CN: Yale University Press, 1996); Gregory D. Black, *The Catholic Crusade Against the Movies, 1940–1975* (New York: Cambridge University Press, 1998). For an excellent biography of the person responsible for administering the Code, see Thomas Doherty, *Hollywood's Censor: Joseph I. Breen and the Production Code Administration* (New York: Columbia University Press, 2007).

Many of the controversial films discussed by Black, especially those produced during the Pre-Code era of 1930–1934, are available on DVD or streaming sources and offer excellent examples of movies that censors and critics considered dangerous. For films dealing with sexuality and "fallen women," see *Baby Face* (1933) and *She Done Him Wrong* (1933); for crime, see *Little Caesar* (1930), *The Public Enemy* (1931), and *Scarface* (1932); for politically controversial films, see *Gabriel Over the White House* (1933), *Heroes For Sale* (1933), and *The President Vanishes* (1934); for the brutality of the southern plantation system, see *Cabin in the Cotton* (1932). For an excellent case study of the outside pressures applied on filmmakers and the ways in which censors forced studios to tone down films they believed were too class conscious, read Francis R. Walsh, "The Films We Never Saw: American Movies View Organized Labor, 1934–1954," *Labor History*, 27 (Fall 1986), 564–80, and then screen the films *Black Fury* (1934) and *Grapes of Wrath* (1940).

5

Confronting the Great Depression: Renewing Democracy in Hard Times

Introduction to Article

Talking pictures emerged during the early years of the Great Depression, a devastating phenomenon that adversely affected all aspects of American life. Unhappy with the inability of politicians and business leaders to solve the crisis, a wide variety of citizens began questioning the dominant values and institutions of American society. Throughout the 1930s and early 1940s, immigrants, workers, women, and people of color – the so-called marginalized of society – fought to institute their vision of a more just nation. Despite hard times, they and millions of other Americans continued going to the movies to be entertained and, perhaps, to find solutions to the problems plaguing their lives.

Lary May shows us how these "marginal" groups moved to the center stage of American film. Challenging earlier scholarship that portrayed 1930s' culture as fundamentally conservative, May argues that Depression-era film played a vital role in reshaping the meaning of nationalism and citizenship. He also demonstrates how films used new ideas about race, ethnicity, gender, and class to forge a more democratic national identity. Well before the New Deal, he writes, "movie makers responded to audience demands by creating a language for what did not yet exist: a pluralistic Americanism that revitalized a republican critique of monopoly capitalism and inequality." Independent filmmakers were

Movies and American Society, Second Edition. Edited by Steven J. Ross.
© 2014 John Wiley & Sons, Inc. Published 2014 by John Wiley & Sons, Inc.

especially active in producing movies with "conversion narratives" that promoted a new, inclusive democratic ethos which heralded the equality of all citizens and called for cooperation between previously hostile groups of elites and outsiders. Films by John Ford, Busby Berkeley, King Vidor, Frank Capra, and Orson Welles offered sympathetic depictions of immigrants, blacks, and various "others" in American society and showed how people could cooperate across class and ethnic lines to create a better world.

Discussion Points

Can movies help restore democracy or is that the job of politicians and government? What can movies do in this regard that other groups and institutions cannot? In addition to arguing on behalf of the redemptive power of cinema, May describes how Depression-era films revised traditional ideas about heroes and villains. This raises another interesting question: What do the cinematic heroes and villains of a particular time period tell us about the values of that society?

The Recreation of America: Hybrid Moviemakers and the Multicultural Republic

Lary May

Source: Lary May, *The Big Tomorrow: Hollywood and the Politics of the American Way* (Chicago and London: University of Chicago Press, 2000), 55–99

Will Rogers often remarked that he neither was self-made nor acted alone: He participated in a wide upheaval in American culture. Yet how did that upheaval inform moviemaking as a whole in the New Deal era? One way to answer that question is to listen to the recollections of another famed artist who came to prominence in the thirties: Orson Welles, the boy wonder and creator of the work that has been acknowledged as the greatest film ever made in the United States, *Citizen Kane* (1941). As he looked back, Welles proudly traced his ancestry to a family whose members fought in the Civil War. Committed to making a republic free of slavery and aristocracy, they hoped to create a democracy where the people controlled their work and participated in civic affairs. By the twentieth century his grandparents backed Theodore Roosevelt's efforts to master big business and order industrial society.

Yet the reform-minded Progressives disdained alignments with immigrants and racial minorities. Instead, they aligned themselves with corporate leaders to pass immigrant restriction and the new southern segregation laws. Welles believed that out of their efforts to save Anglo-Saxon civilization, they became trapped in what they had disdained: the corporate order. Out of that impasse Welles's relatives began to emulate the status symbols of the rich and European high art. Soon his aunts got into the "imitation place business" and decorated their lavish homes with historical styles of a bygone time, a process that had the great advantage of elevating white western culture above the vernacular arts of immigrant workers and minorities.

Young Welles, however, matured at a time when many intellectuals and artists launched a quest for an alternative. Describing his childhood as a "lost paradise," he evoked the imagery of the Edenic West that lay at the heart of the nineteenth-century republic, a vision undermined by the new era of industrialism and his family's emulation of the wealthy. To recover that dream Welles turned to radio and movies as a modern form of "education ... to dramatize the art of imparting knowledge" so that "people will listen to what I have to say politically." Breaking away from the elevated white culture of his ancestors, he joined the Federal Theatre Arts Projects to produce a "Harlemized and gangsterized" version of *Macbeth*. Late in the Depression he gained control over his work in the Hollywood studios to create a "cinema" that "should always be the discovery of something ... revealing the sort of vertigo, unceasing lack of stability, that melange of movement and tension that is our universe." The result yielded *Citizen Kane*, a film that Welles saw as a tragedy about our big "business plutocrats ... who believed that money had automatically conferred stature to a man. Kane is a man who truly belongs to his time."

Welles, like Will Rogers, combined moviemaking with promotion of radical politics. Working as a newsman, he wrote that in the modern world citizens had renewed the faith that "America ... is an adventure ... a new world that for the races of man was a new place, a new beginning." Only now we must realize that "race hate is a disease." Racism formerly had aligned whites with those big business "marauders" who had "greed for all things possessed by the people." These forces together led to the "oppression of the Indians, Blacks, Hispanics and Asians." But Welles retained faith that the New Deal of President Roosevelt and the battle against fascism in World War II made it possible that "America can write her name across the centuries ... if we the people – brown and black and white and red – rise to the great occasions of our brotherhood." Carrying that élan into politics, he backed the "wonderfully encouraging" rise of unions, the New Deal, civil rights, and the Popular Front. But when conservatives called him a "communist," Welles noted that "the idea of interdependency antedates Karl Marx." Evoking the American radical ethos – the "splendour of our republic" – he explained that

> I believe – and this has very much to do with my notion of freedom – I believe I owe the very profit I make to the people I make it from. ... If this is radicalism ... it comes automatically to most of us in show business, it being generally agreed that any public man owes his position to the public. ... A free man owes to the world's slaves all that he can do for them ... free them.[1]

Welles's effort to modernize republican traditions at odds with monopoly capitalism and inequality suggests that Will Rogers was not alone. No doubt backward-looking images and demeaning racial prejudice informed moviemaking and politics. Nonetheless, views that assert that a monolithic, Anglo-Saxon Americanism pervaded popular art and politics cannot account for Welles's view that the film capital provided a site for creating a discourse of nationality and public life. Yet why did this occur and what implications did it have for moviemaking and politics? How was it possible that the young Welles saw that Hollywood moviemaking provided a site for modernizing the "splendour of our republic"?

The Margins Talk Back

To answer these questions, it is important to realize that unlike earlier forms of mass amusements, the film industry provided the means for immigrants to alter the American values that had been promoted by elite tastemakers for over a hundred years. In the teens, small studios aligned with labor unions created films promoting labor–capital conflict, and the industry as a whole allowed non-Anglo-Saxons to alter the contours of traditional American myths and symbols. No doubt the most visible example of that transformation was the rise of Hollywood, where outsiders appeared to dominate the production of movie images. In reaction, state leaders spurred film producers to enact censorship that eliminated overt images of class conflict and defiance of moral codes. The result was that moviemakers contained the moral revolution within standards promoted by the rich. Still, even as this legitimated a new mass consumer culture, moralists were also alarmed that "no American born actors or directors have a prominent part" in Hollywood studios. It was pointed out that the "majority of American movie picture producers are of foreign birth" and over 425 foreign-born directors and players "comprise the leaders of the profession."[2]

No doubt the most visible example of this trend were the founders of the film studios that dominated the scene. Generally, these producers represented first- and second-generation immigrants from eastern and southern Europe. Seven of the eight founders of the studios descended from either Jewish immigrants or their children. Coming from outside the old forms of power, they exemplified what Max Weber aptly called "pariah capitalists." That is, they seized chances in marginal trades shunned by members of the host society. It was these marginal endeavors that served them well as producers. At a time when movies generated a revolution in morals that was feared by defenders of the old order, the Jews had experience in Europe and the United States with marginal trades, ranging from clothing to furs and jewels, where the key to success was the tapping of consumer tastes. ...

The Jews were so successful because they supplanted the original Anglo-Saxon producers and hundreds of independents by making films that catered to audiences' ambivalent approach to the new urban culture of the twenties. ... Having experience on the margins, they could be critical of all closed systems of national blood purity, while advancing visions of a more open life. To the early studio founder Carl Laemmle and the producer Sam Spiegel, the movies provided a way to forge a multicultural public, for as Laemmle observed, "Regardless of creed, color, race or nationality, everyone in the universe understands the stories that are told by Universal pictures."[3]

While Jewish immigrants possessed traditions that made it possible for them to innovate with cultural forms, they also possessed a tradition that placed them at odds with the restrained work ethic and family life promoted by the Anglo-Saxon middle class. Like other ethnic and racial minorities, the Jewish immigrants from eastern Europe possessed a rich life of festivals permeated with humor, exuberant music, and dances. Within their communities there was no concept of the protected, pure woman who remained outside the economy and shunned sexual pleasure. The Jewish immigrants did not sanction premarital sex, but eroticism within marriage was encouraged. When couples found that they were incompatible, divorce was permitted. Unlike the gender divisions of Victorian culture, Jewish women played a major role within the economy. Within Jewish life the enjoyment of material goods – when one could afford it – was not a sin but a part of life's pleasures.

During the twenties, Jewish producers' status as marginal businessmen and cultural brokers made it possible for them to cater to the moral revolution associated with the rise of mass art. The key to their success lay in generating films that sanctioned the new consumer culture and the revolution in morals within the highbrow "foreign" models of aristocracy. ...

The advent of the Depression, however, collapsed the old barriers and allowed the lures of mass culture to move from the private to the public domain, altering both in the process. It began when producers found that audiences now had a mind of their own. Watching that change unfold, a *Variety* reporter noted that "general conditions no longer make theatre patronizing a matter of after dinner routine. The patrons go to pictures these days because there's something specific they want to see. Every thing else gets the go-by."[4] Searching for an explanation for this shift, reporters found that the patrons no longer admired studio formulas derived from "high brow standards." Young people who "cared not a hoot about tradition" showed their displeasure at one local theater by throwing objects at the screen until the projectionist showed a film that they approved. Observers told film producers that the "imitation of successful pictures was passe," for "times were eliminating class distinctions so far as the industry is concerned."[5]

This elimination of "class distinctions" manifests a major realignment of cultural authority. No longer could high art contain the revolution in morals and visions of cross-cultural communication in a realm separate from public life. In the new "catch as catch can" atmosphere, a critic saw that "the industry is finally admitting that its only collateral is the barometer of motion picture mindedness."[6] Those who continued in the old ways got the message as the once invincible studios lost profits and filed for bankruptcy, while firms that tapped the "new audience" generated an upheaval in the structure of Hollywood. Suddenly the assumption that large studios could monopolize production, ward off newcomers, and generate predictable profits gave way before audiences who had a mind of their own. ...

From the late twenties to early thirties several fresh companies – Warner Brothers, Disney, Columbia, Radio Corporation of America – moved from marginal status to that of majors. Unlike the established firms, they were not encumbered either with heavily mortgaged movie houses or silent stars with expensive contracts. Capitalizing on the new sound technology, they hired journalists and writers from New York City, spurring a major turnover in industry personnel. It also appears that they aimed their products more to the vernacular tastes of the lower classes. Illustrating that market segmentation, pollsters found that stars contracted to studios that dominated production in the past – for example, Metro-Goldwyn-Mayer and Paramount – appealed to audiences centered in the upper-income groups. But the newer firms, such as Warner Brothers, featured stars that appealed predominately to lower-income audiences.

To top it off, the major studios' monopolistic control was also challenged by the rise of independent studios, which found their markets among marginal groups. Where in the twenties, fifty-one small firms catered primarily to rural markets, the ranks of the independents rose to ninety-two between 1929 and 1934. These new firms turned over more than 90 percent in every five-year period, but the number of films the small firms made almost equaled that of the majors in any year. In 1932, 1936, and 1938, their film production actually surpassed that of all the majors combined. The independents also had a competitive advantage since they had no high-priced theaters or stars nor did they have to submit their product to the industrywide censorship boards, since the large firms excluded most small independents from the Hays Commission and its censorship panel. ...

Just as the independents and innovative studios catered to a "new audience" arising outside mainstream institutions, they also created a symbiotic interchange with the large studios in making a different type of film. Increasingly, artists who made it in the world of the "indies" took their inspirations to the larger studios. Central to that alteration was the creation of a new type of production, the "talkie" film that interjected into the national civic sphere the voice and views of formerly silenced groups. ...

Once the Depression hit, the power of talkies to strike "deeply home" continued as producers created films that utilized sound to create characters who challenged inherited visions of art and civilization. ... W. R. Burnett, a newspaperman and son of an Ohio politician, recalled that when he wrote the gangster novel and then script for *Little Caesar*, he discarded "literary English ... I dumped all that out. I just threw it away. It was a revolt in the name of a language based on the way the American people spoke." Another writer saw that the key to success was to write dialogue that evoked the way real people spoke, giving it the "Woolworth touch." Furthermore, Edna Ferber, the writer of novels and plays that became the films *Cimarron* (1931), *Dinner at Eight* (1933), and *Showboat* (1936), regarded her work as part of an intellectual revolt against the educated who looked to Europe for models of emulation.[7] ...

It was not accidental that the emphasis of sound to evoke the vernacular speech of the people also brought to the fore moviemakers who drew on their immigrant pasts to reshape the nation's myths. Film industry personnel turned over by more than half from 1929 to 1935. In this context, directors such as John Ford (Irish Catholic), William Wyler (Alsatian Jew), Busby Berkeley (eastern European Jew), Frank Capra

(Italian American), Mervyn LeRoy (eastern European Jew), Edgar Ulmer (German Jew), William Dieterle (German Jew), and Lewis Milestone (Russian Jew) moved from a marginal status in the world of the silent film to the center of the world of the talkies. The success of their films not only allowed them to gain control over production in the studios, but they worked with set companies of actors, crew members, and even writers. Scenarists ranging from Dudley Nichols to Ben Hecht, Robert Riskin to Lester Cole, John Huston to W. R. Burnett and Billy Wilder accordingly found freedom in working with one major director. On the way they carried into movies the public views they developed in the tabloid press, the ethnic stage, and the avant-garde world of New York, Chicago, and Los Angeles.

The Return of the Repressed

So what were the themes of the new talking films? To answer this question it is necessary to realize that trade reporters clearly saw that "subjects which would have been a failure in the past were successes today." Current writers and directors saw the key to success was "less art for more box office." By returning to the industry's roots in the lowbrow "nickelodeon" élan, the new films were, as one producer noted, "cut from the cloth the times provide." The success of one of the new upstarts, Warner Brothers, lay in providing films that were "timely, topical, but not typical."[8]

Along with the shift to "realism" there also occurred a major transformation in cultural authority. From the twenties to the thirties our plot samples showed that the number of characters who dealt with a world out of control increased from 10 to over 50 percent. Businessmen cast as villains similarly rose from 5 to over 20 percent, while the rich portrayed as morally evil or a social danger accelerated the most of all, from 5 to over 60 percent from 1929 to 1940. If this revealed that filmmakers had become more critical of established values, protagonists who met death and defeat increased from zero to over 10 percent through the early thirties.

This alteration in authority had two major themes: the way in which adherence to mainstream values of success and the home created the disasters of the age, and the eruption from below of characters who rebelled against their former status and position as racialized and gendered inferiors. These two themes – the fall of the old order and the rise of marginal characters – ran parallel to each other. ...

Characters in some of the most popular films of the early thirties learn that their personal success and individualism have created not progress, but decline. In *Little Caesar* (1930), *I Am a Fugitive from a Chain Gang* (1932), *An American Tragedy* (1931), *Frankenstein* (1931), *Dracula* (1931), *The Invisible Man* (1933), or *King Kong* (1933), the story focuses on self-made men whose pursuit of gain generates the "lost paradise" of the national promise. Cast as the heroes of the age – soldiers, inventors, explorers, bankers, businessmen, and journalists – these heroes' values lead to destruction. ...

What made these films so "realistic" was that they collapsed the boundaries between popular drama and the stories of chaos and disruption that permeated the newspapers. In order to link these fictions with public events, the new talking films often opened with a panoramic shot of an urban skyline, usually that of New York City. Derived from magazines and advertisements, the skyline image grounded the story less in the myths of the old agrarian countryside than in the modern world of "today." Repeatedly newspaper headlines drove the plot forward and served to root the characters' private lives in historical events and the news, a practice similar to the innovations pioneered by John Dos Passos in his 1936 novel, *The Big Money*.

Trade critics noted that the new icons and stories made moviemaking a form of journalistic muckraking and exposé, a practice that collapsed the barriers between the newspapers' public sphere and the entertainment provided by the movies. Commenting on why films of this journalistic "ilk" and "topicality" had gained popularity, one trade critic noted these works took the viewers "behind the newspaper headlines, behind the scenes of industry and politics." Film productions such as *Washington Show* (1932) revealed the "grip" of " 'big business' ... on the government of this country" and the "ways in which it makes its power work to insure the accomplishment of its own purposes and the defeat of the will of the people." Screenwriter Dudley Nichols noted that "for good or ill" mass entertainment matched the Greek stage of antiquity. Now artists sought to

> deepen our understanding of ourselves and society so that movie making was a tremendous educative force. What we see enacted we unconsciously relate to our immediate problems and draw practical conclusions. ... Our exposure to the theatre is either helping us to resolve our own conflicts and the conflicts of society by making us understand them, or it is engendering more conflicts.[9]

Intimately linked to this effort to "resolve our own conflicts ... by making us understand them," the new films also interjected into the public domain formerly silenced groups and repressed wishes. Moralists criticized these new films and called for censorship, but nothing could thwart the popularity in the early Depression years of gangsters, ribald ethnic comics, and fallen women. In the past, the middle class saw criminals as the exemplars of racial minorities and deviants who disrupted modern life. But the Italian or Irish criminal in *Scarface* (1932), *Public Enemy* (1931), and *Little Caesar* reversed the formula. As one critic noted, the treatment of crime as "picture material has now changed radically." Formerly the "criminal characters were infected with desires for coin and for bloody spoils," but the hoodlum featured in the talking films "thirsts primarily for power." W. R. Burnett, the author of *Little Caesar*, explained that the reason why his work was a "smack in the face ... was the fact that it was the world seen completely through the eyes of a gangster. ... It had never been done before then. You had crime stories but always seen through the eyes of society. The criminal was just some son-of-a-bitch who'd killed somebody and then they got 'em. I treated them as human beings. Well, what else are they?" Burnett observed that in contrast to the moral deviant of the past, the modern gangster was a sympathetic "Gutter Macbeth."

The distinctiveness of the cinematic gangster thus was his capacity to shift the audience's moral viewpoint. That is, he met defeat because he was the victim of official leaders and institutions' false values. At first he rebelled due to the discrimination and exploitation confronted by immigrant workers. As Burnett saw it, if you have "this type of society, you will get this type of man." Ethnic youths facing poverty and a world that excludes them turn to crime to gain money and power. Reinventing themselves with new clothes, cars, and "fast" women, much as Rico Bandello becomes famous in all the newspapers as "Little Caesar," they utilize consumer goods to serve their own purposes. Yet the attainment of the American dream also means that they emulate the laissez-faire capitalist ethos of the robber barons of industry, a flaw that leads to their downfall.[10] ...

The urge to be "different, above, higher," and a "man on his own" identified the gangster not only with revolt against class exploitation but with revolt against the stereotypes that linked the racially marked outsider with passivity before the forces of history dominated by the Anglo-Saxons. The Fu Manchu film series, for example, featured an Asian businessman whose family was destroyed in the Boxer Rebellion. To seek revenge on white colonists, he reinvents himself as an Asiatic gangster. Along similar lines, *The Emperor Jones* (1933) featured a poor southern black who rejects his subordinate status. Derived from a play by Eugene O'Neill, the film featured the black activist Paul Robeson as Brutus Jones. Initially Brutus lives in the segregated South and sings in the local church, but, like many other blacks, he moves North for freedom from segregation. On the way the soundtrack punctuates his travels with the black blues songs "Let Me Fly," "The St. Louis Blues," and "I'm Travelling." Brutus finds employment as a Pullman porter, where a white businessman teaches him how to exploit and cheat others. After killing a man, Brutus works on a chain gang, only to escape to a Caribbean island. There he overthrows rulers who have exploited and degraded him. But as he transforms his identity and gains power over both whites and blacks, he emulates the gangster tactics of whites. When his black subjects revolt, Brutus dies in a jungle dreaming of his youth in an organic African-American community. ...

Films featuring the rebellious outsider shattered stereotypes in what many saw as truly the most sacred realm of all – that of gender. The gangster rebel was in fact often accompanied by his female counterpart, the fallen woman. By the early thirties films like *Rain* (1932), *Blonde Venus* (1932), *Imitation of Life* (1934), *Anna Christie* (1930), *Ann Vickers* (1933), *Back Street* (1932), *Of Human Bondage* (1934), *Red Dust* (1932), and *Dinner at Eight* (1933) were condemned and criticized by moral guardians for undermining the female identity as mother and wife. ... Increasingly "flappers" of the twenties – heroines who linked sex to "girlishness" – gave way to females who exuded "some intelligence behind the performance. Contrary to earlier trends, The Great God Public, formerly considered a Puritan censor, voiced its approval with admission fees that fully endorsed heroines of easy virtue." ...

Each woman of "easy virtue" used sex and glamour either to manipulate men or cross official racial and gender barriers. Instead of uplifting consumer pleasure in the private domain, the heroines entered public life where they took delight in the clothes, cars, and penthouses of the city. Unlike the foreign "vamps," these were American women who sold their bodies to gain material success. In the 1932 film *Call Her Savage*, the white heroine, played by Clara Bow, grows discontent with Anglo-Saxon men and marries an Indian. Similarly, the devoted wife in *Blonde Venus*, played by Marlene Dietrich, leaves her husband and sings hot blues songs like "Hot Voodoo" in nightclubs. Fleeing her husband, she lives with blacks in vice districts, wears a man's suit, and earns her own money. In sum, she has taken on masculine qualities and crossed racial barriers in order to reconstruct the coordinates of female identity.

The assault on convention also gained popular currency in ribald comedy that gave voice to the humor and language of working-class minorities. Here again the innovation on traditional forms was all-pervasive. Over and over the films of W. C. Fields, the Marx Brothers, and Mae West broke from the forms that had pervaded earlier vaudeville and popular entertainments. It had once been necessary for comedians to perform under a minstrel mask. Not only did this degrade blacks, but it linked rebellion against official work, sex, and class roles with African Americans. In a society where work required repression of instincts, a minstrel show allowed whites to put on a black mask and express whites' repressed desires for play and for crossing sexual boundaries. Yet at all times the performer identified the disruptive desires with nonwhites. At the end, the white performer took off the burnt cork and emerged as a dignified Caucasian family and working man. Black minstrelsy thus allowed whites to release their hidden desires without guilt and to degrade nonwhites.

Yet the importance of comedy in the early talking films was that it allowed ethnic comics to validate the desires of whites, once linked to blacks alone, for a different self and society. As these comics shed the minstrel mask, the challenge to racial stereotypes happened on two clear levels. This is exemplified by the rise to success of the black comic Stepin Fetchit. On some levels Fetchit seems to perpetuate the old minstrel stereotype without alteration, yet it is also important to realize that Fetchit was not a white, but a black artist who utilized the old imagery to suit his own purposes. In so doing he was also well prepared. Fetchit honed his art on the black vaudeville stage where his comic style showed black audiences how to exploit demeaning stereotypes to manipulate the oppressor. ... Transferred onto the screen, this subversive mode meant that in films like *Stand Up and Cheer* (1934), Fetchit assumed at first the image of the lazy black but then at the end led a parade to advance the New Deal government hated by the characters who speak for big businessmen.

The undermining of minstrel stereotypes was not confined to blacks. The most famed comics of the early thirties, the Marx Brothers, Will Rogers, W. C. Fields, Charles Chaplin, and Mae West, came to the movies from the urban vaudeville stage. Where in the past vaudeville comics used the black mask to distance the humor that subverted established values, these new comics presented that rebellious stance as part of the white self. Over and over Fields gloried in the cliche of the dumb and lazy Irishman's proclivity to drink and use wordplay to overturn convention. The Marx Brothers similarly exuded the aura of the cliched stingy Jew or the foolish Italian, only to turn the image against their oppressors. Accordingly, Fields in *The Bank Dick* (1940) and the Marx Brothers in *A Night at the Opera* (1935) humorously attacked the pretensions of the rich and status symbols. In a similar vein Mae West celebrated the image of the fallen woman who was not ashamed of her desire for plenty of sex. *I'm No Angel* (1933) portrayed her as "more savage than the savages," a woman who reversed roles by telling a young lady that "marriage is nothing more than contracted prostitution. I believe in a single standard for men and women."[11]

Just beneath the surface of this comic mode can also be found a critique of the new consumer culture. Nowhere was that more evident than in the work of Charles Chaplin. In *City Lights* (1931), for example, Chaplin began his story at the unveiling of a patriotic monument. Chaplin's tramp sleeps at the base and catches his pants on the sword held by one of the classic figures of freedom. Once the police eject the tramp, the scene suggests that public life and "liberty" are the preserve of the rich and their middle-class followers. Moving down the road, the tramp saves a banker who wants to commit suicide because life, so the viewer assumes, is meaningless. Soon the tramp and the rich man share the promise of equality in a night of cabaret hopping. Though they live the promise of democracy in amusements, the daylight world sees realities of power descend. Once the sun comes up, the rich man rejects the tramp as an inferior. The final indignity now occurs: In their nightly frolics, the rich man had given the tramp money to pay for a blind girl's operation, but when the banker awakens he has the tramp jailed for stealing. Years later the tramp returns to encounter the girl whose sight has been restored. To disabuse her of the notion that a rich man saved her, he touches her hands. As she recognizes the truth, their eyes meet and she "sees" at last where true virtue lies: among the poor rather than the rich bankers and industrialists.

Fundamental to these converging trends – the rise of the social problem, gangster, fallen woman, and ribald comic films – is a major transformation in mass art. This shift generated renewed cries for stiffer censorship guidelines than those promoted by the official industry regulatory body, the Hays Commission. During the twenties, producers and ethnic artists had promoted a consumer ethos that preserved Victorian standards and Anglo-Saxon civilization. The Crash saw audiences rejecting the formulas of the twenties. In that vacuum, new producers and independents made sound films that realigned authority from the top to the bottom of society. Increasingly, artists of immigrant stock inverted racial and ethnic stereotypes to give voice to subordinate groups. But that strategy also yielded a sharp and ambivalent duality at the core of the early talking films. On the positive side, rebellious gangsters and fallen women made it possible for marginalized characters to take images that had been rejected by officials and reshape them for their own ends. No longer were they passive recipients of cultural imagery, but men and women of passion who reinvented their identities as modern men and women of desire and instinct. The negative side of this strategy was that it left the established opinion makers with the full power of description.

The rebels might wear a pejorative slur with pride, but they still remained caught in the constructions of their oppressors. Since they were unable to alter established social roles, at the end of the film the outsiders adapted to conventional family values, "hit the road," met death, or were incarcerated.

One might think that such endings satisfied the censors, but there was far more to it. It is worth noting that in recalling the process of writing scripts, John Huston claimed that in the thirties and forties "no picture of mine was ever really damaged by the censors in any form. There was usually a way around them."[12] Yet the ethic that rebels and bandits had to pay for their sins was not simply a formula imposed by external censors. Folk songs, for example, emerged out of a long tradition of oral culture that existed outside the control of moral guardians and commercial pressures. Over and over popular songs such as "Tom Dooley" and "Stagger Lee" and "Frankie and Johnny" evoked the glamour of men and women whose defiance of social convention led to defeat and destruction. These widely held beliefs emanated less from official leaders than the popular consciousness of the people themselves. The problem was that in defining modernity, the quest was conducted in the guise of inappropriate inherited forms. That is, all moviemakers had inherited the strictures of the Victorian artistic canon that defined that a dramatic hero was to be Anglo-Saxon, while criminals, clowns, and fallen women exhibited the qualities of lasciviousness and disorder. It followed that to bring outsiders' desires into the center one had to reimagine an artistic language for what did not exist: a self and nationality that brought artistic and social opposites into an interpenetrating whole altering each other.

The Art of Interpenetrating Opposites

To open the possibility of an alternative public life and culture, filmmakers and audiences had to reimagine the canon and bring together all that Victorians tore apart. Gradually films that collapsed the Victorian hierarchy altered the ideal self and national identity – a trend that set the stage for a new star system and film formula. One of the most significant trendsetters appeared in the form of the Academy-Award-winning film for 1931, *Cimarron*, based on Edna Ferber's novel. In a society in which nationality came to focus on the image of the "West," it was not accidental that the film charted a contest between two competing visions of the frontier for the modern era. The first vision of the frontier was promoted by the family of the heroine Sabra. Believers in Anglo-Saxon superiority, they resist her romance and marriage with Yancey Cravet, a man with a "cimarron" or dark complexion that suggests he is an Indian. Yet the two marry and move to Oklahoma, where Yancey, who owns a newspaper and embodies the second vision of the frontier, defends the rights of fallen women, Jews, a poor black, and Indians.

At first Sabra condemns her husband's actions, enforcing the code of racial purity and Victorian norms of her past. However, when Yancey leaves for another frontier adventure, his wife undergoes a conversion. Taking over Yancey's newspaper, she defends Indians from capitalists and exploiters. Due to her efforts, she becomes a senator from Oklahoma. Combining masculine with feminine traits, she blesses her own white son's marriage to an Indian. At the end, set in 1929, Sabra appears at a banquet in Washington, DC, attended by officials from across the land. There she introduces to the guests her mixed-blood grandchildren. Her speech suggests that marriage across the races, coupled with the capacity of women to reinvent themselves, provides a vision of reform and nationality for the twentieth century. Edna Ferber – the daughter of Jewish immigrants in the Midwest – explained that films like *Cimarron* undermined Anglo-Saxon visions to reveal the truth about the nation and its peoples. That is, the

> United States seems to be the Jews among the nations. It is resourceful, adaptable, maligned, envied and feared … its peoples are travellers and wanderers by nature, moving, shifting, restless.[13]

Once the image of a dynamic democratic republic gained success in *Cimarron*, it also paved the way for films that celebrated the reshaping of cultural authorities from the top to the bottom of society. …

By shedding their psychic dependence on the wealthy, these new heroes and heroines embody the ethos of interpenetrating opposites in that they combine the shrewdness of the fallen woman, the comic, and the gangster with the heroic citizen. That conversion narrative in other films also provides a model for overcoming the cultural barriers that prevent the population from cooperating in order to advance their common interests. Take the most successful commercial film of 1933, *42nd Street*. The music incarnates the show-within-a-show musical, which takes viewers backstage to watch artists and commoners work to create a new culture that earns success and public approval. The narrative of fall and rebirth also echoes one of the most pervasive themes of the Depression era, providing a model of redemption amid hard times.

The means to renewal centers on the symbol of "42nd Street" as the embodiment of the dreams of mass culture. The film opens as the camera glides over New York City, moving down to the main thoroughfare of

Manhattan that links the world of the wealthy East Side with the world of the working class on the West Side. The bonds holding both worlds together exist in the appeal of the new mass art and consumerism. Yet as the story opens we meet Julian Marsh, a showman who symbolizes the contradictions that have led to the Depression. He has speculated and lost on the stock market. Though in poor physical health, Marsh decides to make a new type of "show." Initially he encourages a female star to sell her body to a monopoly capitalist who will finance the new endeavor. Meanwhile, the chorus girls sell *their* bodies, and a cast composed of diverse ethnic comics and dancers cannot get along. Emblematic of the whole, the selfish star breaks her leg, and the financier threatens to withdraw his money.

Yet in response to this fall from grace, the characters are reborn by recreating the basis of American culture itself. The disaster spurs Marsh to turn to outsiders for assistance. So he asks a new dancer, Peggy Sawyer (played by Ruby Keeler), to replace the stricken star. That choice is not accidental. At a time when cultural wars pitted rural areas against the modern city, Peggy comes from a small western town but combines the ethos of the frontier with urban wisdom. Having learned from the fallen women, the ethnic comics, and gangsters how to "make it" in the city, she becomes a composite heroine who inspires the divided group to cooperate. Incarnating a new spirit of interpenetrating opposites, she engages in vernacular dance and jazz derived not from the upper orders but from the "street." At the end the diverse cast sings "42nd Street" while the camera pans down the avenue. As the audience voices its approval, we see that on the street all races and ethnic groups dance and mingle. In the foreground the heroine tapdances, and a skyline filled with towering buildings evokes the city culture. Now Peggy sings to the audience:

> Take your dancing feet down to 42nd Street
> Where the underworld meets the elite
> Little nifties from the fifties, innocent and sweet
> Shady ladies from the eighties who are indiscreet
> They're side by side and glorified
> On naughty, bawdy 42nd Street

The protagonists of the show-within-a-show musical have done the impossible. Instead of undermining society, a moral revolution and a popular art engendered by blacks and the lower classes provide a new cross-cultural exchange. By the mid-forties that fusion bred formula films in which the hybrid heroes and heroines gave birth to a new man and woman. Take the case of the "Thin Man" series. Derived from a famed detective novel by Dashiell Hammett, the series focused on a play-boy citizen and his urbane wife. Unlike the older detective Sherlock Holmes, Nick Charles has little interest in remaining aloof from night-clubs, ribald comedy, and gangsters. On the contrary, Nick and his beautiful young wife Nora are "comedians of no mean ability." Nick stylizes himself as a gigolo who is an "amusing drunk, a smart wisecracker" but "a very devoted husband and detective." Nick and Nora enjoy what her wealthy relatives disdain – drink and nightclubs – and together they exude an identity that defies older gender roles. ...

Other hybrid characters break down cultural barriers that had thwarted cooperation among groups from different regions. The "Hardy Family" films showed that the new culture would not undermine but renew home and public life. Each film in the series focuses on Judge Hardy and his family in Idaho. Symbolic of the western small-town myth, the judge incarnates the ethos of the virtuous citizen. Whether fighting monopolists aligned to corrupt politicians at home or in Washington, DC, the judge cooperates with youthful offspring who embody the élan of the modern age, especially his son Andy, played by Mickey Rooney. Together adults as well as adolescents cooperate to reform and renew the community.

Each of these fresh narratives features a story of fall and rebirth that generates an alternative mode of perceiving the self and society. Whether we consider the Thin Man or Hardy Family series, the Rogers formula films, the show-within-a-show musicals, or *Cimarron*, these films show the main characters initially adhering to the values promoted by the wealthy and established leaders. Yet they soon find that the old faith has led to disaster in the forms of poverty and public chaos. To explain social disorder, the wealthy villains blame crime and disorder on the poor or aliens. Yet as the hero or other main characters learn the truth, they undergo a conversion experience. Overcoming the fall, they are reborn by cooperating with former outsiders to save traditional family and communal life. Their efforts yield a just society and a more inclusive and better tomorrow.

Directors complemented the conversion story with a visual style that emphasized that the world, like the self, was not fixed or static but in metamorphosis. To convey visual forms that evoked these sensations in the audience, the major directors of the day – Busby Berkeley, Lewis Milestone, King Vidor, Edmund Goulding, Frank Capra, John Ford, and Orson Welles – developed an art form that restructured the inherited studio practices of the twenties. King Vidor explained that he wanted to "get away from all those old ways of doing things. ... When I arrived in Hollywood, there was a sort of unreality about a film, a falseness. The acting was overdone. The make-ups were overdone. ... Acting had no connection with reality."[14] To him the films of Cecil B. De Mille and D. W. Griffith conveyed a static Victorian worldview. The camera remained outside the frame, and subtitles written in accord with proper English interpreted the action in accord with the views of official taste-makers. Films constructed around such rules told the viewer that the story conveyed eternal morals. Since there existed only one truth for the audiences, the composition emphasized one focal point, while makeup and lighting ensured that the blonde hero or heroine embodied the ideals of civilization that would eventually triumph over the villains. Within this visual universe villains possessed dark complexions and clothes, linking them to the outsiders in an Anglo-Saxon world.

In reworking these cinematic practices, directors incorporated into the movies some of the central principles associated with modernism, in which the world was seen not as something known but something to be discovered and reinvented. To shatter the older viewpoints, the directors often had their players shed makeup that demarcated the white characters from the dark villains. Frank Capra noted that by photographing a player devoid of makeup the audience saw the "secret beauty" contained in the lowly and despised. Capra and others also used a mobile camera to enter inside the frame to create a story where the characters engaged in a process of discovery rather than reinforcing known truths. ...

The viewers encountered a world where they looked beneath the surface to see the interconnection among apparently isolated events and material things. A society where white and black, men and women, work and play were seen as diametrically opposed gave way to an interdependency. To convey that relational view directors like John Ford often moved the camera from one object to another, avoiding cuts that divided characters and objects from each other. Ford similarly transferred into movies some of the principles of modern art, particularly multiple spaces and scenes photographed within a flat picture plane that suggested that the world was less a transparent set of truths than a work of art made by human effort. His designers conveyed this holistic view with compositions where several spaces overlapped in one multiple image. Unlike in the past, no single focal point or authority figure dominated. Busby Berkeley's musical numbers in *42nd Street*, for example, often have dancers interacting in concentric and asymmetrical circles and layers. The visual effect provided a communal dynamism where change and movement brought things together in a mutual reinforcement of renewal and vitality. Working in a similar vein, Welles and Capra used overlapping dialogue from one scene to the next to reveal their connectedness. Edmund Goulding, the director of *Grand Hotel*, often used a moving camera to focus on one character seated in the foreground, another in a middle ground, and still another in the background. As the parts inter-acted, the viewers saw action unfolding on several layers at once. ...

The total effect of these innovations – the multiple views, the moving camera, the overlapping dialogue, the elimination of makeup – made it possible for the audience to become active rather than passive spectators. Critics saw that in many ways this placed into popular currency the prin-ciples of cubism, for the director asked the viewers to experience the world from many different perspectives – only here the subject matter focused on living characters making choices in the modern world. The directors of thirties films utilized montage principles similar to those of cubism as well. Scenes in a Will Rogers film directed by John Ford or Busby Berkeley's dance scenes in *42nd Street* showed several objects at once in simultaneous images. To Frank Capra, having all parts of the set "equally lighted [in] the back, middle and foreground" meant that all the characters "get equal billing." ...

Noting the way these new techniques altered cinematic aesthetics from the late twenties to the thirties, Lewis Milestone observed that

> before the film had been like the stage ... the camera was in the position of the audience and photographed everything from the same position. We learned how to use the camera from the point of view of the actor. We built our sets differently. We could not just move on one wall, but all of them. We could shoot from any one position and follow the actor around.[15]

Composite Personalities and Interdependent Publics

If the camera followed the actor around in multiple spaces to convey imagery of movement and change, the most prominent films also gave rise to a new, hybrid personality that restored the star system shaken by the Depression. Grounded in a world of change and flux, these new per-sonalities combined formerly dualistic opposites: the comic fool and the dramatic hero. Where the hero had embodied the values of the Anglo-Saxon citizen and the fool the impulses of rebellious youth or minorities, now these opposites fused. Commenting on the reason why this new mode fit audience taste in the Depression, the director Frank Capra explained that comedy was an essential, for the "man in the street has had so many dogmas crammed down his throat that he is prepared to revolt against current underestimation of his intelligence. He's fed up." According to Capra, current politics, Prohibition, patriotism, big busi-ness, and high-powered advertising were all subjects "ripe for ridicule." Comedy also allowed one to imagine not just "what exists" but "the way things should be." Norman Krasna, a writer who was a "big fella for the underdog," noted that comic heroes allowed one a "protest against the existing system and it's all in the framework of comedy." Still another writer, Alan Scott, saw that his goal was to make an "American" character and art that "combined all that anyone knew of the stage, burlesque, black comedy routines – refurbished for legitimate actors and actresses."[16]

Central to the style of characters who brought these influences together was that they exuded an aura of what the critic Gilbert Seldes called the "metropolitan type." Unlike in the past, "the influence of the gangster film has worked through the whole business of making pictures, so that in nearly every picture the adult and intelligent observer catches a glimpse of its factual rudeness; in nearly every one there is a character who drastically or sourly says what human beings really think, or mocks at heroics, or deflates pretensions." This shift in style gave birth to stars like William Powell. When he arrived in Hollywood, his dark, swarthy looks decreed that producers cast him as a gangster. Yet by the thirties these same swarthy looks made Powell an ideal hero for the role of Nick Charles in *The Thin Man*. Along similar lines, the most popular male star of the day was Clark Gable. Initially Gable's dark features meant that he played gangsters, one appropriately named "Blackie" in *Manhattan Melodrama* (1934). Yet two years later trade reporters observed that a "cinema upstart stole the crown that rested on the heads of established knockouts." Becoming the top male player of the era, Gable carried the aura of a "patent-leather-haired, swarthy-skinned, glint-eyed racketeer." Only now he brought that élan to a comic hero in Capra's *It Happened One Night* (1934), to the dark, romantic gunrunner in *Gone with the Wind* (1939), and to the rebellious officer in *Mutiny on the Bounty* (1935). At the same time, James Cagney, Humphrey Bogart, James Garfield, Paul Muni, Spencer Tracy, and Edward G. Robinson incarnated what Robert Sklar has called the ethos of "city boys," who merged their tough-guy gangster style with roles as citizens who served a public good.[17]

A similar combination of opposites characterized the major female stars as well. Myrna Loy, who played Nick Charles's wife Nora in the "Thin Man" series, noted that prior to the thirties she "played orientals" – characters who in those days were invariably "wicked ladies" – in films like the Fu Manchu series because "I with my slanty eyes and my sense of humour – which was unforgivable in a woman – seemed to fit into the category of 'doubtful ladies.'"[18] Loy, however, gained greater success as the "dream wife of a million men" by combining the aura of "doubtful ladies" with the dignity of Nora Charles, a good wife, mother, and public citizen. Other female stars followed suit as Joan Crawford, Carole Lombard, and Bette Davis combined the aura of the "bad girl" with the spunk of the empowered woman. Furthermore, Vivien Leigh as Scarlett O'Hara in *Gone with the Wind* and Claudette Colbert in *Imitation of Life* (1934) shed the refined image of protected sweetheart in favor of the shrewd businesswomen who beat men at their own game. Summarizing these trends, Carole Lombard wrote that she "lived by a man's code."[19]

The ethos of interpenetrating opposites also permeated genres and formula films associated with traditional American myths. The major cowboy stars after Will Rogers's death were Gene Autry and Roy Rogers. Both incorporated the values of a rugged cowboy with the expressiveness of the urban singer of swing ballads. Along the same lines, the major child players of the era, Shirley Temple and Deanna Durbin, incorporated youthful spontaneity with the adult wisdom to help save rather than undermine family life. *Little Miss Broadway* (1938), for example, features Shirley as a young girl who confronts bankers and staid rich matrons when they attempt to evict poor showmen from their homes. In response she mobilizes diverse peoples to overcome the power of these corrupt businessmen and society matrons. Walt Disney's cartoon characters, as Steven Watts has shown, combined animal traits with human sentiments and beliefs. The Soviet filmmaker, Sergei Eisenstein, saw that Disney's cartoon characters were popular because they evoked a vision of wholeness to counter the deep fragmentations of the modern world. ...

The political message flowing from these innovations was also not too hard to find. By incorporating into the self the desires of outsiders, whether they be gangsters, fallen women, ribald comics, or cartoon animals, the new citizen carried into the civic sphere the capacity to cooperate with outsiders to reinvent oneself and society. Nowhere was this more in evidence than in the populist trilogy of Frank Capra, an artist deeply committed to the ideal of the composite personality and film formula. In *Mr. Deeds Goes to Town* (1936), *Mr. Smith Goes to Washington* (1939), and *Meet John Doe* (1941), Capra and writers like Robert Riskin created conversion narratives that focused on competing views of cultural authority. Traditional authority resided in the official leaders and the monopoly capitalists who were his villains. The villains' view of life was complete and closed to new ideas. They manipulate the mass media to gain power over the people and turn to force and power – embodied in their assistants – to impose on the central hero demands to do their bidding.

Typically the environment of the rich reflects the imposition of the power of aristocratic lords and monopolists on the dreams of the old republic. As such the rich threaten to destroy the democracy and impose the values of the "Old World" on citizens dedicated to the public good. The Capra hero thus embodies the ethos of the producers' democracy that is in danger, while the Capra heroine initially works as a reporter or political aide for the rich. Once the hero and heroine meet, they engage in humor, song, and urban nightlife. Slowly they shed their psychic dependency and find in each other what they lack to make themselves complete. Armed with a code that combines both tough realism and idealism, they undergo a conversion experience. Modernizing republican ideals, they align with the lower classes to launch a collective battle for justice as well as a more holistic life. Watching this contest unfold in *Meet John Doe*, a critic saw that

> the text – and it is all entertainment, not screen editorial – is right down the broad highway of human concern. And through the compelling human equation runs a patriotic strain which relies on no flag waving, no stilted eloquence, but is all the more stirring because it leaps from the heart of almost inarticulate folk to confront injustice, oppression, and selfish aggrandizement everywhere around the world.[20]

Importantly Capra and others evoked the myths of American traditions, but did so as a means to critique and alter the present. With names like Jefferson Smith and Long John Willoughby, Capra's heroes embodied the recovery of the traditional republic and democratic community. Much as in the Will Rogers vehicles, the vision of the past in films of this period suggests an alternative American ethos. Take *Stagecoach*, made in 1939 by John Ford. The western charts the journey of a stagecoach across the Southwest. Inside the coach are an outlaw, a fallen woman, a southern gambler, a drunken Irishman, a refined Victorian "lady," and a banker who evokes the image of Herbert Hoover and the corrupt financiers of the day. Under the threat of Indian attack, they expel the banker and learn how to forge a public life where opposites cooperate. Similarly, Ford's *How Green Was My Valley* (1941) showed how rich capitalists exploit poor miners. In response the commoners form a union to advance their class interests. The Soviet director Sergei Eisenstein observed that Ford's *Young Mr. Lincoln* (1939) portrayed a Lincoln who came directly from the "womb of popular and national spirit," of the "progressive tradition of America" that is struggling to restore "harmony" to a fragmented world. Even apparently escapist films turned to an alternative past as a model for public life and republican renewal. *The Wizard of Oz* (1939), for example, originated as a populist novel depicting the farmers' uprising in the 1890s. Transferred into the Great Depression, the novel generated a film that charted the actions of a young girl, Dorothy, and fanciful characters who learn through doing that they are not inferior, and that they can trust their resources to achieve common goals and success through collective effort.[21]

Within these productions, the music often reinforced the theme that American folk culture and modern culture operated on the same tracks. During the thirties, for example, swing bands played at intermissions in urban theaters. An audience could see bands like Benny Goodman's that featured white and black musicians performing together, then see a main feature like *How Green Was My Valley* and *Young Mr. Lincoln* that featured the songs of workers and the folk, a process that would inspire Eisenstein to note that Ford's Lincoln was "half Rabelais and half Michelangelo." Similarly, Paul Robeson sang "Old Man River" in *Showboat* (1936), and the Caucasian heroine did a "sand dance" accompanied by blacks playing music on the Mississippi River. Together these images gave dignity to the music of slaves and suggested that America was rooted in cross-cultural exchange. To immigrants who had been discriminated against, and seen as not "yet white" by official leaders, the effect of talking films was evident. In the twenties minorities had reinterpreted the silent films to suit their own interests. In the thirties there was a much closer relation between working-class spectators and what appeared on the screen. Commenting on that shift, the *Jewish Daily Forward* noted that though silent films encouraged immigrants to model themselves on "Anglo-Saxon austerity," sound films encouraged working-class immigrants to learn that "an accent instead of impoverishing a personality, lends interest to it … [making] accents … into an asset."[22]

The advent of sound film generated a competitive discourse of pluralism as the heart of the national tradition. Yet what about nonwhites? Were they included as well? There is no doubt that many films perpetuated racial stereotypes. While negative images continued, it was also true that in the thirties the racism permeating mainstream culture began to decline and formerly ostracized groups and characters gained dignity. Classic examples of the more complicated portrayal of racial minorities are the Charlie Chan films. Though the series perpetuated many traditional white stereotypes of Asians, the central character, played by Warner Oland, a Finnish actor with Asian features, often turned these views upside down. In the twenties Oland had played the evil Asian gangster, Fu Manchu. Yet as that genre faded in the early thirties, he gained success as the detective Charlie Chan who combined gangster qualities with that of the dedicated detective who served the public good.

Throughout Chan reversed many of the conventional stereotypes that whites had used to subordinate and demean Asians. To begin with, he was a family man with a wife and three sons, all played by Asians. He also appealed to urban whites as well as what reporters called the "oriental trade" at home and in the Far East. At a time when whites forbade Asian immigrants to attain citizenship, and states on the West Coast forbade the Japanese to hold land, Chan was the skilled "urbane oriental who took delight in unravelling the most complicated crime mysteries." A critic said of *Charlie Chan at the Race Track* (1936) that Chan may have "the help of Inspector Fifer of the Scotland Yard and Inspector Flannery of New York. But as far as helping they're a couple of stooges ... baffled by foolish facts which cannot fool Chan." Moreover, Chan emerged as a "witty philosopher" and hero who also delighted in modern consumer goods such as flashy cars, good wine, and nightclubs. Like Nick Charles, Charlie Chan was "full of wise-cracks." He solved crimes that "baffled others," the result being that the Charlie Chan films celebrated Asians as skilled men and women who aided whites and the victims of crime.[23]

A similar alteration informed the portrayal of blacks as well. Though a self-directed detective failed to emerge in the guise of an African American in mainstream Hollywood films, a more inclusive vision of blacks did receive representation. No doubt films like *Gone with the Wind* continued to perpetuate demeaning images. A sample of plot descriptions, gathered by Thomas Cripps from trade journals, shows that during the 1920s black performers were cast in the traditional role of servants in 80 percent of all films; however, during the thirties that number fell to 40 percent. Similarly, our plot samples show that racial minorities cast in favorable roles rose from 4 to about 15 percent from the twenties to late thirties.

Black journalists also perceived that a more dignified black portrayal of African Americans graced the Hollywood screen. Even though they wanted to see blacks in more positive roles, they praised players like Paul Robeson, Bill "Bojangles" Robinson, Rex Ingram, Lena Horne, Hattie McDaniel, and Louise Beavers, who now attained major billing and success in Hollywood films. Rex Ingram told a reporter that things indeed had changed. Where in the twenties Hollywood producers cast him as either a "Nubian slave" or a subordinate servant, he now found more positive roles, playing God himself in films like *The Green Pastures* (1936). Similarly, in the adaptation of Edna Ferber's *Showboat*, Paul Robeson sang "Ol' Man River" to give voice to the reality of blacks' exploitation by whites. As Robeson sang "[we] tote that bale, get a little drunk and land in jail," the lyrics and montage reveal that African Americans have made the South rich but remain racially oppressed.

If major films portrayed minorities in a more positive light, some of the most prominent also challenged the foundation of white superiority: the enforcement in a majority of states of miscegenation laws that outlawed intermarriage between whites and racial minorities. In many ways these select films resemble the beginnings of what literary scholars and students of new nationalities call "foundational myths." That is, stories that focus on unions of lovers of different regions and races often provide models for overcoming divisions that thwart the making of new "imaginary communities." *Cimarron*, for example, portrayed lovers whose romance and marriage created new bonds across the races, foreshadowing the birth of a multicultural America.

This was not an isolated occurrence. *Showboat* as well as Will Rogers's *Steamboat 'Round the Bend* (1935) challenged miscegenation codes. The Academy-Award-winning film of 1935, *Mutiny on the Bounty*, continued that trend by focusing on the adventures of a British ship manned by a tyrannical captain who disdains nonwhites, whom he exploits with shrewd business practices. But when the crew meets South Sea islanders who believe in cooperation and love across the races, the white subordinates revolt and intermarry with the nonwhite islanders, all of whom were played by Polynesian actresses. *Juarez* (1939) told the story of a mixed-blood Indian who defeats an army of French imperialists. Not only does Juarez find inspiration in the ideals of Abraham Lincoln, but to make a republic he foresees that land has to be redistributed so citizens can attain both political and economic independence. Similarly, Frank Capra's *The Bitter Tea of General Yen* (1933) depicted a white woman who falls in love with an Asian. The star of the film, Barbara Stanwyck, recalled that "the women's clubs came out very strongly against it, because the white woman was in love with a yellow man and kissed his hand. So what! I was so shocked [by the reaction]. I accepted it and believed in it, and loved it."[24]

By the end of the decade films that evoked the élan of the composite protagonist gave visibility to the possibility of a more pluralistic and just republic. Our plot samples reveal that this was not an isolated occurrence. As criticism of business and the rich ranged from 25 to 60 percent in plot samples, characters who engaged in a conversion narrative that shifted loyalty from the upper to lower classes occurred in over 25 percent of all plots. Similarly, the lures of mass culture – nightclubs, dance halls, jazz, the new woman, and "youth" – altered as well. In the twenties, mass art was seen as dangerous in well over 50 percent of all films, implying that the characters' desire for a new life should incorporate the status symbols of the wealthy. But fears of mass art – with its links to the expressive culture of blacks and immigrants – receded to almost zero in the thirties. In sharp contrast, the lures of mass art emerged as a force for personal and social renewal. With that change, protagonists linked to the old middle class dropped to less than 40 percent, and a new man and woman came clearly into prominence. Rooted in the new "trades of the city," the new man and woman appeared as urban singers, dancers, comics, radio announcers, sportsmen and women, pilots, and nightclub performers. Along with this shift the new man and woman were disproportionately found in films in which the heroes engaged in social reform, a category that fluctuated from a low of 10 percent to about 25 percent of film plots from the mid-twenties to the late thirties.

"Our Collective Unconscious" or the Audience Takes Command

By the late thirties it was clear that moviemakers were not adapting, as Neal Gabler has told us, to every "old bromide" of society. Instead, major films and Jewish producers displaced an Anglo-Saxon Americanism with an alternative, pluralistic vision. As is so often the case in the study of the popular arts, the question arises: How did the audiences respond to these themes? What was the relation between film content and audience belief and public values? Though a definitive answer is impossible, one thing is clear. Producers' awareness of audience demand spurred them to make productions dramatically different from the formulas of the twenties and to give directors and performers such as Frank Capra, Will Rogers, John Ford, and Orson Welles control over their work in the studios.

The audience had become less of a passive "crowd" than a "public" that made their own choices. A telling testimony to that shift informed the recollections of the screenwriter Lester Cole. Early in the thirties, Cole participated in creating Hollywood guilds that drew on a republican critique of capitalism to mobilize unions. Meanwhile, Cole and his friend Nathanael West – soon to be the famed writer of *The Day of the Locust* (1939) – created scripts based on current news. One featured a lawyer who sides with striking workers. In *The President's Mystery* (1936) Cole recalled that he combined love with "mystery, romance and a generous dash of Roosevelt propaganda." At first Republic studios refused to release the film because it was too radical. Yet when President Roosevelt won reelection in 1936, the producers released it to the tune of great profits. Summarizing the lessons learned from these events, Cole saw that

> certain producers began to see profit in film topics other than sheer escape and inane fantasy. Even though the ideas expressed and social realities depicted caused them some extreme uneasiness, the magnetism of the new fields of profits conquered such misgivings. To show poverty, joblessness and hunger not only awakened the consciousness of millions who saw themselves represented realistically on the screen, but aroused their consciousness and stimulated what was most dreaded by the producers who made the films – a sense of dignity of the common man and woman, their courage and their strength to fight back.[25]

Besides the convergence between market demand and the making of more socially conscious films, popular values did take a leftward swing. As our plot samples recorded hostility to the old order and to business coupled with reformist themes, pollsters found that over 63 percent of the public expressed great fears of unemployment and wished for more security in their lives. At the same time over 65 percent felt that big businessmen and elites had too much power, and that sharp inequalities of wealth were undemocratic. They had not, however, lost faith in the possibility of progressive reform. When asked what class they came from, 88 percent responded they emanated from the solid middle class. When asked about their hopes for the country, the majority had faith in the glories of American democracy and a tomorrow where technology and science created abundance. Most thought that Franklin Roosevelt and the New Deal offered hope for realizing these goals, a faith that was strongest among those under thirty-five years of age and those situated in the middle and working classes – the groups most drawn to the movies.

At the grassroots it appeared that moviemakers' capacity to give form to these beliefs had an impact on political attitudes. The novelist John Clellon Holmes recalled that movies provided him and his friends with "our collective unconscious. I for one still associate certain films with the dawning of certain ideas." Sound made Hollywood films a "universal part of puberty" that generated a "heightening of psychological involvement so pervasive that the gulf between the audience and the image was all but obliterated." In his neighborhood "an entire generation went to the movies two or three times a week." Holmes recalled that it would be "difficult to calculate the number of hours that people of my age spent talking about movies in those years." When he saw *All Quiet on the Western Front* in 1930, or went to a Marx Brothers or W. C. Fields comedy, he learned that the "pompous" world of adults was a fraud, but he went back home "renewed by [the] knowledge that the bores could be foiled by cagey irrationality." By watching films like *Meet John Doe*, Holmes also learned that big business could be a fraud. In fact, when he became involved in "party politics," the memory of this Capra production "and others like it" had an "influence on my decisions and aversions which is incalculable." Movies during the thirties thus provided "a continuation of our schooling by another means," teaching that war and big business constituted the "siren call of the devil."[26]

Just as it appeared that many in the audience altered their political values watching major films, so the critics and the artists themselves saw moviemaking as part of creating an alternative public life. A writer in Tennessee observed after watching *All Quiet on the Western Front* that "this is the first time that those who fought the war with only bonds and thrift stamps have ever been shown what the real thing is."[27] ...

At this point one can also see why Orson Welles recalled that Hollywood provided a site to advance a shift in symbols, racial norms, and politics that would renew the "democratic republic." Public opinion polls, memoirs, audience response, and alterations in narratives showed that even before the New Deal came to power in 1933, many moviemakers created a language for what did not yet exist: a pluralistic producers' democracy rooted in hostility to what President Roosevelt called the new "money changers" and "feudal lords" of industry. Indicative of that political drift, progressive civic associations created a series of film study guides that provided questions to stimulate students to see the civic implications of each story. The guide for John Ford's *How Green Was My Valley* observed that the film "shows admirably the beginnings of the labour movement." Another pamphlet noted that *Fury* (1936), a film about lynching, focused on a white victim. But the story nevertheless helped to promote the national antilynching legislation to protect African Americans. Still another focused on a Hardy Family production that featured the judge protecting an ostracized citizen. To have students think about the story's larger implications, the writer asked, "What if the man had been a Negro, or foreign born? ... Can you think of any instance where your standing in the community is likely to affect the quality of justice which will be meted out?"[28]

Besides the study guides and their encouragement of discussion about the "quality of justice" meted out in the community, Hollywood producers directly combined the élan of the new art with social reform. Such a merger surfaced in the organization of Hollywood unions as well as Will Rogers's radio programs. In public rituals that impulse came inescapably into view with the Roosevelt victory in 1932. The southern California organizers of Roosevelt's campaign came from the Warner Brothers studio. Once Roosevelt won the presidency, Jack Warner organized a streamlined train to participate in the inaugural of the "New Deal Chief." Accordingly, the "42nd Street Special" stopped in major cities to announce the arrival of the "Better Times Special" linking the film *42nd Street* with a "New Deal in entertainment." Citizens groups and Mayor Curley met the train and its stars in Boston, while reporters interviewed the stars, taking care to feature players from the local area. On several occasions, newsmen observed with surprise that the actresses dressed like "men" and enjoyed performing the roles of the "bad girls" in order to let loose their "inhibitions." The actors similarly enjoyed playing gangster roles rather than the "colorless" leading men. Along the way commentators saw that the train embodied the spirit of an alternative public, rising from the ashes of hard times. If we "needed," explained one observer, "to be sold on ourselves" the train with its silver Pullman cars and modern interiors did the trick. The Hollywood stars captured the attention of fans precisely because in days of deflated hopes,

> we Americans must find some hat rack to which we can hang our national affection. At this moment celebrities are the number one vote getter. To be sure we haven't much choice. What with Big Business hiding its naughty face in the drawer and society turning out to be a boring lead-headed princess, there is nothing left for us to idealize except the clan of pretty boys and girls who live on the rhinestone shore of Hollywood.[29]

The heart of the matter lay beyond the lure of the "rhinestone shore of Hollywood." With official institutions in disarray, the train and the film signaled the incorporation of politics and the popular arts into remaking the nation. At a time when established institutions continued to exclude racial minorities and women, a new mass culture arose that evoked dreams of a more inclusive and modern culture. In response moviemakers who themselves were often minorities, immigrants, or the children of immigrants rejected European status symbols and turned to the lower classes and vernacular arts for inspiration for a new public life. On the screen, films evoked the vision of a modernized republic, rooted in citizen action, pluralism, and dreams of contemporary morals and abundance. While the process of cultural and social reform had only begun, there was no doubt that feature films now brought to the fore composite heroes and heroines who combined instinctual vitality with the art of interpenetrating opposites.

Notes

1 On Orson Welles's life, art, and politics, see Welles and Peter Bogdanovich, *This Is Orson Welles* (New York: Harper Perennial, 1993), pp. xxvi, 13, 33, 80, 93–8 (the lost Eden informing work and relation to family), 102, 168, 183–5 (his political activities), 258. The quotation on *Kane* comes from Juan Cobs, Miguel Rubio, and J. A. Pruneda, "A Trip to Don Quixote-land: Conversations with Orson Welles," *Cahiers du Cinema* (English), No. 5 (1966): 34–47.

2 The comments about "foreign-born" domination of Hollywood are from an article entitled "News from Hollywood" in *St. Louis Mo. Post Dispatch*, August 7, 1927, p. 1D.

3 Gabler, *Empire of Their Own*, p. 225.

4 "Phoney Splurges Weakens Sex Lure," *V*, December 10, 1930, p. 1.

5   For "not a hoot about tradition," and throwing items at the screen, see *MPH*, October 8, 1931.

6   *V*, December 29, 1931, p. 4.

7   W. R. Burnett interview, in *Backstory: Interviews with Screenwriters of the Golden Age*, ed. Pat McGilligan (Berkeley: University of California Press, 1986), pp. 56–8; Norman Krasna interview, in ibid., pp. 212–41; Edna Ferber, *A Peculiar Treasure* (New York: Doubleday, Doran and Co., 1939), p. 10.

8   "Hollywood Stops Making Films for Hollywood," *V*, December 29, 1931, p. 7; Cecelia Agar, "Ways and Means to the Screen," *V*, December 29, 1931, p. 18; Ruth Morris, "Screen's Best Liked Men," *V*, December 29, 1931, p. 163.

9   The comment about journalistic productions comes from "Showmen's Reviews" of *Washington Show*, in *MPH*, July 2, 1932, p. 1; Dudley Nichols, "Theatre, Society, Education," *Educational Theatre Journal* (November 1956), p. 183.

10 "Little Caesar," *V*, January 14, 1931; W. R. Burnett, "The Outsider," interview by Ken Mate and Pat McGilligan, in McGilligan, *Backstory*, pp. 56–9.

11 Marybeth Hamilton, " 'A Little Bit Spicy, but Not Too Raw': Mae West and Urban Performance," *The Gateway to Hays* (Venice, Italy: Biennale di Venezia, 1991), pp. 183–7, and Jeanine Basinger, *A Woman's View: How Hollywood Spoke to Women, 1930–1960* (Hanover, NH, and London: Wesleyan University Press, 1993), pp. 17–183.

12 John Huston, *An Open Book* (New York: Ballantine Books, 1980), pp. 94–5.

13 Ferber, *A Peculiar Treasure*, p. 10.

14 King Vidor interview with Kay Mills, *Los Angeles Times*, September 13, 1981, pt. IV, p. 2.

15 Milestone interview, American Film Institute, in Milestone Collection, AMPAS.

16 Ruth Morris, "Capra Foresees Satirical Cycle: Many Subjects 'Ripe for Ridicule,' " *V*, February 2, 1932, p. 2; Krasna interview, in McGilligan, ed., *Backstory*, p. 221; Scott interview, ibid., p. 322.

17 Gilbert Seldes, "The Movies in Peril," first appeared in *Scribners Magazine*, February 1935, reprinted in *The Movies in Our Midst*, ed. Gerald Mast (Chicago: University of Chicago Press, 1982), pp. 427–38. The quotation is on pp. 431–2. The Gable quotation is from Ruth Morris, "Screen's Best Liked Men," *V*, December 29, 1931, p. 163. See Robert Sklar, *City Boys: Cagney, Bogart, Garfield* (Princeton NJ: Princeton University Press, 1992).

18 "Dream Wife of a Million Men," *Look* (November 1937); "Myrna Loy in Colorado," unidentified clipping, Loy file, AMPAS.

19 Basinger, *A Woman's View*; Elizabeth Kendall, *The Runaway Bride: Hollywood Romantic Comedy in the 1930's* (New York: Alfred A. Knopf, 1990); Hart Seymore, "Carole Lombard Tells 'How I Live by a Man's Code,' " *Photoplay*, June 1937, p. 17.

20 *V*, March 13, 1941, p. 2.

21 Sergei Eisenstein, "Mr. Lincoln by Mr. Ford," in Jay Leyda, ed., *Film Essays* (London: Dennis Dobson, 1968), pp. 139–49.

22   Nettie Zimmerman, "Making an Asset of an Accent … Talkies Point the Way," *Jewish Daily Forward*, August 13, 1930, p. 10.

23   The quotations are from reviews in *V*, January 26, 1932; "*Chan at Circus*: Nice B.O.; Story Stacks Up with Predecessors," *The Hollywood Reporter*, March 12, 1936; "Charlie Chan Carries On," *Film Daily*, March 22, 1936.

24   Barbara Stanwyck interview, in McBride, *Frank Capra*, p. 281.

25   Lester Cole, *Hollywood Red: The Autobiography of Lester Cole* (Palo Alto, CA: Ramparts Press, 1981), pp. 143–51.

26   John Clellon Holmes, "15 Cents Before 6 PM: The Wonderful Movies of the Thirties," *Harper's* (December 1965), pp. 51–5.

27   *San Francisco Examiner*, August 8, 1930, unpaginated clipping, *All Quiet on the Western Front* scrapbook, AMPAS.

28   "Progressive Educational Association Study Guides for *How Green Was My Valley*, 1941," in *How Green Was My Valley* file, AMPAS, and "Progressive Educational Association Study Guide for *A Family Affair*, 1937," in *A Family Affair* file, AMPAS.

29   The quotation comes from an unidentified clipping in the AMPAS file.

Documents

Introduction to Documents

May discusses the liberal promise of cinema and its potential for renewing democracy. During the 1930s, many actors fought for democracy off the screen as well as on the screen. Few causes attracted more attention than the rise of Nazism and fascism in Europe. On December 9, 1938, fifty-six prominent stars, writers, directors, and studio heads – including James Cagney, Joan Crawford, Henry Fonda, Bette Davis, and Harry Warner – gathered at Edward G. Robinson's home and signed a "Declaration of Democratic Independence" calling on Congress and the president to boycott of all German products until the nation ended its aggression toward other nations and stopped persecuting Jews and all minorities. It would be heartening to think that Americans embraced the democratic pronouncements of their favorite stars, but that was not the case. While some applauded Robinson's actions, others denounced him as a Communist and as a "cheap, big-mouthed ignorant Jew lacking in a sense of public decency and decorum." The following are some of the letters that Robinson received following the December 9 declaration. The letters lead us to ask: Should movie stars speak out on controversial issues? Why? Why not?

Responses to Edward G. Robinson's "Declaration of Democratic Independence"

Source: Edward G. Robinson Papers, Cinema-TV Library, University of Southern California

---

Henry Bortin Jr. (Laguna Beach, CA) to Edward G. Robinson, December 10, 1938

For a man in your high position to take this kind of stand is to exert a great deal influence with the American public . . . . I myself am unable to exert such influence personally, but I hope I can help a little by carrying out a personal resolve to attend, insofar as possible, all pictures in which you have a part. I hope you will find that your strong stand will pay you financial dividends at the box office as well as spiritual dividends of happiness in your own conscience.

T. Conden (Chicago, IL) to Edward G. Robinson, December 12, 1938

Sir, News reports state that you have organized a crew of Jews to try to force the American Government to break diplomatic relations with Germany. ... The Christian people of this country have been very tolerant of Jewish activities in this country. We all have been conscious of the methods by which Jews attempt to control business, finance and other avenues of business . . . . Once it becomes apparent that you are attempting to supplant your role of stage villain and mendicant with an off-stage role of pseudo-statesman – every Christian in the country will recognize you for what you really are. A cheap, big-mouthed ignorant Jew lacking in a sense of public decency and decorum. I certainly hesitate to believe the news reports which indicate that you have placed yourself on a plane with Jews like Eddie Cantor *et al.* Nothing could be more disastrous for you – or the race which such action would grossly misrepresent. America has been more than kind to the Jews – let them not fail for once in their history to display a spark of loyalty to a Christian nation which has given them citizenship and a haven.

Diego Rivera (Mexico, D.F.) to Edward G. Robinson, January 21, 1939

First, I want very much to congratulate you for your anti-fascist work and action. The step you have taken to have the signatures for the anti-Nazi declaration seems to me excellent. ... I ask of you that you count on me as among your comrades of action, and I wish and hope that there should be more than 20 millions of signatures, if the American men and women have a clear understanding of the real need existing for all of us to destroy the dark power of the crazily savage Hitler, Mussolini, Stalin and all the mad dogs following them.

I. E. Schoening ("A Bible Christian" from Minneapolis) to Edward G. Robinson, December 13, 1938

So you movie executives and actors are entering upon a new field of endeavor – that of advising the President and Congress. What arrogance! Who do you think you are anyway? Because a lot of silly men and women worship you does not prove that you are gods who may tell our government what or what not it is to do. Like fun that movement launched in your home was a spontaneous affair! Anyone who knows enough to put two and two together knows better. That meeting was a planned affair and the idea it advanced was born in the minds of the men who own the movie industry – a group of clever atheistic Jews. ... The movie colony may root for the Jews all they wish – that's their privilege, but don't think that the people of the United States are going to fall in with your plans. ... Those of us who know World History and the Bible know that the Jews have always been in trouble up to their ears. They are troublemakers. They hounded Jesus from pillar to post and finally did away with him and he certainly never harmed them. You set up a howl at what Hitler is doing, but now you are planning to starve innocent Germans. Pray tell me in what way you are better than he?

Walter S. Loebl (Roanoke, VA) to Edward G. Robinson, December 12, 1938

It was an agreeable surprise to read in our local newspaper about the stand regarding Nazi Germany taken by the leaders of the movie industry on December 9, at your home in Beverly Hills. This is a direct refutation of the charge that Hollywood is shallow. It has the character and integrity of those who have it within their power to mold the public opinion of today as well as that of the future. ... I believe if some of our more popular, definitely non-Jewish, motion picture stars would speak from the screen to the audience, the audiences would be glad to sign the document as drawn up at your meeting.

J. O' Connor (Cleveland, OH) to Edward G. Robinson and "Clique," December 9, 1938

You and your bunch are making it your business to boycott Germany. But! Nary a word or statement against Russia and it's persecution of Christians – oh, me!

Readings and Screenings

The period from the late 1920s through the early 1940s witnessed major changes in American society and American film. For a general overview of the transition to sound and the subsequent changes in movies and the movie industry, see Donald Crafton, *The Talkies: American Cinema's Transition to Sound, 1926–1931* (New York: Charles Scribner's Sons, 1997); Tino Balio, *Grand Design: Hollywood as a Modern Business Enterprise, 1930–1939* (New York: Charles Scribner's Sons, 1993); Thomas Schatz, *Boom and Bust: American Cinema in the 1940s* (New York: Charles Scribner's Sons, 1993). Like Lary May, several other scholars stress the democratic uses of film during this era: Michael Denning, *The Cultural Front: The Laboring of American Culture in the Twentieth Century* (London and New York: Verso, 1997); Sam B. Girgus, *Hollywood Renaissance: The Cinema of Democracy in the Era of Ford, Capra, and Kazan* (New York: Cambridge University Press, 1998). Those interested in exploring how movies of the time both reflected and shaped changes in American society should look at Colin Shindler, *Hollywood in Crisis: Cinema and American Society, 1929–1939* (London and New York: Routledge, 1996); Andrew Bergman, *We're in the Money: Depression America and its Films* (New York: New York University Press, reprinted 1997); Peter Roffman and Jim Purdy, *The Hollywood Social Problem Film: Madness, Despair, and Politics From the Depression to the Fifties* (Bloomington, IN: Indiana University Press, 1981). The politicization of movies, movie stars, and studio heads during this era is discussed in Steven J. Ross, *Hollywood Left and Right: How Movie Stars Shaped American Politics* (New York: Oxford University Press, 2011); Saverio Giovacchini, *Hollywood Modernism: Film and Politics in the Age of the New Deal* (Philadelphia, PN: Temple University Press, 2001); Michael Birdwell, *Celluloid Soldiers: Warner Bros. Campaign Against Nazism* (New York and London: New York University Press,

1999); Giuliana Muscio, *Hollywood's New Deal* (Philadelphia, PN: Temple University Press, 1997); Gabler, *An Empire of Their Own*. For the interconnections of race, ethnicity, class, and cinema, see Michael Rogin, *Blackface, White Noise: Jewish Immigrants in the Hollywood Melting Pot* (Berkeley and Los Angeles, CA: University of California Press, 1996); Otto Friedrich, *City of Nets: A Portrait of Hollywood in the 1940's* (Berkeley and Los Angeles, CA: University of California Press, reprint edition, 1997); Robert Sklar, *City Boys: Cagney, Bogart, Garfield* (Princeton, NJ: Princeton University Press, 1992); Mark Winokur, *American Laughter: Immigrants, Ethnicity and 1930s Hollywood Film Comedy* (New York: St. Martin's Press, 1996). For an important look at the power of audiences during the 1930s, see Lawrence Levine, "The Folklore of Industrial Society: Popular Culture and Its Audience," in Levine, ed., *The Unpredictable Past* (New York: Oxford University Press, 1993).

Because there are so many Depression- and New Deal-era films, I will narrow my recommendations to those that deal with themes raised in the May reading. *The Jazz Singer* (1927) is a good starting point for looking at what one critic called the "low group tastes of the masses." Gangster films questioned the premises of the American Dream and recast popular ideas about heroes and villains. The most famous of these films are *Little Caesar* (1930), *The Public Enemy* (1931), and *Scarface* (1932). African-Americans also challenged Anglo-Saxon ideas about their place in American society; see *The Emperor Jones* (1933). The plight of migrant laborers is movingly dramatized in *Our Daily Bread* (1934); several DVD versions of this film also contain footage of the staged 1934 newsreels produced by MGM and mentioned in the Sinclair document. *Blonde Venus* (1932), *I'm No Angel* (1933), and *Imitation of Life* (1934) show how women rejected traditional gender roles. Charlie Chaplin continually challenged all authority figures. His best films of this era include *City Lights* (1931), *Modern Times* (1936), and *The Great Dictator* (1940). The call for a new spirit of cooperation and democracy can be seen in the musical *42nd Street* (1933), the dramas *The Grapes of Wrath* (1940) and *How Green Was My Valley* (1941), and in Frank Capra's populist trilogy *Mr. Deeds Goes to Town* (1936), *Mr. Smith Goes to Washington* (1939), and *Meet John Doe* (1941). For a similar political attack on the power of media moguls, see Orson Welles' most famous film, *Citizen Kane* (1941). MGM's Hardy Family films – the most successful series in the studio's history up until then – offered a conservative alternative to the liberal productions coming out of Warner Brothers. In particular, see *A Family Affair* (1937), *You're Only Young Once* (1938), *Love Finds Andy Hardy* (1938), and *Judge Hardy's Children* (1938).

6

Alternatives Cinemas: Movies on the Margins

Introduction to Article

During the first half of the twentieth century, blacks, workers, socialists, homosexuals, feminists, political activists, and various other minority groups were either stereotyped, underrepresented, or excluded from mainstream Hollywood productions. Expensive feature films, however, were not the only movies seen by Americans. Documentaries, race movies, Yiddish films, and even pornographic movies dealt with the hardships, aspirations, failures, triumphs, and daily problems faced by more "marginal" groups in American society.

Thomas Cripps surveys a wide range of alternative cinemas that appealed to the political, ethnic, racial, sexual, and aesthetic tastes of those often excluded from more traditional Hollywood fare. Beginning in 1918 with the release of *The Birth of a Race*, African Americans, for example, responded to the negative images seen in *Birth of a Nation* (1915) by producing movies and newsreels for black audiences – "race films" as they were known – that offered positive depictions of African-American life and aspirations. Over the next several decades, other groups – including the Workers' Film and Photo League and the government's Office of War Information – made films that depicted themes and events meant to educate, amuse, and inspire audiences.

Movies and American Society, Second Edition. Edited by Steven J. Ross.
© 2014 John Wiley & Sons, Inc. Published 2014 by John Wiley & Sons, Inc.

Cripps suggests that these modest productions, which generally played on the margins in small neighborhood houses, churches, synagogues, union halls, schools, and voluntary associations, often said as much about American society as the lavish Hollywood films shown in first-run theaters and movie palaces.

Discussion Points

Does what we see on the screen really influence the way we view other people? Think of old and new films you have seen that feature homosexuals, African American, Asians, Mexicans, Jews, Arabs, and other minority groups. How are these folks depicted? To what extent are these depictions positive or negative?

Others' Movies

Thomas Cripps

Source: Thomas Cripps, *Hollywood's High Noon: Moviemaking and Society Before Television* (Baltimore and London: The Johns Hopkins University Press, 1997), 118–39

Throughout the classical era of Hollywood, what moviemakers put on the silver screen was determined by the box office; by the mores formulated into the Production Code Administration's censoring system and its forerunners; and by a slyness on the part of some moviemakers in slipping in references to racial, sexual, and political material that the first two forces precluded explicit mention of in the movies. This meant that African Americans, Jews, and other ethnic groups; political ideologues on the extreme left or right; and people whose sexual preferences thrust them into a corner of American life found only undertones of lives on Hollywood's main screens. Indeed, Hollywood often denied the presence of even the undertones, as Vito Russo claims in *The Celluloid Closet: Homosexuality in Movies* (1981). Howard Hawks did in an interview about his classic western *Red River* (1948), in which he denied the gay undertones that homosexuals imputed to the male bondings portrayed in the film. "A goddamn silly statement," Hawks said.

Only blacks, socialists, homosexuals, feminists, members of other sub-jected minorities, or activists acting on behalf of one of these groups decoded the moviegoing experience, focusing careful attention on small bits so as to tease out tonal meanings that mainstream viewers might have missed. Indeed, meanings other than the ostensible ones had a way of slipping into the frame, through moviemakers' inattention or naïveté or sly willfulness – or viewers' imagining. For example, in 1943 a Richmond newspaper critic complained that the camera doggedly, incongruously sought out black Ethel Waters in *Cairo* (1943), as though for some unstated racially driven reason. Glenn Ford recalled that in making the sexually charged noir film *Gilda* (1946), he and George MacCready knew that "we were supposed to be playing homosexuals," but the director, Charles Vidor, could only ask in disbelief, "Really?" ... For homosexual moviegoers on the lookout for a witty parody of gay life, there were always the mincing scenes of Franklin Pangborn and Fritz Feld; there was also the game of rushing to see the latest film by the reputedly homosexual George Cukor or Mitchell Leisen in order to ran-sack it for fey asides directed at the homoerotically inclined. Lesbians on the lookout for a nod in their direction could find Eve Arden playing the wisecracking buddy who has been through a lot with the female star. The slim canon of Dorothy Arzner was also fruitful, not only for the movies but for her "bourgeois butch" mode of dress, a boldly mannish jacket and tie. Feminists searching the frame for signs and omens were rewarded with Rosalind Russell on an adventure in Bombay, alleviating the effects of polio, or even slugging some bad guy with an uppercut. Other offer-ings for feminists were Zona Gale's Lulu Bett throwing off the harness of domesticity with far more rage on the screen than in the book; the biopic of Marie Curie; and the many movies in which the star walks alone when she chooses (Lauren Bacall in *To Have and Have Not* [1944], Marlene Dietrich in *Blonde Venus* [1932] or *Shanghai Express* [1932], Barbara Stanwyck in *The Bitter Tea of General Yen* [1933], and Jean Arthur as Calamity Jane in *The Plainsman* [1937]). Along these same lines, John Schuchman, the historian of Hollywood's treatment of deaf persons, closes *Hollywood Speaks: Deafness and the Film Entertainment Industry* (1988) with not only a ringing appeal for movies worthy of "a society committed to a policy of equal access," but also a forty-nine-page film-ography of bits and sequences that politically centered deaf persons may wish to seek out.

Hollywood's exclusionary posture toward these individuals for whom life "ain't been no crystal stair" and who have responded to this fact with a heightened political consciousness resulted in alternative cinemas only for blacks, Jews, and political extremists (feature films by blacks and Jews and documentaries by political groups). Almost no alternative cinemas for feminists, homosexuals, or persons with physical impairments. It is these alternative cinemas that are the focus of this chapter, rather than Hollywood's sly hints and inadvertent leaks, whereby it, for example, through Katharine Hepburn's androgynous character in *Sylvia Scarlett* (1936) merely "introduced the possibility of homosexual activity into the film for a covert gay audience while providing laughs for the majority," as Russo writes.

In addition to these political subcultures was another taste-culture, one that was driven by an appetite for the erotic and was hellbent on violating convention. Indeed, its tastes serve as a loose definition of pornography, the medium that titillates by violating prevailing norms of taste, behavior, and expression. Catering to its fans' insistence on pressing against the limits of convention, this genre drove them through an endless cycle of first arousal by violation of norms, and then jadedness as violation became norm, and then revival of arousal by the next round of deviance from norms already stretched. These films suggest not so much a common taste that impelled a politics as a politics of alienation symbolized by the lone, joyless men who patronized pornographic movies. The movies warrant our attention not as an alternative sociopolitical cinema on the model of African American race movies or Nykino's politically radical movies, but as an example of a cystlike subculture within the main culture.

An outlaw form of cinema, pornography films have stood outside the protection of the First Amendment, and to their devotees that is part of their allure. Before the existence of the present system of rating movies by letter grade, with X indicating the intent to trade in the porn houses, most porn movies played in private venues, such as a war veterans' post, a political club-house, or a stag party. In its marginal forms – striptease movies, nudist camp frolics, patently fraudulent "educational" films, and anthropological films unerringly focused on brown-skinned breasts – such fare played the side streets of urban rialtos. The west 40s in Manhattan, "the Block" in Baltimore, south State Street in Chicago, and Turk and Eddy in San Francisco were a few of the notorious scenes. Even when censorship began to crumble in the late 1960s, purveyors of pornography preferred their side-street grind houses, perhaps for the anonymity they provided. Since its earliest days it was here that pornography in all its genres – skin flicks, nudies, exploitation movies, and burlesque reels – offered its nips of arcana, curiosa, erotica, and fetishism in perpetual sideshow seediness. Neither the puritans who assailed these movies nor the fans who knelt before them cared whether the movies were beautiful; roués and puritans alike shared an interest only in their excesses.

In *Sinema* (1974), Stephen Zito and Kenneth Turan report that such movies were offered in the penny arcades as early as 1908 and were not driven underground until the age of the Hays office began in the early 1920s. Thereafter, in the grind houses they always promised more than they delivered, a fact that helped stimulate their audiences' obsessive behavior. ... Topping the bill might have been *Jungle Siren* (ca. 1935) starring Ann Corio, a sometime stripper who might have been playing in the flesh across the street at the Gayety, followed by a well-worn print of Armand Denis's *Goona Goona* (1932). Closing the show might have been a burlesque reel with Hinda Wassau removing far less of her clothing than she would have in one of her shows at the Gayety.

Such fare reached all the way to the 1960s and the implementation of the Motion Picture Association of America (MPAA) ratings system. Thereafter, pornographers displayed a movie's X rating as prominently in its ads as if the movie had won an Oscar, and there was actually a movement among pornographers to attain styles, forms, and conventions of the old classical Hollywood style. No longer restricted to back rooms and grind houses, the "blue movies" were shot in color; were plot- and even character-driven; and were structured in classical linear fashion with beginnings, middles, and ends.

The person responsible for bridging the old and the new was Russ Meyer, a former combat photographer who combined a voyeuristic sensibility with a knack for recruiting and casting women with outrageously, almost pneumatically, endowed bodies. He arrived at his formula as early as 1959, with *The Immoral Mr. Teas*. In this movie he linked his voyeur's eye to the threat of censorship by offering a sort of erotica interruptus in which the plot began with a sexually frustrated man, desperate to satisfy his lust, and ended with the urge thwarted. Replicating Meyer's typecasting of the audience, the protagonist was a wool- gathering nebbish who, while on his rounds as a delivery man, mistakenly receives an anesthetic that provides him with the voyeur's nirvana – the power to see through clothing! The result for Meyer: a $1 million return on a $24,000 nut, earned partly because the film broke into the disused downtown palaces (which soon would fill with black kids in search of "blaxploitation" movies) and the flagging art houses that the end of World War II had brought about and partly because it broke into the columns of the daily press. "More female nudity than ever before," said *Variety*. Such movies scratched their clientele's itch (simple to do, really, when one considers that it was entirely innocent of any ethnic, political, or gender loyalty and driven only by anomic obsessions) and became the most persistently successful of alternative movie products.

The other alternative cinemas, those based in political and ethnic taste-cultures, had a more difficult time of it in serving their audiences, who were sectored and poor and made fickle by Hollywood slickness.

The inexperienced alternative moviemakers and their scant budgets made the creation of an alternative aesthetic elusive. Moreover, these moviemakers were often driven by cross-purposed ambitions to be both objective and advocative, authentic and propagandistic, magisterial and engaging.

Turning first to the documentary, until World War II there was no political tradition in this cinema. A couple of leftist groups attempted to change the apolitical stance of the documentary in the 1930s, and the right wing occasionally attempted an ideological movie, but it would take World War II to create a strong political vein of documentary.

At the mercy of corporate sponsors, most documentarists adopted a pose of disinterested objectivity that disqualified them from asserting a politics. By default, they spoke for the status quo. (Even Joris Ivens, a lifelong Dutch leftist, made commercial reels for Philips Radio.) In addition, their urge to document cultures in the rimlands could not help but confirm in their viewers a sense of cultural chauvinism. Whether it was Edison making his early vignettes of black Caribbean life, featuring women bathing babies and men coaling ships; Robert Flaherty making his long-lived classic, *Nanook of the North* (1922); or even the more raffish makers of "adventure yarns," most documentarists edited their subjects into Procrustean beds in order to contrast their savagery with Christendom.

In making *Nanook*, Flaherty trekked north of the Arctic Circle in search of the Inuit he had known as a boy; his sponsor was the furrier Revillon Freres, who expected an image-enhancing film. The mixed motives could not help but lead to bread buttered on both sides, an outcome Flaherty achieved much as the photographers for the Farm Security Administration would do later in recording the responses of American folk to the Great Depression: by dressing, posing, cropping, and otherwise shaping his subjects into images fit for America's gaze. Sometimes Flaherty went so far as to put his Eskimo subjects at risk, rolling film beyond the moment when a prudent walrus hunter would have called "cut" and sectioning igloos in order to shoot their interiors. However, "authenticity of result" was these moviemakers' goal, even though, as Erik Barnouw explains in *Documentary: A History of the Nonfiction Film* (1974), their tools included the "machinery of the fiction film."

Although upon its completion in 1922 *Nanook* was not picked up by Hollywood, its opening at the Capital in New York reaped a "substantial profit" as well as the praise of critics, who found it "in a class by itself." Only then did Hollywood chase Flaherty, if only to do another *Nanook*. The moguls' enthusiasm soured, however, after Paramount sent Flaherty to the South Pacific, where he shot *Moana* (1926), an idyll that lacked the dramatic danger of life inside the Arctic Circle. After having a go at other cultures of the rimlands, in F. W. Murnau's *Tabu* (1931) and Merian C. Cooper and Ernest B. Schoedsack's *Grass* (1925) and *Chang* (1927), Hollywood resumed business as usual, symbolized most patently by Cooper and Schoedsack's reward – the opportunity to make *King Kong* (1933) for RKO.

The only exception to Hollywood's retreat from the genre was the occasional film of an actual anthropological expedition, which, for the sake of heightening interest (at the expense of verisimilitude), would be shamelessly recut until it bore little resemblance to its makers' intentions. It was as if the studios' credo became, as one mogul said, "Let's fill the screen with tits." In the late 1920s, Martin and Osa Johnson roamed Africa, often at great risk, recording its peoples, only to arrive back home and lay in voiceovers dripping with racial humor. Among their imitators, Frank Buck won a following for his "animal pictures," the most famous among them *Darkest Africa*, which played the Century of Progress Exposition in Chicago in 1933. Buck's pseudoscholarly detachment from the "childlike," even "weird," subjects in his staged fragments of African culture encouraged his audiences' sense of cultural superiority. ...

In the 1930s some documentary filmmakers to the left of this mainstream tried to take the documentary beyond fluff. William Alexander begins *Film on the Left* (1981) by conveying the hopes Lenin and Seymour Stern had for the cinema. "The cinema can and must have the greatest significance," said Lenin. "It is a powerful weapon." Stern called for "a working-class cinema" free of capitalists, censors, the merely pink left, and Hollywood. "What a possibility!" he wrote in 1931. "What a vision!"

Though leftist documentarists struggled to gain access to the theaters, they often had to settle for preaching to the converted in union halls and church basements. Typical of those on the left was the Marxist Film and Photo League, which, as part of its cultural activities, one evening might have shown Sergei Eisenstein's *Battleship Potemkin* (1925) or one of its own films, such as *Fighting Workers of New York* (ca. 1932), or a *Worker Newsreel* that covered strikes, "Hoovervilles," and, in 1932, a national hunger march. In *Filmfront*, *The Left*, and other hand-cranked magazines, the left debated the place of film in dispensing "organically" grown ideology. And throughout the 1930s leftists working under the colophon of Frontier Films shot footage that ultimately became *Native Land* (1942), an alarm sounded about the shadowy interests conspiring against workers. As World War II approached, they directed their attention to the rise of fascism in Spain, rational city planning, and social justice.

Through it all, however, leftist cinema suffered not only from lack of access to theaters, but also from the divisiveness of the left. When Pare Lorentz's New Deal film *The Plow That Broke the Plains* was able to break into the theaters in 1936, for example, having been made with the help of a federal agency, it still suffered from the factionalism of the left. Although Lorentz had guarded his script against rewrites by cautious federal agencies, the Film and Photo circles still attacked the bland politics of *The Plow* as a sign of government control. Nonethless, Lorentz had the support of a few members of the Film and Photo League, King Vidor in Hollywood (whose populist *Our Daily Bread* had just appeared in 1934), and various federal agencies, and the movie's lyricism earned it a Broadway opening and bookings in three thousand theaters (bookings that often superseded those of its Hollywood rivals). Lorentz's second offer, *The River* (1937), enjoyed a tenfold increase in nut; was praised by Roosevelt himself; and won Lorentz not only the award for best documentary at the Venice Film Festival, but also the satisfaction of probably having influenced the tone of Ford's *The Grapes of Wrath* (1940).

Whereas the leftists tried to reach a left audience, the right wing aimed more toward the center. It had even less to say and, when it spoke, only muttered under its breath. So only in Hollywood Depression movies were any solutions offered, many of which were simply appeals to a führer. Sometimes they called for a populist rising against cabals who ran everything and championed the rise of authoritarian, even secret, leaders who knew what was good for the nation. In the first half of the 1930s, the repetition of the theme of a populist movement led by a "man on horseback" so closely paralleled the rise of Hitler and Nazism in Germany as to seem prescient. In *The Secret Six*; *Gabriel over the White House*; *The President Vanishes*; and even a musical comedy, *Stand Up and Cheer*, America's social dysfunctions are portrayed as the result of cabalistic villains (standing in for Hitler's Jews), rather than social forces. The apparently invincible heavies drive men to reckon that "there is no time for rules of evidence," the volatile mood leads to a publicly approved vigilantism, and finally a powerful lone figure rises to the presidency. In *Stand Up and Cheer*, a vast chorus rises to sing a rousing double-entendre song, "We're Out of the Red," as a voiceover to a shrewdly handled montage. Like the New Deal, the movie dismayed leftists by using radical means merely to save capitalism from itself.

More overtly ideological films that would have appealed to more rightist audiences rarely emerged from the right wing of Hollywood, if for no other reason than it would have sectored the audience and broken with the duty to earn profits. Here and there an exception emerged. Warner Bros.'s World War I hit, *My Four Years in Germany* (1916), a diplomat's autobiographical warning against Teutonic militarism, reached an alarmed audience. Al Woods's handmade *The Toll of Justice* (1924), a Ku Klux Klan tract, managed to offend almost everyone, including Thomas Dixon, the literary source for *The Birth of a Nation* (1915). No chance of even "a nickel," said *Variety* of this extremist flop. Hollywood's one successful attempt at overt rightist politics was one of Felix Feist's *Metrotone News* films, which Mayer and Thalberg (and others) commissioned to defeat the candidacy of the socialist Upton Sinclair for governor of California. Surprisingly, Sinclair had carried the Democratic primary, and Feist's film, a string of talking heads of Californians, successfully challenged him in the general election by stacking the opinions of clean-cut citizens for the Republican candidate against those of the pro-Sinclair forces, who seemed uniformly to speak for the vagrants and hoboes of the state.

Not until World War II approached did the right wing attempt another movie of political advocacy, and this offering conveyed not so much an explicit rightist ideology as a preparation for war. Throughout the late 1930s, Henry Luce's *The March of Time* series had provided an unrivaled movie magazine that met theaters' need for "shorts." In a strident voice that seemed to speak for a broad American center, the series twitted or viewed with wry irony almost any cultural expression that departed from the sentiments of middle America. The producer of Luce's series, Louis DeRochemont, gradually assumed a degree of control and used it to prod the nation to prepare for war. Indeed, as Raymond Fielding reports in his book *The March of Time*, DeRochemont mounted a feature-length *March of Time* film entitled *The Ramparts We Watch* (1940) in which he warned of impending war. Senator Burton K. Wheeler charged DeRochemont with warmongering, to which the filmmaker replied by branding Wheeler and his clique "intemperate and reckless" in their ignoring of the "tragic fate of millions who have come under the tyranny of the Nazis."

A similar film greeted the throngs at the 1939 world's fair in New York. *Land of Liberty*, a patriotic pageant drawn from historical scenes from a dozen Hollywood features and presented by the Motion Picture Producers and Directors of America, offered only a butler as a black historical presence and described Americans' westward migration as seeking "a new home for the white man." Even a black biography, that of the agronomist George Washington Carver, suggested that the only proper political behavior was individual effort, either as a form of racial self-help or as a form of white "philanthropic efforts on behalf of the Negro." By inspiring individuals to aim toward personal goals, such films tended to endorse things as they were while at the same time paying homage to the oppressed, such as Carver, whose vision of personal achievement consisted solely of self-help. ...

With the onset of World War II, both the left and right experienced a boom in documentary filmmaking, perhaps because, as both James Feibleman in *Theory of Culture* (1946) and Antonio Gramsci presciently argued, war against foreign enemies drew the citizenry together while at the same time the prospects of the oppressed were enhanced by the nation's need for their services. And of course, white America, caught up as it was in a war against Hitler's racism, suddenly found its goals conjoined with those of blacks.

Thus the propaganda celebrated the triumph of "teamwork" over robotic foreign enemies. William Wellman's *Memphis Belle* (1943) and John Ford's *The Battle of Midway* (1943), along with others that drew African Americans into the war, such as Stuart Heisler's *The Negro Soldier* (1945) and Edmund North's *Teamwork* (1945) are a few examples. Certainly the balance tipped toward the patriotic right. Nonetheless, the war brought forth a new agency, the Office of War Information (OWI), that differed from many peacetime agencies in that its lifers, career civil servants, were joined by "social engineers" (as they liked to be called) and liberals of various stripes for whom the war seemed a moment of opportunity. Almost predictably, the OWI and other agencies colored their official work of promoting the national war effort with a drop or so of the liberal change they promised would be an outcome of the war. Typifying the spirit, the New School professor Saul Padover, a wartime recruit in agriculture, proposed a film in which the African American appeared as "an average human being."

In the case of the Pentagon film *The Negro Soldier*, apart from its merely inclusionist goals, the National Association for the Advancement of Colored People (NAACP) viewed it as a prospective postwar voice of liberal advocacy and successfully demanded of the Pentagon that it prepare a version for civilians as well as soldiers. Echoing the NAACP's assertion that wartime propaganda could be used after the war to promote social change was Philleo Nash, an anthropologist in the OWI and a liberal whose work had resulted in an invitation from Lockheed Aircraft to use "wartime experience in the utilization of ... physically handicapped, minor and overage, part-time workers, Negro, and Mexican workers." Optimistically hoping for a sort of peacetime version of the OWI that would carry American attitudes "away from the tolerance and good will aspects of minority group relations toward [solving] ... an industry and community problem," Nash turned down the offer in anticipation of a more active postwar government.

The war was startling in its impact on documentary movies. Not only did it make racism a national issue for the first time since the *Plessy v. Ferguson* (1896) "separate but equal" decision, but it rendered it part of American propaganda. After all, ran the logic, Hitler had given racism a bad name.

The result was the training and political maturing of a generation of filmmakers who advanced documentary from its noncontroversial roots into a postwar alternative cinema of liberal advocacy. *The Negro Soldier* stood out as an instance of the liberal drift toward using movies as propaganda. Originally written by the black radio writer Carlton Moss as *Men of Color to Arms*, the War Department diluted its black nationalism, asked that it be reworked into a call for national unity across racial lines, previewed it before a panel of black journalists, ordered its showing to all training companies, released it rent free to civilian audiences, and at the end of the war gave it away as surplus to any liberal group who asked. Considered "painfully, pitifully mild" by James Agee, the film nonetheless became the NAACP's call for "living together ... now and for the future." In a press release, the Congress of Industrial Organizations (better known as the CIO, the union that later linked with the American Federation of Labor to form the AFL-CIO) stated that because "commercial movies [promote] intolerance through stereotyped characterization ... perhaps the industry can profit" from a look at these government films.

Immediately after the war, advocates of social change through film, such as the American Council on Education, the Educational Film Library Association, the American Film Center, and others, together formed an "audio-visual movement." "The whole AV field was starting up fresh," recalled Emily S. Jones, one of its leaders, "and new people were appearing ... out of service in the armed forces." The studios themselves finished their war contracts with government agencies and released *It Happened in Springfield* (1946), *Don't Be a Sucker* (1946), and other films that turned racist incidents into little liberal victories. No longer dependent on corporate angels, filmmakers raised funds by turning to the NAACP, the United Auto Workers, the American Jewish Council, and other activists on the left. One survey indicated that one exemplary library acquired some two hundred movies that played to a quarter of a million viewers.

Joining this trend, various religious faiths put out their own advocacy films. Jews made a particular impact, because their films were more ecumenical than most and because some of them echoed the race movie movement. Indeed, Jews and blacks alike had first entered the documentary field by making lantern slide shows of Palestine. Two pioneers, Jewish Joseph Seiden and black Reverend Kieffer Jackson, shot their plates on location and then provided voiceovers to scenes of Old Testament parables, much as Catholic producers made continuities from the Stations of the Cross. By 1940, the black actor Spencer Williams and his white angel, Alfred Sack, had built on these frail beginnings to produce two feature-length race movies that caught the spirit of African American religion: *The Blood of Jesus* (1940) and *Go Down Death* (1946).

During their halcyon days, both groups released newsfilm to their clienteles. Seiden's sequences of Jewish life on the Lower East Side played to nostalgic dinner meetings of Jewish businessmen – "the Grand Street Boys," as one such group called itself. Leigh Whipper's Renaissance firm was a contemporary of Seiden's, to be followed by Bert and Jack Goldberg's studio, The Negro Marches On (named for a documentary of black soldiers in World War I); Claude Barnett's extension of his Associated Negro Press, which he called All America News; and, after the war, Liberty Films and an offshoot of Barnett's firm that made television magazine shows for Chesterfield cigarettes. Of this group, only Whipper and Barnett's colleague, William D. Alexander, was black.

This pattern was followed in the production of feature films: Jewish feature films reached some fifty in number, while the black total reached a few hundred. Other ethnic groups made do with a thin stream of imports from Europe. Jewish exhibitors played it both ways, importing a few and making a few more. The most famous of the European imports was Paul Wegener's *The Golem* (1913 and 1920), a sort of positive-thinking Frankenstein tale based on a medieval legend in which Rabbi Loew of the Prague ghetto heads off a pogrom by raising up a golem.

In its way, the golem story spoke for all the alternative cinemas, in that the heroes affirmed or defended the group, the heavies embodied negative traits meant to be scorned, and the plots consisted of each group's following a roadmap to its collectively defined Holy Grail. In addition to the main story, such movies often provided an anatomy of a ghetto social order and celebrated folkishness over assimilationism. ... Meanwhile in Jewish America, Seiden and Edgar G. Ulmer made a few Yiddish movies in disused studios on both banks of the Hudson. Ulmer, who spoke on Yiddish, shared direction with the theatrical actor Jacob Ben Ami in *Green Fields* (1937) and *Yankel dem Schmidt* (1938), for which they roamed New Jersey in search of shtetl-like settings.

What was the difference between Yiddish alternative movies and Hollywood fare? Easy, reports Patricia Erens in *The Jew in American Cinema* (1984): Movies like *The Cantor's Son* (1937) placed high value on the continuation of the Jewish ethos, whereas Hollywood's *The Jazz Singer*, of course, played an angle of assimilationism that echoed *Abie's Irish Rose* and *The Cohens and the Kellys*. "Most specifically, [Yiddish cinema] rejects intermarriage," concludes Erens.

Curiously, the year of epiphany for Yiddish films, and perhaps for all other ethnic cinemas as well, was 1939, which in the eyes of many critics was also Hollywood's pinnacle. For Roger Dooley, 1939 was Hollywood's "fabulous zenith," for Larry Swindell it was "the apogee," and Ted Sennett devoted an entire book to the year. Clearly, these critics spotted a transcendant moment in movie history, but perhaps their sense of Hollywood's having reached a crest also derived from a memory without pain, a nostalgia for the last year before the world plunged into war for the second time in twenty years.

African American race movies were shaped by the same forces that defined Yiddish cinema or, for that matter, any ethnic cinema: a sense of a common past, a setting forth of issues, a lightly sweetened nostalgia, and an anatomy of the group's interior life, all of it meant to cultivate a warm cultural chauvinism. They differed from European movies only in the details of their group's otherness. Along the way, the movies helped mediate between the pull-and-haul of opposing forces of assimilation and ethnic nationalism. On one hand, there were the "other directed" (to use David Riesman's term) African Americans who were bent on "making it" and lived in the cold wind of urban anomie, adrift from the warmth of the group. On the other hand, there were those who clung to language and culture, embraced religion as a conduit of culture, and ached with a nostalgia for community. The former ingested mass culture because it seemed more polished and grasped at mobility and its attractions, whereas the latter clung to folkish culture, rejected mobility, and stayed in the old neighborhood.

Only the black inventory of details seemed different. Their first culture came less from Africa or Europe than from "down South" or merely "down home." Segregation, by limiting interracial cultural contact, diminished the threat of assimilation, but upward mobility seemed an equal threat to cultural cohesiveness, in that the higher the black aspiration, the more likely that black bourgeois culture would intersect with the white, thereby setting apart the black riffraff from the black talented tenth. Moreover, just as the mafia or the tong provided Italians and Chinese with alternative, often criminal, paths to success, black outlaws often intersected with black bourgeois circles, sometimes even serving as their bankers and capital sources. The resulting claustrophobic social structure often thrust black respectables and riffraff into the same ghetto circles, and race movies necessarily struggled with how to handle the heroism of characters who also happened to be outlaws.

Black filmmakers considered how to take this into account while formulating a cinematic alternative to Hollywood. Should they admire indigenous black institutions at the expense of the increasingly sharply defined goal of integration? As a grudgingly liberalizing white America faced the social changes brought about by the Great Depression and war, would race movies behave like the black church or black baseball? Would they remain staunchly black, or would they, as black baseball did, fold up in anticipation of a surge of black athletes into formerly lily-white arenas?

At stake, for example, was black dignity. . . . Mary Carbine and Gregory Waller have reported that blacks often went to theaters in Chicago and

Lexington, Kentucky, respectively, not so much to see a movie as to be in clean and dignified surroundings remote from white rejection and black riffraff. Thus they carried with them to their movies an ideology rooted in both race and class. Paradoxically, class pride induced them to seek dignity within the situation of their rank, while race pride induced them to find movies that stressed black optimism and uplift.

Race movie firms outdid themselves in appealing to one or both of these urges while at the same time playing to differing tastes that had evolved in the black North and the black South. Northern and urban movies often seemed irreverent, jiving, even outlaw in their heroes' style, while southern and rural movies reached out to a folkish, pastoral, pious taste-culture. Each mode also acted as a sort of anatomical drawing of the social system of the other group. Thus a southern rural moviegoer might learn a bit about urban life from the Harvard-trained hero of the Lincoln Company's *The Realization of a Negro's Ambition* (1916), while an urban audience might relive the fervor of old-time religion in Spencer Williams's *The Blood of Jesus* (1940). Either way, race movies challenged Hollywood movies in that they took black aspiration seriously and formulated it into generic melodramas of scaling a black ladder of success, struggling against demons of cupidity within the race (never any off-screen white demons), and reworkings of white genres such as musicals, westerns, and film noir.

The first race movie that caught national black attention, *The Birth of a Race* (1918), grew out of a wish shared by Emmett J. Scott (Washington's secretary at Tuskegee), a committee within the NAACP, and a few whites in Laemmle's Universal studio to offer a rebuttal to Griffith's *Birth of a Nation*. At first financed in part by Julius Rosenwald of Sears Roebuck, a philanthropist of black education, the movie eventually fell victim to a "mammoth swindle" by shady brokers of its stock who scared off Rosenwald and his allies; a string of white directors, each of whom stirred in his own themes; and, finally, the onset of World War I, which resulted in a tacked-on justification of America's entry into it. Drifting every which way from Scott's original idea of the "strivings of the race" told from "the colored man's viewpoint," *The Birth of a Race* pleased no one. *Variety* called it "grotesque" and said it was remote from its original "preachment."

The most famous black pioneers, who are famous mainly for the simple reason that their archives survive (although their films do not), are George and Noble Johnson, whose Lincoln Company defined its ambition as "to picture the Negro as he is in everyday life" and to stand against the stereotype that "the brother is not up to the times in handling such fast business [as moviemaking]." If they failed in any respect, it was in garbling the success myth by failing to take into account off-camera white obstacles to its attainment, an ideological glitch that few black moviemakers were able to overcome. This is not to minimize their ideological rigor, but only to point out the political impediments embedded in an all-black genre in which whites were absolved by their absence of complicity in black plight and in which the race's goals seemed too linked to the sort of lone, laissez-faire hero that Hollywood movies offered.

Partly, they struggled with the black audience itself, which was divided into southern rural and northern urban taste-cultures as well as respectables and riffraff (the "talented tenth" versus "submerged tenth" as Du Bois put it). Moreover, it was tempted by the gloss of Hollywood movies, while wishing for better race movies, and was resistant to "colored theaters" that were too financially strapped to offer amenities. And yet, what else might have the race moviemakers expected? Except for the small group of employed, churched, socially affiliated black bourgeoisie, African Americans simply lacked the discretionary income and leisure for the movies. Moreover, politically, black audiences were of two minds. On the one hand, the Baltimore *Afro-American* praised "sensible producers like [Oscar] Micheaux," a black producer, and called for organized protest against Hollywood fare. On the other, the *California Eagle* praised a black western for its avoidance of politics: "No tragic race issue is involved; no tiresome sermon preached."

Oscar Micheaux most exemplified both the achievement and the plight of race moviemakers. Like the Johnsons, he insisted on a black identity apart from the white world, an identity often defined in his movies by a dramatic conundrum over whether to marry across racial lines. But like the *Eagle*, the Johnsons guessed that "our people do not care for propaganda." Between these two poles stood Micheaux, acutely black but seldom an overt advocate of a specific black cause, instinctively cinematic but too poor to be an artist, and avidly sensational and thus alien to the respectables, who thought him "not elevating" and short on the "high moral aim" of upbuilding the race.

Ambiguity colored Micheaux's entire life and thus his movies, so that the black respectables seemed at once appalled at his raffishness and lifted by his sense of bourgeois aspiration. Micheaux was both the primly correct Pullman porter and the lone wolf homesteader on the Dakota frontier, the suitor of a white fiancee and the husband of a solidly loyal black woman, the vendor of his own books to white midwesterners and a lifelong sojourner in black Harlem and the south side of Chicago. But it was his capacity for survival in the face of a countrywide influenza epidemic; the rise of white rivals; the black imitators who diverted attention from actual black achievers; and eventually the Great Depression, which forced him into bankruptcy, retrenchment, and indebtedness to white angels that marked him as a success. The dichotomies of his life leached into his movies in almost predictable ways. *The Homesteader* (1919) was an autobiography of life on the prairie (and on the border between black life and white life). *Body and Soul* (1925) challenged the hegemony that black preachers often held over their flocks. *Within Our Gates* (1921) assailed lynching by placing a white miscreant at the center of a plot. *Ten Minutes To Live* (1931), *The Girl from Chicago* (1932), and *The Exile* (1931) reworked in soundfilm the nagging theme of urban versus rural life.

These ambiguities that often exercised Micheaux's black moviegoers have, in recent years, caused critics to debate not only the merits of his work, but also the place of race movies in the canon of movies. At issue are such questions as whether race movies were an emergent African American art form or merely a blackface extension of Hollywood style. If they were a black art form, were they marked by specifically "black" shots, cuts, and other devices? If not, what made these movies black? Mere advocacy of uplift? If so, why did Micheaux often eschew uplift in favor of the lowlife? Were his movies "black" merely because they were peopled by Hollywood's "others"? If they were demonstrably black, how come the black press harped on the unfriendly audiences who laughed in the wrong places, catcalled, and, worse, often preferred the sleek Hollywood product? If the denouements were dictated by the group's collective wish for uplift or positive images, were their darkened versions of Hollywood happy endings politically sufficient? Or was the black essentialism of race movies embedded in the very fact of their poverty, their making necessity a virtue, their shameless pride in the benchmarks of one-take flaws? These issues have been raised in tandem with redoubled academic attention to race movies previously regarded as lost, unremarkable, or merely eccentric.

The issue matters to students of race movies partly because with each new rediscovery, these movies have been held up to aesthetic scrutiny against conventional critical canons that have found many in the genre wanting. For example, the Colored Players firm in Philadelphia, which had a white producer–director team, turned out *The Scar of Shame* (1927), a startlingly polished social drama in the mode of the Hollywood problem movie. Some recent critics have debated whether its mise-en-scène and its tragic plot were class or caste based, and others have debated its subtle congruence with American stereotyping of African Americans according to light-skinned virtue and dark-skinned vice. Finally, in the eyes of some critics the movie's obvious cinematic polish has artificially called attention to its flawed race movie rivals. In their view, to claim as an *Amsterdam News* critic did at the time, that the movie attained "a new standard of excellence" or to find, as one recent critic wrote, that it approached Hollywood quality was to miss the point.

The quality of race movies varied more with the coming of sound, as may be seen in, for example, the gulf between Micheaux's naturalistic silents and his stagey soundfilms. Because soundfilms cost more to make, race moviemakers leavened their products with musical vaudeville turns that allowed them to cut down on the expense of dialogue. Nonetheless, these jazzy scenes provided a culturally blacker idiom. Paradoxically, soundfilm technology and its costs also brought greater numbers of more experienced white entrepreneurs into the field, thereby blurring the definition of the race movie.

At the same time, as though anticipating the decline of the race movie, many Hollywood studios spent the Depression years and World War II adding increasingly sophisticated black roles to their product (while slowly giving up their reliance on older forms of stereotyping). It began to play to black audiences in 1929, with *Hallelujah!* and *Hearts in Dixie*; later came *The Green Pastures* (1936), which strove for a black folk idiom played with quiet dignity. Universal's film of Fannie Hurst's *Imitation of Life* (1934) treated the taboo theme of "passing." *So Red the Rose* (1935) and *Slave Ship* (1936) toyed with the theme of slave revolt. And Hattie McDaniel won an Oscar in 1939 for her "Mammy" in *Gone with the Wind*, the movie that David O. Selznick changed from southern lost cause to a national *Iliad*. During World War II, each of the major studios made a combat film in which a black character had been integrated – *Sahara* (1943), *Crashdive* (1943), *Bataan* (1943), and *Lifeboat* (1944). This trend persisted into civilian life in 1949 as a cycle of movies with major black protagonists, including *Pinky, No Way Out* (1950 release), *Intruder in the Dust, Lost Boundaries,* and *Home of the Brave*, each successive movie revealing audiences' increasing desire to see social drama. Parallel to this trend and even anticipating it, the increasingly politicized Paul Robeson appeared in his own cycle of British movies that featured a black hero, among them *Sanders of the River* (1935), *Jericho* (1937), and the overtly socialist *Proud Valley* (1940). Taken together, these movies of the Depression and war eras held out hope to African Americans that a national cinema might make ideological room for a black political aesthetic.

Clearly, the crises provided a moment of racial conscience that opened to the "other" a place in formerly white movies, thereby leaving open the question of the raison d'être of race movies. Increasingly, their former supporters in the black press reflected the anomalous place the movies had assumed. Critics either reckoned them, as the *Amsterdam News* viewed Bill Robinson's *Harlem Is Heaven* (1932), as "positively objectionable" or, as James Asendio did, praised them for conforming to Hollywood standards of "modern story, setting, and costumes." Those who made race movies increasingly touted them, as the Popkins did their *Bargain with Bullets* (1937), as "up to the Loew standard" and so devoid of "race propaganda" as to preclude "trouble" in the South. Indeed, at the height of the 1939–40 boom in race movies, the *Amsterdam News* praised *Mystery in Swing* (1938) and *Double Deal* (1939) as "the best to come out of black Hollywood" and dubbed their director Arthur Dreifuss "the Frank Capra ... of the Colored motion picture industry." So ethnically ecumenical had they become that directors Joseph Seiden and Edgar Ulmer easily crossed over from Yiddish movies to race movies.

Unfortunately, its makers miscalculated in trying to become more like their Hollywood rivals; all this tactic accomplished was to unfairly thrust these movies into direct competition with the glossier Hollywood product. "Why have [race movies] failed to make the instantaneous hit with the public and what must be done," asked critic Dan Burley, to erode the black preference for Hollywood? Why, asked others, did black viewers laugh at scenes intended to be tense? Why support Micheaux's *God's Step Children* (1937) asked the Young Communists of Harlem, when it "creates a false splitting of Negroes into light and dark groups?" And as to standing up to Hollywood's production values, Hubert Julian, the black aviator and occasional movie angel, pleaded with *Amsterdam News* readers, "Don't expect the perfection of a Hollywood picture, but know that we have done our very best." ...

The watershed year during which African Americans signaled an end to their support of race movies and the NAACP mounted an organized effort to affect movies at their Hollywood sources was 1944, in the midst of world war. As early as 1942, Walter White of the NAACP had held his group's convention in Los Angeles in the hope of pledging the moguls to succumb to the rhetoric of the war and amend their portrayals of blacks in movies. Some of them complied and produced parallel cycles of combat films and musicals in which black actors held roles to which they had never before had access. Abetting the NAACP campaign was the OWI. As mentioned earlier, the OWI pressed the Army to make a propaganda film, *The Negro Soldier*, and then prepared a civilian version of it. Horrified at surveys that revealed deep black disaffection, the OWI and the NAACP combined to block the efforts of the makers of race movies to retail their own propaganda films. The coalition denied race movies an allocation of raw film stock, used the courts to stymie efforts to promote race movies, and promoted Hollywood movies as harbingers of the improved racial arrangements that awaited blacks at the end of the war.

The impact on African America's alternative cinema was devastating. The combination of the demands for change asserted by William Nunn's "Double Victory" campaign, the implicit messages in the government's propaganda movies, and the strictures imposed by shortages of film guaranteed that race movies would engage in a struggle they could not win. Unavoidably, they faced the same fate the Negro National Baseball League faced after Jackie Robinson signed on with the white Brooklyn Dodgers: both Hollywood and major league baseball, by holding out a promise of black integration into a classier product than blacks could provide for themselves, ensured that the black audience would desert in favor of an integrated future. Not all black institutions faced such ruin; primary groups into which blacks were born rather than bought tickets to – such as the African American church – became instruments of future change, rather than its victims.

In this sense, the NAACP and OWI's collaborative wartime achievement anticipated the postwar era of Hollywood's message movie cycle, in which the studios made movies directly influenced by propagandists who believed, along with many social engineers, that prejudice could be irradiated by the light of reason and knowledge. Thus this peacetime outcome of the war's propaganda of liberalism helped create a taste-culture that drew its sense of advocacy from formerely stodgy Hollywood. This is not to argue that Hollywood was innocent of the charge leveled by the Frankfurt school of social critics that it acted as a form of state apparatus that spoke as the voice of the ruling class. Rather, in classic Gramscian fashion, World War II had provided the critical occasion when the social goals of the left and right, particularly with respect to race relations, briefly intersected, giving class and race antagonists an opportunity to bargain for change. The resulting postwar "thinking picture" was far more self-congratulatory than substantive, but nonetheless it provided a basis for hope that drew African America away from race movies.

Moreover, the war had matured documentary film from its infancy stage as sterile educational film into yet another voice of activism that eventually spoke to the television age. Indeed, the documentary became the voice and "the chosen instrument of the civil rights movement," according to the broadcaster William Monroe. Thereafter, despite a narrowing of the range of racial alternative cinema, documentary film found its voice as an advocate of, if not racial radicalism, at least a "liberalism of the heart."

Immediately after the war, educational institutions and other users of documentaries laid claim to the government's surplus documentaries that had taught Americans, as Frank Capra's War Department series put it, "Why We Fight." In the ensuing months, other signs of the birth of a documentary of persuasion appeared. In 1947, a British "docudrama" (to use a later coinage) entitled *Day Break at Udi*, an account of health agencies' assault on the tsetse fly in Nigeria, won an Oscar, while in the same year *To Secure These Rights*, the report of Harry Truman's Civil Rights Commission, was made into an animated film that provided a lexicon for teaching racial liberalism. In a typical press release, the CIO urged its members to see *The Negro Soldier* as a weapon in "the battle against bias" and a call for "a better world for all the people."

Soon the American Jewish Committee, the International Ladies Garment Workers Union, the NAACP, and other advocates of leftist causes joined up as angels for documentaries. The American Film Center, the National Film Cooperative, the Educational Film Library Association, and commercial distributors such as Thomas Brandon ensured easy access to these films, which were not likely to reach mainstream theatrical screens.

Parallel to this movement, yet another alternative cinema emerged. This cinema consisted of foreign films made in a "neorealist" or documentary "style," and it immediately found an audience in so-called art houses, the small theaters, often independent from the major chains, that were locally owned by exhibitors intent on creating an ambience of understated amenities. These movies brought a new social dimension to American commercial movies. When Roberto Rossellini's *Open City* came to America in 1946, it took off at the box office, leading to a cycle of domestically produced, grainy, realistic movies such as Jules Dassin's *The Naked City* (1948).

Some of the imports, notably *Paisan* (1946), *Senza Pieta* (1948), and *Vivere In Pace* (1946), wove in black characters of such uncommon humanity that *Ebony* and other glossy black magazines allocated them equally uncommon coverage. As was typical of Marxist movies, in *Paisan* the black hero, a soldier made cynical by the thieving children of the streets of Livorno, comes to see in the poverty of the Italian proletariat a parallel with his own. The success of such gently political movies soon created a similar American genre in such movies as Helen Levitt and Janice Loeb's *The Quiet One* (1947), with their blend of fiction and location-shot documentary. Each new decade brought with it another *Nanook*, not of the North but of Harlem: Shirley Clark's *The Cool World* (1964), Gene Persson and Anthony Harvey's version of Amiri Baraka's *Dutchman* (1967), and Michael Roemer's *Nothing But a Man* (1964), each one a gem that diverted black moviegoers from any notion of a need for an essentially black cinema. Their sheer quality as well as box office take seemed to announce that black material had arrived and therefore the issue of an alternative cinema was moot.

Documents

Introduction to Documents

George Johnson, Noble Johnson, and Oscar Micheaux pioneered independent African-American filmmaking in the United States. Micheaux, the most prolific of the three, produced his first "race film," *The Homesteader* in 1918, and his last, *The Notorious Elinor*, in 1949. The first document discusses Micheaux motivations for making movies, while the second document offers a brief review of his film *The Symbol of the Unconquered*. In the third document, John Winge discusses how leftist filmmakers of the 1930s made documentaries aimed at renewing the spirit of democracy and activism among the great mass of citizens.

The Negro and the Photo-Play

Oscar Micheaux

Source: *The Half-Century Magazine*, May 6, 1919

"How can I break into the movies?" is the question I am asked daily which is no surprise, for it is the question every producer is asked and has been asked for years. Of all the things appealing to the vanity in people, no doubt the photo-play is the center of most. I do not consider it worth while to dwell upon this question of "how can I break into the movies," but will deal more largely with a more essential point.

"How is the Negro to break into the movies?" will, I am sure, concern the race more directly. Of one thing I can say now without fear or favor, the Negro will break into the movies, in the way he wishes to see himself portrayed when members of the race open the way, and only through race people. To illustrate this point, I had occasion, following one effort on the part of certain race men to prevent the showing of "The Homesteader" before the Chicago Board of Censors, on account, they claimed, I had chosen to portray one of their ministers in a hypocritical role, to appear before the State of Kansas Board of Censors, whom, after viewing the play, making only one cut out, I was confronted with a statement from the head lady member to the effect that she had prepared a Scenario concerning Colored people that she would like to have me consider with a view to producing the same. She then gave me a synopsis of it, ending with the statement, "And you cannot imagine what a perfectly lovely and original title I have given it!" I admitted that I couldn't. "A Good Old Darkey," she replied, sweetly, and looked kindly up into my face for approval.

Now the point is here clearly illustrated. As in the case of this kindly disposed northern woman, it seems the white race will never come to look upon us in a serious light, which perhaps explains why we are always caricatured in almost all the photo-plays we have even the smallest and most insignificant part in. Always the "good old darkey," our present environments and desires seem under a cover to them, and as the time is here when the black man is rightfully tired of being looked upon only as a "good darkey," my statement that the race will only be brought seriously into the silent drama when men of the race, through whose veins course the blood of sympathy and understanding of our peculiar position in our Great American Society puts him in. So, on the whole, it is of this question I feel it more timely to write.

The first thing to be considered in the production of a photo-play is the story. Unfortunately, in so far as the race efforts along this line have been concerned, this appears to have been regarded as a negligible part. I personally know that a large share of the few plays featuring Negroes and produced by Colored people, have been made without a scenario. ...

It is a common thing to see a poster advertising an interesting photo-play where the same has been "adapted" from a novel of the same name, or at the worst, a magazine story. In view, therefore, of the fact that the race has written only a small number of novels as well as magazine stories, among many things, this will help explain the fewness of Negro photo-plays. ...

What I want to emphasize is, the Negro nor any other race can ever be thoroughly appreciated until he appears in plays that deal in some way with Negro life as lived by Negroes in that age or period, or day. The fact that we can with a degree of success portray all the leads in the great plays that we are and have been in, the public will never accept us fully until the play is written to fit the people who appear and their particular condition, for every play has in some way a moral or an immoral.

So I have contended that I will never produce a photo-play in which to star Colored people until I have a story of the same time, for, as I see it, if we are able to act a thing in all completeness and detail, we should at the same time be able to write the play.

So getting back to the subject, before we expect to see ourselves featured on the silver screen as we live, hope, act and think today, men and women must write original stories of Negro life, and as the cost of producing high class photo-plays is high, money must be risked in Negro corporations for this purpose – some, many will perhaps fail before they have got to going right, but from their ashes will spring other and better men, some of whom in time will master the art in completeness, and detail and when so, we will have plays in which our young men and women will appear to our credit, as finished silent drama artists.

"The Symbol of the Unconquered," New Play

Source: *The Competitor*, 3, January–February 1921

"Moving pictures have become one of the greatest vitalizing forces in race adjustment, and we are just beginning." Thus spoke Oscar Micheaux, the leading and most successful producer of the race for the Associated Negro Press. Mr. Micheaux spent a few days in Chicago at the western opening of his latest and most pretentious picture, "The Symbol of the Unconquered."

This production demonstrates beyond question what the producer meant in his statement, and proves that there has been an arrival not only in the producing field, but in the wide and necessary field of sentiment making, and a better understanding between the races.

The story of the picture is a stirring tale of love and adventure in the great and unsheltered and open northwest, but through it all are impressive lessons on the folly of color, both within and without the race.

"There is one thing aside from the story interesting, that is I strive to demonstrate in all my pictures," said Mr. Micheaux, "and that is, it makes no difference what may be a person's color, or from where a person comes, if the heart is right, that's what counts, and success is sure."

"The Symbol of the Unconquered" takes a significant thrust at the "more than 500,000" people in America who, with American blood in their veins, are "passing for white."

One of the most thrilling and realistic scenes is that of the Ku-Klux Klaners, who ride forth "on the stroke of twelve," to pursue their orgy of destruction and terror. Coming at this time when there is an attempt to revive this post-civil war force of ignominy and barbarism, denounced by the leading people of both races, in speech and editorials, North and South, the effect of disgust and determination are heightened.

Mr. Micheaux announces that his productions are now being shown in all of the leading countries of Europe, including England, France, Italy, Spain, and in Africa and the leading South American Republics. Arrangements have practically been concluded to make at least one production a month, in which scores of the leading performers of the country are to be used.

Some New American Documentaries: In Defense of Liberty

John H. Winge

Source: *Sight and Sound*, Spring 1939

"Democracy depends upon the easy and prompt dissemination of ideas and opinions. The motion picture is potentially one of the greatest weapons for the safeguarding of democracy. But if it is hobbled and haltered – if it cannot speak truthfully and freely where great issues are involved – then it can be a weapon turned against democracy. Democracies, unwisely fearing the power of the medium, have not allowed it to speak for democratic principles, whereas the totalitarian States have used it to the nth degree to spread their doctrines. What we who believe in our democracy would like to do is to make films that would counteract these totalitarian ideologies, and make ours more effective by using the truth that is on our side. I do not call this propaganda. I call this a necessary patriotic service." ...

As you have already guessed – it was indeed an American who spoke these remarkable sentences. But not a temperamental after-dinner-speaker, who likes to indulge in commonplaces, no outsider who puts his nose in another's business, but a very well known and successful producer, acknowledged even by Hollywood: Walter F. Wanger. ...

As you know, Hollywood is the capital of the picture business, but even in the United States itself there are other places where movies are made. I mean the modest city of New York, where the studios on Long Island are used every day in what may be called a boom. Because some democratically minded people living in New York City had the idea of using the film to put over democratic propaganda.

The Mexican government, filled with enthusiasm by the gorgeous stills taken by Mr. Paul Strand of New York in 1935, ordered him to produce a film dealing with the strike of the much exploited Mexican fishermen.

The picture was *The Wave,* a much discussed, beautifully photographed documentary, in which the fishermen themselves were featured.

Even at that time there was a small group of young aspirants around Mr. Strand, from the Film and Photo League, all amateurs, and all particularly interested in the problem of making better and truer films.

First they discussed films only aesthetically, but during the election of 1936 they discovered that the great excitement of the country about the problems surrounding Franklin Delano Roosevelt was to be seen everywhere except in the charming dreams from the Hollywood factories. Thus they were awakened to reality. They realized in 1936 the necessity to use the films as an instrument for democracy and progress. And now Strand and Leo Hurwitz had the opportunity to do the photography of *The Plow That Broke the Plains,* first progressive documentary film produced by the American government.

The small group around Mr. Strand, consisting of young writers, photographers, and even poets, used its leisure time for making its first picture, *The World Today.* The rather pathetic title, apparently inspired by *The March of Time,* headed a picture of two reels, the first about the evictions of Sunnyside. Half a year before there had been a lot of trouble with evictions of residents of a New York settlement called Sunnyside, and this rather sensational affair was remade by the group. Most of the parts were played by the real heroes of the affair, the inhabitants of the settlement.

Afterwards they hired little-known actors and made a second short (with the eviction-story as a story, *Black Legion*) and previewed it together with *The Wave* and *World Today* before an audience of artists and people interested in progressive films. It was a tremendous success and they dared then to invite the visitors to help so that they could found a special group to produce progressive films. The exalted visitors understood and in 1937 Strand's group founded Frontier Films. ...

Eager to make pictures about the reality of American life, their first picture was, paradoxically, *Heart of Spain.* The former editor of New Theatre, Mr. Herbert Kline, and Mr. Geza Karpathi had returned from Spain with lots of interesting picture material for the North American Committee to Aid Spanish Democracy. Creating a new scenario and adding to this material the best newsreel clips on the Spanish War, Paul Strand and Leo Hurwitz edited this footage into a moving documentary film. Thus they produced *Heart of Spain* with a commentary written by David Wolff and Herbert Kline, and for seven weeks the audience of the Playhouse on New York City's 55th Street enjoyed the close-ups of transfusions of blood to badly wounded Spanish warriors.

Heart of Spain was already running in numerous cinemas, in clubs and trade unions on 16 mm films, when in 1938 the new film company handled the material Harry Dunham had brought home from China, mostly photographs taken in districts never seen before by white men. Mr. Dunham was sponsored by interested Chinese and American people and so Frontier Films was able to edit a very topical picture, *China Strikes Back*, an even bigger success than the Spanish beginning. Forty-five theaters in New York City played it and the audience devoured the heavy stuff which did not pretend to be a fairystory despite the fact that the commentary was sometimes a genuine poem by Mr. Wolff.

Now partly aided by a regular distributing company, Garrison Films, in 1938 Frontier Films was able to make the first real American picture, *People of the Cumberland*, which started as a bitter document of the miserable life of the people in that section of the country and became a rather sweet one of the favorable influence of the newly founded Highlander Folk School. You could see for the first time in a picture the folkdances of the Cumberland, truly American scenes, encouraged and managed by the very active school. This interesting and often remarkable film had the advantage of a commentary by the famous writer Erskine Caldwell, author of "Tobacco Road."

After this vivid picture the company returned to the business of editing. A French director Henri Cartier[-Bresson], having brought material from fighting Spain, Frontier Films was again ordered by the Committee to Aid Spain to produce the English version and commentary of *Return to Life*. Favored by the reception of *Heart of Spain*, the new Spanish picture also got enthusiastic approbation from the United States, nearly as much as *People of the Cumberland*, which succeeded especially because of its realistic theme. ...

But more interesting is the newest picture about certain strange incidents gathered in documents by the famous Civil Liberties Committee, which is headed by Robert La Follette, Jr., and Elbert D. Thomas. This first feature of seven or eight reels, made by Frontier Films, will deal with some notorious violations of civil liberties in the United States of America which happened recently and were recorded by the Committee. Both La Follette and Thomas helped the young people of Frontier Films to gather materials and the original heroes of the events. But, of course, the "villains" would not like to repeat their crimes before a camera, therefore only the heroes are the same as in the real events and the less reputable parts are taken by actors. The background remains realistic. In contrast to customary Hollywood usage, the foreword will read, "Everything herein is related to real people and real events."

The picture is nearly completed. To finish it they need only means and it is the old tragedy of people with common sense being hardly able to raise money. What Frontier Films has done on this picture so far presages an unusual, daring, and courageous film.

Readings and Screenings

There is a substantial literature on race films and the rise of an independent African-American cinema. The most useful books include Thomas Cripps, *Slow Fade to Black: The Negro in American Film, 1900–1942* (New York: Oxford University Press, 1977); Thomas Cripps, *Making Movies Black: The Hollywood Message Movie from World War II to the Civil Rights Era* (New York: Oxford University Press, 1993); Donald Bogle, *Bright Boulevards, Bold Dreams: The Story of Black Hollywood* (New York: Ballantine Books, 2005); Patrick McGilligan, *Oscar Micheaux: The Great and Only: The Life of America's First Black Filmmaker* (New York: HarperCollins, 2007); Pearl Bowser and Louise Spence, *Writing Himself into History: Oscar Micheaux, His Silent Films, and His Audiences* (New Brunswick, Canada: Rutgers University Press, 2000); Jane Gaines, *Fire and Desire: Mixed-Race Movies in the Silent Era* (Chicago, IL: University of Chicago Press, 2001); Judith Weisenfeld, *Hollywood By Thy Name: African-American Religion in American Film, 1929–1949* (Berkeley and Los Angeles, CA: University of California Press, 2007). Yiddish filmmaking is discussed in J. Hoberman, *Bridge of Light: Yiddish Film Between Two Worlds* (New York: Museum of Modern Art and Schocken Books, 1991). For a general look at race and ethnicity in American cinema, see Lester D. Friedman, ed., *Unspeakable Images: Ethnicity and the American Cinema* (Urbana and Chicago, IL: University of Illinois Press, 1991). Depictions of homosexuality are discussed in Vito Russo, *The Celluloid Closet: Homosexuality in Movies* (New York: Harper and Row, 1981); William J. Mann, *Behind the Screen: How Gays and Lesbians Shaped Hollywood, 1910–1969* (New York: Viking, 2001); Patricia White, *Uninvited: Classical Hollywood Cinema and Lesbian Representability* (Bloomington, IN: Indiana University Press, 1999). Documentary film-making during the 1930s and 1940s is explored in William Stott, *Documentary Expression and Thirties America* (New York: Oxford University Press, 1973); William Alexander, *Film on the Left: American Documentary From 1931 to 1942* (Princeton, NJ: Princeton University Press, 1981); Robert L. Snyder, *Pare Lorentz and the Documentary Film* (Reno, NV: University of Nevada Press, 1967). For an excellent examination of gov-ernment filmmaking during World War II, see Clayton Koppes and Gregory Black, *Hollywood Goes to War: How Politics, Profits and Propaganda Shaped World War II Movies* (New York: Free Press, 1987); Allan M. Winkler, *The Politics of Propaganda: The Office of War Information, 1942–1945* (New Haven, CN: Yale University Press, 1978). For a look at exploitation films, see Eric Schaefer, *Bold! Daring! Shocking! True!: A History of Exploitation Films, 1919–1959* (Durham, NC: Duke University Press, 1999).

Midnight Ramble: Oscar Micheaux and the Story of Race Movies (1994) is a fascinating documentary that looks at the history of race films from the silent era through the 1940s. Micheaux's films are occasionally shown on public television and Turner Classic Movies. Several of his productions are available on DVD: *Symbol of the Unconquered* (1920); *Within Our Gates* (1920); and *Body and Soul* (1925). *Reefer Madness* (1936) is one of the best known early exploitation films and a hit with students. Pare Lorentz's documentaries, *The Plow that Broke the Plains* (1936) and *The River* (1937), can be found along with several documentaries in the DVD collection titled, *Our Daily Bread and Other Films of the Great Depression*. For a documentary and docudrama, respectively, produced by radical filmmakers, see *People of the Cumberland* (1938) and *Native Land* (1942). The government's *Why We Fight* series offers an interesting look into the uses of film as wartime propaganda. Those interested in screening Yiddish films can purchase DVDs from the National Center for Jewish Film in Waltham, Massachusetts.

7

Seeing Red:
Cold War Hollywood

Introduction to Article

Movies have played a vital role in shaping the ways in which Americans think about Communists, socialists, leftists, and the desirability of radical change. The Cold War did not start in the late 1940s, as most Americans generally believe, but began in the days following the Russian Revolution of October 1917. For the next eighty years, Hollywood filmmakers rarely presented any serious analysis of the causes that led people to engage in radical activities. Instead, they depicted radicals and political activists as generic "Red" agitators responsible for all that is wrong in American society – especially during times of economic and political unrest.

John Belton traces Hollywood's depiction of Reds from 1919 until the breakup of the Soviet Union and seeming end of the Cold War in 1991. In order to understand why anti-Red images assumed the form they did, Belton goes beyond the screen and analyzes the pressures placed on Hollywood studios by censors and government agencies to avoid any taint of radicalism either in their films or among their employees. These pressures were especially pronounced during the Red Scare and House Un-American Activities Committee (HUAC) hearings of the late 1940s and early 1950s. Individuals who resisted government demands were blacklisted from the industry. Belton also shows how fears of Red invaders made their way into westerns, science-fiction films, and even biblical epics of the 1950s and reappeared again in militarist films of the 1980s.

Movies and American Society, Second Edition. Edited by Steven J. Ross.
© 2014 John Wiley & Sons, Inc. Published 2014 by John Wiley & Sons, Inc.

Discussion Points

How does Hollywood teach us to think about radicalism and the desirability of radical change? What images of Communists and radicals do you remember seeing in films? Should filmmakers with political views to the far left or far right be allowed to make movies for mass audiences?

Hollywood and the Cold War

John Belton

Source: John Belton, *American Cinema/American Culture* (New York: McGraw-Hill, Inc., 1994), 233–54

Origins: Communism, Hollywood, and the American Way

Revolution and repercussion

Unofficially, the Cold War began in 1917, when the Communist Bolsheviks came to power in Russia, after unseating the more moderate Mensheviks who ran the country after the overthrow of the Czar. The Cold War officially ended more than 70 years later, in 1991, when the Soviet Union began to unravel. America responded to the Russian Revolution with a "red scare," which was triggered in 1919 by labor unrest, strikes, and the growing unionization of the work force. Even the Boston police force formed a union and went on strike, leaving the city defenseless and forcing officials to call out the state guard. The official responsible for breaking this strike, state governor Calvin Coolidge, parlayed his antiunion stance into a probusiness platform, which later won him a nomination for Vice-President in 1920. When President Warren Harding died in 1923, Coolidge found himself President.

In 1919, anarchists, Bolsheviks, and other radical groups were suspected of sending a series of bombs through the mails to prominent political leaders and industrialists, terrorizing government officials and capitalists. In 1920, five socialists were elected to the New York State Assembly, then expelled by that body because, as socialists, they were members of "a disloyal organization composed exclusively of perpetual traitors." To many, it seemed as if the forces of revolution had spread beyond the borders of Russia and the Communist goal of worldwide revolution was threatening the United States as well. Blaming the postwar strikes by steel workers and coal miners on "the red menace," the US Attorney General ordered that all Communists be rounded up and deported. Over 6,000 men were arrested and over 500 were deported as undesirable aliens.

At the same time, Hollywood produced a number of anti-Communist films, including *Bolshevism on Trial* (1919), which was based on a novel by Thomas Dixon, the author of D. W. Griffith's *The Birth of a Nation* (1915). Playing upon popular fears of worldwide revolution, publicity for the film asks, "Shall [Bolshevism] travel to America, gathering in its net Western peoples and Democratic organizations?" *The Right to Happiness* (ca. 1919) seeks from its viewers the answer to a similar question: "Which would you rather have in this country – destruction under the Red flag or construction and co-operation under the American Flag?" Griffith's *Orphans of the Storm* (1922), which ostensibly dealt with the French Revolution, warns its audiences in an opening intertitle of the dangers of "Anarchy and Bolshevism," suggesting that the film be seen as a lesson in history. "The lesson: the French Revolution RIGHTLY overthrew a BAD government. But we in America should be careful lest we with a GOOD government mistake fanatics for leaders and exchange our decent law and order for Anarchy and Bolshevism." ...

Fear of potential "reds" spread to the motion picture industry. In 1922, the FBI opened a file on Charles Chaplin, after he had entertained a leader of the American Communist Party in his home. They continued to document his supposedly "subversive" activities and associations until 1952, when Chaplin left the United States and his reentry permit was revoked by the State Department.

The threat of worldwide revolution in the wake of the 1917 Russian Revolution began to seem a bit less likely when postwar leftist movements in Germany, Hungary, and other European countries failed to succeed in establishing Communist or socialist governments. As a result, concern about domestic radicals gradually subsided in the United States. At the same time, the prosperity of the American economy in the 1920s appeared to undermine Communist critiques of capitalism – that is, until the stock market crash in 1929.

In the red: The Depression era

Hollywood has never attempted to glamorize bankers, industrialists, and stock speculators. After the crash, these capitalist figures tend to be regularly identified with the fiscal mismanagement that had brought about the Great Depression, but their villainy is more often seen in terms of individual greed than of class oppression. Decades later, during the Communist witch-hunts of the late 1940s and early 1950s, right-wing novelist Ayn Rand, author of *The Fountainhead*, would read these characterizations of the business community as Communist-inspired. In her booklet *Screen Guide for Americans*, Rand warns Hollywood filmmakers "Don't Smear Industrialists," "Don't Smear the Free Enterprise System," and "Don't Smear Success." Rand also advises screen-writers, "Don't give your character – as a sign of villainy, as a damning characteristic – the desire to make money."

But the depiction of capitalists in 1930s Hollywood films, ranging from Charles Chaplin's *City Lights* (1931) to Frank Capra's *You Can't Take It With You* (1938), is inspired more by the reactionary spirit of populism, which seeks reform, than by the radical spirit of communism, which preaches revolution. In other words, the "system" works, though it often needs watching. Indeed, for every "bad" capitalist or millionaire, these movies suggest that there is a "good" capitalist, who might make things right.

However, the films that depict Communists continued to portray them negatively. In Depression-era comedies, Bolsheviks not only behave like deranged lunatics but – even worse – they have no sense of humor, style, or wit. Thus the Bolshevik in Ernst Lubitsch's *Trouble in Paradise* (1932) denounces the heroine (Kay Francis), a wealthy cosmetics manufacturer, and lectures to her that "any women who spends a fortune in times like these for a handbag – phooey, phooey, phooey!" In topical melodramas, such as *Heroes for Sale* (1933) and *Little Man, What Now* (1934), Communists are exposed as essentially selfish phonies who are unconcerned with the genuine poverty and hardship of others. ...

Anti-Fascists, populists, and "dupes"

During the Spanish Civil War, Hollywood's anti-communism was tempered somewhat by its anti-fascism. The specter of yet another Fascist dictatorship in Spain, supported by those already in place in Hitler's Germany and Mussolini's Italy, prompted many liberals to support the Communist-backed Loyalists in their fight against Generalissimo Francisco Franco's Fascists. Screenwriter Dorothy Parker and playwright Lillian Hellman organized a group of Loyalist supporters in

Hollywood into the Motion Picture Artists Committee to Aid Republican Spain. Members included writers Dashiell Hammett, Dudley Nichols, and Julius and Philip Epstein; directors John Ford and Lewis Milestone; and actors Louise Rainer, Melvyn Douglas, Fredric March, Paul Muni, John Garfield, and others. ...

Producer Walter Wanger, together with screenwriter John Howard Lawson, made a film about the Spanish Civil War, *Blockade* (1938), which was released by United Artists. However, pressure from the Hays Office and the Roosevelt administration, which were nervous about taking sides in the conflict, undermined the project, which had been designed as a warning about the dangers of the spread of fascism in Europe. As a result, the film becomes a simple love story about an idealistic farmer (Henry Fonda), whose political affiliation is never stated, and a beautiful spy (Madeleine Carroll), who works for "the other side." The Loyalists and the Fascists were never identified by name and viewers had difficulty knowing whether Fonda was a Loyalist or merely a humble advocate for the universal rights of man. ...

Populist films that exposed the predicament of the working class took pains to make it clear that the support of labor was not to be confused with Communist propaganda. Ford's adaptation of John Steinbeck's *The Grapes of Wrath* (1940) explores the ways in which migrant farm workers were exploited, but it carefully distances itself from anything that might be considered un-American. Thus Tom Joad (Henry Fonda), though "radicalized" by his experiences at the hands of farm owners and their company police, remains ignorant of the larger political debates that surround the plight of labor in the film. Someone mentions to him that "reds" are suspected of causing trouble by organizing the workers, and he responds by asking, "Who are these 'reds' anyway?"

By the late 1930s, the government had begun to take greater and greater interest in Hollywood's anti-fascism, which was considered to be Communist-inspired. In 1938, Representative Martin Dies, the first chair of the House Un-American Activities Committee (HUAC), declared that those members of the industry who had joined the Hollywood Anti-Nazi League (whose list of sponsors included moguls Carl Laemmle, Jack Warner, and Dore Schary) were "Communist dupes." In 1940, Dies opened hearings to investigate the presence of Communists in Hollywood, naming actors Fredric March, Humphrey Bogart, and James Cagney, and screenwriter Philip Dunne as suspected "reds." All four successfully cleared themselves in testimony given to the Dies Committee, but a precedent had been set. Witch-hunters such as

Dies discovered that they could generate enormous publicity by using Hollywood as the target of their investigations.

World War II and government policy

During World War II, the government put a hold on its inquiries into communism in Hollywood. Industry personnel had been suspected of being Communists largely because of their participation in anti-Fascist causes and organizations. With American entry into the war, anti-fascism suddenly became national policy, and, with the exception of a brief period during which the Soviet Union and Germany had signed and observed a non-aggression pact (1939–41), Russia was an ally in America's fight against Germany, Italy, and Japan. For the time being, HUAC kept a low profile.

However, right-wing elements within the Hollywood community continued the anti-Communist campaign which the Dies Committee had begun. In February 1944, they organized themselves into the Motion Picture Alliance for the Preservation of American Ideals, which dedicated itself to purging the industry of "Communists, radicals, and crackpots." Members of the Alliance included director Sam Wood, producer Walt Disney, actors Robert Taylor, Barbara Stanwyck, Adolphe Menjou, Gary Cooper, Clark Gable, John Wayne, and Ward Bond, writers Ayn Rand and Borden Chase, labor representative Roy Brewer of IATSE (the International Alliance of Theatrical Stage Employees), and Lela Rogers, the mother of actress Ginger Rogers.

During the war, the Alliance issued statements calling upon patriotic elements within the film industry to combat "totalitarian-minded groups working within the industry for the dissemination of un-American ideas and beliefs." In response, Dies and his committee returned to Hollywood to investigate the Alliance's charges. In 1945, HUAC, which had originally been a temporary committee, was made permanent, partially in response to the publicity it and the Alliance generated investigating radicals in Hollywood.

During the war, Hollywood produced a number of films designed to give support to American allies. Thus, in addition to celebrating England in *Mrs. Miniver* (1942) and *The White Cliffs of Dover* (1944), the major studios produced several pro-Soviet films, including *Song of Russia* (1943) and *Mission to Moscow* (1943). These works were commissioned, in part, by the US government, which sought to familiarize Americans with the plight of our allies. But these productions would come back to haunt Hollywood in the postwar years, when any support of the Soviet Union was deemed traitorous.

Inquisition: HUAC, McCarthy, and the Hollywood Ten

Friends and foes

Immediately after the war, the long-time tensions that had existed between the United States and the Soviet Union were renewed. In March 1946, former British Prime Minister Winston Churchill gave voice to the concerns of the West in response to the threat of Soviet postwar expansion. After observing the fate of Eastern Europe after its "liberation" by Russia, Churchill declared that "from Stettin in the Baltic to Trieste in the Adriatic, an Iron Curtain has descended across the continent." Churchill identified the spread of communism with the imprisonment of innocent nations behind an "Iron Curtain." Churchill's phrase succinctly conveyed the fears of the West that it was also in danger of being swallowed up behind the ever-expanding walls of totalitarian oppression. At the same time, communism began to play a greater and greater role in the postwar political landscape of the Far East, especially in North Korea, China, and Indochina.

In the United States, business feared that labor unions would be "taken over" by Communists in a somewhat similar way. In 1945, the Conference of Studio Unions (CSU) (those unions not represented by IATSE) began a strike against the studios which lasted for over eight months. Warner Bros. relied on scabs, fire hoses, tear gas, and other violent means to disperse union pickets and break the strike. During the fall of 1946, another industrywide strike by the CSU resulted in charges, from opponents of the strike, that the unions represented by the CSU had become infiltrated by Communists.

Meanwhile, a nationwide strike by coal miners, which began in April 1946, was followed by a national strike of railway workers in May. These strikes were resolved only after President Harry Truman threatened to draft striking workers into the Armed Forces.

The elections of 1946 witnessed a number of races in which Republican candidates accused the Democratic opponents and the Democratic New Deal administration of Communist sympathies. Both Richard Nixon and Joseph McCarthy relied upon red-baiting to gain their seats in Congress. In 1947, President Truman, in an attempt to demonstrate his administration's own anti-Communist bias, officially declared a "Cold War" against the Soviet Union which was designed to contain the spread of communism abroad. Funds were allocated to assist anti-Communist forces in Greece and Turkey in their struggle against "armed minorities" within their own countries. At the same time, Truman initiated a series of domestic loyalty probes to root out Communist infiltration of government and labor in the United States. As a result of Truman's loyalty review program, between March 1947 and December 1952, over 6.6 million people were investigated and over 500 were dismissed because their loyalty was deemed to be in question.

"Are you now or have you ever been ... ?"

It was in this atmosphere of governmental distrust and suspicion that the House Un-American Activities Committee renewed its investigation of subversives within the film industry. Preliminary, closed-door hearings were held in May 1947 by new Committee Chair J. Parnell Thomas. After hearing testimony from members of the Motion Picture Alliance for the Preservation of American Ideals and others, Thomas announced that Hollywood filmmakers "have employed subtle techniques in pictures in glorifying the Communist system and degrading our own system of Government and Institutions." Later that year, in October, Thomas conducted public hearings in Washington DC, during which his committee interviewed 24 "friendly" and 11 "unfriendly" witnesses (18 had been called but only 11 testified). The friendly witnesses, including actors Robert Taylor, Robert Montgomery, Adolphe Menjou, Ronald Reagan, and Gary Cooper, director Sam Wood, and producer Walt Disney, complained about the subversive activities of Communists within the film industry and identified as many of them as they could by name.

The "unfriendly" witnesses, many of whom had been named as Communists, attended the hearings but refused to cooperate with the Committee, contending that its investigation was illegal and in violation of their rights under the First Amendment of the Constitution. These witnesses included German playwright Bertolt Brecht, who testified that he had never been a member of the Communist Party and then fled the United States on the following day (thus, this eleventh witness avoided making the "Hollywood Ten" the "Hollywood Eleven").

The remaining ten "unfriendly" witnesses were subsequently known as the "Hollywood Ten." They included writer Alvah Bessie (drama critic for *New Masses* and coscreenwriter of *Objective Burma*, 1945); director Herbert Biberman (*Meet Nero Wolfe*, 1936); writer Lester Cole (*Objective Burma*); director Edward Dmytryk (*Crossfire*, 1947); screenwriter Ring Lardner, Jr. (*Woman of the Year*, 1942); founder and first president of the Screen Writers Guild, John Howard Lawson (*Action in the North Atlantic*, 1943); writer Albert Maltz (*Pride of the Marines*, 1945); writer Sam Ornitz; writer–producer Adrian Scott (*Murder, My Sweet*, 1944; *Crossfire*, 1947); and writer Dalton Trumbo (*Thirty Seconds Over Tokyo*, 1944).

They were accompanied to the hearings by an independent group of famous Hollywood celebrities, such as Edward G. Robinson, Humphrey Bogart, Lauren Bacall, Danny Kaye, John Garfield, Gregory Peck, John Huston, and others (such as writer Philip Dunne) who had become members of the Committee for the First Amendment. During the hearings, these celebrities participated in a radio broadcast from Washington, which denounced HUAC and supported the First Amendment, but which gave no direct support to any individual "unfriendly" witnesses with whose confrontational tactics they disagreed.

The Hollywood Ten initially sought to use the hearings as a platform for exposing the dangers of anti-communism and for protesting the way in which the Committee threatened their rights under the First Amendment of the Constitution (although none of the "Ten" chose to invoke the First Amendment, preferring instead to answer the Committee in their own words). Each came with a prepared statement to read, but only one, Albert Maltz, was permitted to present it. They were all asked by members of HUAC, "Are you now or have you ever been a member of the Communist Party?" Because they all refused to answer, they were cited with contempt of Congress, were tried and convicted, and sentenced to from six months to one year in jail. After exhausting their appeals (and after the US Supreme Court refused to hear their case), they began serving their sentences in 1950.

Blacklisting

Shortly after the October hearings, more than 50 studio executives, members of the Motion Pictures Producers Association, met secretly at the Waldorf-Astoria Hotel in New York to discuss steps that the industry might take to protect itself from the "fallout" from the hearings. In particular, the producers feared threatened boycotts of their films, organized by the Hearst newspapers, the American Legion, and other "patriotic" national organizations. Much as the industry had earlier adopted self-censorship, through the agency of the Hays Office, in order to prevent the creation of external censorship review boards, here it adopted a policy of "self-regulation" which was coupled with the institution of "blacklisting."

Issuing what would be known as "the Waldorf Statement," the studio heads agreed to suspend the Hollywood Ten without pay, deny employment to anyone who did not cooperate with HUAC's investigations, and refuse to hire Communists. In this way, the industry effectively instituted a blacklist of unemployable talent. The numbers of those blacklisted ultimately extended beyond the Hollywood Ten and those who refused to testify before the Committee at subsequent hearings to include any employees who were suspected of Communist sympathies and who were unable to clear themselves to the satisfaction of the studios. By the mid-1950s over 200 suspected Communists had been blacklisted by the Hollywood studios. The blacklist remained unchallenged from 1947 until 1960, when screenwriter Dalton Trumbo, one of the original Hollywood Ten, worked openly in the industry and received screen credit for his work on producer–director Otto Preminger's *Exodus* (1960) and actor–producer Kirk Douglas's *Spartacus* (1960). However, the blacklist did not begin to give way until the mid-1960s and it remained in effect for a number of artists well into the 1970s.

Alger Hiss, the Rosenbergs, and Senator McCarthy

A second round of HUAC hearings on Hollywood took place in 1951. In the interim, the Cold War had dramatically escalated. A Communist coup had taken place in Czechoslovakia in 1948. In July 1948, a federal grand jury indicted (and subsequently convicted) eleven leaders of the American Communist Party with conspiracy to overthrow the United States government. In 1949, Mao Tse-tung defeated the forces of Chiang Kai-shek and China became a Communist nation. That same year, the Soviets exploded their first nuclear weapon, launching an arms race that would continue for over four decades. In January 1950, former New Deal official Alger Hiss was convicted of perjury charges, stemming from a 1948 accusation by admitted former Communist Whittaker Chambers, a senior editor at *Time* magazine, that Hiss had sold government documents to the Soviets in the 1930s when he worked in the State Department. Hiss's apparent guilt enabled Republicans to portray the Roosevelt administration as thoroughly infiltrated by Communists, a notion that would subsequently be exploited by Senator Joseph McCarthy in his attack on Communists in government. (The release of secret Soviet records in 1992 ultimately cleared Hiss of any association with Communist espionage.)

In February, the British arrested Dr. Klaus Fuchs, an atomic scientist who had worked with the Americans on the A-bomb at Los Alamos, charging that he had spied for the Soviets. The arrest of Fuchs led to the subsequent arrest and conviction of his supposed accomplices, Americans Harry Gold, Morton Sobell, and Julius and Ethel Rosenberg. The Rosenbergs were ultimately executed for espionage in 1953. Several days after the highly publicized arrest of Fuchs, Senator McCarthy launched a witch-hunt of Communists working in government. Speaking in Wheeling, West Virginia, McCarthy declared that he had in his possession a list of 205 names of Communists who were knowingly employed by the State Department.

Even though McCarthy's charges were investigated and proven false by a special committee of the Senate, the press continued to publish his accusations and headline the threat of the red menace until the Army–McCarthy hearings, which were held from April through June 1954. The televised hearings exposed the senator as a bully and a self-serving demagogue, who would do anything to advance his own career. Later that year, in December, the Senate voted to censure McCarthy, whose credibility as a force in national politics quickly crumbled.

Naming names

During the 1951 HUAC hearings, dozens of former Communists and suspected Communists chose to cooperate with the Committee in an attempt to clear themselves. Unlike the Hollywood Ten, they chose to identify other supposed Communists by name. In April of 1951, Edward Dmytryk, one of the Hollywood Ten, reappeared before HUAC in a carefully orchestrated attempt to clear himself and regain employment in Hollywood. He answered the Committee's questions and identified 24 former Communists. Within a matter of weeks, he was back at work, directing a low-budget film for the King Brothers. The following year, he returned to work at the major studios.

Dozens of other Hollywood artists cooperated with the Committee and chose to name names, although most of them held out for several months or even years before doing so. ... The victims of this round of testimony included writers Dashiell Hammett, Paul Jarrico, Michael Wilson, and Carl Foreman; actors Mady Christians, Canada Lee, John Garfield, Larry Parks, Howard da Silva, Paul Robeson, and Gale Sondergaard; and directors Abraham Polonsky, Joseph Losey, and Jules Dassin.

Actor Lionel Stander, who is known to audiences today for his role as the chauffeur in the TV series "Hart to Hart," was perhaps blacklisted for the longest period – from the late 1940s until 1965. Stander's 1951 testimony provided one of the few lighter moments in the saga of the blacklist. When questioned by HUAC, he offered to cooperate with them in exposing "subversive action." Stander declared "I know of a group of fanatics who are desperately trying to undermine the Constitution of the United States by depriving artists and others of Life, Liberty, and the

Pursuit of Happiness without due process of law. ... I can tell names and cite instances and I am one of the first victims of it. And if you are interested in that and also a group of ex-Fascists and America-Firsters and anti-Semites, people who hate everybody including Negroes, minority groups and most likely themselves ... and these people are engaged in a conspiracy outside all the legal processes to undermine the very fundamental American concepts upon which our entire system of democracy exists." Stander was referring, of course, to HUAC itself.

The hearings produced very little evidence of Communist influence upon the motion picture industry. One witness recalled that Stander had once whistled the Communist anthem, "The Internationale," in a film while waiting for an elevator. Another noted that screenwriter Lester Cole had inserted lines from a famous pro-Loyalist speech by La Pasionaria about it being "better to die on your feet than to live on your knees" into a pep talk delivered by a football coach.

The Cold War on Screen

Pro-Soviet wartime films

Chief targets of HUAC investigators were a handful of pro-Soviet films, such as *The North Star* (RKO, 1943), *Song of Russia* (MGM, 1943), *Days of Glory* (RKO, 1944), and *Mission to Moscow* (Warner Bros., 1943), which had been made during the war by major studios as part of the war effort. *The North Star*, which celebrates the resistance of a small Russian village to the Nazis when they are invaded, was written by Lillian Hellman and directed by Lewis Milestone, both of whom were subsequently investigated by HUAC. *Mission to Moscow*, which was based on the autobiography of Joseph Davies, the US Ambassador to the Soviet Union, was supposedly made at the request of Franklin Delano Roosevelt in order "to show American mothers and fathers that ... the Russians are worthy allies." This piece of obvious pro-Soviet propaganda demonstrated the virtues of our new allies and whitewashed, in the process, their faults, including Stalin's infamous purge trials of the late 1930s.

HUAC focused on this film in particular in an attempt to suggest that the Roosevelt administration was pro-Communist and that Hollywood had served as FDR's unwitting tool, producing pro-Soviet propaganda. But it was difficult to fault Hollywood for its support of an acknowledged American ally in its war against Germany. Indeed, in a 1947 statement delivered to HUAC in defense of the film, producer Jack Warner argued that "if making *Mission to Moscow* in 1942 was a subversive activity, then the American Liberty ships which carried food and guns to Russian allies and the American naval vessels which convoyed them were likewise engaged in subversive activities." In his testimony, Warner "protected" FDR, denying that the President played any role in encouraging the studio to make the film.

However, Warner later named the film's screenwriter, Howard Koch, as a Communist, insisting that whatever pro-Soviet sentiments anyone could find in the film had been slipped into it by Koch. Koch, who had co-authored such patriotic scripts as *Sergeant York* (1941) and *Casablanca* (1942), became, as a result of Warner's desperate need for a "fall guy" on whom to pin responsibility for the film's obvious sympathy for the Soviet Union, yet another victim of the blacklist, remaining out of work for over ten years.

The anti-commie cycle

Ironically, Hollywood produced more films with "subversive" messages after HUAC began its investigations than it did before them. For every anti-Communist picture released in the wake of the first HUAC hearings of 1947, there was another film that attacked the scapegoating and witch-hunting tactics of HUAC and the anti-Communist far right. With films such as *The Iron Curtain* (1948), *The Red Menace* (1949), *The Woman on Pier 13* (aka *I Married a Communist*, 1949), *I Was a Communist for the FBI* (1951), *The Whip Hand* (1951), *Walk East on Beacon* (1952), *My Son John* (1952), *Big Jim McLain* (1952), and *Pickup on South Street* (1953), Hollywood openly condemned Communists, associating them with espionage and with plots involving the violent overthrow of the American government.

The Iron Curtain, which is based on the confessions of a real-life Russian defector, exposes the operations of a Soviet spy ring in Canada. In *The Red Menace*, a disillusioned war veteran falls victim to Communist propaganda, which the film's narrator describes as "Marxian hatred … intent upon spreading world dissension and treason." In *Big Jim McLain*, John Wayne plays an FBI agent who tracks down Communist spies in Hawaii for HUAC; the film's end credits even thank the members of the Committee, who "undaunted by the vicious campaign against them" continue to fight against Communist subversion. *Pickup on South Street* portrays Communists as more treacherous and corrupt than common criminals, who at least observe the codes of the underworld. The film's hero, a small-time pickpocket, is no patriot, but he learns that you can't "play footsie" with the "commies," who are even less trustworthy than police stool pigeons and prostitutes.

Us vs. them: Science fiction and paranoia

Few of these blatantly anti-Communist works made a profit at the box office, but virtually every studio made them in order to demonstrate their anti-Communist zeal. Films dealing with the Korean war, such as *The Steel Helmet* (1950) and *Fixed Bayonets* (1951), or with the war in Indochina, such as *China Gate* (1957), provided a more traditional formula for the expression of anti-communism by removing the conflict between "us" and "them" from within the borders of America itself to foreign shores. These movies tended to fare somewhat better with audiences. Even more successful than these overtly anti-Communist films were the covert "war" films – science-fiction films. These works captured the decade's greatest fears – fear of the bomb and fear of a Communist takeover – but did so without the crude tactics of the more flagrantly political films that merely restaged the HUAC hearings in a somewhat more dramatic form or simply reworked recent events that had taken place in Korea.

In *Them!* (1954), gigantic ants, who appear to be mutations produced by nuclear testing, attack Los Angeles, while in *The Incredible Shrinking Man* (1957), a radiation shower serves as the source for human mutation. But instead of producing giant insects, fallout from the bomb actually diminishes the size of the film's hero, who then struggles to survive in a world in which the everyday (in the form of household pets and spiders in the basement) threatens his very existence. Cold War tensions also find expression in films in which invaders from outer space threaten to take over the Earth. In *The Thing* (1951), a creature from outer space that feeds on the blood of its victims and plants seeds that will enable it to reproduce, gives monstrous form to contemporary fears about the spread of communism.

Invaders From Mars (1953) and *Invasion of the Body Snatchers* (1956) exploit the association of communism with "brainwashing," which had developed in the aftermath of the Korean war when American prisoners of war were said to have been indoctrinated with Communist ideology. In *Invaders*, Martians implant crystals in the brains of local citizens, transforming them into slaves who do their bidding. In *Invasion*, aliens take over the bodies of the local residents by placing "seed pods" in their houses. The pods copy their features while they sleep, taking them over, "cell by cell." Once they have been taken over by the pods, the film's characters lack individuality, feeling, and emotion; they have, in short, become Communist dupes.

God and country

Even biblical epics took up the issues of the Cold War. In *The Ten Commandments* (1956), the right-wing director Cecil B. DeMille provides a prologue to the movie in which he asks "whether men are to be ruled

by God's law – or whether they are to be ruled by the whims of a dictator." He stresses the relevance of these issues by then asking, "Are men
the property of the state? Or are they free souls under God?" And he
finally links these issues to the current Cold War by observing that "the
same battle continues throughout the world today."

Yet, it is in this same genre that the radical left was able to make a case
for the Hollywood Ten and the evils of repressive government. The original script of the first CinemaScope blockbuster, *The Robe* (Fox, 1953),
for example, was, according to Philip Dunne who rewrote it and received
sole screen credit for the film, written by a blacklisted writer. It casts
Caligula as a witch-hunting, McCarthyesque figure and the Christians as
persecuted victims of his demonic attempts to purge the Roman empire
of potential subversives – that is, of Christians. The hero, Marcellus, is
converted to Christianity and publicly tried for treason at the end of the
film. The film's Christians meet in underground caverns (i. e., cells) and
resist the fascism of the Roman state. The pagan villain in *Prince Valiant*
(Fox, 1954) captures Prince Valiant and refuses to release him unless he
betrays his Christian comrades. The villain literally asks the hero to name
names, demanding that the Prince "confirm this list – your father named
them all." Needless to say, the Prince stoically refuses, remaining silent in
spite of being tortured.

Subversions

Subversive messages also surfaced in the Western. Because he was ultimately blacklisted, Carl Foreman's script for the critically acclaimed,
box-office success *High Noon* (1952) emerges as an obvious example of
resistance within the industry to outside investigators, such as HUAC.
The film's hero, ironically played by a real-life friendly witness, Gary
Cooper, is threatened by a gang of cutthroats (HUAC) who are on their
way to town (Hollywood). The sheriff–hero is unable to find allies to help
him within the (Hollywood) community. He nonetheless confronts and
defeats them, waging a battle alone which the townspeople ought to have
fought together with him.

A few years earlier, hard on the heels of being blacklisted as one of the
original Hollywood Ten, Alvah Bessie wrote the screenplay for *Broken
Arrow* (1950), which proved to be one of the highest-grossing films of
the year. Bessie was able to accomplish this by using a "front," another
screenwriter (Michael Blankfort) who pretended to be the author of the
script and who received screen credit for it. ... The story, which later
served as the basis for a highly popular television series of the same
name in the mid-1950s, involved the unusual friendship between a
white man, Tom Jeffords (James Stewart), and an Apache, Cochise

(Jeff Chandler). In befriending the Indians, Jeffords is regarded as a traitor to his own people, who attempt to lynch him. Jeffords, however, is rescued by the Army. He subsequently marries an Indian girl and plays the role of peacemaker between the Apaches and the whites, but the leading citizens of a nearby town attack the Indian camp, killing Jeffords's wife in the process.

In Bessie's scenario, Jeffords's friendship with the Indians and his campaign for peaceful coexistence between reds and whites marks him as a traitor (a Communist or Communist sympathizer) in the eyes of his own community. The townspeople emerge as barely disguised Communist witch-hunters. The film's sympathies clearly lie with Jeffords, who, like the blacklisted writer, is not only rejected by society but becomes the target of its violence and anger.

A similar scenario crops up in *Johnny Guitar* (1954), which was written by Philip Yordan and directed by one of Hollywood's young rebels, Nicholas Ray. The film's plot reworks the HUAC confrontations between suspected subversives and local vigilantes in terms of a typical Western. Again, the community is seen to be intolerant of those within it who are not like themselves. And the unconventional, nonconformist hero and heroine are forced to defend themselves against the false accusations of society. The casting of the film makes its allegorical status as an anti-HUAC vehicle even clearer. The hero, whom the town suspects of having robbed the bank, is played by confessed former Communist Sterling Hayden. One of the chief leaders of the vigilantes is played by Ward Bond, a member of Hollywood's most vocal anti-Communist group, the Motion Picture Alliance for the Preservation of American Ideals. The final shoot-out dramatizes the central battle between the forces of conformity and those of nonconformity. However, it does not take place between the two former cold warriors, Bond and Hayden, but between two women, who, in the form of the neurotic and sexually repressive Emma (Mercedes McCambridge) and the former prostitute Vienna (Joan Crawford), reconfigure the political extremes of the film in sexual terms. Though carefully disguised, the anti-HUAC and antiauthoritarian sentiments of the film clearly encourage audiences to root for Hayden and Crawford, as the victims of social oppression.

As in the case of Alvah Bessie, blacklisted writers continued to work secretly in Hollywood and were often drawn to projects that provided a platform for the expression of "liberal" ideas. On more than one occasion, blacklisted writers even won Academy Awards for their work. In 1956, the (unclaimed) Academy Award for best story went to *The*

Brave One, which was written by "Robert Rich," one of Dalton Trumbo's aliases. The story deals with the efforts of a Mexican peasant boy to rescue his bull from slaughter in the arena. Next year, the Academy Award for best screenplay went to *The Bridge on the River Kwai* (1957), which explores life in a Japanese prisoner-of-war camp, questions blind obedience to authority, and takes a critical stance toward those who collaborate with the enemy. The script for this box-office blockbuster was signed by Pierre Boule, author of the original novel on which the film was based. Boule, however, did not speak a work of English; the script was actually written by two blacklisted writers, Carl Foreman and Michael Wilson.

The secret work of blacklisted writers tended to fare better at the box office than did the one or two projects which directly attacked the system. In 1954, a group of blacklisted filmmakers, including Herbert Biberman, Michael Wilson, and Paul Jarrico, worked on an independently made feature, *Salt of the Earth*, which was a prolabor film dealing with the 1951–2 strike by Mexican-American zinc miners. The film exposes a double standard whereby minority workers were paid less than their white coworkers and were forced to work under hazardous conditions. In addition, it celebrates the efforts of the miners' wives in winning the strike. Its feminist narrative perspective, unique for the 1950s, provided a model for Barbara Kopple's *Harlan County, U.S.A.* (1977), a documentary about a strike by Kentucky coal miners.

American immigration officials attempted to halt production of *Salt of the Earth* by deporting its Mexican star as an illegal alien before the film was completed. Laboratory technicians and projectionists, members of the anti-Communist IATSE union, refused to process prints of the film or to project them in theaters. And right-wing organizations, such as the American Legion, threatened to organize boycotts if exhibitors attempted to show the film. As a result, the film played in only a limited number of situations in the United States.

Chaplin in exile

The most overt attack on HUAC came from Charles Chaplin, whose prior association with "known Communists" such as composer Hanns Eisler and writer Bertolt Brecht put him under suspicion as a Communist sympathizer. In 1952, Chaplin's apolitical, semiautobiographical drama about a music hall comic, *Limelight*, became the target of a nationwide boycott, organized by the American Legion. Chaplin, who had never become an American citizen, had embarked on a worldwide tour to promote the film, after first securing a permit from the State Department to reenter the United States on his return. In September, 1952, shortly after Chaplin had left the country, the US Attorney General suddenly revoked Chaplin's reentry permit on the grounds that Chaplin was an "unsavory" character. The Attorney General insisted that Chaplin answer questions about his political beliefs before he would be granted permission to reenter the United States.

A few weeks later, the American Legion denounced Chaplin as a Communist "fellow traveler" and launched a boycott of *Limelight*, vowing to sustain their protest until Chaplin returned to the United States to answer questions about his political sympathies. Refusing to submit himself to the ordeal undergone by other members of the Hollywood community who had been forced to testify before HUAC, Chaplin gave up his residence in the United States and moved to Switzerland, where he lived until his death in 1977. Chaplin did not return to the United States until 1972 – 20 years later – when he journeyed to New York City, where he was honored by the Film Society of Lincoln Center in a special tribute, and then to Los Angeles to receive an honorary Oscar from the Academy of Motion Picture Arts and Sciences.

During the period of his European exile in the mid-1950s, Chaplin wrote, starred in, and directed *A King in New York* (1957), which was a bitter denunciation of American McCarthyism, in general, and HUAC, in particular. Chaplin, however, did not release the film in the United States until 1973. In the film, Chaplin plays the dethroned king of a fictional European country who flees to the United States. There he meets and befriends a young boy, whose parents are Communists who have been called to testify before HUAC. The boy, played by Chaplin's son, Michael, denounces the government for its totalitarian behavior, including acts similar to Chaplin's own experiences, such as depriving citizens of passports to travel. Chaplin's king shields the boy from HUAC, which has subpoenaed him to testify about his parents' political beliefs and loyalties. The FBI eventually tracks the boy down, takes him into custody, and forces him to "name names" in order to secure the release of his parents.

Because he has helped the boy, the king is called to appear before HUAC to explain his actions and to give testimony about his political sympathies. On his way to the hearings, the king's finger becomes accidentally caught in the nozzle of a fire hose, which he is forced to bring into the hearing room with him. The water is turned on and the king "inadvertently" ends up dousing the members of HUAC with a stream of water. In spite of this mishap, the Committee clears the king of the charges that he is a subversive. He is, after all, a monarch and thus, by profession, an anti-Communist. However, at the end of the film, Chaplin's king decides to return to Europe rather than live in a society dominated by the forces of fear and political repression.

In defense of the informers: On the Waterfront

Perhaps the most curious film to be "inspired" by the HUAC hearings, however, was *On the Waterfront* (1954), which was written by Budd Schulberg and directed by Elia Kazan. Both Schulberg and Kazan were friendly witnesses who had named names when they testified before HUAC. Voted Best Picture of the Year by the Academy, *Waterfront* functions as a cleverly disguised defense of those members of the Hollywood community who informed on their colleagues. In the film, ex-prizefighter Terry Malloy (Marlon Brando) is a union (read "Communist") "dupe" who slowly discovers just how corrupt and vicious the local longshoremen's union actually is. The union leadership, which is dominated by mobsters, is seen to be responsible for the death of a potential "stool pigeon," who threatens to inform on them. It also exploits the very workers it claims to protect. Near the end of the film, union boss Johnny Friendly orders the murder of Terry's protective brother Charley (Rod Steiger) and Terry then testifies against the union in hearings held by the Waterfront Crime Commission. The film concludes with Terry's return to the docks, where he openly confronts the union's hired thugs, who beat him up. Terry's defiance of the union, however, wins him the support of the other workers, who join him in his repudiation of the union leadership. The message of the film was clear: it's not only okay to inform, but those who do are the real heroes.

Aftermath

The fight continues

By the late 1950s, the political power of HUAC and Senator McCarthy had declined. In 1953, the Soviet Union's hard-line premier, Joseph Stalin, died and the Korean war came to a conclusion. At the end of 1954, the Senate voted to "condemn" McCarthy for his verbal abuse of fellow senators and for his contempt for the Senate itself. McCarthy's influence quickly faded, and he died three years later. During the early

1960s, Hollywood slowly began to abandon the blacklist, openly acknowledging the work of Trumbo (*Exodus*, *Spartacus*) and other black-listed individuals.

However, Hollywood continued to fight the Cold War, though the hysterical anti-communism of the 1950s quickly gave way to a cooler, more calculated manipulation of Cold War fears for dramatic effect rather than for political propaganda. In other words, Communists began to function more as traditional villains than as real-life threats to our national security. The paranoid vision of *The Manchurian Candidate* (1962) suggests that brainwashed Korean prisoners of war have been programmed to assassinate American political candidates. Yet, the film also condemns a McCarthyite politician who is, ironically, revealed to be an unwitting pawn in the larger game plan the Communists have devised to take over the United States.

Rabid anti-communism and nuclear anxiety are still strong enough in the mid-1960s – the Barry Goldwater era – to provide the stuff of black humor in Stanley Kubrick's *Dr. Strangelove* (1964), which explores the political "fallout" after a fanatical anti-Communist in the American military deliberately launches a nuclear attack on the Soviets. ...

John Wayne's *The Green Berets* (1968) takes a hard line against those who oppose the war in Vietnam, suggesting that they are the unfortunate victims of Communist propaganda. Even more recently, *Rambo: First Blood Part II* (1985) attempts to keep the Cold War alive by mixing old-fashioned, us-vs.-them anti-communism with a new ingredient – the revelation of treachery from within. As a result, Rambo takes on not only the Vietcong and its Russian military advisers, but also the American CIA and the political establishment, who attempt to undermine Rambo's mission to rescue POWs. Sylvester Stallone successfully manipulates anti-Communist sentiment again that same year in *Rocky IV* (1985), which pits Rocky against a Soviet boxer who is responsible for the ring death of Rocky's old friend, Apollo Creed.

Red Dawn (1984), a right-wing fantasy written and directed by John Milius, imagines what it would be like if the Cubans and the Soviets invaded the United States, transforming rural Colorado into a battle-ground in which American teenagers wage a guerrilla war with the Communist invaders. Cold War tensions also fuel *Top Gun* (1986), in which Navy pilots test their mettle against Soviet migs, and *No Way Out* (1987), in which Russian agents are found working in the Pentagon. The fact that the latter film was a remake of an apolitical film noir, *The Big Clock* (1948), further illustrates the way in which the Cold War had been reduced to the status of a timely convention, which could be plugged into virtually any traditional narrative formula.

The rise to power of Mikhail Gorbachev in the Soviet Union in 1985 and the advent of the era of *glasnost* further served to undermine the viability of Cold War rhetoric in American films. *Rambo III* (1988) attempts to prolong the anti-Soviet sentiments which had helped to make *Rambo II* a box-office hit by sending Rambo to Soviet-occupied Afghanistan to fight Russians, but the film did not do well commercially, putting an end to the highly successful *Rambo* series. By 1990, the relaxation of US/Soviet tensions could be dramatically seen in the adaptation of Tom Clancy's 1984 Cold War novel, *The Hunt for Red October*, into a suspense melodrama in which Sean Connery's Soviet submarine commander emerges as the film's hero, successfully outwitting both his Soviet superiors and his American counterparts.

Win, lose, or draw?

From the vantage point of the 1990s, the Cold War, the HUAC hearings in Hollywood, and the blacklist emerge as nightmarish aberrations which properly belong to another time, another place, and another generation. Recent attempts to recreate this world, such as *Guilty by Suspicion* (1991) in which Robert De Niro plays a director forced to give testimony to HUAC, have failed to connect with contemporary filmgoers who find little in these dramatic situations with which they can identify. Even before the Cold War officially concluded, Hollywood discovered that audiences could not care less about the supposed "red menace" threatening us from without and from within. If then-President Ronald Reagan, an old Cold Warrior from the 1950s, could come to terms with the "evil empire" of the Soviet Union, then so could the rest of us.

During the presidential campaign of 1992, George Bush insisted that the United States had "won" the Cold War, forcing the collapse of communism. What is more likely is that both the United States and the USSR "lost" it by spending themselves into a state of economic disaster, characterized by rampant inflation, recessions, and escalating deficits. Day by day, the Cold War is emerging as a common enemy of the peoples of both the United States and the Soviet Union. At any rate, this appears to be the message that Hollywood is sending in films like *The Hunt for Red October* in which lower-echelon officers in the Soviet navy, such as nuclear submarine commander Marko Ramius (Sean Connery), and in the American CIA, such as analyst Jack Ryan (Alec Baldwin), join forces to outwit the doomsday scenario being written by their political superiors and to establish the grounds for a post-Cold War alliance of Soviet and American peoples.

Set "shortly before Gorbachev came to power," the film documents the attempts of Ramius and his fellow officers to defect from the Soviet Union and the political and military responses of both the United States and the Soviet Union. In the final scenes, American and Soviet officers collaborate, jointly serving as the crew of the Soviet typhoon-class submarine, *Red October*, as it evades destruction by Cold War forces which emanate both from within (a KGB saboteur) and from without (an overzealous Soviet submarine commander). Unconventional naval tactics, including the cooperation of an American submarine, result in the self-destruction of the Soviet Union's representative of Cold War philosophy, the promise of a "healthy" revolution in the Soviet Union itself, and the suggestion of peaceful coexistence between the two countries in the future.

HUAC remained in existence until 1975 and the Cold War finally came to an end in the 1990s, but it owes its conclusion not to politicians or governments but to those who have most often been subjected to its tensions – its victims.

Documents

Introduction to Documents

Federal authorities have long feared the potential impact of movies on American political consciousness. The following Federal Bureau of Investigation report from 1943, offers a glimpse into the mindset of the government agency and its fear that Reds and radicals had penetrated the movie industry and were inserting dangerous Communist propaganda into American films. Four year later, the government crusade against alleged Reds heated up as the House Un-American Activities Committee (HUAC) began investing Communist activity in Hollywood. When ten writers and directors, known as the Hollywood Ten, refused to answer any questions regarding their political affiliation, they were indicted and eventually sent to jail. Nervous studio leaders responded to threats of boycotts and federal censorship by issuing the "Waldorf Statement" (named after the New York hotel that hosted their meeting) in which they condemned the actions of the Hollywood Ten and pledged that they would not knowingly employ Communists.

FBI Report, "Communist Political Influence and Activities in the Motion Picture Business in Hollywood, California"

Source: Report of special agent, "*Communist Infiltration of the Motion Picture Industries,*" Internal Security-C. File No. 100–15732, Los Angeles, October 11, 1943

An analysis of the Hollywood motion picture industry from that period when it first began to be recognized as a stable institution in American life which period began about 1910 or 1911 up to the present time, will show that it has undergone a definite change in its relations with the national life of the United States. In order to show this change clearly it is necessary to treat the subject by dividing it into two distinct periods of development, the first and the second.

The first period extended from the beginning of the industry to the advent of the so-called "talking picture" in about 1930. The second extending from that time up to the present.

During the first period, when motion pictures depended on the pantomimic method, commonly known as the "silent picture," the motion picture industry was strictly a commercial one and completely free of political implications of an ideological nature. Pictures produced during this period were for entertainment purposes only. Propaganda of any serious type had no place in picture production; in fact, had there been occasion for such propaganda of a subtle political nature it would have been ineffective in the silent picture, a fact which is obvious.

As a consequence, the motion picture industry and those individuals prominent therein were not involved, or even concerned, with political matters or with any attempt to influence the public mind along those lines. Neither was there any attempt, organized or instinctive, during this period to undermine by ridicule or direct attack upon the ideals and traditions upon which the government of the United States was based.

It can be said that the motion picture industry of the first period was strictly an American institution reflecting American ways of life; that it was free from any form of propaganda inimical to the American way of life.

But with the perfection of sound recording instruments and the adaptation of sound to the motion picture, the "talking picture" came into existence. This innovation changed the entire course of the motion picture industry and made it possible for the industry to be used for purposes other than pure entertainment. This revolutionary innovation paved the way for the use of the motion picture as a propaganda instrument.

The development along these lines has been so rapid and the expansion so great that today the motion picture industry is beginning to be recognized as one of the greatest, if not the very greatest, influence upon the minds and culture, not only of the people of the United States, but of the entire world. It has been said by A. P. Giannini the well-known banker and representative of those banking interests which finance the making of motion pictures, that "The nation which controls the cinema can control the thought of the world."

This idea did not escape notice of certain political groups, international in scope which, with the development of the talking picture, began to utilize this field for their purposes.

At the same time, about 1930, a change in the personnel of control and management of the industry took place. Slowly at first but with increasing tempo, a different type of individual filtered into the industry and began taking it over. This type of individual can be described as one either of foreign birth or extraction. By this is meant persons who were either born abroad or immediate descendants of such, for the most part native or naturalized citizens, whose ideas and culture were much closer to the land of their birth or extraction than they were to the ideals and traditions of America. ...

With the phenomenal growth of the industry it was only natural that this industry should be concerned with political matters in the United States. ... But the political influence of the motion picture industry has not ... confined itself to American politics on the home field. In fact, it seems to be taking an entirely different course, one which can be described as international in a political sense. And there can be no doubt that the national origins and inherited "ideologies" of those now in control of the motion picture industry are determining these developments and bending them in a direction unfavorable to American ideals and customs – and it can be said, in the long run, democracy.

The predominating political influence in the motion picture industry at this time is one which has its origin in a combination fostered by a foreign "ideology" which in turn stems from Soviet Russia and its growing influence on the affairs of the world.

In about 1934, Soviet Russia began to show an intense interest in the American motion picture industry. Operating through the Communist International (Comintern) and the Communist Party of the United States, it began an intensive campaign to penetrate the industry by placing communists and fellow travelers in responsible positions and at the same time conducting a propaganda campaign within the industry to convert employees in all departments to the cause of communism and draw them into the Communist Party or subject them to its influence.

There were two lines of attack, one to influence the cultural and creative arts and their exponents and another to capture and control the trade unions. Both lines of attack apparently operated separately, but in reality they were parallel efforts secretly cooperating with one another and directed at all times by functionaries of the Communist Party.

Progress was slow at first, but by 1938 it had developed to such a degree and its importance to the communist cause had been so thoroughly demonstrated that it was necessary to make the Hollywood communist groups a distinct section of the Communist Party apparatus, responsible directly to the Central Committee of that Party in New York. Thus the Communist Party recognized this importance of the motion picture as a weapon in its cause and that it could not risk exposure of its activities by permitting them to be associated with local communist groups. The individual responsible for setting up this plan was Victor J. Jerome, a member of the Central Committee and a leading communist of national importance who was sent to Hollywood for the purpose.

Up to the signing of the Hitler–Stalin pact in August 1939, the communist influence in the Hollywood motion picture industry was such that, taking the lead by reason of prestige and financial resources derived from high-paid actors, writers, etc., it had not only grown to alarming proportions within the industry, but had penetrated the political apparatus of the Democratic Party in the state of California to such an extent that it was able to elect to state, county and city offices persons who were either direct communists, fellow travelers or just plain politicians who were willing to cooperate and follow the party line. ...

During the period of the Hitler–Stalin pact, from August 23, 1939 to June 22, 1941 there was a lull in the more open activities of the Communist Party in Hollywood. ... But with the attack on the Soviet Union by Hitler and the attendant change in the Communist Party line from one of isolation and opposition to aid to England and France to one of violent patriotism for Russia's sake, the influence of the Hollywood communists on the production of motion pictures and the industry itself immediately became alarmingly apparent. It could now be plainly seen what the effects of the long years of agitation in Hollywood had brought about.

It now being possible to amalgamate their efforts with the honest efforts of the loyal American people to win the war, they took advantage of this situation and, using their highly disciplined members and followers, they succeeded to such an extent that at the present time, posing as good loyal Americans, they have practically assumed control of all Hollywood pro-war activities. They have set up front organizations to operate in the political field; they have penetrated government agencies; they have set up propaganda agencies; they have utilized their controlled trade unions, creating coordinating bodies, presumably to aid the war effort; and what is most important is their success in influencing the production of a type of motion picture that can be used as a medium for carrying out the Communist Party line and glorifying the Soviet Union as a democratic, progressive state and economy which could well be adopted elsewhere and, by implication, right here in the United States.

Communist activities in the Hollywood area are at the present time confined roughly to the following efforts:

1   Production of a type of motion picture favorable to Communism and the Soviet Union.
2   Creation of propaganda agencies and groups to work within the industry and with outside governmental agencies such as the OWI.
3   Directing the political influence of the motion picture industry toward support for candidates for public office who are secretly known to be sympathetic to the communist cause.
4   Utilizing the trade unions under the guise of all-out war effort to cooperate with organizations controlled by the Communist Party.
5   Set up front organizations to overlap into all groups on a basis of anti-Fascism, Russian Relief, Spanish Relief, Refugee Relief, etc. utilizing the efforts to spread propaganda for the Soviet Union and Communism.
6   Call mass meetings and demonstrations in the … [support] of the war program, using these gatherings to raise funds for communist purposes.
7   Work secretly to have known communists and fellow travelers placed in responsible positions in the motion picture industry, using the man-power shortage as a golden opportunity.
8   And last, but not least, take advantage of the fact that the Soviet Union is still an ally of the democracies and therefore enjoys prestige and use this factor to recruit members for the Communist Party, and develop a new crop of fellow travelers and sympathizers.

... [The FBI] will continue this investigation at Los Angeles and Hollywood, California, and will obtain information relative to the Communist activities in the motion picture industry and in the political situation as it exists in Hollywood.

Will also continue to observe the production of motion pictures having a propaganda effort favorable to Communist ideology and will obtain evidence of the activities of directors, producers, writers, actors, distributors engaged in producing and distributing pictures of a propaganda nature.

"The Waldorf Statement," Issued by the Association of Motion Picture Producers

Source: Issued December 3, 1947 at the Waldorf-Astoria Hotel, New York City

---

Members of the Association of Motion Picture Producers deplore the action of the ten Hollywood men who have been cited for contempt. We do not desire to prejudge their legal rights, but their actions have been a disservice to their employers and have impaired their usefulness to the industry.

We will forthwith discharge or suspend without compensation those in our employ and we will not re-employ any of the ten until such time as he is acquitted or has purged himself of contempt and declares under oath that he is not a Communist.

On the broader issues of alleged subversive and disloyal elements in Hollywood, our members are likewise prepared to take positive action.

We will not knowingly employ a Communist or a member of any party or group which advocates the overthrow of the government of the United States by force or by illegal or unconstitutional methods. In pursuing this policy, we are not going to be swayed by hysteria or intimidation from any source. We are frank to recognize that such a policy involves dangers and risks. There is the danger of hurting innocent people. There is the risk of creating an atmosphere of fear. Creative work at its best cannot be carried on in an atmosphere of fear. To this end we will invite the Hollywood talent guilds to work with us to eliminate any subversives, to protect the innocent, and to safeguard free speech and a free screen wherever threatened.

Readings and Screenings

For a look at radical and anti-radical filmmaking during the silent era and early 1930s, see Michael Slade Shull, *Radicalism in American Silent Films, 1909–1929: A Filmography and History* (Jefferson, NC: McFarland and Company, Inc., 2000); Steven J. Ross, *Working-Class Hollywood: Silent Film and the Shaping of Class in America* (Princeton, NJ: Princeton University Press, 1998); Russell Campbell, *The Cinema Strikes Back: Radical Filmmaking in the US 1930–1942* (Ann Arbor, MI: UMI Research Press, 1982). The literature on HUAC, the Hollywood Ten, and Hollywood politics – onscreen and offscreen – from the 1930s to the 1950s is massive. The best overall history of the subject is Larry Ceplair and Steven Englund, *The Inquisition in Hollywood: Politics in the Film Community, 1930–1960* (Berkeley, CA: University of California Press, 1983). For a brief but excellent overview of how external politics effected the ideology of the era's films, see Stephen Whitfield, "Reeling: The Politics of Film," in his book *The Culture of the Cold War* (Baltimore, CN: John Hopkins University Press, 2nd edition, 1996). For longer looks at Cold War films, see J. Hoberman, *An Army of Phantoms: American Movies and the Making of the Cold War* (New York: The New Press, 2011); Nora Sayre, *Running Time: Films of the Cold War* (New York: Dial Press, 1982). Recent works on the subject include John Joseph Gladchuk, *Hollywood and Anti-Communism: HUAC and the Evolution of the Red Menace, 1935–1950* (New York and London: Routledge, 2007); Tony Shaw, *Hollywood's Cold War* (Amherst, MA: University of Massachusetts Press, 2007); Frank Krutnik, Steve Neale, Brian Neve, and Peter Stanfield, eds., *"Un-American" Hollywood: Politics and Film in the Blacklist Era* (New Brunswick, NJ: Rutgers University Press, 2007); Patrick McGilligan and Paul Buhle, *Tender Comrades: A Backstory of the Hollywood Blacklist* (New York: St. Martin's Press, 1997); Kenneth Lloyd Billingsley, *Hollywood Party: How Communism Seduced the American Film Industry in the 1930s and 1940s* (Rockland, CA: Forum, 1998); Gerald Horne, *Class Struggle in Hollywood, 1930–1950: Moguls, Mobsters, Stars, Reds, and Trade Unionists* (Austin, TX: University of Texas Press, 2001); Paul Buhle and David Wagner, *A Very Dangerous Citizen: Abraham Lincoln Polonsky and the Hollywood Left* (Berkeley, CA: University of California Press, 2001).

The earliest anti-Communist films available on DVD are *Bolshevism on Trial* (1919) and *Dangerous Hours* (1920). The latter film, which revolves around the nefarious activities of secret Bolshevik agent Boris

Blatchi, is especially valuable for showing the ways in which Hollywood represented – or misrepresented – the Russian Revolution. Red activists, secret and otherwise, can be found in 1930s films such as *Heroes for Sale* (1933) and *Red Salute* (1935). After the Soviet Union broke with Germany and joined the Allied forces, Hollywood welcomed our new allies with pro-Soviet films such as *Mission to Moscow* (1943) and *The Song of Russia* (1943). By 1948, the anti-Soviet chill that fell over the nation prompted a series of anti-Communist films; those available on DVD or VHS (most are not, in part because the genre proved a box-office flop) include *The Red Menace* (1949), *Big Jim McLain* (1952), *My Son John* (1952), and *Pickup on South Street* (1953). Fears of brainwashing by foreign invaders were played out in science fiction films such as *Invaders from Mars* (1953) and *Invasion of the Body Snatchers* (1956). The dilemma faced by the Hollywood Ten as to whether or not to testify against friends is at the heart of Elia Kazan's *On the Waterfront* (1954). Two films that challenged the climate of fear and offered a positive look at radical activity are *Salt of the Earth* (1954) and *A King in New York* (1957). For an excellent documentary on HUAC, blacklisting, and the trial of the Hollywood Ten, see *Hollywood on Trial* (1976).

8

Eisenhower's America: Prosperity and Problems in the 1950s

Introduction to Article

The 1950s were rife with paradoxes: they were a time of prosperity and poverty, of freedom and discrimination, of domestic tranquillity and fear of nuclear war. Growing up in Queens, New York, during the 1950s, my elementary school classmates and I all had to do regular A-bomb drills where we ducked under our desks and shielded our eyes in case the Russians bombed Manhattan. The Cold War, the Civil Rights movement, suburbanization, the Beat generation, corporate culture, rock and roll, and the rise of the television were all hallmarks of the mid-century decade.

Leonard Quart and Albert Auster present a broad survey of the decade's political, social, and cultural landscape. Far from seeing the 1950s as extraordinarily dull and bland, the authors show how filmmakers interpreted the era's most provocative and often contradictory issues for a mass audience: McCarthyism, optimism and pessimism about the future, women's consciousness and identity, teenage rebellion, racism, social justice and injustice, and the threat of militarism. Movies were often able to say what political leaders could not. Although the "economy of abundance helped create a powerful suburban culture where the pursuit of success and an emphasis on social conformity became the dominant values of the era," Quart and Auster argue that the era's films "managed to contain a deeper sense of uneasiness and urgency, and a greater sense of the imperfections of American society, than in the past."

Movies and American Society, Second Edition. Edited by Steven J. Ross.
© 2014 John Wiley & Sons, Inc. Published 2014 by John Wiley & Sons, Inc.

Discussion Points

How do the films described by Quart and Auster reflect the contradictions, problems, and possibilities of the 1950s? Compare and contrast the ways in which contemporary films deal with similar issues.

The Fifties

Leonard Quart and Albert Auster

Source: Leonard Quart and Albert Auster, *American Film and Society Since 1945* (New York and Wesport: Praeger, 1991), 41–70

The fifties began on an ominous note with America, as part of a nominally United Nations-led force, becoming involved in a war in Korea, and the repressive and paranoid investigations of Senator McCarthy and company in full throttle. The decade, however, ultimately evolved into one permeated by a broad political and cultural consensus.

The first years of the decade were dominated by the stalemated Korean War, where the Truman administration was willing to eschew military victory for a limited war and a negotiated settlement. Truman's military policies were challenged by World War II hero General Douglas MacArthur, who was then commander of the United Nations forces. Cloaking himself in his own sense of omniscience and nineteenth- century patriotic pieties, MacArthur saw Truman's policies as the appeasement of communism and committed himself to total victory in Korea. Truman, in turn, responded by firing MacArthur for insubordination and subsequently discovered himself the object of intense public rage.

That rage soon found a home in the McCarthy, HUAC, and Senate Internal Security Subcommittee investigations of a domestic communist conspiracy. This conspiracy was seen as a threat to take over a number of American institutions, like the church, universities, private industry, and Hollywood. During the fifties the anticommunist crusade elicited the involvement, whether out of fear, political self-interest, or conviction, of a number of liberal groups and individuals. It included the American Civil Liberties Union, which from 1953 to 1959 refused to defend communists who were under attack or lost jobs, and Hubert Humphrey, who as a senator proposed a bill to outlaw the Communist party. Interestingly enough, many liberal intellectuals placed the blame for men like McCarthy on the actions of the left rather than on the right, at times even supporting the general public's view that the rights of communists and communist sympathizers should be denied. ...

The prime American political symbol of the fifties, however, was not Joe McCarthy but General Dwight Eisenhower, the Republican president from 1952 to 1960. Ike was a World War II military hero, whose calm, avuncular, optimistic public presence helped create a nonideological political mood that muted controversy and offered something both to liberals and to conservatives. Though disliking the welfare state, Ike accepted the reforms of the New Deal without extending them and was prepared to use fiscal and monetary measures to maintain full employment. Despite believing in the Cold War, and unable to see the differences between communist and nationalist revolutions (e.g., CIA interventions in Iran and Guatemala occurred during his administration), he believed in a nuclear truce, refusing to engage in an arms race with the Soviets, and studiously avoided getting the United States involved in a war.

Eisenhower was a cautious president who, though unsympathetic to the growing civil rights movement, reluctantly sent troops to Little Rock to ensure school desegregation in 1957 and in crisis after crisis kept political tensions beneath the surface. By dint of his confident cautiousness and political skills, Eisenhower was able to preside over a national political consensus that excluded only paranoid right elements, southern reactionaries, segments of the old left, and the few independent radicals who were still functioning as critics.

This political consensus was built on and reinforced by an intellectual consensus shared by most American intellectuals. Some, like John Kenneth Galbraith, believed in a theory of "countervailing power" where big business power would be balanced by the power of big labor and government. Others held that the age of ideology was over (e.g., Daniel Bell, *The End of Ideology*) and in its place substituted an optimistic faith in capitalism, political pluralism, and the uniqueness and perfectibility of American society. These tough-minded anti-ideologues had constructed their own ideology, building it on a belief that economic growth and the practical application of social science principles would provide social justice and solve social problems. In their social vision there would be no need for economic redistribution (many of them were ex-radicals and leftists who out of a complex of motives rejected their own political past), for the American people were supposedly becoming more economically equal. And poverty, during the rare times it was acknowledged to exist, was seen as gradually disappearing. In turn they also read the idea of class conflict, and even the significance of class, out of the American social and political landscape, promoting their own liberal mythology that in a totally middle-class society everybody had an equal opportunity to succeed. The other prime element of this ideological consensus was the aforementioned rise of liberal anticommunism (e.g., *The Partisan Review*, once a critical, sophisticated Marxist journal, became an avid defender of the West), which viewed Cold War politics as far more significant than domestic affairs. This commitment was so potent that even the newly merged American Federation of Labor and Congress of Industrial Organizations (AFL-CIO) gave more attention to the anticommunist struggle than to organizing the mass of workers who remained outside the unions.

However, though most intellectuals either were utterly at home with the direction of American politics or turned to contemplating existential and religious questions emphasizing the limitations of human nature, simply ceasing to be political dissenters and critics, there were still a number of them who preserved their critical skills by analyzing and attacking the character of American mass culture. In the fifties the economy of abundance helped create a powerful suburban and consumer culture where the pursuit of success and an emphasis on social conformity became the dominant values of the era. As novelist Edmund White wrote about growing up in the Midwest in the fifties: "That was a time and place where there was little consumption of culture and no dissent. ... It felt, at least to me, like a big gray country of families on drowsy holiday, all stuffed in one oversized car and discussing the mileage they were getting."[1]

College students were in harmony with this mood and were for the most part apolitical ("a silent generation"), interested in a fraternity–sorority-based social life and in preparing for future careers. The Reverend Norman Vincent Peale, with his message of "positive thinking," became the country's most popular moralist and preacher, and the country's growing religious interest seemed built on sociability rather than spirituality.

The mass media of the fifties reflected and reinforced these values. Television was dominated by entertainers like the droning, folksy Arthur Godfrey, who became one of its most powerful personalities, by the skilled slapstick of *I Love Lucy*, and by the naked greed of quiz shows such as *Twenty-one*. And though there were imaginative comedy programs like *Your Show of Shows* and original television drama on *Playhouse 90*, the most popular programs were often built on the most inane premises and on the marketing of personal comfort and instant gratification. One interesting statistic that conveyed something of the anti-intellectual taste of the times was that "about four times the expenditures on public libraries were paid out for comic books."[2]

In books like William H. Whyte's *The Organization Man* (1956) and David Riesman's more scholarly and complex *The Lonely Crowd* (1950), American middle-class life was criticized for its penchant for uniformity, social role-playing, and privatism. Other critics, both liberal and conservative, poked fun at the mass media, advertising, the automobile culture, and the anxiety-laden drive for social status and material goods. However, though the banality and tastelessness of much of what appeared on television and the blandness of suburban life were criticized, there was no attempt by these critics to break from the political and social consensus of the fifties. For the most part, they accepted the political and social system that helped shape the culture, and most of the targets they attacked were not particularly controversial ones.

Nevertheless, despite the serene and confident veneer of the Eisenhower years, there were subversive currents that, though barely recognized, coexisted with the dominant mood of stability and complacency. The threat of nuclear war shadowed the period, creating among a number of people a sense of fatalism and despair and leading to protests in the late 1950s against the civil defense program. The program was seen as treating nuclear war as an acceptable military alternative which people had to prepare themselves to survive.

The fifties also saw the civil rights movement begin to take shape. Whites may have been content with the political and social world of the fifties, but black needs and problems were clearly left unmet by an indifferent Republican administration and a Congress paralyzed by the southern Democratic bloc. The only arm of government responsive to black grievances was the Supreme Court led by Chief Justice Earl Warren. In 1954 the Court came to a monumental decision. In *Brown v. Board of Education of Topeka* it outlawed segregation in the public schools. There were violent reactions in the South, but de jure segregation of the schools (de facto segregation is a continuing and deepening reality) was at the beginning of its end.

The Court decision led to the 1955 Montgomery bus boycott – a grassroots black protest against segregation in public transportation. The boycott was followed by protest movements in other southern cities and, most importantly, marked the ascent to national black leadership of Martin Luther King Jr.

The movement to the suburbs by urban whites also carried a critical, even dark, undercurrent. For though it was viewed either satirically – as a flight to a sterile, tedious, and vulgar world – or sympathetically – ordinary Americans achieving their small portion of the American

Dream – the radical consequences of this flight (by 1950, 40 to 50 million Americans lived in the suburbs) for the inner city of the 1960s and 1970s were not foreseen. The departure of a white middle and lower middle class from the cities and their replacement by black and Hispanic poor led in the following decades to the erosion of the urban tax base (built on the sales and property taxes of its inhabitants), the escalation of often insoluble urban problems, and even greater residential segregation than had existed in the past.

There were also other fifties' currents that indicated resistance to the conservatism of the decade. The Beat movement, which was an attack on both the middle-class conformity and hypocrisy of the Eisenhower years and the elite literary culture of the universities, came of age in the 1950s. Led by serious poets like Allen Ginsberg and Gregory Corso and novelists like Jack Kerouac (*On the Road*), the Beats modeled their writing on poets like Walt Whitman and novelists like Henry Miller and on the improvisation of jazz musicians like Charlie Parker. In their writing and lives they emphasized spontaneity, personal freedom, a contempt for authority, and spiritual exploration. The Beat movement did not consist only of artists; there were other young people – beatniks – who, taking their lead from the Kerouacs and Ginsbergs, adopted or mimicked a more natural, antibourgeois life-style (symbolized by pot, jazz, and free sex). And, though the Beats were never a part of a political or social movement, their writings rejected racism and the nuclear arms race and treated homosexuality without contempt or condescension.

The fifties also saw the development of a distinctive youth culture accompanied by a new (though derived from black rhythm-and-blues music) form of music – rock and roll. For many older Americans rock music was too loud and overtly sexual, and sounded to them like aimless noise. However, at its best and most innovative (e.g., the rock of Chuck Berry and Elvis Presley) the music had an energy, freedom, and earthiness that offered the possibility of an undefined new life-style, which strongly contrasted with 1950s conventionality. Of course, by the late 1950s much of rock music's class and regional identity had been bleached out and transformed into the mass-produced, soporific sound of Frankie Avalon and his clones.

Clearly these deviant currents and dark strains were not the preeminent ones in fifties' America. It is important, however, to recognize that the era was more complex than is implied by the usual images and descriptive phrases evoking a time supposedly dominated by a passive "silent generation."

Similarly, the films produced in Hollywood defied facile labels and categories. In the early 1950s, as in the late 1940s, HUAC garnered publicity by investigating the film industry. Its hearings helped buttress the already powerful blacklist of actors, writers, and directors, and created in its wake a "clearance" industry that passed judgment on the political purity and future employment of the people who worked in Hollywood. And, just as in the late 1940s (*I Married a Communist*, 1949), cheap genre films were produced to purge the Hollywood image of any taint of radicalism. A film like *Big Jim McLain* (1952) used a documentary style, including an author-itative narrator, to exalt the FBI and HUAC while condemning communists more for their character traits (they were criminals, idealistic dupes, nym-phomaniacs, or disturbed fanatics) than for their ideology. In fact, the ideology was never defined or explored. Communists were reduced to caricatures who saw human life as dispensable, had no room for private feelings, and were even in opposition to God and motherhood. ...

Undoubtedly, a direct or even an oblique commitment to dealing with political issues was far from the dominant force in the Hollywood of the fifties. Given decreasing movie theater attendance and the competition from television, Hollywood gave a great deal of thought to recapturing its audience. Using color more heavily and then seeking out new technological processes, the studios attempted by overwhelming the viewer to attract him back to moviegoing. Processes such as Cinemascope, Vista-Vision, Cinerama, and 3-D were introduced, exploiting the size of the film image and experi-menting (unsuccessfully) with the creation of the illusion of depth.

Ultimately, the widescreen processes led to a number of expensive, lengthy blockbuster films like *The Robe* (1953), *The Ten Commandments* – which cost thirteen and a half million dollars to make – (1956), and *Ben Hur* (1959). These epics were on one level part of the religious revival of the fifties – cartoons of religious piety – and, more importantly, with their color, crowds, chariot races, and crucifixions they were the last great flings of studio excess (where "only too much is really sufficient"),[3] which allowed these films to fully exploit the vastness of the new screen.

The new Hollywood could be glimpsed in Billy Wilder's smart *Sunset Boulevard* (1950). The plot centers on an aging, once famous and glam-orous silent screen actress, Norma Desmond (Gloria Swanson), who lives in a decaying mansion as if time had stood still. She fantasizes about making a comeback film with the aid of a decent, weary, and hungry screenwriter, Joe Gillis (William Holden), who becomes first her collabo-rator, then her lover and kept man. *Sunset Boulevard* follows a number of the conventions of film noir, using voice-over narration and flashback and centering on a possessive, hysterical, sexually devouring heroine and a morally ambiguous hero. However, the film's prime focus is not on the corruption of Joe Gillis but on the contrast between the old Hollywood and the new – not necessarily to the latter's advantage.

Though Billy Wilder and his cowriter Charles Bracket depict Norma Desmond as something of a wild-eyed, campy grotesque, the film is still an idiosyncratic homage to the absurdity, excess, and graciousness of the flamboyant old Hollywood. Luminaries of the old Hollywood like Buster Keaton, Cecil B. De Mille, and Erich von Stroheim (who plays Max, Norma's first director, ex-husband, and present-day protector and servant) are treated sympathetically, while the plainer, sharp-tongued, grasping new Hollywood producers dismiss the "message kids," want to make Betty Hutton musicals out of baseball stories, and have no time for truth or art. For Wilder, the old Hollywood had style, if nothing else, which made the more pragmatic, businesslike Hollywood of the fifties (which he was an integral part of) pale in comparison.

Contrary to *Sunset Boulevard's* sour view of the contemporary Hollywood scene, many producers still felt optimism about the future. Some of that hopefulness was based on the success of big-screen musical comedies, particularly adaptations of Broadway hits like *Oklahoma* (1955) and *Guys and Dolls* (1955). However, these musicals, though commercially successful, suffered from ponderous and inflated production values. It also began to seem ridiculous for characters to break into song and dance at the slightest provocation. The best musicals of the decade appeared in the early fifties and came from the illustrious Freed unit at MGM. These medium-budget original musicals included Vincente Minnelli's decorative and stylized *An American in Paris* (1951), with an athletic Gene Kelly; his somber and witty *The Bandwagon* (1953), with the elegant and feathery Fred Astaire; and Stanley Donen and Gene Kelly's classic show-business musical *Singin' in the Rain* (1952).

Singin' in the Rain is a breezy, good-natured satire of Hollywood's Busby Berkeley musicals, film premieres, star biographies, and the introduction of sound, written by the urbane Betty Comden and Adolph Green and starring Gene Kelly as an earthy, dynamic, ordinary American Hollywood star, Don Lockwood. Kelly is, as always, brashly self-confident and jaunty, and in the film's title number he wistfully stamps around in rain puddles, and, holding his sole prop, an umbrella, exultingly embraces the studio rain. With its pastel colors, cheerful songs ("Good Morning"), and acrobatic pratfalls (Donald O'Connor energetically dancing through cardboard sets), *Singin' in the Rain* created a world where any action could spontaneously, calmly, and naturally be turned into music and dance. It was a world where despair and doubt do not exist and where the happy ending continues to survive. And if *Singin' in the Rain's* plot about the transition to sound is a metaphor of the challenge that Hollywood faced from TV, it is also an indicator of just how much carefully honed optimism still dominated the studio product.

A few years later, a much more melancholy and despairing note was conveyed in Donen and Kelly's final collaboration, *It's Always Fair Weather* (1955), in many ways a successor to *On the Town*. Here three GI buddies (Dan Dailey and Michael Kidd recreating the Jules Munshin and Frank Sinatra roles) decide to get together ten years after the war is over. It is a measure of the sour mood of the film that the three find they have very little in common and do not really like one another. Although both Dailey and Kidd are better dancers than Munshin and Sinatra, there is very little chemistry between the three – even their bravura garbage-can dance together, though clever, has none of the inspired warmth of the numbers in *On the Town*. Also indicative of the darkening Hollywood mood is the film's negative response to the world of media and TV. It takes satiric potshots at advertising – Dan Dailey as an ad executive singing the drunken "Situationwise" – and at TV shows like *This Is Your Life*.

Even if *It's Always Fair Weather* did sound a despondent chord and if few fifties' films had *Singin' in the Rain*'s charming airiness and feeling of being at home in the world, the era still contained many genre films that upheld traditional virtues and values and were commercially successful. In George Stevens's carefully composed, beautiful *Shane* (1955), a blond, mysterious stranger in white named Shane (Alan Ladd) is befriended by a group of homesteaders and protects them in turn from a predatory rancher and his psychopathic hired killer dressed in black (Jack Palance). *Shane* tries hard not to be an ordinary western: It is a self-conscious attempt to create a mythic West populated by archetypes – with the enigmatic, perfect-featured, sententious Shane seen continually from the perspective of a hero-worshipping young boy (Brandon de Wilde). However, despite its portentousness, it was a more conventional film (for all his grandiosity, Shane is not that much different from the more pedestrian radio and TV hero, the Lone Ranger) than the 1950s westerns of Anthony Mann (*The Naked Spur*, 1953), austere, bleak films built around a revenge motif, or John Ford's epic western *The Searchers* (1956), with John Wayne as the most ambiguous of Fordian heroes.

Ford's later films like *The Searchers* depicted a darker, less morally defined world than earlier works like *Stagecoach* (1939) and *My Darling Clementine* (1946). The plot of *The Searchers* revolves around a driven ex- Confederate soldier named Ethan Edwards (Wayne) who searches for years for his niece Debbie (Natalie Wood). Debbie has been kidnapped by Indians – who for the most part are treated here as savages or childlike, comic foils – whose way of life she has adopted. Edwards still has enough left of the character of the old Wayne–Ford hero to display indomitable courage, rescuing Debbie from the Indians he passionately hates and returning her to Ford's ideal world of family and community – the garden in the wilderness.

But nothing is quite the same in Ford's world in this film. Everything has become grimmer: The landscape is more threatening; Ford's beloved cavalry both less noble and more absurd; and his sullen, violent hero consumed by murderous rage. Ford's heroes can usually reconcile their individuality with community – nature with civilization. But Ethan is the "man who wanders" who is unable to enter the door of the hearth again. The stirring long shot of him riding away, framed by the doorway of the house, is not an affirmation of the romance and freedom of a Shane-like hero who can never be domesticated, but a tragic, desolate image of a man doomed to solitude. (In the 1980s *The Searchers* became a model for films like *Rambo: First Blood Part II*, where the freeing of MIAs from the barbaric captivity of the North Vietnamese followed the pattern of Ethan's quest to free Debbie from the Indians.)

Despite the sense of unease that began to creep into fifties' film, neither Hollywood nor the public were particularly open to films that took formal or intellectual risks. Exemplifying this attitude was the popular comedy team of the fifties, Martin and Lewis (*Artists and Models*, 1955), whose slapstick routines, and Jerry Lewis's twitchy, idiotic victim's persona, did not differ much from the style of earlier B-film comic teams like Abbott and Costello.

Just as indicative of the basic conservatism of popular taste and values were films dealing with women's consciousness and identity. During the decade not only were there fewer films about independent women than in the thirties or forties, but there were fewer films dealing with women at all. In the literate, epigrammatic Academy Award-winning *All About Eve* (1950), a temperamental, sarcastic, ambitious star of the theater, Margo Channing (Bette Davis), is also a vulnerable, insecure woman underneath all her wit and drive. She ultimately sees her career as insufficient, as something separate from being a real woman, and opts for marriage, children, and retirement. Her mousy and devoted protégé Eve (Anne Baxter) turns out to be a predatory and manipulative actress who wants to be a star and is willing to use any means to supplant Margo. In *All About Eve* successful women are either unhappy or so distorted by their ambition that they lose their humanity in the process.

In a minor role in the same film, Marilyn Monroe, the sex symbol of the fifties, plays another of her dumb blondes, a woman-object, whose sexuality is unthreatening, guileless, and childlike. Towards the end of the decade, in films such as Billy Wilder's frenetically paced, transvestite sex farce, *Some Like It Hot* (1959), she added vulnerability to her victim's persona.

While Monroe was more a male fantasy figure than a woman that other women could identify with, the freckled, eternally sunny Doris Day was one female star capable of eliciting both male and female sympathy.

In a period where being popular had become a prime cultural value, Day's persona in battle-of-the-sexes comedies such as *Pillow Talk* (1958), with Rock Hudson, conveyed a super-hygienic, wholesome cheerfulness. However, though these comedies were built on an extremely puritanical, timorous form of sexiness, with Day remaining always the virgin, her supposed sexual innocence was less significant than her drive, ambition, and spunkiness. In fact, so potent were those qualities that as a tailored-suited journalism professor in *Teacher's Pet* (1958) she is tough enough even to put to rout Hollywood studs (albeit in this case an aging one) like Clark Gable. Despite Day's girl-next-door looks and behavior, her characters often had jobs and projected a tougher, more independent persona than most of the other major female stars (e.g., Grace Kelly, Audrey Hepburn) of the decade.

But though the characters Doris Day played may have held down jobs, most women in the 1950s' films were housewives or women seeking to avoid spinsterhood, who found salvation in marriage. In one traditional genre, however – the soap opera – German-born director Douglas Sirk made films that used the genre's conventions to make oblique criticisms of traditional female roles and middle-class conformity.

Backed by one of the most commercial Hollywood producers, Ross Hunter, Sirk's *All That Heaven Allows* (1955) was characterized by artificial studio landscapes and townscapes, melodramatic, fortuitous accidents, a saccharine score, and a predictable, neat conclusion. Despite the clichés that permeated the film, Sirk was a consummate stylist who could use color, light, clothes, and furniture to express his sensibility and capture his heroine's state of mind. Throughout the film Sirk uses reflections on TV screens, mirrors, and piano tops and ubiquitous screens and doors both to evoke a middle-class world dominated by gleaming surfaces and appearances and to catch the heroine's feelings of imprisonment. It's an eloquent use of cinematic form to comment on content and, at moments, transcends the lack of subtlety and soap-operatic quality of the script.

The film presents the world from the point of view of an older heroine, Carrie (Jane Wyman) – an upper-middle-class widow with few interests, little emotional connection between herself and her unpleasant, grownup children, and a number of stolid, acceptable men desiring to marry her. She breaks from the mores of her country club set and arouses the disapproval of her children by becoming involved with a young, passive, handsome hero, Ron Kirby (Rock Hudson). He is not only much younger than her, but a landscaper who lives a comfortably bohemian life dimly committed to simplicity, love of nature, an uncompromising belief in being autonomous, and a disdain for snobbery and status-seeking.

But he's also college-educated and refined, and his home and friends look more like models for a Norman Rockwell magazine cover – cute and unnaturally wholesome – than some bohemian enclave.

For all that, Kirby is not the usual alternative for heroines in fifties' and women's pictures. Carrie chooses to fulfill her own emotional and sexual needs, and not only rejects her friends but decides she won't be a Stella Dallas (the heroine in Vidor's film of the same name in 1937) or Mildred Pierce and sacrifice her life for her children. Sirk's film, however, was clearly no feminist work. Carrie's choice of a new way of life is predicated on the existence of a man to provide her with an alternate set of values and a refuge in marriage – in terms of the narrative a very safe sort of rebellion. But its criticism of middle-class materialism, hypocrisy, and emptiness (more telling in the film's mise-en-scène than its narrative) was symptomatic of much less oblique works that rebelled against the complacency and conformity of Eisenhower America. In these films, male stars such as the aforementioned virile, angry Brando (*On the Waterfront*), the brooding, vulnerable Montgomery Clift (*A Place in the Sun*, 1951; *From Here to Eternity*, 1953), and James Dean (Kazan's *East of Eden*, 1955) played anti-heroic heroes who in different ways were at odds with the prevailing social order.

In *A Place in the Sun* (1951) Clift plays a haunted, sensitive outsider in a dark, romantic version – all dramatic tight close-ups, shadows, superimpositions, and dissolves – of Dreiser's naturalistic novel *American Tragedy*. George Eastman (Clift) is a quietly ambitious, uneducated young man who wants to escape his street missionary boyhood and enter the world of his wealthy relatives. However, the film's emphasis is much less on the nature of social class and the hunger for success in America than on Eastman's doomed relationships with a clinging, drab, working-class woman (given texture and poignancy in Shelley Winters's performance) and with Angela Vickers (Elizabeth Taylor), who is the embodiment of glamor and wealth. In the Oscar-winning *From Here to Eternity* (1953) Clift played another vulnerable, doomed outsider (Prewitt), brutalized by a corrupt army on the eve of Pearl Harbor. Prewitt is here a man of courage and integrity who is unwilling to bend to the dictates of an institution he loves.

The rebellion expressed by three actors was, however, neither political nor social in nature, nor were the characters they played artists, beats, or bohemians. They were just sensitive, sensual, and often anguished young men seeking to discover and define their identities. In the process they raised doubts about the values and behavior that dominated American culture and society, and indirectly conveyed some of the undercurrent of dissatisfaction that existed during the decade.

Of the three stars, James Dean had the most profound effect on the consciousness of the young in the fifties. Dean had an aura – a mythic presence – and with his abrupt and tragic death in a car crash in 1955 generated a cult and became a legend. His film career was a brief one, but in Nicholas Ray's extremely popular *Rebel Without a Cause* (1955) he left his unique mark on the fifties.

Rebel Without a Cause was less about rebellion than about the anger of Jim Stark (James Dean) towards his middle-class parents and the world. Jim is a brooding, suffering, isolated high school student who hates his apron-wearing father's (Jim Backus) flaccid amiability and weak submission to his self-involved, backbiting wife. Mumbling, slouching, hunching his shoulders, curling up in a fetal position, cigarette dangling from his mouth, the tormented Jim is like a coiled spring ready to cry and rage. Surrounding Jim are two other pained, rejected adolescents, Judy (Natalie Wood), stunned and emotionally thrown by her father's sudden rejection, and Plato (Sal Mineo), a morbid, friendless boy who lives alone with a black maid because his divorced parents have deserted him.

Rebel Without a Cause's uniqueness rests more in its cinematic style and Dean's performance than in its script. Ray uses a variety of camera angles, a dislocated mise-en-scène, tight close-ups, point-of-view shots, intense color, and rapid, turbulent cutting to successfully project the tension, anger, and sense of almost metaphysical alienation that permeates the film. There are also luminous, metaphoric sequences: the "chicken run," with a pinkish-white specter, Judy, signaling the beginning of the race in the center of a pitch-black runway lit by car headlights – an initiation rite or journey confronting death; and the scene shot in the vastness of the planetarium (which is located on a precipice) with its apocalyptic, end-of-the-world images of the galaxy exploding as the three alienated kids sit alone in the dark watching – all providing a powerful metaphor for the insecurity and isolation of adolescence.

Rebel Without a Cause's dialogue and narrative are much more pedestrian than its imagery. In terms of the narrative, the film sees the causes of adolescent turmoil as solely psychological – caused both by the instability and conflict within families and by their failure to communicate and provide understanding. There is an implicit critique of upper-middle-class status striving and conformity, but the script's emphasis is not on social or class reality. In fact, the film even introduces an understanding detective who acts as a social worker (the helping professions, such as psychologists and social workers, became commonplace in fifties' films) and surrogate father to Jim.

The film's conclusion is both clichéd and sexist, the submerged father taking off his apron, asserting his authority and embracing Jim, and reconciliation and love triumphing over fragmentation. However, what is most memorable is not Jim's opting for a 1950s affirmation of domesticity – shedding his asocial self for a responsible familial one – but those powerful existential images of lostness, of being a romantic outcast alone in the world.

Dean departed from this image in his third and last film, George Stevens's *Giant* (1956), which was adapted from Edna Ferber's novel. He plays Jett Rink, a sullen, inarticulate ranch hand who becomes an oil millionaire. Rink is the only character in the film with the suggestion of an internal life – a tribute to Dean's gift for giving nuance and complexity to even this most seemingly stereotypical of characters. Although in *Giant* Dean continues to mumble and slouch, he is transformed from a hostile, arrogant outsider, filled with resentment of those who have power, to a wealthy but pathetic power-wielder consumed by alcoholic self-pity, racism, and the resentments of youth. Dean's Jett is not a particularly sympathetic figure, but the tension and energy he conveys in the role are among the few vital elements in this inflated and trite epic about Texas culture and society.

However, in contrast to Dean's earlier films, *Giant* does make some interesting social points, albeit they are built on a sentimental, liberal point of view characteristic of the Hollywood social films of the mid-1950s. For *Giant* is both a ponderous soap-operatic chronicle about a wealthy ranching family and a critique and a bit of a satire of Texas materialism, anti-intellectualism, machismo, and racism. Unfortunately, the critique is subverted both by the long shots exalting an almost mythic Texas landscape and by the beautiful and somewhat progressive eastern heroine's, Leslie's (Elizabeth Taylor), ultimate embrace of Texas and its ethos. And her acceptance of that world after years of ambivalence only occurs when her stolid rancher husband Vic (Rock Hudson) displays his humanness and manliness by brawling for the rights of his half-Mexican grandchild. *Giant* contains no real political critique; Leslie does not want to give up her privileges or make changes in the political and economic structure, she merely wants the elite to be more paternalistic (to sustain the values of her Maryland adolescence) and demonstrate some kindness to the poor Mexicans who work for them. However, she is bold enough to accept intermarriage, and the film clumsily suggests, through its final shots of Leslie and Vic's white and copper-skinned grandchildren sitting together in their playpen, that the answer to racism may lie in the coupling of the races – the traditional Hollywood embrace of personal rather than political solutions.

Richard Brooks's *Blackboard Jungle* (1955) was a fifties' film carrying more social bite and tension than *Rebel Without a Cause* or *Giant* and dealing with similar issues – delinquency and racism. In fact, when the film was screened at the Venice Film Festival it elicited a diplomatic protest from Claire Booth Luce (ambassador to the Vatican) because she felt it exported a squalid, unfavorable image of American life.

Blackboard Jungle centers around a tough, crew-cut idealistic teacher, Mr. Dadier (Glenn Ford), who believes in education and democracy and must tame a group of violent young hoods. In true 1950s style the actions of the hoods are given no social roots or explanation, merely psychological chatter about permissive childrearing. Nevertheless, these hoods are no Bowery Boy cream puffs, but alienated, resentful, and vicious, especially their leader, West (played with an imitation Brando–Dean posture by Vic Morrow). *Blackboard Jungle* is a perfect example of what in Hollywood passes for social realism and social exposé. New York is reduced to a studio set devoid of any sense of texture or place, and the teachers in the main are stereotypes, ranging from Murdoch (Louis Calhern), a cynic who calls the school a "garbage can," to the frustrated Miss Hammond, who wears tight, sexy clothes and is almost raped by one of the students. The plot is also built on a series of contrived, mechanical twists featuring sudden shifts of destructive or cynical characters to the side of virtue, and of course offering Hollywood's usual solution to complex social problems: the concern and commitment of one courageous, caring individual – Dadier.

Despite these discordant elements, the film was still capable of capturing some of the difficulties involved in teaching tough, disruptive adolescents (it uses the dissonant sounds of a machine shop class and the passing elevated subway train to help evoke feelings of oppression). The potent use of one of the first rock hits, "Rock Around the Clock," conveys a strong feeling of the unbridled energy and antagonism of 1950s' youth culture. The issue of racism is also raised with the introduction of the character of Miller (Sidney Poitier in one of his early, more complex roles). Miller is a sensitive, strong, intelligent underachiever, who at first, angry and resentful of what he perceives to be a white education system, baits and torments Dadier. But by the film's climax he turns into a noble hero joining Dadier against West and his brutish allies.

Blackboard Jungle is filled with embarrassing clichés about the promises of equal opportunity in America – Dadier attempts to get Miller to continue to go to school by invoking the careers of black success stories like Joe Louis and Ralph Bunche. Nevertheless, the film does touch on the reality of black anger, and that is a positive step in a decade where, excepting *No Way Out* (1950) – Poitier as a middle-class doctor – there were no other films dealing with black consciousness and problems until Martin Ritt's *Edge of the City* (1957). However, in *Edge of the City* Poitier plays a longshoreman-saint who sacrifices his life for a confused, neurotic white friend, played by John Cassavetes, and no real feeling of black life or problems is conveyed.

In Stanley Kramer's *The Defiant Ones* (1958), Poitier plays an escaped convict (Cullen) in the South whose character is given enough pungency and reality to directly express his anger at southern racism. Because Poitier is a symbol of virtue, his rage is balanced by qualities like intelligence, tenderness, loyalty, and courage. *The Defiant Ones* is a conventional, contrived work of liberal poster art whose key image – a close-up of two hands, black and white, manacled together – is an obvious metaphor for Kramer's view that blacks and whites are inescapably linked to each other in America. Cullen has escaped chained to a white convict, Jackson (Tony Curtis), who is morally and physically much weaker than he. Jackson is an insecure, petty criminal, who dreams of the big money and lives by the southern racist code. But it is predictable from the very beginning that Jackson will be transformed and the hate between him and Cullen will turn into concern and love.

The Defiant Ones, like *Blackboard Jungle*, has a great deal of surface excitement and even some dramatic punch – the cross-cutting between the convicts on the run and the liberal sheriff (Theodore Bikel) in pursuit is especially effective. However, like *Jungle* it offers a simplistic social answer – the achievement of racial solidarity through the commitment of individual blacks and whites to each other. And there is no attempt in the film to depict or even suggest the complex economic, political, and cultural dimensions of the race problem. Of course, integration is made easy for whites, because the black character is Sidney Poitier, a charismatic, seductive, and superior presence, who at the film's climax even sacrifices his freedom for his white friend (invoking jeers from the blacks in the audience). Indeed, it was this dignity and transcendent humanness that made Poitier the one black star who was consistently successful and acceptable to white audiences. Poitier never bowed or scraped to whites, but he was so reasonable and humane that the white audience knew that his anger would always stay within acceptable bounds and that there was nothing to fear from the characters he portrayed. They were men who could arouse the hatred or abuse only of the most ignorant or reactionary of whites.

Later on, during the more militant sixties, blacks often put down Poitier's persona as middle-class, masochistic, and liberal. Nevertheless, he was one black actor who no longer had to sing, dance, and roll his eyes to have his image appear on the screen. And though Hollywood's handling of the race problem was neither bold nor imaginative, given the conformist political tenor of the time the emergence of a token black star could still be viewed as a minor triumph.

Ultimately it was this lack of political and artistic ferment or originality in 1950s Hollywood that allowed an opening for a group of independently produced films such as the Academy Award-winning *Marty* (1955). Ironically, it was Hollywood's bête noir, TV, that was the inspiration for *Marty* and other films of this type. For along with the hours of dross that dominated 1950s TV there were some moments that broke the mold. Under the inspiration of innovative spirits such as NBC's Sylvester "Pat" Weaver new forms like the magazine concept show ("Today"), talk shows ("Tonight"), and spectaculars ("Peter Pan") were produced on TV. Producers such as Fred Coe and Worthington Minor created original live drama shows such as "Studio One" and "Philco Playhouse," featuring the talents of new writers (Paddy Chayefsky, Rod Serling, Horton Foote), directors (Sidney Lumet, John Frankenheimer), and actors (Paul Newman, Kim Stanley, Rod Steiger).

Marty was the first and most commercially successful of these films adapted from live television. Written by Paddy Chayefsky and made on location in the East Bronx in low-budget black and white, it dealt with the daily lives of ordinary people. *Marty*'s major achievement was in evoking the tedium and loneliness that permeates the life of an unattractive Bronx butcher (Ernest Borgnine), who ultimately finds happiness by going out with a shy, homely teacher. Although Chayefsky claimed that his work opened up the "marvellous world of the ordinary," *Marty* was a dialogue-bound, formally inexpressive film, whose camera did not probe deeply into the faces and behavior of lower-middle-class life. It was merely a quietly sentimental story, touched with a fine ear for Bronx dialogue and syntax – for instance, answering a question with a question (e.g., "What do you feel like doing tonight?" "I dunno, what do you feel like doing?") – and offering Hollywood's predictable, all-purpose solution – love – to give Marty's life some purpose.

Marty's commercial success led to other "small" films, the most distinctive being Sidney Lumet's *Twelve Angry Men* (1957), adapted from a television play by Reginald Rose. *Twelve Angry Men* is an account of a jury's deliberations over a murder case where the defendant is a Puerto Rican boy. Using a single set of a New York City jury room on the hottest day of the year, Lumet succeeded in adapting most of the conventions of the television play – tight close-ups, medium group shots, panning, and fluid and precise cutting from sweating face to face – to build a dramatically effective film. He was especially gifted directing actors, and a cast that included a combination of New York character actors (Lee J. Cobb, Jack Klugman, E. G. Marshall) and a Hollywood star, Henry Fonda, as the jury gave a seamless illustration of ensemble playing.

Twelve Angry Men was a socially committed work which raised questions about the nature of the jury system and, by extension, the nature of American democracy itself. The jury is a gallery of social types: bigots, a shallow, spineless advertising man, a decent working man, an immigrant deeply committed to the democratic process, a cold, logical stockbroker, and the hero, an intelligent, decent, liberal architect (Henry Fonda) who must convince the rest of the jury members that what seems like an open-and-shut case is liable to reasonable doubt. He is a resolute man with a soft, cultivated voice, who ingeniously and logically succeeds in convincing the other jury members that the prosecution's case has holes. Despite the doubts the film raises about a system where bigotry, complacency, and convenience (one juror wants to resolve the case quickly so he can get to a Yankee game) become the sole basis for deciding the guilt or innocence of a defendant, the film ends on a positive note, with the defendant allowed to go free and the American system of justice affirmed.

Twelve Angry Men's strength lies in its dramatic fireworks and its well-drawn social types rather than in the depth of its social critique or the psychological complexity of its characters. It is a film where the villains sweat, rage, and bellow a great deal, and whose hero is a totally admirable and reasonable man. Every scene in the film is neatly choreographed and calculated for dramatic impact, with each of the characters given a single note – the old man on the jury is observant and notices details – to define themselves, and a significant moment where they shift their vote. And though the film does not gloss over the fact of how ambiguous and complex the meting out of guilt and innocence in a criminal case can be, it still holds that for our institutions to be just they merely need one good man who will tap the basic virtues of other ordinary Americans. It is the type of Hollywood political fantasy that such vastly different directorial sensibilities as Frank Capra and Sidney Lumet could share.

Besides *Marty* and *Twelve Angry Men* there were other small films that elicited critical attention during the late fifties, such as Richard Brooks's *Catered Affair* (1956) and Delbert Mann's *Middle of the Night* (1959). But the production of these small films began to decrease at the same time as live drama was replaced on television by filmed series. And although good, small, realistic films were still produced during the next three decades – *The Luck of Ginger Coffey* (1964), *Hester Street* (1974), *El Norte* (1984) – after the fifties there never again was a time where the small film seemed capable of becoming one of the dominant cinematic forms in Hollywood.

The small, realistic films did not attempt to subvert either Hollywood conventions or the dominant political and cultural values of the fifties. However, in the late fifties two films were made which were critical of the military mind and of the development of nuclear weapons – *Paths of Glory* (1957) and *On the Beach* (1959).

Of the two, the more formally distinctive and politically subversive was Stanley Kubrick's independently produced *Paths of Glory*. Despite the fact that the film takes place within the confines of the French Army of World War I rather than in the more charged and contemporary setting of the US Army of the Korean War, *Paths of Glory* trenchantly conveys the cynicism, hypocrisy, and careerism of the French officer class and provides a powerful indictment of war.

In what was to become his characteristically cool, dazzling, and original style, Kubrick evokes an unjust and death-saturated world through sound (drum beats, whistles), camera movement, lighting, and vivid imagery rather than through antiwar sermonizing. The two prime villains of the film are the calculating, subtle, and insidious General Broulard (Adolphe Menjou) and the neurotic, murderously ambitious General Mireau (George Macready), who live in opulent châteaux and hold glittering formal-dress balls. They are totally contemptuous of their men, treating them like chess pieces to be manipulated or ants to be casually slaughtered – "scum" who can be sacrificed to their own career ambitions. Mireau watches the battle through binoculars (one of Kubrick's many devices conveying war as a voyeur's sport of the officer class) and hysterically rages at the soldiers' retreat.

Though the film puts greater emphasis on the class structure and inequity of the war machine than on the horrors of the war, Kubrick still evokes the advance and retreat of the soldiers in nightmarish, richly textured battlefield scenes. The battlefield is a lunar landscape of craters, mud, and puddles, littered with bodies, barbed wire, and the wreckage of a plane, punctuated by whistling shells and enveloped by a flare-lit sky. The camera relentlessly tracks the men as they scramble to their anonymous deaths through the debris and smoke.

The hero of *Paths of Glory* is the granite-faced, courageous, and compassionate Colonel Dax (Kirk Douglas), who is at one with the men. Dax is an uncomplicated idealist who can openly say to Mireau that "patriotism is the last refuge of scoundrels." He also defends three innocent, court-martialed soldiers – he is a defense lawyer in civilian life – who have been chosen arbitrarily from the mass of soldiers to be punished for their supposed cowardice (in reality to cover the general's mistakes) in battle. Though Dax is a jut-jawed hero and idealist, the three soldiers are fallible, frightened men who cry and rage and whose death is absolutely barbaric and meaningless. Kubrick concludes the film without a glimmer of hope: Dax not only fails to prevent their deaths but, almost immediately after the court martial, is forced to lead his exhausted troops, who are longing for home, back to the murderous trenches. The system has him in its hands, and there is no escape.

Stanley Kubrick went on to make much more mordant and outrageous films, where strong, noble figures like Dax not only rarely appear but would be parodied and undermined if they did (e.g., *Dr. Strangelove*, 1963; *A Clockwork Orange*, 1971). For the smug fifties, a film that portrayed the military hierarchy as moral monsters and maintained such a bleak view of the human condition was a radical work and, of course, doomed to commercial failure. *Paths of Glory* did not offer the facile, personal, and liberal solutions of *Blackboard Jungle* and *The Defiant Ones* or the leftist optimism of *Salt of the Earth*. It was a profoundly pessimistic work that offered only contempt for the conduct of war and the corruptions of power and privilege, and nothing more.

In contrast, Stanley Kramer's disaster movie *On the Beach* (1959), although it is built around the notion that the world is on the verge of extinction by nuclear war, ends on a curious note of hope. Based on Australian novelist Nevil Shute's best-selling book, the film was seen in some ways as a small step towards the easing of Cold War tensions because it was screened almost simultaneously in Moscow and Washington. But despite its political pretensions, this tale about the aftermath of World War III, and a last surviving American submarine arriving in Australia just ahead of a postnuclear exterminating cloud, seems nothing more than a backdrop for a doomed love affair between Ava Gardner, an alcoholic war widow, and Gregory Peck, the submarine commander.

Stanley Kramer's aim to make a star-laden film (Fred Astaire also had a role in it) that would act as a warning about the consequences of the nuclear arms race had good intentions. In fact, few people could take exception to the film's decent instincts, but only in Hollywood would bromides like the need to preserve the wonder of life be seen as socially significant. There is also something bland and antiseptic about the images of the nuclear holocaust that the film projects. However, there are moments when the film captures the kind of despair that might become an integral part of the lives of the doomed survivors, particularly in a car race in which the drivers drive with a consciously suicidal recklessness and abandon. These scenes are rare, and *On the Beach*'s real purpose is revealed in its final image of a Salvation Army banner proclaiming the message that "there is still time, brother!"[4]

Though the film was intended as a cautionary message about the apocalyptic consequences of the arms race and nuclear war, the implications of this message might also serve as a convenient summary of Hollywood's passage from the optimism of the forties to the anxiety of the sixties. On the one hand the film evokes the complacency of an industry that despite economic decline and political problems still went on churning out films built on the ersatz emotions, melodramatic conventions, and evasive political and social formulas of previous decades. On the other hand, however, a number of these films managed to contain a deeper sense of uneasiness and urgency, and a greater sense of the imperfections of American society, than in the past. Of course, the fifties ended with Eisenhower in the White House and Doris Day starring in *Pillow Talk* (1958), but inherent in all that manufactured calm and good cheer was a sense of disquiet, perhaps even of time running out on a period of stability and consensus.

Notes

1   Edmund White, *The Beautiful Room Is Empty* (New York: Ballantine, 1988), pp. 7–8.
2   Eric Goldman, *The Crucial Decade – and After, America 1945–1960* (New York: Vintage, 1960), p. 291.
3   Michael Wood, *America in the Movies: or, "Santa Maria, It Had Slipped My Mind!"* (New York: Basic Books, 1975), pp. 180–1.
4   Donald Spoto, *Stanley Kramer: Filmmaker* (New York: G. P. Putnam's Sons, 1978), pp. 207–15.

Documents

Introduction to Documents

The 1950s were a time when youth culture and especially youth rebellion made it into the newspapers and onto the nation's movie screens in a major way. The presence of gangs and widespread reports of increased juvenile delinquency presented major challenges to the ideals of prosperity, consensus, and conformity. In the first document, prominent gossip columnist Hedda Hopper interviews *Rebel Without a Cause* (1955) star James Dean – whose mystique grew even greater following his untimely death in a car crash a few months later. The thoughtful teen idol was not at all what Hopper had expected. The two remaining documents show how a movie critic's personal politics can affect how he or she feels about a film. The *Cue* review of *Rebel Without a Cause* is sympathetic to the plight of modern teenagers; *New York Times* critic Bosley Crowther expresses a far less positive view toward the film and the problems of teenage life.

Teen Idol: Hedda Hopper Interviews James Dean

Source: *Chicago Tribune – New York News*, March 27, 1955

I can't remember when any screen newcomer generated as much excitement in Hollywood as did James Dean in his first picture "East of Eden." Word got out that we had a "young genius" in our midst who was as rebellious as he was talented. Producers, directors, critics flocked to see the film before its release. Inevitably they found their attention, despite the fine work of the other actors, riveted on a twenty-three-year-old ex-farm boy from Indiana.

I was cautious. In my business I get "genius" dished out as the regular meal. I generally take it with a grain of salt. I'd seen Dean only once. Slumping, surly looking and carelessly dressed in the studio commissary, he was not impressive. But after watching his performance, I admitted he was worth all the praise given him – and perhaps more. On the screen he has about him an almost unbearable tenseness; a subdued spirit leaping to be heard; and an ability to project an ever-changing, fleeting mood.

Wanting to know what made him tick, I invited him to my house for a chat. He arrived on the dot, wearing a charcoal-colored suit, black shirt and tie, and on his feet heavy riding boots. When you see him on the screen, you're not aware that he's not quite six feet tall. His height is a sore spot with him. Ask him how tall he is, and he'll retort: "My feet just touch the ground. Abe Lincoln said that – I didn't." A serious and thoughtful and amazingly articulate youngster, he takes you completely by surprise with unexpected flashes of humor.

"From the farm to the movies is quite a jump," I said. "I'd like to know how you managed that."

Jimmy leaped up from his chair, the only straight-backed seat in the room ("I don't like to be too comfortable"), strode over to the fireplace, whirled around and after a long pause, said, "When I was four or five my mother had me playing the violin – I was a blasted child prodigy. My family came to California and before it was over my mother had me tap dancing. Not at the same time I was playing the violin," he added with a twinkle. "My mother died when I was eight – and the violin was buried, too. Then I left California. I was anemic –." He stopped suddenly and said, "What this story needs is a background of music."

"I've got it," said I and turned on some records.

"I was anemic," he continued, "so I went back to the farm. I don't know whether I was looking for greater source of life and expression – or blood."

"You're killing me," I laughed.

Dean gave me a knowing look and said, "Oh, you've got a lot of work to do yet." Then he continued: "Getting healthy can be hazardous. You have to assume more responsibility. Now this was a real farm I was on and I worked like crazy – as long as someone was watching me. The forty acres of oats was a huge stage and when the audience left, I took a nap and things didn't get plowed or harrowed.

"I made high marks in school until I met a friend who taught me to wrestle and kill cats and fight and other things boys do behind barns, and I began to live. My grades fell off. This was taken a dim view of. But I was gaining my health.

"I felt a need to prove myself and I had the facility to do so. I began doing dramatic readings for the WCTU [Women's Christian Temperance Union]. I was that tall (he measured about half his present size) and instead of doing little poems about mice, I recited gory odes. This made me a straight little harpy in short pants. But I won all the medals the WCTU had to offer; then I became proficient at wielding a paint brush and sketching. I became an athelete and won the state pole vault championship. I played basketball and baseball. I won the Indiana State dramatic contest reading Charles Dickens' 'The Mad Man.'" He paused and explained, "The decision to act was never prompted. My whole life has been spent in a dramatic display of expression.

"When I graduated from high school, I enrolled as a pre-law student at UCLA [University of California, Los Angeles]. But I stayed only two years. I couldn't take the (he searched for the right words) tea-sipping, moss-walled Academicians. There's always somebody in your life who opens your eyes and makes you see your mistakes and stimulates you to the point of trying to find your way. Not of rectifying your mistakes but of growing. In my life that somebody was James Whitmore. He encouraged me to go to New York and with the fortification of his knowledge of theater and the right way of working, I went. After several jobs on TV, I did a couple of plays.

"Whitmore was working at Warners when I came out, and I wanted to thank him for his kindness and patience, but he said, 'It's not necessary. Elia Kazan (director of "East of Eden") did the same thing for me, and you will do the same for someone else.' I feel I have been of some benefit to young actors – it's the only way to repay Jimmy. But let me say this. No one really helps you; you do it yourself."

"Your performance in 'East of Eden' showed a great understanding of people and character. How did one so young achieve that?"

"This gift astonishes me," he said. "An actor must observe. He must feel the need to become involved in many things; he must have a cardinal interest in all things. Aristotle said, 'A gentleman should play the flute, but not too well.' At the time of youth when all your interests and dreams are coming into focus, you find a craft – acting – to help you untangle your natural resources, everything you've been interested in. Trust and belief are two prime considerations. You must not allow yourself to be opinionated. You must say, 'Wait. Let me see.' And above all, you must be honest with yourself.

"Acting is wonderful and immediately satisfying, but it is not the end-all, be-all of my existence. My talents lie in directing even more than acting. And beyond direction, my great fear is writing. That's the god. I can't apply the seat of my pants right now to write – I'm too youthful and silly, but someday. ..."

That someday will never come if his studio bosses have anything to say about it. His Warners contract calls for nine pictures in six years. He will play the brooding Jett Rink in "Giant" for George Stevens, and he also has been announced for Nick Ray's "Rebel Without a Cause," a story of extravagant youth from a higher social strata than most delinquents.

Jimmy gets 1956 off from pictures to return to Broadway. He says he will never give up New York entirely: "It's a fertile, wonderful, generous city, if you can accept the violence and decadence. There are so many things to do. I go to dancing school, take percussion lessons, acting lessons, attend concerts, operas. ..."

"And Hollywood?" I asked.

This took some thought on his part. Obviously, James Dean will never become part of the hard core of Hollywood, the swimming pool, Cadillac, party-giving brigade. "I was raised in a simple way," he said. "We learned that the church and the theater are not just structures of brick and mortar. Hollywood is brick and mortar. So is New York. But within the confines of that brick and mortar, you find perceptive, receptive people which compensate for the exterior."

He walked over to the fireplace again, raised the lid on one of my bristol boxes, and aping the doorman at a big Hollywood premiere, said, "Send up Mr. Dean's car."

"Speaking of cars," I said, "I understand you have a motorcycle and tear around town on it."

He frowned at me like a teacher trying to be patient while correcting a stubborn pupil: "I have a motorcycle. I do not *tear around* on it, but intelligently motivate myself through the quagmire and entanglement of your streets.

"A lone wolf," he began, "is a four-legged animal who by his own efforts ..."

He was off on another of his scholarly descriptions, so I interrupted with, "Tell me, don't you mind live television? – you do a lot of it."

"I don't mind anything that's good and live."

"Doesn't it scare you?"

"Not if I have a good grip of the character I'm playing and know what I'm doing. Cannons could go off and it wouldn't bother me."

I sized up this pint-sized but giant-talented 23-year-old and said, "You've got a long and beautiful life ahead of you."

"I hope the second adjective is the more abundant," he replied as he smiled his way out into the twilight.

Reviews of Rebel Without a Cause

Source: "What Makes Juveniles Delinquent?," *Cue*, October 29, 1955; Bosley Crowther, "Juvenile Misfits," *New York Times*, October 30, 1955

What Makes Juveniles Delinquent?

REBEL WITHOUT A CAUSE – (*Warner*) *At the Astor*. What makes kids go haywire? What sets them off into almost unbelievable and seemingly senseless acts of violence, vandalism and anti-social behavior? Juvenile delinquents (perhaps it would be better just to call them the mixed-up kids they so frequently are) are not always the product of slums, poverty and ignorance. Many come from "nice" neighborhoods and schools, good homes and well-educated parents. Some may share their elders' restlessness and uneasiness in the shaky times in which we live – and seek in sudden excitement and "kicks" emotional release from pressures they cannot understand, or resist.

Certainly, a good number of off-bounds youngsters seem to have lacked the stabilizing security of a united family: an emotional fortress buttressed against the harsh world outside. When the rapid pace of modern living spins this family circle too fast, its parts tend to fly apart – leaving behind a frightening emptiness. Children cannot exist in a vacuum, and so seek elsewhere for the comforting things they miss most – companionship, love, the acceptance of others, and a place in the world.

"Rebel Without a Cause" is an absorbing, poignant drama on this theme. It carries a terrific wallop and conviction in its tense story of three mixed-up youngsters in a "nice" community who get trapped, along with similarly rootless schoolmates, in a series of shocking social messes for which no one seems to have a ready explanation, or an easy solution.

Co-authors Nicholas Ray and Stewart Stern – basing their fictional drama on factual police-court research – attribute the wild behavior of their three leading juvenile characters to lack of family unity in the homes they came out of: a youth whose parents are interminably bickering; a girl whose parents don't understand her because they've never taken the trouble to try; and a younger boy, starving for affection because he's never had any – both his parents finding it more convenient to live away from home most of the year.

These three teen-agers are the core of the drama – although many of their school pals in somewhat similar predicaments also bounce around from escapade to escapade, just for kicks. One, sneered at for being a "wise guy," is challenged to a switch-blade battle – and later to a "chickie run." Getting no help or intelligent counsel from his squabbling parents, he lets himself be taken into this dangerous game, in which he and another boy are to race stolen cars at high speed up to the edge of a cliff – and then jump out just before the car leaps into space. First boy "out" is chicken. Unfortunately, one youth, trapped in his car, goes over the cliff with it and is drowned in the sea below. Another gets drunk and runs beserk; a third gets a gun to protect his friend in the inevitable fight and flight, shoots a cop and is himself slain by police bullets in a night-time siege. The girl, running away from home, finds a kindred "lost soul" in the victor of the chickie run.

The drama, vivid, unreeled in almost documentary style, is first rate "theatre," intelligent in its writing and direction, and superb in the high quality of its performances. James Dean, the young actor who made so great an impression last spring in John Steinbeck's "East of Eden," and who died so tragically a few weeks ago in an automobile accident, gives a memorable performance as the rebel of the title. Others who contribute toward the tremendous impact of the film are Natalie Wood and Sal Mineo, Corey Allen and Dennis Hopper, and Jim Backus and Ann Doran. Mr. Ray directed.

Cue, October 29, 1955

Juvenile Misfits

"Rebel Without a Cause" depicts another set

The recognized increase in the number of youngsters in our society who are emotionally disturbed and who manifest their disturbance in various manners, including delinquency and crime, offers a strong temptation to film makers to move in on that theme. Goodness knows, it is infinitely dramatic and full of possibilities. But it is also exceedingly delicate and subject to easy abuse by those who, either willfully or blindly, might misrepresent or sensationalize.

Certainly there was no intention on the part of Metro-Goldwyn-Mayer to make its "Blackboard Jungle" an exaggeration of the general nature of the boys and the conditions that prevail in a typical big-city vocational high school in a low-class area. But some of the critical reactions to that picture were almost as strong as the resentments and violences in it. The feeling was that it had gone overboard.

So, we suspect, many people will feel that Warner Brothers' "Rebel Without a Cause" is a desperate and dangerous distortion of another aspect of modern disturbed youth. For there is a tendency in this picture to toss every bit of the blame for the insecurity and rebelliousness of its three key youngsters upon their parents and the police – the former for not "understanding" and the latter for being dull and dumb.

No "chicken"

The main character in this item at the Astor is a handsome teen-age lad who has a phobia about being tagged a "chicken" (a coward) by his unstable friends. This is because his well-off father, whom he apparently once loved, has lacked the "guts" to stand up to his nagging mother in the forcible manner the boy thinks he should. And so our restless, mumbling misfit, played intensely by the late James Dean, is indecisive himself and is groping for security and an understanding love.

The person from whom he gets it, all in the course of one mad day, is a girl his own age of good background who is also emotionally disturbed. Her trouble is that her father stopped kissing her when she was 16 and this has filled her with such a sense of not belonging in her family that she has taken up with high school "cow-boys" and "goons."

In the course of proving he isn't "chicken" by fighting a switch-blade knife duel with one of these lads and then by vying with him in a desperate and suicidal game with automobiles, Mr. Dean wins the admiration of the young lady, played prettily by Natalie Wood. Together they seek a lonely exile, from which they are soon returned home when a young friend, also a misfit, tragically is killed by the police. Fortunately, at this point, dawn breaks in the parents' minds.

There is a great deal in this picture that does reflect the attitudes of certain teen-age elements, particularly in their bullying braggadocio and their mania for pointless violence. But the insistence with which the scriptwriter and director address sympathy to the youngsters at the expense of their parents and others who represent authority (even an innocent schoolteacher also comes in for a passing knock) renders this picture's likely influence upon real youngsters with emotional disturbance questionable. There is a deception in its pretense of "understanding" that can gravely mislead.

Little egos

We certainly would not want to argue for the prohibition of such films, but we continue to insist that producers be more careful and responsible in what they say. To paraphrase an old axiom, little egos have big eyes.

Speaking of prohibition, we hope everyone took careful note that the United States Supreme Court has swung another wallop at the pre-release censorship of films. In giving a decision last Monday on an appeal of the distributors of "The Moon Is Blue" against the banning of that film in Kansas, the court repeated what it has said – that it is a violation of the guarantees of free speech for a state to condemn a film for being "obscene." In four decisions, now, the Supreme Court has invalidated censorship laws. How long will it take state legislators to get this through their heads?

Bosley Crowther, *New York Times*, October 30, 1955

Readings and Screenings

Peter Biskind's *Seeing is Believing: How Hollywood Taught Us to Stop Worrying and Love the Fifties* (New York: Pantheon Books, 1983) provides a comprehensive and entertaining look at film and society in the 1950s. The broad spectrum of the decade's social problem films are discussed in Peter Roffman and Jim Purdy, *The Hollywood Social Problem Film: Madness, Despair, and Politics from the Depression to the Fifties* (Bloomington,

IN: Indiana University Press, 1981); David Manning White and Richard Averson, *The Celluloid Weapon: Social Comment in the American Film* (Boston, MA: Beacon Press, 1972); Robert B. Ray, *A Certain Tendency of the Hollywood Cinema, 1930–1980* (Princeton, NJ: Princeton University Press, 1985); Wheeler Winston Dixon, *Lost in the Fifties: Recovering Phantom Hollywood* (Carbondale, IL: Southern Illinois University Press, 2005). The problems and pleasures of teenage life are discussed in Thomas Patrick Doherty, *Teenagers and Teenpics: The Juvenilization of American Movies in the 1950s* (Boston, MA: Unwin Hyman, 1988); Jon Lewis, *The Road to Romance and Ruin: Teen Films and Youth Culture* (London: Routledge, 1992). Fears and cinematic depictions of nuclear war are analyzed in J. Hoberman, *An Army of Phantoms: American Movies and the Making of the Cold War* (New York: The New Press, 2011); Joyce A. Evans, *Celluloid Mushroom Clouds: Hollywood and the Atomic Bomb* (Boulder, CO: Westview Press, 1998); Alan Nadel, *Containment Culture: American Narrative, Postmodernism, and the Atomic Age* (Durham, NC: Duke University Press, 1995). For an examination of gender and film, see J. David Slocum, ed., *Rebel Without a Cause: Approaches to a Maverick Masterwork* (Albany, NY: State University of New York Press, 2005); Jackie Byars, *All that Hollywood Allows: Re-Reading Gender in 1950's Melodrama* (Chapel Hill, NC: University of North Carolina Press, 1991). The link between westerns and American ideology is explored in Will Wright, *Six Guns and Society: A Structural Study of the Western* (Berkeley, CA: University of California Press, 1975).

The optimism and seeming innocence of the 1950s can be gleamed in lavish musicals such as *Singin' in the Rain* (1952), *Oklahoma* (1955) and *Guys and Dolls* (1955). Westerns such as *Broken Arrow* (1950), *High Noon* (1952), *Shane* (1955), and *The Searchers* (1956) offered audiences more complex visions of battles between good and evil. The conformity demanded by the new corporate culture of the 1950s is dramatically displayed in *The Man in the Gray Flannel Suit* (1956), while reluctance to conform is stressed in *East of Eden* (1955). Teenage rebellion was an especially popular cinematic subject and can be seen in dramas such as *The Wild One* (1953), *Rebel Without a Cause* (1955) and *Blackboard Jungle* (1955); in youth culture rock and roll films such as *Rock Around the Clock* (1956), *Rock, Rock, Rock!* (1956); and in the slew of Elvis Presley films such as *Love Me Tender* (1956), *Jailhouse Rock* (1957), and *King Creole* (1958). The fear of prosperous teens falling prey to drugs is the subject of *High School Confidential* (1958); a harder hitting view of drug addiction is presented in *The Man With the Golden Arm* (1955). Prominent social problem films of the era touched on issues of race – *No Way Out*

(1950) and *The Defiant Ones* (1958); corruption on the waterfront – *Edge of the City* (1957); the criminal justice system – *Twelve Angry Men* (1957); organized crime – *The Racket* (1951); media manipulation of politics – *A Face in the Crowd* (1957); alcoholism – *I'll Cry Tomorrow* (1955); and the dangers of militarism and nuclear war – *Paths of Glory* (1957) and *On the Beach* (1959). For markedly different views of women and gender roles, compare *All About Eve* (1950), *Pillow Talk* (1958), and *Some Like It Hot* (1959). Those interested in Cold War films of the era should consult the titles suggested in the previous chapter.

9

Race, Violence, and Film: From the Blaxploitation Era of the 1960s to the "Hood-Homeboy" Movies of the 1990s

Introduction to Article

From the beginning of the film industry, African Americans have generally been portrayed in patronizing and derogatory ways. Yet, from time to time, minority groups get so fed up with the ways in which they are depicted on screen that they create a whole new set of cinematic images about themselves. Between 1969 and 1974, independent black filmmakers and studios created a new genre of violence-infused movies known as Blaxploitation films. These were the first films since race movies aimed specifically at black audiences – especially inner-city youths. They contained themes and values that, while popular among young African-American moviegoers, generated a great deal of debate and concern among critics and community leaders, black as well as white. During the 1990s, however, images and explanations of black violence took a markedly different turn.

Ed Guerrero analyzes the politics and evolution of black cinematic violence – and heroism – from the Blaxploitation era of the 1960s to the "Hood-Homeboy" and black-themed historical films of the 1990s. He explains how these movies reflected many of the changes experienced by the African-American community during the last four decades of the twentieth century. For all their problems, Guerrero argues, Blaxploitation films spoke to the optimistic collective fantasies of black liberation while

Movies and American Society, Second Edition. Edited by Steven J. Ross.
© 2014 John Wiley & Sons, Inc. Published 2014 by John Wiley & Sons, Inc.

the far more pessimistic "Hood-Homeboy" action films of the 1990s were more concerned with the "grim, violent struggle for individual survival left in the wake of the faded collective dreams of the 1960s." Yet, Guerrero also shows how a new generation of male and female African-American directors hoped to educate as well as entertain audiences by making films such as *Malcolm X* (1992), *Rosewood* (1997) and *Beloved* (1998) that placed violence by and against blacks – as well as stories of black struggles for freedom – in a broad historical context.

Discussion Points

To what extent did images of blacks in Blaxploitation and Hood-Homebody films remedy previously negative stereotypes of African Americans? To what extent did they create new stereotypes? Were these films ultimately positive or negative? For whom? Why? What were the main messages of the black-themed historical films of the 1990s?

Black Violence as Cinema: From Cheap Thrills to Historical Agonies

Ed Guerrero

Source: J. David Slocum, ed., *Violence and American Cinema* (New York and London: Routledge, 2001), 211–25

The painful collision of comedy and history is a revealing place to start this exploration of black violence on the cinema screen. Americans living in the 1990s, a full thirty years after the end of the civil rights movement, are confronted with many unsettling paradigm shifts. As Chris Rock, the raw, funky heir to the politicized early comedic style of Richard Pryor, acidly notes in his stage act, wherever you find a boulevard named after Dr. Martin Luther King Jr. "run ... because there's some violence going down." With racism recoding and rearticulating its hegemony and privilege in the neoconservative language of the 1990s, the ironies are sharp, sad, and very obvious. For starters, all too many black people still remain poor, disenfranchised, and trapped in urban ghettos. The only "progress," it seems, is that now the main boulevards and public schools are named after the last generation's martyrs. Moreover, the great collective ideal of liberation, across the political spectrum, from nonviolent action to "by any means necessary" militancy, has eroded into an ambivalent, self-focused consumerism of brand-name jeans and sneakers, and intra-communal annihilation through gun-drug-gang violence.

… Despite the limited gains of the black middle class and the cosmetic rhetoric of "black progress," for all too many African Americans, mean ghetto streets are the lived reality, a reality that has been refracted in the hood-homeboy action flicks that have become such an influential, though now fading, staple of what critics have dubbed the "new black film wave" of the 1990s. Although hood-homeboy violence stands out, it is only one of many expressions and styles of black violence in contemporary cinema. For the purposes of this essay I would like to historicize, interrogate, and critically comment upon some of the varied social political, and psychic conditions, along with some of the many representations, that constitute the construction of black violence on the commercial cinema screen. In the process perhaps I can address a few salient questions raised about black violence in the movies. For instance, what is the general framework within which dominant cinema violence, black and white, expresses itself? What are the origins of black violence in contemporary commercial cinema and are there variations on the theme? And is black violence held to prefigured historical codes and a double standard by the dominant movie industry and its mainstream audience?

First, it is important to note that most black-focused films or black characters in mainstream films are not unique in their expressions of violence, and that blacks got into the screen violence game late. With few exceptions, the stylistic range of black violence follows the overall configuration of mainstream white cinematic violence, which escalated in 1966 with the collapse of the Production Code and the advent of such technology-driven, stunningly violent successes as *Bonnie and Clyde* (1967), *Bullitt* (1968), and *The Wild Bunch* (1969).[1] Since then, we as a nation have become increasingly entertained by, and addicted to, ever more graphic representations of violence expressed across a broad field of commercial movies with two loosely defined categories at either end. At the most popular pole, we have action-adventure or "popcorn" violence, with its emphasis on shootouts, car chases, pyrotechnics, quadraphonic noise, and ever increasing body counts. Other than shouted threats and screams, these films are light on dialogue, character development, and intellectual or psychological complexity. In industry terms, they are "sensation driven" and are made for Hollywood's biggest and most influential audience, the young.[2] Consequently, the violent, action-adventure blockbuster delivers a jolting cinematic experience that's more akin to the thrill of a hyperkinetic amusement park ride or an action-packed computer game. At the less profitable pole are the social, psychological or political dramas, and historical epics, made for an older, baby boomer audience seeking an aesthetic or intellectual experience at the movies. These films are considered by the industry as "plot and character driven," and when violence is depicted it is aesthetically, socially, or morally edifying, erupting in such contexts as dramatic, character-focused conflicts or the broader sweep of history – in genocidal cataclysms, mass movements, political struggles, and social upheavals.

Dominant cinema productions structured on action-adventure violence abound, as exemplified by films like *True Romance* (1993), the *Die Hard* saga (1988–95), *Terminator I* and *II* (1984 and 1991), *Independence Day* (1996), *Air Force One* (1997), and *The Replacement Killers* (1998). Appealing to adolescent fantasy, this is Hollywood's biggest money-making category. At the other end of the spectrum, films that try to historicize, comment on, or dramatize the psychic, moral, social, or political consequences of violence, like *Schindler's List* (1993), *Gandhi* (1982), *Michael Collins* (1996), *Dr. Zhivago* (1965), and *The Pawnbroker* (1965), are less common industry features. However, since some sort of violence is a necessary plot ingredient for box office success these days, our polarities are not discrete, and we find a great many feature films alloyed with violent moments regardless of their themes. ...

...

In black-focused commercial films we find a similar spectrum between the polar ends of cheap thrills and historical agonies. Features like *New Jack City* (1991), *Juice* (1992), *Menace II Society* (1993), *Trespass* (1992), *Set It Off* (1996), *Posse* (1993), and *Bad Boys* (1995) are all centered on violence as action-adventure entertainment and make up the popular end of the field. At the other end, examples of black-focused films that attempt to represent violence in a historical, moral, or epic context would include *Malcolm X* (1992), *Rosewood* (1997), *Amistad* (1997), and *Beloved* (1998). Those films that are a mix of action-adventure violence and politicized or historicized theme would include *Dead Presidents* (1995), *Boyz N the Hood* (1991), and *Panther* (1995). Moreover, both *Boyz N the Hood* and *Menace II Society*, as well as *Clockers* (1995), all make varied claims that their depictions of violence are meant to help stem black urban violence.

However we map this complex and tangled field, we find that the origins of contemporary black screen violence are located in Hollywood's blaxploitation period, which consists of sixty-something cheaply made black-focused action-adventure flicks released between 1969 and 1974. Representationally, things started to stir when, to the cheers of blacks and the applause of the mainstream white audience, star athlete turned actor Jim Brown sprinted down a line of ventilators, dropping grenades into them and blowing up a gathering of the elite Nazi German command in *The Dirty Dozen* (1967). The industry's long unspoken but strictly observed rules regarding the expression of black violence toward whites were beginning to erode under the political pressures of the civil rights movement and the surging "black power" aspirations of urban blacks. Before this defining cinematic moment, with rare exceptions, like Paul Robeson killing a prison guard (not even seen in today's prints) in *The Emperor Jones* (1933), or the obligatory threat of savage tribesmen in the Tarzan flicks or the Mau Maus in *Something of Value* (1957), black lives were expendable and spectacularly devalued. Except for the functional purposes of staging threats and challenges to white supremacy to which whites could heroically respond, nonwhites were prohibited from inflicting violence upon whites, for compared to black life, white life was sacrosanct on the cinema screen.[3]

However, it was not too long after Jim Brown's grenade attack that a black superhero outlaw with revolutionary pretensions emerged in *Sweet Sweetback's Baadasssss Song* (1971) to maim or kill several white policemen, enjoy various dubious sexual escapades, and then escape a citywide dragnet to brag about it all. Thus the blaxploitation formula, which generally consisted of a black hero out of the ghetto underworld, violently challenging "the Man" and triumphing over a corrupt, racist system, was born. What followed was a succession of detectives, gangsters, ex-cons, cowboys, dope dealers, pimps, insurgent slaves, and women vigilantes in flicks like *Shaft*, *Superfly*, *Across 110th Street*, *Black Caesar*, *Drum*, *Black Mama*, *White Mama*, and *Boss Nigger*, in which the protagonists shoot, punch, stab, and karate chop their way through a series of low-budget features that garnered mega-profits for Hollywood.[4] A couple of things are notable about the construction of violence in most blaxploitation period pieces. For one, because the technological advances of today's cinematic apparatus allow the industry to ever more convincingly represent or simulate anything that can be written or imagined, blaxploitation violence in many instances now appears crudely rendered and visually "camp" or naive in comparison to graphic blood- and brain-splashing shoot-outs in contemporary hood-homeboy action flicks. Also, the blaxploitation genre had a place for macho women in its pantheon of fierce action stars, women who echoed and upheld the cultural moment's call for a reclamation of black manhood in the most violent, masculinist terms. Pam Grier in *Coffy* (1973) and *Foxy Brown* (1974), and Tamara Dobson in *Cleopatra Jones* (1973) play sexy black women adventurers configured to the social message of the times and black male adolescent fantasies that largely determined the success of blaxploitation films at the box office.

But perhaps most important, while the genre is full of fantastic moments of popcorn violence, like Foxy Brown (Pam Grier) triumphantly displaying the genitals of her archenemy in a jar, or vampire Blacula (William Marshall) energetically dispatching several white L.A. cops in *Blacula* (1972), blaxploitation violence, in most cases, referenced black social reality, or transcoded, however fancifully, black political struggles and aspirations of the times. When outside the movie theaters urban blacks were increasingly becoming disenchanted with the limited gains of the civil rights movement, and black militancy was on the rise with insurrections in hundreds of U.S. cities, these social energies found barely containable expression on the blaxploitation screen.

Transcoding the energy of the moment, the box office hit *Superfly* (1972) exemplifies blaxploitation violence's social grounding in a variety of expressions, even though the film was considered regressive by many black critics because of its blatant celebration of cocaine use and the hero's self-indulgent, drug pushing, hustling lifestyle. In the film's opening the protagonist dope dealer, Superfly (Ron O'Neal), chases down and then brutally stomps a junkie mugger. However, the mise-en-scène is insistently socially contextualized as the foot chase winds its way through the grimy alleys and dilapidated tenements of Harlem and culminates with this hapless derelict getting the vomit kicked out of him in front of his impoverished wife and children; and all this to the over-dub refrain of Curtis Mayfield singing the hit "Little Child Runnin' Wild." No matter what we think of Superfly, or this nameless junkie, the social setting of this opening vignette forces us into a disturbing awareness of urban poverty, drugs, and the wicked symbiotic power relation between the junkie and the pusherman.

In contrast to the gritty realism of the black underworld informing *Superfly*, where, interestingly, no guns are ever fired and most of the violence wears the cool mask of macho gesture, threat, and intimidation, the movie concludes with a rather fantastic athletic explosion of fisticuffs. In a cartoonish allusion to Popeye's love of spinach, Superfly toots up on cocaine and then singlehandedly whips three police detectives (in slow motion, no less), all while the corrupt police commissioner, literally known as "the Man," holds him at gunpoint. The social issues of this violent denouement emerge when Superfly informs the Man that he's quitting the dope business, with a million dollars in drug profits. However, this retirement speech is also meant to recuperate the film's reactionary attitude and align it more closely with the political energies of the times. For Superfly dramatically tells the Man off in the collective voice and terms of the black social insurgence of the late 1960s, thus framing what would be a totally implausible scene, and the film, in the social yearnings of the historical moment. This type of politically conscious speech is fairly standard throughout the genre, from Ji-Tu Cumbuka's rousing gallows speech after an aborted slave revolt in *Mandingo* (1972), to Pam Grier's call to black unity and arms, against the backdrop of a wall-size George Jackson poster, in *Foxy Brown*.

It can be argued that society's racial power relation hasn't changed all that significantly in the past twenty years,[5] but it's clear that the psychic and social influences impelling the construction of black cinematic violence most certainly have changed. In comparison to the blaxploitation era, the hood-homeboy films of the 1990s are less obviously politically focused, and in their violent nihilism (and sometimes self-contempt) they hardly suggest the possibility of social change. Violence in the blaxploitation genre, in all of its expressions, no matter how crude or formulaic, transcoded the black liberation impulse of the 1960s. By contrast, the depiction of violence in the new black film wave, and especially the home-boy-action flick, rather than mediating black social and political yearnings, is concerned more with depicting the grim, violent struggle for individual survival left in the wake of the faded collective dreams of the 1960s. In white commercial cinema, films such as *Being There* (1979), *The Big Chill* (1983), *Wall Street* (1987), and *Running on Empty* (1988) mediate aspects of the shift away from a 1960s cultural orientation. *The Toy* (1982) and *Trading Places* (1983) certainly signal this shift for black-focused mainstream cinema as surely as the rise of their respective stars, Richard Pryor and Eddie Murphy, followed the end of blaxploitation. The concentration of Hollywood's attention and production budgets on the rise of Pryor and Murphy coincides with the political and cultural shift from "we" to "me" in mainstream culture and in representations of African Americans in commercial cinema. For no matter how imperfectly rendered its narratives, violence in much of Blaxploitation either depicted or implied the shaking off of the oppression of "the Man," and, significantly, the movement toward the dream of a liberated future.

By contrast, violence in the new black film wave for the most part transcodes the collapse of those very hopes under the assault of the Reagan and Bush years and their rollback policies on affirmative action, black social progress, multiculturalism, and the welfare state in general. And perhaps that is the ghettocentric hood-homeboy flick's most salient political point. With black inner-city neighborhoods ringed and contained by police departments, totally deindustrialized, poisoned with abundant drugs, fortified with malt liquor, and flooded with cheap guns, ghettos have become free fire zones where the most self-destructive impulses are encouraged by every social and economic factor in the environment. Or as a white cop in Spike Lee's *Clockers* (1995) coldly analogizes, the urban ghetto has become "a self-cleaning oven." At best, then, 1990s cinematic hood-homeboy violence is socially diagnostic in an attempt to raise consciousness by depicting the symptoms of a failed social and racial system. These depictions amount to endless variations on scenes of black and other nonwhite people trapped in ghettos, and killing each other. Note (Ice Cube) Doughboy's "either they don't know, or they don't care" appeal for an awakening of conscience (and consciousness) at the end of *Boyz N the Hood*. The Hughes brothers, the directors of *Menace II Society*, say it another way, declaring that they are not here to give people hope but rather to depict the realities of those trapped in the urban hood.[6] Thus one can discern the great distance between the political consciousness underpinning even the cheapest of blaxploitation, ghetto thrillers, and the hood-homeboy flicks of the 1990s black movie boom.

Yet, as with blaxploitation, the success of any commercial black film today is still eminently configured by the tastes of its (and Hollywood's) biggest aggregate, the youth audience, which mainly consumes action-adventure and generalized comedy and eschews drama and character-focused vehicles.[7] Consequently, the popular end of the spectrum of 1990s black-focused films is crowded with those productions deploying violence very much in the style of dominant cinema, as a necessary action-adventure ingredient for box office success. Moreover, one can perceive a definite escalation or acceleration of violence from film to film. John Singleton's *Boyz N the Hood*, while punctuated with explicitly violent scenes, structures its narrative and ideology around the fates of good and bad brothers, Tre (Cuba Gooding) and Doughboy (Ice Cube). In this way the film at least holds out the possibility of escape from the hood through the time-honored, black race-building route of education. Conversely, the fates of Caine (Tyrin Turner) and O-Dog (Larenz Tate) are sealed when O-Dog brutally murders two Korean grocers in the opening moments of *Menace II Society*. From this gruesome beginning, the trajectory is straight down. And compared to *Boyz* the body count increases exponentially; the action in *Menace* is best described as sort of a gruesome hyperviolence.

Consequently, many of the issues and debates regarding the depiction of extreme graphic violence as entertainment or realism were brought into high focus with the release and box office success of *Menace II Society*. The Hughes brothers have claimed that their depiction of violence in *Menace* was a means to promote anti-violence efforts in the urban hood, telling the *New York Times*, "we wanted to show the realities of violence, we wanted to make a movie with a strong antiviolent theme and not like one of those Hollywood movies where hundreds of people die and everybody laughs and cheers."[8] However, the film's violence and impact on its audience would seem to annul this claim. As the brothers say, throughout most of *Menace* violence is handled in an ugly, brutal fashion, as in the killings of the Korean grocers that open the film. However, the narrative is saturated with so many intensely violent scenes that violent action becomes the main structuring, captivating – and thus cumulatively entertaining – device in the film. What is more, in *Menace*'s final moments, when Caine is cut down in a hail of bullets, the scene is filmed in close-frame slow motion, thus fetishizing violence and evoking a style in the grammar of representational violence going back to Hollywood's foundational *Bonnie and Clyde* (1967).[9] But perhaps more disturbing was *Menace*'s social impact, with film and media critics noting that youth audiences cheered the violent scenes – particularly the one in which the Korean grocers were killed. Because film is an intensely visual medium, audiences, whether impressionable or sophisticated, will always look past what a director says about a film's lofty intents to the visible evidence of what a film actually shows them on the big screen.

It is also important to note that ghettocentric violence is not always revealed through the lens of the hood-homeboy action formula and that in various ways some black artists have tried to counter its exploitation on the screen. When he stands up to the neighborhood bully, Ice Cube comes to a critical moment of extreme provocation in his popular hood-homeboy comedy *Friday* (1995). Flush with anger, Ice Cube pulls a gun, but instead of following the protocols of homeboy realism and "bustin' a cap" in his adversary, he pauses and reflects on the dire outcomes of such an act. Spike Lee's character-focused drama *Clockers*, about a low-level drug dealer, covers the same issues and the same deadly turf. Like Ice Cube, Lee turns his eye more to the destructive consequences and grief that violence brings to the community and people's lives. The violence in *Clockers* is minimal, low-key though realistic, and decidedly not of the action-entertainment variety. Marking the contrast between anti-violence strategies in *Clockers* and *Menace*, critic Leonard Quart comments that "Lee truly wants to turn his adolescent audience away from violence, rather than ostensibly moralize against it like *Menace* which simultaneously makes the gory spectacle of people being slaughtered so exciting that the audience could howl with joy while watching."[10]

Nowhere are the contrasts between sensation-driven and character/ plot-driven films more evident than between the filmmaking practices of black men and black women, and how these gender differences are perceived by the dominant film industry. Since the breakthrough of Julie

Dash's *Daughters of the Dust* (1991), which had a reflective, dreamlike surface and no action-adventure violence, Hollywood has released into mainstream distribution a meager handful of features directed or written by black women, films like *Just Another Girl on the I.R.T.* (1993) directed by Leslie Harris, *I Like It Like That* (1994) directed by Darnell Martin, and *Eve's Bayou* (1997), written by Kasi Lemmons. When it occurs, violence in all of these films is understated, it causes the protagonists a great deal of anguish, and it is used to dramatize the complexities of broader social or psychological situations. Film industry exclusion intensifies according to the number of out-groups one belongs to. So, reinforcing the bias against black women's filmmaking, Hollywood's executive offices, in general, tend to view women's narratives as "soft," centered on drama and character, and outside of their most reliable money-making formulas, which, of course, means liberal doses of action and violence. These differences in industry perception and audience consumption of black men's and women's products, especially concerning the uses of violence, in part explain the box office success of *Menace II Society* and the comparative failure of *Just Another Girl on the I.R.T.*, which were both modest-budget black films released at the same time.

It is also interesting to note that the gender hybrid originating in blaxploitation, the woman-focused action-adventure flick, has risen again in a series of variations and specific moments in films. *Set It Off*, featuring Queen Latifah, Jada Pinkett, and Vivica A. Fox, is about an all-girl gang that tries to escape the ghetto by pulling a series of increasingly violent bank jobs. In Quentin Tarantino's blaxploitation reprise *Jackie Brown* (1997), the undisputed queen of black camp violence, Pam Grier, returns to play a somewhat more subdued, middle-aged airline stewardess who rooks the streetwise gunrunner Ordell (Samuel L. Jackson) out of $500,000. One of Grier's big Freudian moments of reversal and castrating violence comes when she presses a gun to Ordell's dick and talks bad to him. And again recalling blaxploitation's sexual ideology, in Ice Cube's *The Player's Club* (1998), homosexuality, the great threat to cultural nationalism, is punished as the beautiful stripper protagonist brutally defeats the "wicked" lesbian stripper in the film's culminating woman-on-woman fistfight.

If violence is the principal and profitable cheap thrill in the hood-homeboy action flick, it also finds expression at the other end of the black cinema spectrum as historical agony in such recent films as *Malcolm X, Rosewood,* and *Amistad, Beloved,* and to a lesser degree in *Panther.* As Spike Lee's most ambitious and publicized project to date, *Malcolm X* grapples with a routine industry contradiction: it is a Hollywood bio-pic with crossover money-making intentions, but at the same time, it aims to portray the life of a black revolutionary hero with some historical veracity. In pursuit of the broad audience in the middle, Lee mixes his renderings of violence by first entertaining us with the adventures of Malcolm as a hoodlum with his sidekick Shorty as they pursue the transgressive adventure of the hustling life. Lee even throws in a dance-musical number in zoot suits. But in the latter half of *Malcolm X*, the mood shifts and culminates with the brutally drawn out and explicit assassination of Malcolm X before a public assembly; the moment is both stunning and ambivalent in its effects. This scene has complex crosscurrents of political meaning, first working as historiographic realism to psychically shock us into fully recognizing the sacrifice that Malcolm X (and his family) made for black liberation and social progress. Yet the graphically violent surplus of the scene also turns it …, into spectacle, a public execution by firing squad rendered in brutal detail, punishing Malcolm for his beliefs. …

Like Lee's *Malcolm X*, Mario and Melvin Van Peebles's *Panther* aspires to historical distinction, this time by sympathetically depicting the rise of the Black Panther Party, and the grievances of the black community that brought the party into being – police brutality, ghettoization, economic marginalization, and disenfranchisement. However, while grappling with the same recurring contradictions between commerce and politics that appeared in *Malcolm X*, *Panther* relies mostly on the action-adventure violence of the Hollywood heroic individual in pursuit of profits at the box office. Thus beyond the political insights about its historical moment the film articulates, like in the shoot-out in which Bobby Hutton is killed, the film's deployment of popcorn violence in other scenes tends to undermine *Panther*'s claims to a historically realist style. Moreover, this tangle of issues involving varied styles of violence is certainly relevant to John Singleton's *Rosewood* and Steven Spielberg's *Amistad*. And perhaps these issues can be best explored by considering a question salient to both films: How does one make a feel-good Hollywood movie, with big box office expectations, about some of history's most wicked crimes: racism, genocide, and slavery?

John Singleton answers, in *Rosewood*, by formulating his tale about the real-life 1923 destruction of the all-black Florida town of Rosewood by a white mob as a revisionist Western, replete with an opening scene of the loner hero Mann (Ving Rhames) riding into town on a black "hoss," packing two .45 automatics, and "lookin' for a nice place to settle down." As Lee did in *Malcolm X*, Singleton opts for a mix of action-adventure moments of popcorn violence, enveloped in a more shocking overall rendering of historicized violence. In one scene depicting the former, Mann hurries out of town to escape a deputized lynch mob, but he is set upon by a gang of white men and chased deep into the woods. Finally, Mann turns, stands his ground, and opens up with both of his .45s. Cut to the whites hauling ass out of the woods, with the punchline coming when they later excitedly exclaim that they were ambushed by a gang of "ten or fifteen niggers." The audience explodes with laughter. Singleton's timing and editorial touch with this classic scene from the archives of the cinematic Old West proves just right.

Overall, however, what happens to Rosewood on that gruesome night, as rendered by Singleton, is not at all funny or entertaining. At the height of the film's action, the disturbing sight of black men and women hanging from trees and telephone poles illuminated by the flames of their burning community, seamlessly merges with those old *Life*, *Jet*, and archival photographs of the very real lynchings in America's gallery of horrors. Consequently, *Rosewood*'s panorama of violence is decidedly not escapist entertainment in the Hollywood sense. Violence here provokes the return of barely repressed collective nightmares and guilty complicities, as well as a painful examination of the national conscience. These are all things we as a national audience don't like to address, even in the darkness and anonymity of our cinemas. The historical agony of genocidal violence is brought into sharp focus in one of *Rosewood*'s culminating scenes, in which one of the mob's prime instigators, proud of his crimes, forces his young son to look at a pile of black bodies awaiting disposal. Here, all of humanity's body counts are evoked, from Auschwitz to Wounded Knee to Mylai. Singleton's obvious point is that hope resides in the next generation, as the child rejects his father's wretched path and runs away from home.

Yet, as noted, *Rosewood* is a mainstream commercial vehicle, and as such, its approach to violence is necessarily a mixed bag. If the film aspires to social conscience by shocking us with the historically repressed and oppressed, the lynch mob and its victims, it unfortunately lapses into the delusion of Hollywood formula in its portrayal of violence against women, black and white. ...

Rosewood ends with the camera looking down in a long shot of a shack as we hear the screams of the white woman Fannie (Catherine Kellner), who initially yelled "nigger" to set things off, being brutally beaten by her husband, mixed with an over-dub of lush, poignant cinematic music of the type used to signal narrative and ideological resolution. In Singleton's defense one can speculate that a society that could burn an entire black town on impulse would have no trouble thrashing one defenseless, lower-class white woman of loose reputation, especially one who has been set up by the narrative. Fannie does bear the historical burden of the oft-deployed false rape charge against black men. Yet with this beating the film reverts to a final cheap thrill amounting to another act of symbolic punishment that displays the sacrificial offender/victim as spectacle, while hiding the intrigues of the much more guilty and powerful. Coming in the film's closing moment, then, this beating concentrates blame for the genocide of a racial minority on yet another Hollywood out-group, disenfranchised women.[11]

In dominant cinema, moreover, the representation of black violence in the service of white narratives still circulates powerfully, animating some of Hollywood's most popular features. This is in part because the sign of blackness has become so indispensable as the implicit, negative standard in neoconservative political rhetoric and moral panics about family, education, welfare, and crime. Simultaneously, however, the stylistic inventions and expressions of black culture powerfully influence every aspect of mainstream culture, especially urban youth styles, language, music, and dance. In many ways the films of writer-directors David Lynch and Quentin Tarantino epitomize the utility and profitability of black violence, as well as the deeply rooted psychological fantasies about the sign blackness in the white popular imaginary. David Lynch's crime-action-romance *Wild at Heart* (1990) opens with the gratuitous and brutally graphic murder of a black man who gets his brains publicly stomped out for the entertainment, and perhaps wish fulfillment, of the action-adventure audience. In this scene, in fact, David Lynch treats us to a "lynching," which also happens to be a play on his name and his style as invoked by the popular press.[12] More broadly, Quentin Tarantino, in films like *True Romance, Reservoir Dogs, Pulp Fiction, Get Shorty*, and *Jackie Brown*, appears to be deeply disturbed by barely repressed, ambivalent feelings about race in general, black masculinity in particular, and the issues of violence, miscegenation, and sex. Black male delinquents, while hip and alluring in Tarantino screenplays, wind up eliminated, raped, or murdered, with black male–white female miscegenation always punished. Conversely, black women are the exotic trophies of white male desire. ...

...

The big-budget, mainstream feature at the end of the scale of black violence as historical agony and realism is Steven Spielberg's *Amistad*, weighing in with production costs totaling $75 million. *Amistad* fits into a trajectory well established by a number of films made during the blaxploitation period, like the action- and sexploitation-driven *Mandingo* and *Drum* (1976), and sustained in the 1990s with *Sankofa* (1993) and *Beloved*, which sharply reverse or debunk Hollywood's genteel sentimental depiction of slavery over the eighty-year span of its "plantation genre."[13] Because *Amistad* recounts the actual events of a slave revolt on the high seas, and the successful repatriation of the rebellious Africans after an extensive court case, the film struggles in its narrative with two issues pertaining to black violence that are not given much exposure in dominant cinema. The first concerns the right, the necessity, of the slave to rebel against tyranny. The second issue has to do with the graphic revelation of the violence and oppression routinely inflicted upon blacks by the daily operations of the slave system.

Of course it's a long way from historical actuality to the big-budget Hollywood canvas, with its ultimate imperative that everybody's story be measured by its box office potential – that is, reduced to the compromises of its commodity status. Given the pressures on any blockbuster to return a profit at the ratio of three to one on an already hefty investment, it seems that in search of the broadest audience (read: white approval), Spielberg approaches the issue of black revolt against white systems of tyranny, or even the frank depiction of those systems, with narrative restraint, to say the least. Yet, due to the inherent violent and irrepressible surplus of the subject matter, *Amistad*, unavoidably perhaps, unmasks the extreme cruelty of the slave system in historical realist terms. Consequently, as in Spielberg's *Schindler's List* (1993), as well as the work of Lee and Singleton, here again we see the containing power of delimiting form and formula aimed at ensuring the biggest audience, in direct conflict with the insurgent tendency of *Amistad*'s inherently emancipatory content.

Amistad opens with a spirited, furious, and successful shipboard rebellion that soon goes adrift, with the black rebels being recaptured, imprisoned, and put on trial in New England. From here on the Africans are enslaved by the representational chains of Hollywood liberalism as they are portrayed as confused, exotic creatures and denied all agency, voice, and centrality in what one would expect to be their story. The narrative drags, then turns into a two-hour civics lesson about noble, well-intentioned whites defining and securing black freedom.[14] When it comes to Hollywood's standard depiction of black liberation struggles, black characters tend to have no agency in the production of their own history, and are reduced to passive victims emancipated by courageous whites (like the FBI in *Mississippi Burning* or the white lawyers in *Ghosts of Mississippi*). In fact, this stratagem is so worn that Matthew McConaughey was recruited from *A Time to Kill* (1996), to play yet another dedicated white lawyer in defense of a black cause in *Amistad*. This convention is also present in *Schindler's List*, in which the narrative focus is on factory owner Oskar Schindler and concentration camp commander Amon Goeth, with the Jews mostly reduced to the passivity of a grim historical backdrop. ...

The slave revolt in *Amistad*'s opening, a revolt of oppressed against oppressor, has considerable action-adventure impact and historical appeal.

Yet its placement is a subtle form of co-optation: staging the insurrection in the opening moments of the narrative denies it any conclusive, cathartic force, thus displacing the insight that resistance against oppression in defence of one's freedom is a form of justice, one afforded every white hero from John Wayne to Gary Cooper and Henry Fonda onward. As we come to see, *Amistad*'s version of justice is a weary court case that essentially celebrates constitutional definitions of *white* freedom. It is important to note that while the *Amistad* court case freed thirty-eight Africans, it did nothing to alter the fate of millions of black people enslaved in the United States, or the efficient workings of the slave system itself. If anything, the slave system was further legally entrenched and refined by such sanctions as the Fugitive Slave Act of 1850 or the Dred Scott decision of 1857. In contrast, note who has agency, and the narrative positioning of the violent slave insurrection, in Haile Gerima's *Sankofa*. Coming at the film's conclusion, this slave rebellion works as a resolution, underlining the brutality inflicted upon *Sankofa*'s blacks, broadcasting that they have agency, history, and justice in their own hands. What's at issue here is how the big-budget mainstream blockbuster, regardless of what its producers claim its subject is, almost always winds up talking about whiteness, guided by the persistent refrain of Eurocentrism that subtends its narrative.[15]

In fairness, however, *Amistad* is punctuated with scenes that cannot be entirely repressed, scenes that are quite disturbing and challenging to comfortable, dominant notions of slavery, cinematic, psychic, or otherwise. As noted, Hollywood's depiction of slavery has experienced a sharp reversal of meaning since the resistant blaxploitation of the 1970s. By now, the plantation resembles the blood-soaked ground of the concentration camp more than it does the majestic site of aristocratic Southern culture and gentility. So the irrepressible horror of the slave trade comes into disturbing focus with *Amistad*'s depictions of the infamous Middle Passage, and with one particularly stunning scene in which commerce and mass murder converge with brutal clarity, when the Spanish slavers discover that they don't have enough rations to keep their entire human cargo alive for the Atlantic crossing. Echoing the death camp scene in *Schindler's List*, in which the weak are culled from the strong, in *Amistad* the cargo's weak and sickly are stripped naked, chained together, and very efficiently thrown overboard. Besides the naked, chained bodies, underscoring a basic humanity, what is more disturbing about the scenes violence is the banal utility seen in the practices of maintaining human beings as slaves for profit. This insight is reinforced by other scenes of maintenance and discipline, in which slaves are fed, flogged, and washed in order to enhance their commodity value on the auction block in the

New World. Very much like *Schindler's List, Amistad*'s true force resides in its visual shock value, and in those resistant images, currents, and arguments that escape the policing of Hollywood's liberal, paternalist discourse. Relevant to the fundamental problem with both *Amistad* and *Schindler's List*, one critic puts it succinctly when he asks why *Schindler's List* "is so complicit with the Hollywood convention of showing catastrophe primarily from the point of view of the perpetrators."[16]

In conclusion, I have no doubts that the cinematic depiction of black violence expressed in a variety of mixtures between the poles of cheap, pyrotechnic thrills and the collective agony of historical catastrophes, between entertainment and edification, will continue to evolve as a deeply imbricated and, often, inseparable part of Hollywood's accelerating commitment to all forms of cinematic violence as a technology-enabled, profit-driven industry strategy. Predictably, even though the genre is played out,[17] the film industry will continue to produce a certain number of popcorn violence-saturated hood-homeboy flicks like the recent *Belly*, and the more restrained and socially grounded *Slam* (both 1998). Hope resides in the more innovative ways in which black filmmakers deploy violence in the service of their takes on realism, or the revision of social or historical issues from the black point of view. Suggestions of new directions can be seen in several recent black-inspired, black-cast commercial productions, including the Spike Lee-produced *Tales from the Hood* (1995) and the Oprah Winfrey-inspired and -produced *Beloved*. A horror flick, *Tales from the Hood* makes it clear that for blacks, the horrific repressed fears returning in the form of the monster are markedly political and have to do with the great violent horrors of African-American life: police brutality, lynching, racism, and the catastrophic effects of social inequality. In its mix of popcorn and historical violence, the monsters that arise in *Tales*, are more literal than metaphorical: corrupt, brutal cops framing black citizens, criminally violent hood-homeboys bent on autogenocide, and spouses who turn into violent monsters in front of their wives and children. Similarly, *Beloved* struggles to innovate and frankly depict the reality and consequences of slavery's violence through the metaphor of scarring, both physical and psychic. The violent horror of slavery is revealed in "rememory," in a series of flame-lit, nightmarish flashbacks of hangings, whippings, and bizarre mutilations that continue to haunt and scar the psyches, the narrative present, and the bodies of the film's black cast. Ultimately, then, what will continue to subtly influence the trajectory of black screen violence and suggest new creative directions for its expression and critical understanding will be the persistent and conscientious visions of wave after wave of new black filmmakers in all of their racial and heterogeneous incarnations – as gays, women, men, subalterns, artists, intellectuals – and their ability to bring fresh narrative, social, and representational possibilities to the big screen.

Notes

1 Martin Amis, "Blown Away," in *Screen Violence*, ed. Karl French (London: Bloomsbury, 1996), 12–15.

2 Neal Gabler, "The End of the Middle," *New York Times Magazine*, November 16, 1997, 76–78.

3 Ella Shohat and Robert Stam, *Unthinking Eurocentrism* (New York: Routledge, 1994), 23–25.

4 Ed Guerrero, "The Rise and Fall of Blaxploitation," in *Framing Blackness: The African American Image in Film* (Philadelphia: Temple University Press, 1993).

5 Derrick Bell, "Racial Realism—After We're Gone: Prudent Speculations on America in a Post-Racial Epoch," in *Critical Race Theory: The Cutting Edge*, ed. Richard Delgado (Philadelphia: Temple University Press, 1995), 2–8.

6 Jeff Giles, "A 'Menace' Has Hollywood Seeing Double," *Newsweek*, July 19, 1993, 52.

7 Geraldine Fabrikant, "Harder Struggle to Make and Market Black Films," *New York Times*, November 11, 1996, D1.

8 Bernard Weintraub, "Twins' Movie-Making Vision: Fighting Violence with Violence," *New York Times*, June 10, 1993, C13.

9 Paula Massood, "*Menace II Society*" *Cineaste* 20, no. 2 (1993): 44–45.

10 Leonard Quart, "Spike Lee's *Clockers*: A Lament for the Urban Ghetto," *Cineaste* 22, no. 1 (1996): 9–11.

11 René Girard, *Violence and the Sacred* (Baltimore: Johns Hopkins Univeristy Press, 1972), 1–38.

12 Sharon Willis, *High Contrast: Race and Gender in Contemporary Hollywood Film* (Durham, N.C.: Duke University Press, 1997), 131–32.

13 Guerrero, *Framing Blackness*, 10.

14 Maggie Montesinos Sale, *The Slumbering Volcano: American Slave Ship Revolts and the Production of Rebellious Masculinity* (Durham, N.C.: Duke University Press, 1998), 84–86. Besides an excellent historical survey of the *Amistad* affair, Sale here gives a good account of how the *Amistad* rebels were constructed as passive "happy-go-lucky children in need of protection" at the bottom of the abolitionist defence council's hierarchy.

15 Richard Dyer, *White* (London: Routledge, 1997), 3–4.

16 Michael Andre Bernstein, "The *Schindler's List* Effect," *The American Scholar* 13, no. 3 (summer 1994): 429–32.

17 Ed Guerrero, "A Circus of Dreams and Lies: The Black Film Wave Reaches Middle Age," in *The New American Cinema*, ed. Jon Lewis (Durham, N.C.: Duke University Press, 1998), 328–52.

Documents

Introduction to Documents

During the 1960s, many black activists regarded liberal integrationist films and African-American stars such as Sidney Poitier with great disdain. Yet, as the first documents taken from movie industry periodical *Variety* reveal, audience responses to the opening of Poitier's *Guess Who's Coming to Dinner* (1967) suggest that any film that portrayed a black–white love relationship proved far too radical for many whites. In the second document, Alvin Poussaint, a psychiatrist and descendant of Haitian emigrants, criticizes Blaxploitation films for creating new stereotypes that proved harmful to African-American youth and to the African-American community as a whole. What do you think?

Variety Reports Reactions to Guess Who's Coming to Dinner?

Source: Issues of *Variety*, February 28 to October 16, 1968

February 28, 1968: Atlanta, February 27 When Columbia chose to have Atlanta preem [sic] date of "Guess Who's Coming to Dinner?" at the northside Capri Cinema rather than at a downtown house, it meant that hordes of Negroes plus hippies of both races flocked into the community of Buckshead to see the recordbreaking click film on miscegenation.

Undoubtedly many residents were shocked by this unusual influx, and last week their anger was expressed by Lamar Q. Ball, the segregationist editor of the North Side News. "Never in your life have you Northsiders ever seen such a crowd in Buckshead. For three nights in one incomprehensible row!" he said in a front-page editorial. "Blacks and mulattos in part of the line outnumbered whites. This was anything but the usual North side Sunday night crowd."

He went on: "Black escorts for dun-colored girls could be seen enviously eyeing the blonde and brunet dates of white college students eager to have their turgid minds with an A for effort in mental development. ... The subject of the picture is what attracted these hordes, many of whom have

become contemptuous of their elders for denouncing those who are willing
to destroy the white race just by encouraging moron Negroes to vote."

In questioning the offbeat booking, he asked, "Why wasn't this movie
presented at the Fox or Loew's Grand? Because no one would have
noticed the race-mixing downtown!"

And he approvingly quoted "a woman who has had years of stage
experience" about the film's story of a Negro man marrying a white girl:
"Here is a subject that's fit only for secret discussion by young and old in
small private gatherings or in the late evenings by husbands and wives
who are fearful for the future of their sons and daughters. This is nothing
to be brought out in the open for sound-minded people to view in a
theatre, shoulder to shoulder with perverts."

Ball's viewpoint is obviously a minority one. Reviews in the general
press were favorable in Atlanta, which has long been considered one of
the South's most liberal cities. And, as implied above, business at the
Capri has been outstanding.

March 13, 1968: Cincinnati, March 12 Columbia's "Guess Who's
Coming to Dinner?" with Sidney Poitier got a record-making and a rock-
throwing reception in southern Ohio cities 26 miles apart.

In Cincinnati – which had riots last summer – the picture is jamming
the 3,000-seat Albee with mixed race audiences setting record grosses for
the Negro-engaged-to-white-gal tale.

In Hamilton robed Klansmen picketed the Court Theaters, Wednesday
night [March 6]. Next came counter-picketing and window smashing of
nearby stores and a filling station. Damage $1,840. No arrests.

March 20, 1968: Chicago, March 19 An undercover Chicago police
officer who infiltrated the Ku Klux Klan's Chicago Police Department
operation, last week revealed a Klan scheme to set off a couple of tear-gas
bombs during a performance of Columbia's "Guess Who's Coming to
Dinner?" It's understood that the attack was planned because Klan leaders in the south are enraged at film's portraying a high IQ romance
between Sidney Poitier and Katherine Houghton.

The tear-gas assault, however, was subsequently ditched when local Klan
bosses discovered that "Dinner" hadn't begun its engagement, and that the
only Poitier film playing the Loop at the time was "To Sir, With Love."

October 16, 1968: Lexington, NC, October 15 About 20 to 25 Ku Klux
Klansmen, wearing robes and security guard uniforms, picketed the
Lexington Drive-In urging people not to patronize Columbia's "Guess
Who's Coming to Dinner?"

The klansmen were carrying signs, which said "Fight For Your Rights"
and "Mom and Dad, It Could Happen To You," in protest of the film

portraying an interracial marriage between Sidney Poitier, a world famous MD, and Kate Houghton as daughter of a white publisher.

A representative of the drive-in theater estimated that about 200 cars had driven into the lot for the first night's showing of the feature.

Blaxploitation Movies: Cheap Thrills That Degrade Blacks

Alvin F. Poussaint

Source: *Psychology Today*, 7(4), February 1974, 22, 26–7, 30, 32, 98

Black youth in Brooklyn dramatically increased their use of cocaine after the movie *Super Fly* glamorized the narcotic; Beny Primm, the black physician who picks up the pieces in his drug clinic, knows. On the other side of the continent, practically the entire student body of a high school in Los Angeles is wearing the gold "coke" spoon necklace after a showing of the same movie. ... These latest film-inspired events are having an insidious effect on young lives. ... And in my judgment, these films, especially "blaxploitation" films, have their heaviest impact on black youths. ... They mimic the stars' hip, violent personalities that suggest that success comes with a cool "rap," flashy clothes, big expensive cars, and a gun.

These movies glorify criminal life and encourage in black youth misguided feelings of machismo that are destructive to the community as a whole. ...

Violent, Criminal, Sexy Savages

These films, with few exceptions, damage the well-being of all Afro-Americans. Negative black stereotypes are more subtle and neatly camouflaged than they were in the films of yesteryear, but the same insidious message is there: blacks are violent, criminal, sexy savages who imitate the white man's ways as best they can from their disadvantaged sanctuary in the ghetto.

Many cast members try to dismiss the possibility that blaxploitation films have a negative effect on audiences. They assert that movies featuring heroes who push dope, peddle women's bodies, and routinely mutilate their foes are "mere entertainment" and have no lasting effect on theatergoers. That view assumes that audiences can distinguish black fictional characters and situations from reality, and keep the two separate in their daily lives. But this response is an attempt to dodge an important issue. Movies of any type are seldom mere entertainment because they teach cultural values and influence behavior. Herbert Eveloff, a research child psychiatrist, warns that a "factor that has compounded the struggle to find a reliable value system is related to the manner in which our culture, past and present, has been portrayed by the communications industry – the culture from which adolescents must draw guidelines for future roles." ...

Movies have lied to us before. The movies were at least partially responsible for teaching blacks and whites that Africans were savages, and that their Afro-American descendants were lazy, happy-go-lucky, thieving, sexually promiscuous, and mentally inferior. ...

In the 1960s blacks developed a new pride and self-consciousness that showed up in the "black is beautiful" and "black power" ideologies. And the white establishment gained a lucrative yet untapped market.

Among the first to discover the black market was the movie industry. Films such as *Putney Swope*, and *Sweet Sweetback's Baadasssss Song* showed, by soaring box-office receipts, that there was a tremendous profit to be made from an audience starving to see its image on screen. So, with little regard for content, the movie industry began grinding out blaxploitation films at a phenomenal rate. ...

These recent movies for the most part reinforce negative images of black people, despite claims that such films give the black man "a chance to portray himself as he really is." In the standard scenario, the heroes or heroines are usually caught up in crime, the drug traffic, and acts of excessive violence that leave the impression that most members of the black community have few redeeming features. *Gordon's War* and two films featuring black heroines, *Coffy* and *Cleopatra Jones*, show the heroes leading the fight against drugs, but the plots rely heavily on fantasy, James Bond-style high jinks, sex, and violence. While these films and the sequels to *Shaft* and *Super Fly* represent an improvement in tone and outlook, distortions of black life still abound.

Catharsis of Aggression?

Some blacks and whites argue that such films are psychologically beneficial to the black viewer. They reason that these films show the black man or woman as a hero, successfully defying the system and making it. For the first time, black youths can see a black dude outfoxing and killing the white man. Their hope is that black people watching the carnage will feel less inferior and better able to overcome oppression by "whitey." Blacks will be able to see that the white man is neither omnipotent nor invincible.

At first glance, this argument seems to be convincing, and youthful black audiences seem to support it. They generally cheer and screech with excitement whenever a black person punches, kicks, mutilates or kills a white person. Some directors, producers, and actors see this as a "catharsis of aggression" and a release of violent impulses. But few thoughtful psychologists or psychiatrists would support the view that encouraging violence in young people leads to greater self-esteem. Frantz Fanon, the revolutionary black psychiatrist, suggested that violence against the oppressor was therapeutic for the oppressed, but he did not present a shred of evidence to support his theory. ...

I must reiterate that black youth do identify seriously with these new movies. And by taking advantage of blacks' desire to see themselves on the screen, the producers of these films have exposed black youth to images that undermine an already poor self-concept. Numerous psychological studies, such as those conducted by Kenneth B. Clark, a black psychologist, have documented black self-abnegation. These studies have pointed out that black juvenile delinquents in particular have poor self-concepts. It is little compensation that the black film heroes punch and kill "whitey" and "honkies." Such vicarious thrill-seeking does little to touch the deep social problems that lead to black despair. And the portrayals of super black men are absolute fantasy. ...

Films like *Sweet Sweetback's*, *The Legend of Nigger Charley*, *Super Fly*, *Shaft*, and *Slaughter* reinforce the superstud stereotype but have substituted new sharp-shooting, "dealing" characters for the mentally dull blacks of early movies. To encourage black males to demonstrate personal achievement and manhood through sexual conquest is subtle racism and a blatant distortion of reality. White men in this society do not achieve manhood primarily through promiscuous sex, but by controlling the seats of economic and political power. ...

These black films also feed the viewer stereotypes that perpetuate myths about women. The common portrayal of both black and white women as frivolous sex objects good for a quick lay and little else is subtle and devastating exploitation. The films encourage illicit, short-term sporadic relationships with women rather than stable family life. These stereotypes also perpetuate serious conflicts, specifically in relationships between black men and black women. ...

The new black films also may impede the movement for black unity. Too often the film heroes act independently; they are selfish, egotistical, unscrupulous, and as quick to inflict violence upon other blacks as they are to hurt racist and exploitive whites. ...

Pimps and drug dealers are not civil-rights leaders. In fact, the absence of a strong movement for social justice in the black community today may be largely attributable to the loss of manpower from among the youth because of the drug and hustling culture. ...

Blacks who pay three or four dollars to see these new movies should be reminded that white studios generally produce them, white distributors circulate them, and white-owned movie houses show them.

Given the perennial unemployment among blacks in all fields, we should not be quick to condemn the black artists who take part in the production of these films. But we should be aware of the source of the economic rip-off, the white movie industry. The moviemaking conglomerates are demonstrating that they feel little sense of social or moral responsibility to the black community and to the healthy development of black youth.

It is most disturbing that the American public, and particularly the black sector, supports the new black films. As long as they are profitable, however, these films will be made and shown. I believe everyone who is interested in the positive development of the black community should speak out against these movies, demand enforcement of the rating restrictions to reduce the number of teen-age viewers, and urge community-wide boycotts until the movie industry produces more positive forms of entertainment.

Readings and Screenings

The Blaxploitation genre is thoroughly explored in Ed Guerrero's *Framing Blackness: The African American Image in Film* (Philadelphia, PN: Temple University Press, 1993); Lawrence Novotny, *Blaxploitation Films of the 1970s: Blackness and Genre* (New York and London: Routledge, 2008); Mikel J. Koven, *Blaxploitation Films* (Harpenden, UK: Oldcastle Books, 2010); Stephane Dunn, *"Bad Bitches" and Sassy Supermammas: Black Power Action Films* (Urbana and Chicago, IL: University of Illinois Press, 2008); David Walker, Andrew J. Rausch, and Chris Watson, *Reflections on Blaxploitation: Actors and Directors Speak* (Lanham, MD: Scarecrow Press, Inc., 2009). The best overviews of changing black images in film can be found in Thomas Cripps, *Slow Fade to Black: The Negro in American Film, 1900–1942* (New York: Oxford University Press, 1977); Thomas Cripps, *Making Movies Black: The Hollywood Message*

Movie from World War II to the Civil Rights Era (New York: Oxford University Press, 1993); Donald Bogle, *Bright Boulevards, Bold Dreams: The Story of Black Hollywood* (New York: Ballantine Books, 2005); Donald Bogle, *Toms, Coons, Mulattoes, Mammies, and Bucks: An Interpretive History of Blacks in American Films* (New York: Bantam Books, 1973); Mark A. Reid, *Redefining Black Film* (Berkeley, CA: University of California Press, 1993); Bell Hooks, *Reel to Real: Race, Sex, and Class at the Movies* (New York: Routledge, 1996); Colin MacCabe and Cornel West, eds., *White Screens, Black Images: Hollywood from the Dark Side* (New York: Routledge, 1994). African-American cinematic images of the 1960s are explored in Christopher Sieving, *Soul Searching: Black-Themed Cinema from the March on Washington to the Rise of Blaxploitation* (Middletown, CN: Wesleyan University Press, 2011). For the intersection of race and gender in post 1960s films, see Keith M. Harris, *Boys, Boyz, Bois: An Ethics of Black Masculinity in Film and Popular Media* (New York and London: Routledge, 2006); William R. Grant, IV, *Post-Soul Black Cinema: Discontinuities, Innovations and Breakpoints, 1970–1995* (New York and London: Routledge, 2004); Peter Lev, *American Films of the 70s: Conflicting Visions* (Austin, TX: University of Texas Press, 2000).

For studies of other racial and ethnic groups that were represented, or misrepresented, on the screen, see Daniel Bernardi, ed., *The Birth of White: Race and the Emergence of U.S. Cinema* (New Brunswick, Canada: Rutgers University Press, 1996); Randall M. Miller, ed., *The Kaleidoscopic Lens: How Hollywood Views Ethnic Groups* (Englewood, NJ: Jerome S. Ozer, 1980); Allen Woll and Randall Miller, eds., *Ethnic and Racial Images in American Film and Television: Historical Essays and Bibliography* (New York: Garland, 1987); Chon Noriega, ed., *Chicanos and Film: Essays on Chicano Representation and Resistance* (New York: Garland Publishers, 1992); Linda Rosa Fregosa, *The Bronze Cinema: Chicana and Chicano Film Culture* (Minneapolis, MN: University of Minnesota Press, 1992); Charles Ramírez Berg, *Latino Images in Film: Stereotypes, Subversion, and Resistance* (Austin, TX: University of Texas Press, 2002); Clara Rodriguez, *Heroes, Lovers, and Others: The Story of Latinos in Hollywood* (New York: Oxford University Press, 2008); Peter X. Feng, *Screening Asian Americans* (New Brunswick, Canada: Rutgers University Press, 2002); Eugene Wong, *On Visual Media Racism: Asians in the American Motion Pictures* (New York: Arno Press, 1978); Gina Marchetti, ed., *Romance and the "Yellow Peril": Race, Sex, and Discursive Strategies in Hollywood Fiction* (Berkeley, CA: University of California Press, 1994).

The 1960s were filled with a numerous films that explored racism and the condition of African Americans. The more interesting productions include *A Raisin the Sun* (1961), *Nothing But a Man* (1964), *One Potato, Two Potato* (1964), *A Patch of Blue* (1965), *Guess Who's Coming to Dinner* (1967) – the last three films all deal with interracial love relationships – *In the Heat of the Night* (1967), and *The Learning Tree* (1969). The Blaxploitation era began with *Sweet Sweetback's Baadasssss Song* (1971) and was quickly followed by films such as *Shaft* (1972), *Superfly* (1972), *The Mack* (1973), *Black Caesar* (1973), and *The Black Godfather* (1974). More than sixty Blaxploitation films were eventually released. African-American women get a star turn in Blaxploitation features *Cleopatra Jones* (1973), *Coffy* (1973), and *Foxy Brown* (1974). Films of the early 1970s that countered the Blaxploitation formula include *Cotton Comes to Harlem* (1970), *Watermelon Man* (1970), *Sounder* (1972), and *Black Girl* (1972). For a sampling of what Guerrero refers to as "Hood-Homeboy" action films, see *New Jack City* (1991), *Boyz N the Hood* (1991) *Menace II Society* (1993), and *Friday* (1995). Historically themed films that deal with incidents of violence by and against blacks include *Mandingo* (1972), *Malcolm X* (1992), *Rosewood* (1997), *Amistad* (1997), and *Beloved* (1998). Spike Lee's *Do the Right Thing* (1989) stands out as one of the best cinematic portrayals of the very personal causes and perceived insults that lay behind black–white violence.

10

Vietnam and the Crisis of American Power: Movies, War, and Militarism

Introduction to Article

Since the early days of the motion picture industry, movies have been used both to defend and to criticize war. During and after World War II, Americans were exposed to dozens of films that portrayed our men and women fighting in Europe and the Far East as heroic liberators defending the cause of democracy. The same did not hold true for our involvement in Vietnam. Hollywood was conspicuously silent about the war. The first major Vietnam film, *The Green Berets* (1968), which offered a staunch defense of our involvement, did not appear until well into the conflict and came at a time when domestic opposition to the war was growing increasingly stronger. Once the war ended in 1975, Hollywood producers began turning out a spate of controversial, seemingly anti-war films such as *Deer Hunter* (1978), *Coming Home* (1978), *Go Tell the Spartans* (1978), and *Apocalypse Now* (1979). Yet, several years later, as the New Right rose to power in American politics, films like *Rambo: First Blood Part II* (1985) helped conservatives renew citizens' faith in our military.

Surveying the varied images of militarism in films of the 1970s and 1980s, Michael Ryan and Douglas Kellner show how movies of the era reflected – and shaped – changing attitudes about the war, the American military, and the effectiveness of military solutions to political problems.

Movies and American Society, Second Edition. Edited by Steven J. Ross.
© 2014 John Wiley & Sons, Inc. Published 2014 by John Wiley & Sons, Inc.

They explore the ambiguous legacy of post-Vietnam War films and analyze the ways in which movies of the early 1980s helped restore American confidence in the military and its ability to triumph in foreign battles. Ryan and Kellner argue that militarist films – which ranged from love stories such as *An Officer and a Gentleman* (1982) to action films such as *Red Dawn* (1984) and *Rambo* – helped end the "post-Vietnam War syndrome" of national doubt and paved the way for greater public acceptance of military actions taken by Presidents Reagan and Bush.

Discussion Points

What we *see* on the screen often has a longer lasting impact than what we *hear*. How did anti-war and pro-military filmmakers of the 1970s and 1980s go about visualizing their political messages? How did films of the era explain the reasons for our failure in Vietnam?

Vietnam and the New Militarism

Michael Ryan and Douglas Kellner

Source: Michael Ryan and Douglas Kellner, *Camera Politica: The Politics and Ideology of Contemporary Hollywood Film* (Bloomington and Indianapolis; Indiana University Press, 1988), 194–216, 316–17

Halloween and *Dressed to Kill* appear around 1978–80, at the same time as *The Deer Hunter* and *Apocalypse Now*, two major conservative Vietnam films. All four are distinguished by regressive portrayals of women combined with assertions of male power and right-wing violence. That ideological conjunction, we suggest, is not accidental. It is symptomatic of a turn occurring in American culture at that time, a turn whose trajectory intersects eventually with the rise of the New Right as a force in American politics and with the renewal of militarism during the Reagan eighties. It is also symptomatic of the necessary connection between representations of paranoid projection in the horror genre as a reaction to feminism and representations of revived military might as a result of threats to national self-esteem. The psychological source was similar in each case as was the representational violence that emerged as its solution.

In American culture, film representations of military prowess seem inseparable from national self-esteem. For conservatives especially, greatness as a nation means the ability to exercise military power. In war, the strength and courage of the soldiers who represent male national prestige are tested and proven. In post-World War II cinematic representations of this ritual, proof of manhood was accompanied by a nationalistic idealism that pictured the American fighting man as a heroic liberator of oppressed people and as a defender of freedom. This ideal legend was justified by World War II, when American forces did indeed help defeat right-wing fascist regimes. After the war, however, the defense of political freedom against the right-wing corporatism of the fascist movement was replaced by a defense of free enterprise capitalism against both Soviet communism and national liberation movements throughout the world, from Latin America to Southeast Asia. The legend of the freedom-defending US fighting man soon began to be tarnished by the frequent sacrifice of political freedom and democratic rights that the defense of capitalism entailed. While the overthrow of democratic leftist governments in places like Guatemala and Iran could be tolerated in the Cold War climate of the fifties, in the sixties a new generation, nurtured in a more liberal cultural atmosphere and faced with having to risk their lives in the defense of capitalism overseas, began to question the right of a corporate controlled US government to suppress democracy and socialism throughout the world in the name of "freedom." The equation of "freedom" and "democracy" with capitalism became increasingly strained because antidemocratic military dictatorships were more often than not US allies in policing Third World liberation movements. During the 1960s, the Vietnam War became a focus of popular contestation. American youth refused to fight an unjust war, and by the early seventies, a majority of the people came to oppose the war. In addition, the army began to look increasingly incapable, undisciplined, and demoralized. In 1975, the United States suffered its first military defeat in its history with the liberation of Saigon. The loss created a lesion in the sense of national prestige, and it provoked a heated debate over American foreign policy.

We shall argue that Hollywood military movies of the seventies and eighties need to be read, first, in the context of the national debate over Vietnam, and, secondly, in the context of the "post-Vietnam syndrome," which was characterized by the desire for withdrawal from "foreign involvements" after the debacle in Vietnam and epitomized by the Clark Amendment forbidding intervention in Angola.

In the decade following the end of the war, America's military posture shifted from doubt to assertiveness, as the liberal tide of the mid-seventies receded and a rightist current came to dominate American political life.

Films during the period articulate the arguments that led to this change and point the direction American culture was taking regarding the war long before actual political events confirmed the shift. Around the issues of Vietnam and war in general, the failure of liberalism took the form of an inability to transform the widespread antiwar feelings of the time into a permanent institutional change in foreign policy. Once again, in this regard as in economic policy, the liberals were victims of historical circumstances. As Carter and the Democrats staved off new military programs like the B-1 bomber, the Soviets invaded Afghanistan, the Sandinistas overthrew a US-supported dictator in Nicaragua, and Iran's revolution led to the taking of American hostages all in 1979 and 1980. The American empire, which had lasted from 1945 to 1970, was crumbling, and the triumph of conservatism around military policy resulted from the ability of conservatives to take advantage of these circumstances to promote the sort of military buildup they favored. Many films of the period argue the conservative position.

One major factor in the conservative triumph was the social psychology of shame that was a significant motif of American culture after the military defeat in Vietnam. It is for this reason that the returned vet motif is so important in contemporary Hollywood film. Those whose self-identity is in part constructed through the internalization of representations of the nation as a military power no doubt felt a loss of self-esteem as a result of the nation's failure. That sense of loss generated resentment as well as a yearning for compensation. One aspect of the failure of liberalism is the inability of liberals to provide a redemptive and compensatory vision that would replace military representations as a source of self-esteem. Conservatives, on the other hand, managed successfully to equate self-restoration with military renewal.

I   Debating Vietnam

The posture Hollywood initially adopted toward Vietnam is best summed up in the title of Julian Smith's book – *Looking Away*. With the exception of *The Green Berets* (1968), a jingoist war story, no major films dealt directly with the war until the late seventies. Nevertheless, war itself was a topic of great debate in films of the late sixties and early seventies, and many of these touch covertly on the issue of Vietnam. Blacklisted screenwriter Dalton Trumbo's thirties antiwar novel *Johnny Got His Gun* was made into a film in 1971, a time when opposition to the war was peaking, and films like *M*A*S*H* and *Soldier Blue* of the same period indirectly criticized Vietnam era militarism. A similar sort of indirect message from the conservative side was delivered in *Patton* (1970), a promilitarist film scripted by Coppola that supposedly helped inspire Nixon to bomb Cambodia. Indeed, Patton's opening speech, shot against an immense American flag, which exhorted Americans never to give up the fight, probably had a subliminal topical resonance for many prowar hawks.

The first major 1970s Hollywood film to deal directly with the issue of the war was the independently made feature documentary *Hearts and Minds* (1975), directed by Peter Davis. If *Patton* demonstrated that the conservative militarist pathology is inseparable from male self-aggrandizement, an authoritarian model of social discipline, and the skewing of the personality away from a composite of affectionate and aggressive traits and toward a hypertropism of violence, *Hearts and Minds* by combining clips from war films with scenes of football games, shows how militarism emerges from a culture that promotes aggressivity in young men and furthers a racist attitude toward the world. The film juxtaposes defenders and critics of US policy, and the accompanying documentary footage of the ravages of war positions the prowar speakers as being arrogant and cruel. For example, General Westmoreland's remark that Asians do not value human life is juxtaposed to long and painful scenes of the Vietnamese mourning their dead.

The film is also significant for attempting to establish the historical context and social system out of which the war emerged. Unlike later fictional narrative war films, *Hearts and Minds* adopts a multiple perspective that undermines the power and the blindness of a monocular subjective position. What other films pose as an object (the Vietnamese), this film grants some subjectivity, as when the Vietnamese themselves express their anger and suffering. And it situates the war in a historical context that displaces the conservative concern for violent redemption or the liberal focus on the fate of individual (usually white, male) characters.

It was not until the war was over that fictional films began to appear that dealt directly with or were explicitly critical of the war. The first films to appear concerned returned veterans, frequently portrayed as dangerously alienated or violent (*Black Sunday*, *Stone Killer*). Later films take a more sympathetic point of view; films like *Cutter's Way*, *Who'll Stop the Rain?*, and *Some Kind of Hero* portray the vets as confused and wounded victims. Another strain of returned vet films uses the motif as a springboard for justifying the kind of violent and racist disposition that initiated the war in the first place (*Rolling Thunder*, *First Blood*, *Firefox*). And finally, the vet motif in the eighties (*Uncommon Valor*, *Missing in Action*, *Rambo*) becomes a means of affirming the militarism of the new era.

Liberal vet films focused on personal issues at the expense of the historical and global systemic concerns of *Hearts and Minds*. They criticized the war for what it did to good, white American boys, not for what ruin it brought to innocent Vietnamese. The first major liberal vet film – *Coming Home* (1978) – was also the first major Hollywood feature film to deal seriously with the issue of the war from a critical perspective. It skillfully manipulates the personalist and emotive codes of Hollywood to elicit sympathy for a wounded antiwar vet and to generate an empathetic yet critical stance toward a gung-ho soldier who is driven suicidal by the war experience. The scenes of the military hospital filled with the victims of war lifted a veil of silence, yet at the same time the film reproduces the traditional, Hollywood, sentimentalist vision of postwar experiences (as in, say, *The Best Years of Our Lives*).

Both *Who'll Stop the Rain?* (1978) and *Cutter's Way* (1981) use the figure of the returning vet to engage in social critique. In *Rain* a vet tries to help a buddy's wife who is victimized by drug dealers with whom her husband was involved. He is killed, and his death is cast in such a way as to evoke a sense of victimage. In addition, the fact that the final fight takes place in a carnival atmosphere suggests a critical parallel with the fruitless struggle in Vietnam. Passer's *Cutter's Way* is even bleaker. A bitter disabled vet becomes obsessed with revealing that a wealthy capitalist has murdered a young girl. He associates the man with the class he feels sent him to Vietnam to do its dirty work. Again, the vet dies, while riding a white horse through a lawn party on his way to have justice done. Such liberal vet films are distinguished by the hopeless vision they project, a vision reinforced in *Cutter's Way* by the use of somber color tones and confined spaces that suggest desolation and despair. Yet both direct the violence of the vet against groups or elites who clearly profited from the war at the expense of ordinary working-class soldiers. Conservative vet films turn shame into violent affirmation, but to do so they direct violence against the Vietnamese, in an attempt to win the lost war.

Rolling Thunder (1977) is an example of an extremely reactionary representation of the veteran issue. A veteran returns home to find his wife having an affair (a familiar cultural motif at the time expressed in the popular song "Ruby," concerning a woman who betrays a wounded vet). In this reprise of the post-World War II classic *The Blue Dahlia*, the wife and children are brutally murdered, and the veteran seeks out and kills the perpetrators with the aid of another veteran. Male bonding heals female betrayal, and violence, as usual, cures all ills. The wife's murder could be seen as a symbolic projection of the husband's revenge (his hand is mangled by the attackers, and the two events seem interrelated). And the rest of the violence is directed against non-whites. In this vision, the Vietnam War is not left behind; it is brought home to roost.

The film depicts the psychological basis upon which post-Vietnam Americans are enlisted into the new militarism. The hero is depicted as being shamed ("castrated"), and his reaction is to become violent against non-Americans. The shame associated with sexuality in the film is linked both to military defeat and to being deprived of money (the attack on his family is a burglary attempt). Thus, the denial of self-esteem around economic matters is also in part signaled as a source of resentment.

Returning veteran films range from the critical vision of films like *Coming Home* and *Cutter's Way* to the military revivalist vision of *First Blood, Firefox,* and *Rambo.* Films directly about the war experience itself are equally mixed, although, as in the returning vet subgenre, none adopts an explicitly oppositional posture toward the war.

Go Tell the Spartans (1978) and *The Boys in Company C* (1978) both criticize the US involvement in Vietnam while forgoing more radical critiques of the military, US foreign policy, or the values that support militarism. *Spartans* shows the army blundering deeper into the war during its early stages, and it stands as an allegory of the futility of the war effort as a whole. A small group of US soldiers in a provincial outpost are ordered to occupy another, even more obscure position. They are overrun, and many are killed in the senseless action. Nevertheless, the critique of the war is executed against the standard of the "good war," which reproduces a traditional trope of critical Hollywood war films in that it criticizes a specific war while celebrating military values in general. *The Boys in Company C* suffers from a similar drawback. The story follows a platoon of young marines from boot camp through combat in Vietnam. Along the way, they discover that their officers are corrupt and only interested in high body counts. The film points to the futility and misguidedness of the American war effort. It criticizes both the US-supported Vietnamese bourgeoisie and the Army high command that treated genocide against Vietnamese as a numbers game and as an excuse for using fancy high-tech weaponry. The common soldiers, in alliance with the Vietnamese people, symbolized by the children, are pitted against these two groups. They and the children are slaughtered in the end. *The Boys in Company C* constitutes one of the few overt statements against the war to come out of Hollywood, yet it resorts to the traditional Hollywood convention of valorizing "good grunt soldiers" over officers, and avoids criticizing the military as such.

Vietnam combat films like *Spartans* and *Boys* share the same limits as the liberal vet films. Liberals usually avoided the broader implications of the war, its origin in a desire to maintain access to Third World labor, markets, raw materials, etc., and to forestall the rise of noncapitalist sociopolitical systems. The traditional liberal focus on individuals implies a personalistic account that easily permits larger geopolitical issues to be displaced. And the sorts of self-replicating identifications that such an account invites usually evoke sentimentalist reactions to individual suffering rather than outrage at national policies of genocide. What needs to be determined is whether or not such personal evocations can translate into broader systemic lessons.

The rhetoric of liberal films nevertheless marks an advance on that used in conservative films. In simple thematic terms, the liberal films are critical of figures of authority, while conservative films like *Patton* metaphorically elevate such figures to an ideal position. There is a singularity of focus in conservative war films that is lacking in liberal rhetoric. *Boys* concerns a multiplicity of characters, and no one point of view is privileged. The "other" in *Patton*, a German officer assigned to study the general, is there simply to instantiate the implicit narcissistic male (self-) gaze, which takes the empirical form of the German's adulation for the great American hero. *Boys* draws Vietnamese into the narrative and grants them empathy not as admirers of the Americans but as their victims. ...

By the late seventies Vietnam was no longer an explosive issue. Conservatives decried the slow erosion of American international power in the face of Third World liberation movements, and in response to what they perceived as an expansionist USSR, they called for an end to the "post-Vietnam War syndrome." What began was a period of resurgent militarism, and Vietnam films of the time take part in the conservative backlash. They do so in part by rewriting history.

If, from a conservative political point of view, the period of the "post-Vietnam War syndrome" was characterized by national self-doubt, military vacillation, and a failure of will to intervene overseas, then the appropriate counter in the "post-syndrome" period of national revival was a triumph of the will, a purgation of doubt through action, and an interventionist military stance that brooked no restraint of the sort that led to the United State's first military defeat, tarnished national prestige, and shamed American military manhood. Both *The Deer Hunter* and *Apocalypse Now* contribute to that revival by incorporating Vietnam not as a defeat from which lessons can be learned, but as a springboard for male military heroism.

The Deer Hunter, directed by Michael Cimino, won the Oscar in 1978. The film is more about the accession to leadership of the seer–warrior–individualist hero, Michael Vronsky (Robert DeNiro), than about the war. But this turning away from defeat, loss, and responsibility to an emblem of male strength might itself be symptomatic of a denial of loss through a compensatory self-inflation of the very sort that helped initiate and prolong the war. Nevertheless, the film is multivalent politically.

It appealed to working-class viewers who saw in it an accurate representation of the dilemmas of their lives. Radicals praised its implicit critique of certain male myths. And its bleak, ambiguous ending inspired many to read it as an anti-Vietnam-War statement. We respect all of these positions, but we read the film from the perspective of the critique of ideology, and in that light, it seems less progressive.

The story concerns three steeltown buddies – Michael, Steve, and Nick – who are shown united in the first part in a highly ritualized wedding scene that conveys a sense of strong community. The church steeple, a symbol of unreflective faith, spontaneous adherence to hierarchy, and paternalistic authority, rises above the community as its guiding axis. It is returned to repeatedly by the camera, and the gesture underscores the church's centrality as a locus of social authority and an anchor securing community cohesion. All three men go to Vietnam, where they are reunited as prisoners of the Vietcong, who force them to play Russian roulette. Michael outsmarts the VC and saves his buddies. But Nick, apparently unhinged by his experience, remains in Vietnam playing roulette for money. Steve, now confined to a wheelchair in a stateside hospital, refuses to leave and return home. Michael returns to establish a relationship with Linda, Nick's old girlfriend. He forces Steve to overcome his shame, to be a "man" and leave the hospital. Then, Michael returns to Vietnam at the time of the fall of Saigon to witness Nick kill himself in his last roulette game. The film closes with Nick's funeral and the group of surviving friends singing "God Bless America."

Like so many films of the seventies, *The Deer Hunter* offers as a solution to complex political and social problems the exercise of power by a male individualist who is charged with saving a community through strong leadership. The community is patriarchal; women are present to be fought over, as bossy mothers, and in the role of not altogether faithful, weak, yet at the right moment supportive partners. War breaks the community, and its worst effect is the transformation of men into willless weaklings (Steve) or addicted obsessives (Nick). It falls to Michael to exercise his natural power of leadership to restore the communal cohesion and order at the end of the film. That restoration requires the sacrifice of Michael's weaker counterpart, Nick, with whose funeral the film ends. The reaffirmation of male military power in the character of Michael is predicated upon the purgation of weakness, vacillation, and the obsessively suicidal behavior in which the country was engaged in Vietnam, all of which seem embodied in Nick. It is important that in the scene immediately following Nick's suicide, the audience sees documentary footage of the US Army's "disgraceful" flight from Saigon. The juxtaposition associates Nick's weakness and self-destructiveness with the military defeat of 1975. The film, then, can be said to work in two dimensions. It concerns the restoration of community through strong patriarchal leadership. And it offers an allegorical solution to the problem Vietnam poses by symbolically purging the source of defeat and proposing a way to renewed national strength and patriotic cohesion.

The call for strong leadership as a solution to historical crises is a political version of the aesthetic transformation in the film of actual history into a moral allegory. Just as the warrior–leader–savior resolves vacillation into a triumph of heroic will, so also the romantic, allegorical form of the film attempts to resolve the contradictions, meaninglessness, and ambiguity of the actual historical war into a meaningful and apparently noncontradictory quest narrative executed in a synthetic style that balances the unity of the individual leader with a formal or aesthetic unity. It is not surprising that a political ideology of the superior individual subject should seem inseparable from an aesthetic of romantic, quasi-mystical exaltation, since both are forms of empowerment. The romantic aesthetic overpowers history and incorporates it into highly subjective fantasy representations. The problem of realistically depicting history, which is linked to the political problem of acknowledging responsibility and loss as a nation, is solved by sublimating history into a stylized, ceremonial fusion of color, sound, and theme that elevates contingent events to a moral allegory of redemption and an ordinary human to secular divinity. It is important that the most stylized and allegorical representations appear while Michael is hunting. The aesthetic transformation of the mountains into a mystical temple (replete with choir) parallels the political and ideological elevation of the member of the gang into the strong, mystical leader, naturally destined to lead the lesser mortals around him. It is also, of course, a means of attaining the sorts of separation we have described as necessary to the more pathological forms of male sexual identity. Heightened mental representations of the sort evident in the mountain scenes are themselves ways of denying connection to the world and to others who might transgress the boundary between self and world which a reactive male sexual identity must establish. It is significant, then, that Michael is most alone in the mountain scenes, most separated from others, and most protected from them by a representational boundary that makes him seem transcendent, unique. Those scenes are also, of course, the most metaphoric.

Yet affirmations of transcendence are necessary only when the actual world is fallen (meaningless, hopeless, unhappy). "My country right or wrong" makes sense or is necessary only if the country can be or is frequently wrong. The quest for transcendence, for turning the everyday into the grandiose, the monumental, and the meaningful, presupposes the absence of the empirical equivalents of these spiritual ideals in the actual world. Indeed, the actual world has to be a positive negation of such things as fulfillment, self-worth, and significance for the quest for other-worldly, transcendent meanings to be activated. The metaphor exists in necessary tension with a more metonymic or worldly and material set of constraints which bring the metaphor into being as a reaction against them.

The transcendent moments of the film can thus be read either as successful enactments of the attainment of a spiritual ideal just short of the clouds that are the floor of heaven, or as the neurotic symptoms of this-worldly victimization, attempts to secure a sense of self-worth against a world that denies it nine to five and only allows a few leisure-time pursuits, like the male rituals of drinking and hunting, as metaphoric alternatives. The film depicts both, and our point is that its progressive potential resides in the fact that it cannot avoid this undecidability. The transcendental moments can only appear as such in contrast to a detailed description of a fallen everyday reality. This is why the film is so incredibly dense with ethnographic detail from everyday life, from the long marriage celebration to the scenes inside the industrial workplace. It is important, therefore, that the film opens in the factory, with an establishing shot from under a viaduct at night that makes the factory world seem enclosed and oppressive. The colorful mountain scenes of transcendence gain their meaning from their difference from the darkness of the workplace and the squalor of ethnic neighborhood life. And Michael's individuation is defined as a separating out, a denial of "weakening" social links of the sort that characterize his less strong male cronies.

Thus, the film permits a deconstruction of the premises of its idealization of Michael as the seer–leader. His elevation occurs through the metaphor of the deer hunt, which transforms a literal leisure-time activity into a higher ideal meaning that transcends literality, just as Michael comes to transcend the literal and material social texture, to rise above it. He must do so if he is to give it order, but the metaphor cannot fully rise above the literality that is its vehicle. Part of its literality is that it exists in metonymic or contiguous relation to the opening factory scene of fallen fire, confinement, and darkness where the men seem all alike. Michael's distinction as the superior individual who can read sunspots, like a shaman, or who knows the mystical meaning of a bullet ("This is this"), or who takes down deer with one shot like a true hunter has meaning only in differentiation from the other men, from their sameness in the factory. And the metaphor of transcendental leadership takes on meaning only in distinction from the workaday world; without that contrast, that determining difference, it makes no sense. Yet the film's ideology depends on the assumption that the metaphor subsumes the literal event into an ideal meaning which transcends wordly materiality and meaninglessness (nondistinction) entirely.

The film thus puts on display the interconnections between wage labor oppression and white male working-class compensations for that oppression. In this film, a mythic idealization of the individual counters the reduction of all the men to faceless and impersonal functions in the industrial machine at the beginning of the film. An idealized meaning substitutes for the fallen reality of everyday life. The powerful emblem of the church, the extremely ritualized wedding, the mythologized hunt, and the strong bonding between the men should thus be seen as ways of counteracting the banality of life on the bottom of capitalism.

Like many populist films, this one therefore has a double valence. Its depiction of the accreditation of right-wing political leadership points to the way pre-class-conscious working-class men can have their resentment against oppression channeled into conservative, even fascist forms in a highly individualistic and patriarchal cultural context that limits the means of attaining communal cohesion to strong male individual leadership. Yet it also points to potentially radical desires to transcend the cruel material conditions to which working-class people are reduced (or were being reduced, in the late seventies particularly), conditions that deny a sense of worldly meaning or worth to people, who, as a result, overcompensate for those lacks by turning to either religious or political idealizations.

If both *Deer Hunter* and *Apocalypse Now* indicate the reactionary way of dealing with the Vietnam War, they also testify to something amiss in the country's prevailing conception of itself. The need, demonstrated in these films, to repudiate the war as history and to transfer it into an allegory of militarist manhood is itself symptomatic of a wound, a sense of shame, that seems resistant to the sort of healing these films attempt. And the films merely reproduce the desire to realize a totality of American will in the world that reveals its own problematic anchoring in a web of serial, contiguous non-totalizable relations with other people the more it asserts itself so hyperbolically and hysterically.

By the mid-eighties, the Vietnam syndrome had been at least partially overcome, and conservatives once again felt a pre-Vietnam license to exercise US military power overseas. Yet the country remained convinced by the experience of Vietnam, and it refused to back full-scale interventions that might lead to wars in places like Central America. Our poll suggests that American viewers tended to turn even conservative war films like *The Deer Hunter* into antiwar statements: 69 percent felt that it portrayed the war as a mistake, and 93 percent said that it confirmed their opposition to the war. The ending made 27 percent feel patriotic, while it made 51 percent feel disheartened. Perhaps the most disturbing result we found was that 74 percent felt that the representation of the Vietcong in the film was accurate. Even if Americans had learned some lessons regarding foreign wars, they still seemed to need to learn lessons regarding foreigners. And this perhaps accounts for the fact that, although they continued to oppose interventionism on a large scale, they overwhelmingly approved Ronald Reagan's strikes against Grenada and Libya during this period.

2 The Military Rehabilitated

One consequence of the Vietnam War and the draft that supplied it with men was an undermining of the US Army. By the end of the war, soldiers were "fragging" (deliberately killing) their officers, rather than obeying orders to fight. As a result of this, as well as of the widespread opposition to war that the draft helped inspire, the draft was eliminated, and the army was transformed into an all-volunteer force. That new force was heavily minority, since nonwhite minorities in a retrenching capitalist society dominated by whites had few other career opportunities. Advertisements for the army began to appear on diversionary television shows (sports and MTV especially) that might attract working-class, unemployed, and minority viewers. The restoration of the army became a more pressing concern in the late seventies, when events such as the Soviet invasion of Afghanistan and the taking of US hostages in Iran made it clear that American imperial interests were no longer going to be taken for granted or allowed to go uncontested in the world. Hollywood joined in the effort, and a number of early eighties films "humanize" the army by turning it into a scene for family melodrama, liberal ideals, and humor. The link seemed so overt that one suspected that some Hollywood filmmakers had not heard that culture is supposed to be at least relatively autonomous in relation to political power and the state.

These films are generally liberal in tone; their humanization of the military is laudable in contrast to the more conservative exaggeration of the worst traits of the military – violence, discipline, intolerance, masculinism, etc. – in such films as *Rambo*. Yet these films appear at a time when the country, in the hands of conservatives, was adopting increasingly militarist poses in the world theater and when a "culture of militarism" was developing (in the form of toys, magazines,

TV shows, and films). Whatever the intention of these films, their political valence was reinflected in a conservative direction by their historical moment and their social context. Moreover, the liberal vision takes for granted the necessity of an institution like the military. Liberals fail to see the deep structural roots and systemic relations that link the military per se as an institution to the patriarchal socialization patterns that are partly responsible (as we have argued) for war. It is in light of a broader radical critique of the military itself that the liberal position must be judged. Such a critique would see the military as an instrument of class defense, as well as a machine for producing a model of a general social discipline of the sort capitalism (or any work-oriented, inegalitarian society) requires. In addition, the military from this perspective is less a protection than a threat. In the modern world especially, the very existence of the military poses a danger, and it is no longer possible, because of modern weapons, to justify the military as a defense against aggression. Defense and a war of total annihilation are no longer separable concepts.

The format of humanized military films like *Stripes*, *Private Benjamin*, and *An Officer and a Gentleman* consists of the transformation of an unsuccessful person into a very successful one. Thus, an affirmative personal narrative is laid over an attempt at institutional reconstruction, and, like the ads for the army on television ("Be all that you can be"), the films identify personal achievement with military life. In this way, the films seem to participate in an attempt in the culture to restore the army to its pre-Vietnam credit and, in certain instances, to reintegrate it with a lost patriotic vision of the United States.

Private Benjamin (1980) incorporates feminism into this process. It recounts the transformation of a dependent and ineffectual woman who is at a loss when her husband dies on the night of their wedding into a strong, independent figure. The change is marked by the difference between the first wedding scene, in which she is little more than a sexual servant of her husband, and the last, when she socks her husband-to-be on the jaw because he is a philanderer and stalks off alone. The ideological dimension of the film consists in intimating that the army is what has made her strong. Thus, a very antifeminist institution is made to appear an ally of feminism.

Stripes (1981) and *An Officer and a Gentleman* (1982) both concern the transformation of ne'er-do-wells into successful soldiers and "men." But more important, both are allegories of the metamorphosis of the Vietnam generation, with its anti-bourgeois and antiauthoritarian dropout values, into the fighting machines of the eighties, who believe in patriotism, nationalism, and militarism. In *Stripes* an underemployed goof-off whose girlfriend has left him is transformed by the army into a good soldier who becomes a leader of his squad as well as a sexual success.

The most popular humanized military film, *An Officer and a Gentleman*, is neo-forties in outlook and tone; advertisements made it seem like a story out of the past, but that attempt to step back into the generic form and style of an older, more innocent male military ethos was very much a statement about the present. The film recounts the transformation of Zack (Richard Gere) from an undisciplined, motorcyle-riding, down-and-out tough guy into "an officer and a gentleman." Brutality saves, the film says, as the hammer shapes steel. Foley, Zack's black drill instructor (Lou Gossett), brutalizes him until he renounces his selfishness and becomes a team player. Zack stops treating women badly and does the honorable thing by carrying off his working-class girlfriend (Debra Winger) at the end. And he sacrifices his chance to set a new obstacle course record by returning to help a female classmate. The film elicits audience sympathy (even applause) at points like this. It plays on human, even liberal sentiments (integrationist and token feminist), but it does so in order to reinforce the military institution. Zack's military training seems to make him a better man, a "gentleman." We would argue that the film should be understood, then, as an allegory of a transformation being promoted by the Right in contemporary US society. Zack represents a generation of youth who grew up disaffected with traditional institutions like the military. Through Zack, we see that generation overcome its alienation and accept such values as military honor and team play. The price is submission to discipline, authority, and brutality, but the prize is self-respect and love.

The love story is sweet and reassuring; its retreat from modernity to the sort of "torrid romance" of early Hollywood films invests libidinal energies into militarism – soldiers get the "girls," the film suggests. In a film where men must learn to be "men," it is fitting that women's goal should be portrayed as "getting a man." The love story, in fact, depicts the real state of affairs of many working-class women in a society that fails to satisfy real human needs and that makes women's survival often depend on men. Such romance has a double edge. It permits a hothouse closure to be established which reinforces the film's masculinist–militarist ideology. But romance also testifies to structural differences between male power and female dependency that could never be fully sublated to an ideological closure and are underscored, even as their reality is denied in a film like this. They remain outside such closure always, for they are the very things that make ideology necessary in the first place.

Films like *Officer* were some of the most successful ideological narratives of the era. Yet for that very reason, they are some of the most interesting for understanding the rhetorical procedures of ideology as well as the social system of militarism. They are open to deconstruction precisely because they seem such perfect exercises in ideology. Strong personal needs for romance or family are transferred metaphorically or by analogy onto the military. And by virtue of metaphoric substitution, the military stands in as the answer for the personal desires. Yet this exercise in metaphoric closure also signals literal connections between the realms which are joined metaphorically. The films do not merely compare male-dominated romance or the patriarchal family to the military; they inadvertently dramatize the real material or metonymic relations between these realms of socialization.

For example, in *The Great Santini* (1982), a narrative of intergenerational strife between a gung-ho old-style military man and his son is mapped over a justification of the military. The narrative proceeds as a movement toward a moment of recognition when the children finally see that the father was a good man despite his excesses. He becomes a locus of sympathy when he dies sacrificing himself so that a town will not be destroyed by his crashing jet. The son, who seemed to reject his father's values, dons his flight jacket, assumes his father's position at the driver's wheel of the family car, and begins to act like him. The gesture is indicative of the patriarchal character of the military. It is passed from fathers to sons, bypassing women, who serve in this film as breeders. If the family is not just a legitimating model by metaphoric analogy for the military, but also a literal seed-bed of militarist values, then this division of labor is not accidental. The socialization patterns of the two seemingly separate domains form a continuum.

Liberal films like *Taps* (1981) and *The Lords of Discipline* (1983) criticize military excess in the name of a humanized military, one in which militarism must be tempered by restraint and respect for life. Indeed, *Taps* thematizes this very position. Cadets at a military academy, in order to defend the existence of the academy, engage in an armed revolt, which results in the deaths of several of them. The most fervent apostle of military honor, an aging general, also dies, and his disciple, the young cadet who leads the revolt, learns that militarism must give way to good judgment. Yet the military itself is affirmed.

Films like this display the crucial ingredients of the failure of liberalism to develop a program for significantly transforming American society. Liberalism operates from within patriarchal presuppositions, which, like the similar procapitalist presuppositions liberals hold, limit the ability of liberals to see beyond the walls of the ideological prison in which they operate. Militarist patriarchs are okay, these films seem to say, though we'd be better off with nicer ones. But in a world in which one trigger-happy fool can send everyone to happy vaporland, even nice militarist patriarchs must be seen as pathological. It is such a shift of vision, whereby the most everyday assumptions of patriarchy and capitalism, especially the assumption that strong, rambunctious men are needed to lead and defend us, are relinquished forever, that lies beyond the capacity of liberals. Indeed, liberals should probably be defined as people incapable of such structural conceptualizations.

Liberals do not see the military as a social problem that must be eliminated, in part because they accept the patriarchal logic of the Cold War – that the only way to keep peace with an antagonist is through the threat of aggression or annihilation. Yet this position is itself a product of a patriarchal socialization to competition and power. In other words, if you only look at the world with sunglasses, you'll never see anything but a dark world. In order to perceive the military itself as an unnecessary and potentially dangerous institution, liberals would have to step outside their own socialization, exit from the structure they inhabit, question the very words that come automatically to their lips.

A more radical position would argue that the outlawing of armies and weapons is not a utopian dream; it is a precondition of the modern world's survival. Beyond patriarchal and capitalist socialization to competition, aggression, and domination reside alternative socialization possibilities, and alternate ideals of cooperation, demilitarization, and peaceful communal existence. But that would require a different set of structuring assumptions, as well as a different set of social institutions. If the problem of the military is wedded to the social institutions that justify it metaphorically, then it is not likely to change until they are changed. Indeed, one could say that something of that potentially emergent reality is signaled by even the ideology of some of the humanized military films. For by comparing the military with the family, they indicate the possibility of a breakdown of the boundaries that separate the two realms. The family is a patriarchal form, and for this reason, it can successfully legitimate the military. But it is also a communal form. The very "humanity" that it lends the military also threatens the military. The price of analogy is comparison. And in comparison to the family, the military can only ultimately appear as being inhumane. For if the family breeds children, the military murders them. *Taps* and *Lords* at least point this out. They just don't follow the point to its logical conclusion. And they couldn't, because of the very patriarchal assumptions which underwrite the military, assumptions which also limit any critique of the military by immediately branding accurate critiques as unreal, utopian, or, worse, not manly enough.

3   The New Militarism

Liberals succeeded in stemming the growth of the military in the mid to late seventies, but they were incapable of turning the loss in Vietnam into a permanent structural reform of US militarism. This was so in part because of historical events that made a renewed defense of the American empire necessary. That empire consisted of a network of client states overseas, in places like the Philippines and Iran, that were tied into the imperial economic and military system by treaty and corporate investment. These states helped assure that leftist or anticapitalist governments would not come to power in areas American corporations deemed necessary to their interests. Usually they brutally repressed liberation movements, in places like Indonesia and Chile, for example, and they protected the flow of raw materials and the supply of cheap labor for American firms. Military buildups within the United States were thus closely related to the status of the imperial client states, and they both have an economic dimension. In the late seventies and early eighties several client states fell to liberation movements (Nicaragua, Iran, the Philippines), others (South Korea, South Africa, El Salvador) were troubled by incipient liberation movements or unrest, and other US-supported military regimes (Argentina, Brazil, Peru, Chile) were subject either to internal disturbances or to overthrow by democratic forces repulsed by the exercise of state terror in the name of defending capitalism. At the same time, several previously "secure" colonial nations became socialist – Angola, Ethiopia, Mozambique – as a result of revolutions. The empire was trembling, and the Iran hostage crisis of 1979–80 heated up jingoist sentiment enough in the nation to give the new conservative power bloc the support it required to begin carrying out a momentous military buildup decked out in militarist and anticommunist rhetoric.

Yet public sentiment was not entirely homogeneous on the subject of militarism. Polls indicated that in general people opposed foreign interventionism. For this reason, perhaps, there was a cultural offensive to enlist support for the conservative ideals of an aggressive, combative defense of imperial interests. If the public didn't need to be whipped up, there would not have been so much whipping going on in the early to mid-eighties, especially in films.

The revival of militarism was not spontaneous, however. Conservative groups like the Committee on the Present Danger campaigned throughout the seventies for greater "defense" spending and for a firmer foreign policy. The new militarism is not an effect of the Reagan era; rather, Reagan himself is in part an effect of the culture of militarism born in the late seventies, with some help from Democrats like Jimmy Carter.

The Final Countdown (1979) is an example of a film that prefigures the conservative military buildup of the early eighties. It concerns an aircraft carrier that travels through a time warp to emerge on the day before Pearl Harbor. The captain has to decide whether to intervene and change the course of history. The purpose of this historical displacement is to suggest that the United States needs a powerful military in order to prevent another Pearl Harbor. Indeed, in a number of new militarist films, the Vietnamese, the Russians, or the "enemy" are decked out in uniforms that markedly resemble Japanese and German World War II battle gear. This evocation of the notion of the past "just war" in the contemporary context recalls the American Right's persistent equating of communism with German Nazism, a movement which was in fact conservative and rightist in character as well as being devoted to the eradication of communism.

Militarism in the United States is inseparable from anticommunism. Although anticommunism has been a staple of post-World War II culture, after the late sixties, during the period of détente, it faded somewhat from American consciousness and from Hollywood film. But in the late seventies and early eighties it was revived and promoted in conjunction with the new militarism. It ranged from military revival allegories like *Firefox* to dance musicals like *White Night*. The new anticommunism worked either by projecting its own aggressive animus onto the "enemy," thus justifying itself as a "defense" against a hypothetically offensive Red Terror, or by dehumanizing the ideological adversaries of the United States through the use of racial and social stereotypes in such a way as to excuse the use of violence against them. For example, *Megaforce* (1982) was a Pentagon-supported advertisement both for military hardware and for elite military manpower. It concerns an elite group of fighters known as "Megaforce" (who look and taste like the Pentagon's Rapid Deployment Force). They use some of the most sophisticated military technology available to fight Castro-like, south-of-the-border bandits and their communist allies, who overthrow governments like dominoes, not for social ideals, but out of greed for money. The film presents social revolutionaries as venal criminals. And this criminalization and dehumanization of foreign people struggling for liberation from capitalism and feudalism seems to be essential to the promotion of weapons designed for their liquidation.

Perhaps the most audacious anticommunist film of the era was John Milius's *Red Dawn* (1984), about a hypothetical Soviet invasion of the United States. A group of youngsters hide out in the mountains and become a successful guerrilla unit. In the end, they are all killed. Along with the usual right-wing themes (the Soviets are subhuman concentration camp guards, Latin American revolutionaries are merely their agents, the United States is the last bastion of justice and freedom), the film is distinguished by certain ideological motifs that hark back to fascist and national socialist ideologies of the twenties and thirties. At one point, an intellectual liberal and a jock conservative fight over how to proceed in the group. The liberal's call for democracy loses out to the conservative's assertion of his right to command the others. The authoritarian leadership principle is linked to the assumption that those with greater force or power should prevail – not those with the best principles or rational arguments. Such force derives its authority from nature, from what the Nazis called "blood and soil." The blood motif in the film appears as the ritual drinking of a deer's blood as proof of one's warrior manhood; it refers to the Nazi fetishizing of powerful animals, and it elaborates the conservative idea that human life is primitivist, a struggle for survival in a civil society that is no different from nature. The soil motif appears at those moments when Milius's camera meditates on nature, positioning it as a still, immense, unmoving presence. The existential loneliness of the individualist warrior leader is associated with expansive fields and high mountains, fetishes of power and strength.

Thus, the film displays the close relationship between contemporary American right-wing ideology and Nazism. Indeed, one curious dimension of the film's argument is that what it poses against communism, depicted as totalitarian domination, is a social model of authoritarian leadership. The authoritarian camp in the mountains is not much different from the totalitarian "camp" in the town. At this point in history, conservatives like Jeane Kirkpatrick argued for a distinction between totalitarianism (authoritarianism for the sake of communism) and authoritarianism (totalitarianism for the sake of capitalism). The film shows why such a distinction might have been necessary to avoid confusion.

While films like *Red Dawn* were not particularly successful at the box office, they are shown repeatedly, for months on end, on cable television. In fact, this phenomenon points to the breakdown of the distinction between film and television as well as to the eventual erosion of the importance of box-office figures in the determination of the potential effects of films. Since blockbusters must be kept off the market in order to maintain their scarcity and value, lesser films arguably acquire a greater ability to influence audiences by virtue of saturation showing on TV.

In the late seventies and early eighties, the "world communist conspiracy" becomes associated with "terrorism," the use of non-state-sanctioned violence to gain political ends. Conservative fantasists like Claire Sterling made careers out of tracing all violent opposition to US interests back to an "international terrorist network" emanating from

Moscow. Numerous Hollywood films transcode this discourse, from Stallone's *Nighthawks* (1981) to *The Final Option* (1983), which suggests the peace movement is communist-inspired, and Chuck Norris's *Invasion U.S.A.* (1985), in which terrorists invade the United States. Norris and Stallone were also involved in promoting fantasies of veterans who return to Vietnam to free American POWs – *Missing in Action* (*I* and *II*) and *Rambo*.

In *Rambo* (1985), a veteran, who is depicted mythically as a super-killer, is enlisted to rescue missing POWs in Vietnam. He succeeds through heroic effort and a display of primitive violence that kills off numerous Russians and Vietnamese. The film satisfies several contemporary conservative prejudices. Asian communists are portrayed as sub-human. The film rewrites history in a way that excuses American atrocities against the Vietnamese. And it portrays Americans, not the Vietnamese, as the ones fighting for liberation. The overall significance of the film seems to be to try to make certain that the Vietnam War would be won in Nicaragua. It is less about an event than an attitude. The theme of betrayal that characterized the conservative attitude toward the liberal critics of the war (Reagan's remark that the army did not lose the war but was prevented from winning it) – and that is also reminiscent of post-World War I German attitudes that aided the rise of Nazism – appears in the way Rambo is misled by a Washington bureaucrat who wants him to fail in his mission so that the book can be closed on Vietnam. Yet we suggest that a film of this sort needs to be read as a symptom of victimization. A paragon of inarticulate meatheadedness, the figure of Rambo is also indicative of the way many American working-class youths are undereducated and offered the military as the only way of affirming themselves. Denied self-esteem through creative work for their own self-enhancement, they seek surrogate worth in metaphoric substitutes like militarism and nationalism. Rambo's neurotic resentment is less his own fault than that of those who run the social system, assuring an unequal distribution of cultural and intellectual capital.

We read the new militarist phenomenon as being both a psychological problem of patriarchal society and a problem of a threatened and defensive capitalism. Reagan's "hard line on defense," his stubborn hewing to a stern, punitive, and intolerant attitude toward the world, is symptomatic of patriarchal pathology, as much a matter of socialization as of social organization. *Rambo* is important because it displays the roots of that pathology. The male need to feel singular, to separate out from dependence on initial caretakers, is metaphorized in Rambo's mythic isolation. Because the social world is necessarily interdependent, such isolation is necessarily aggressive. Aggression separates, whereas affection binds and makes one dependent. The isolated male is therefore without affectionate ties. Freedom of action is his norm; it requires the repudiation of anyone who threatens his space or his sense of singular importance, from the communists to the federal bureaucrats – both enemies in the film. War is, as we have argued, in part a matter of representation, images that people identify with and internalize which mobilize action. Loss in war can in consequence be experienced as self-diminution, damage done to internal representations that have become inseparable from the self. Given the prevailing socialization patterns, such loss draws out male dependence and vulnerability, male "femininization." It is the rejection of this possibility, of its intolerable shame, that results in the sorts of hypertropic representations of violence in *Rambo*.

Yet within this problem lurk the rudiments of a solution. For the need for a confirmation of manhood signals a broader need for a feeling of self-worth of a sort that can only be provided by others. It depends on others' affection, just as all singularizing metaphors depend on contextualizing metonyms. To a certain extent, Rambo's violence is simply an expression of such a need. Such a radical compensation for lost self-esteem is in some respects a demand for a return of the other's recognition. If we call such needs "socialist" it is because the ideals of socialism are communal support, mutual help, and shared dependence. Even the male militarist's pathos articulates needs for such social structures. Even as he rejects dependence as shame, he affirms its necessity as the need for self-worth. And such unrecognized dependencies and unrealized desires cannot be recognized or realized in a patriarchal and capitalist social context. Indeed, this film is a testament to that reality.

One major consequence of this argument is that it is not only male sexualization that is at stake in militarism. Women, as they are socialized to be passive, to need strong men in order to survive, are complicit in the socialization process of men for war. This was made particularly clear to us at a viewing of *Rambo*. Women in the theater were especially loud in their demands for blood and vengeance. We were reminded of the housewives of Santiago de Chile who beat their pots at night to help bring down the leftist government. The sort of male self-display evident in *Rambo* requires an adulatory other in conservative women whose applause validates male violence. Thus, a reconstruction of male psychology is inseparable from a broader reconstruction of the patriarchal socialization system that produces both sexes.

The new militarism did not go uncontested. Films like *War Games*, *Wrong Is Right*, *The Dogs of War*, *Blue Thunder*, *Full Metal Jacket*, and *Platoon* opposed certain forms of militarism in the eighties. And several films like *Testament* and *Countdown to Looking Glass* during the same period criticized nuclear war policy. This cultural mobilization, in conjunction with public protests, had an effect. Reagan moved from statements regarding the feasibility of limited nuclear wars in the early years of his tenure to a defensive and somewhat disingenuous call for the avoidance of all nuclear war in his later years. Comedies also contributed to the continuing liberal critique, especially such Chevy Chase vehicles as *Deal of the Century*, a satire of the arms industry, and *Spies Like Us*, a satire of Reagan's "Star Wars" program (the "Strategic Defense Initiative") and of the militarist–Americanist mentality in general. In *Spies*, two trickster figures (played by Chase and Dan Ackroyd) overturn the military's plan to initiate a nuclear attack by the Soviet Union in order to use a new space defense system. The system fails, and one character remarks: "Such a short time to destroy a world." In the film's carnivalesque vision, military authority figures are little worthy of respect, and the irrationality of conservative nostrums ("To guarantee the American way of life, I'm willing to take that risk" [of nuclear destruction]) is underscored. What is noteworthy in this and other antimilitarist films is the attempt to depict alternative social attitudes (toward gays or sexuality, for example) that are necessary correlates of a post-repressive, post-militarist social construction. What the comedies underscore is the importance of irony and humor to such a process, since so many of the militarist films are distinguished by high levels of self-seriousness and an inability to engage in the plunge into indeterminacy that the carnivalesque inversion of hierarchy entails.

What all of this points to is that if militarism is a public projection of private or personal human relations and attitudes, then its reconstruction is something more than a matter of foreign policy. Liberal antimilitarist films like *War Games*, *2010*, *Testament*, or *Platoon* frequently contain images of nonauthoritarian, nonexploitative, equal relations between people. Many conservative films offer just the opposite sorts of relations, and the positive relations are frequently oiled with sentimentalism, a form of alienated positive affect that often accompanies an equally alienated aggressivity that takes authoritarian and militarist forms. What this suggests is that one necessary route to a world free from militarism is a reconstruction of the alienated and skewed affective structures feeding the distrust and enmity that operate behind militarism. Militarism is a collective neurosis, not just a foreign policy alternative. The micrological or interpersonal dimension of human existence, therefore, is not apolitical, nor is it entirely distinct from the macrological dimension of political interaction. A different nonantagonistic structure of international relations, one purged of genocidal impulses, would be predicated in part on a different psychology and a different social construction of interpersonal affection and aggression.

Documents

Introduction to Documents

The line between propaganda and entertainment is often difficult to determine. From the late 1960s through the early 1990s, filmmakers on the political left, center, and right presented audiences with their vision of the rights and wrongs of our involvement in Vietnam. In the first documents, movie star John Wayne asks President Lyndon Johnson for government help in making *The Green Berets*. The subsequent correspondence reveals Wayne's motives and the reasons why the Johnson administration, though generally more liberal than the conservative star, agreed to cooperate with him. The second set of documents explains how former "grunt" Oliver Stone was politicized in Vietnam and how he brought his new awareness to the screen. In the "Reunion" article from the *Los Angeles Times*, members of Stone's former platoon comment on their experiences in Vietnam and the ways in which those experiences were depicted in Stone's *Platoon* and in other films.

Correspondence Regarding the Making of The Green Berets

Source: The Lyndon Baines Johnson Library, Austin, Texas

John Wayne to Lyndon B. Johnson, February 15, 1965

> 5451 Marathon Street
> Hollywood, California
> December 28, 1965

The President
The White House
Washington, D. C.

Dear Mr. President:

When I was a little boy my father always told me that if you want to get anything done see the top man – so I am addressing this letter to you.

We are fighting a war in Vietnam. Though I personally support the Administration's policy there, I know it is not a popular war, and I think it is extremely important that not only the people of the United States but those all over the world should know why it is necessary for us to be there.

The most effective way to accomplish this is through the motion picture medium. Some day soon a motion picture *will* be made about Vietnam. Let's make sure it is the kind of picture that will help our cause throughout the world. I believe my organization can do just that and still accomplish our purpose for being in existence – making money. We want to tell the story of our fighting men in Vietnam with reason, emotion, characterization and action. We want to do it in a manner that will inspire a patriotic attitude on the part of fellow-Americans – a feeling which we have always had in this country in the past during times of stress and trouble. I feel my organization can make a vehicle which will accomplish this. We want to do it through the use of the point of view of our Special Forces. In order to properly put it on the screen we are going to need the help and cooperation of the Defense Department.

My record in this field I feel is a worthy one. Thirty-seven years a star, I must have some small spot in more than a few million people's lives. You cannot stay up there that long without having identification with a great number of people. It has been my good fortune to be associated with some motion pictures which portrayed the integrity and dignity of our military, and imbued our people with pride. In films such as "The Longest Day", "The Sands Of Iwo Jima", and "The Fighting Seabees" we worked closely with the branches of the military involved, and the pictures turned out to be something of which everyone could be proud.

Perhaps you remember the scene from the film "The Alamo", when one of Davy Crockett's Tennesseans said: "What are we doing here in Texas fighting – it ain't our ox that's getting gored." Crockett replied: "Talkin' about whose ox gets gored, figure this: a fella gets in the habit of gorin' oxes, it whets his appetite. May gore yours next." Unquote. And we don't want people like Kosygin, Mao Tse-Tung, or the like, "gorin' our oxes".

Perhaps it is presumptuous on my part to write direct to your Office for guidance, but I feel this picture can be extremely helpful to the Administration. Your assistance in getting us Defense Department cooperation will certainly expedite our project, as we are anxious to move ahead on it immediately. Therefore, we would appreciate hearing from your Office concerning your reactions.

Best wishes for the coming year.

Respectfully yours,
John Wayne

Jack Valenti to Lyndon B. Johnson, January 6, 1966

THE WHITE HOUSE
WASHINGTON
January 6, 1966

Mr. President:

You asked Bill Moyers to look into the proposal made by John Wayne – who wants to make a picture about Vietnam, focusing on our Special Forces.

Bill is investigating this now.

Meanwhile, I think Wayne ought to get an acknowledgement of his letter to you promptly and courteously.

Do you want such a letter prepared – which would be signed by someone on your staff. (I attach a sample letter)

My own judgment is that Wayne's politics are wrong, but insofar as Vietnam is concerned, his views are right. If he made the picture he would be saying the things we want said.

Moreover, a commercial film about Vietnam, with popular stars in it, would probably have a more beneficial effect, and seen by more people than any film the government could make, or any documentary other people would make. The principal defect of a documentary is that we have no film of the Viet Cong and no depiction of their atrocities. Documentaries have to be factual.

In a commercial film, however, there is no restriction on actual film. The film makers can portray the Viet Cong as they really are.

So I recommend we give Wayne permission to make the film – and also give MGM (our friends politically) who also want to make a similar film. The quicker the better. It will take about six months, minimum, to turn out a quality film.

Jack Valenti

Platoon Marks "End of a Cycle" for Oliver Stone

Sean Mitchell

Source: *Los Angeles Herald-Examiner*, December 21, 1986

You look into the smile of a man like Oliver Stone and try to see the molars grinding, the tiny crease of insincerity, a sharp tooth – something, anything to give the lie to amiability in a man who chucked an Ivy League education for a chance to fight, kill and die in Vietnam. The Ivy League did not lose many defectors to the 25th Infantry Division but it did lose Stone, who dropped out of Yale in 1965, volunteered for the Army, asked no favors and went into combat alongside teen-agers who had not finished high school.

Stone's experience as a grunt from the right side of the tracks happens to correspond pretty much to that of the character played by Charlie Sheen in "Platoon," the somber new movie about men at war that Stone has written and directed. Like the Sheen character, who serves as the film's narrator, Stone was a privileged kid who wanted to start over, measuring himself in a crucible of fire.

This is what he is saying, anyway, one evening in the living room of his new home in one of the better parts of Santa Monica. He sits dressed in loose-fitting black clothes, a glass of red wine in front of him on a coffee table. His face is weathered to the emotional climate of the picture business, expressive but hard.

"All my life I've definitely been involved in the extremes of humanity – gangsters, soldiers," he says, referring to the movies he has written or directed, which include "Midnight Express," "The Hand," "Scarface," "Year of the Dragon" and "Salvador," a list that could be recited as a rosary of fear and brutality. "I think I've come to the end of a cycle with 'Platoon.' I've said what I had to say. It was a tremendous release for me."

Stone actually wrote "Platoon" 10 years ago. It has taken this long to get it made.

It is his second movie to be released this year, following "Salvador," the bloody, low-budget thriller about a maverick American newsman trying to get at the truth in Central America. Stone made "Salvador" for no salary after becoming convinced that the United States has betrayed its own revolutionary past by backing the military in El Salvador's civil war.

The movie, starring James Woods, surprised a number of critics who had relegated Stone to the John Milius quarter of film politics (Stone and Milius collaborated on the screenplay for "Conan the Barbarian") based on his collection of menacing portraits of people not native to the US. Stone says his interests are much broader than some people think.

"I'd like to do a comedy. I thought 'The Jerk' was a great picture. I love that kind of humor. I'd like to go more into the areas of romance. I've written a great love story, set in Russia."

He admits, however, that his thinking about America and its place in the world has changed considerably since he volunteered for the nation's longest war. Even then, he insists, he was motivated by the fact that the poor were doing all the fighting.

"I wasn't that intelligent in terms of politics. I was raised right wing. My father was deeply conservative and we were a very politically conscious family. I supported Goldwater in '64; I loved the war movies, I loved John Wayne, I fell for the whole thing. I believed in my country."

When he got to Vietnam, Stone avoided becoming an officer. "I wanted to be a grunt. I wanted to be at the lowest level. I wanted to go to the root of passion, which war was supposed to represent."

The Hemingway idea?

"Yeah. Very much so. Well, actually more Conrad because I'd read 'Lord Jim.' That was one of my favorite books."

Nothing could have prepared him for the experience of combat, which followed less than two weeks after his arrival in the country. He was caught in an ambush at night, a scene that is recreated in "Platoon."

"They just appeared, these guys, and my reactions were dead, I was numb from the neck down. I got wounded that night, a boy got killed, another boy lost part of his arm. After that I got better and better. I started to learn. It takes a few firefights to really figure out what's going on. The first firefight, you don't know if the artillery is coming in or going out. You don't know – the bullets – where they are. You don't know where anybody is. It's a lot of confusion. As you can see in the movie, you get killed a lot from your own side."

It never used to happen that way to John Wayne for some reason.

"Platoon" doesn't hurtle directly into the political questions of the war, but its version of the day-to-day struggle of the infantryman assembles snapshots of US troops that disturb some patriotic cliches. The story develops a simmering feud-to-the-death between two US officers, played by Tom Berenger and Willem Dafoe, making a bold point in Stone's scenario: that the enemy we faced in Vietnam often turned out to be ourselves. These guys would have fragged John Wayne before the third reel.

There are also scenes of vicious cruelty carried out against local farmers and villagers.

"Take a healthy teen-age boy out of Dayton, Ohio," Stone says. "He's 19 years old, and you give him a gun and tell him you can do anything you want, he'll do it. There's a dark side to the American soul and I think a lot of people have a problem with that."

Stone learned this and other things in Vietnam. He learned about drugs and about rhythm and blues. "My soul got out intact because of the blacks and the potheads who turned me on to pot and music. I'd never heard black music until I went to Vietnam. I didn't know about rock 'n' roll. I discovered the Doors there. Hanging out with them in the bunkers, doing dope, restored me between the times when we had to be in the field, which deadened me."

The future filmmaker's political awakening did not come from listening to rock 'n' roll or during the war at all. When he returned from Vietnam he submerged himself in drugs. "I went into a real tailspin," he says. "I thought the war was over, but it was just beginning." After a few years of drifting, he entered film school at NYU, where one of his instructors was Martin Scorsese. "I tried to stay out of it (politics). I did not like the protesters because of the baby-killing image they used to stick the vets with.

"It was only about 1974 or '75, after Watergate, which changed my perceptions about a lot of things. Partly from maturity, partly from thinking about it. Watergate certainly uncovered a lot of things."

Stone doesn't think any of the movies yet made about Vietnam have got it down right. "I'm not going to be so pretentious as to say this is *the* Vietnam War movie. I think there are many more that can be done. There are a thousand stories, a million stories."

"Platoon," which takes as its dominant piece of scoring music Samuel Barber's mournful "Adagio for Strings," heals no wounds the war opened. Stone thinks of the film more as "scar tissue."

"The war is still undecided. Our country is split between left and right factions essentially."

He wants Vietnam veterans to be proud of the movie, though, "proud of what their contribution was and that it's finally being seen by others. I think that what a lot of vets went through was incapable of being communicated or shared.

I honestly hope that teen-agers see the movie and take stock of what a war really means. They do fire back. They kill us as well as we kill them, which has been forgotten in a slew of movies recently. I hope they see real violence as opposed to that obscene TV violence where somebody just raises a gun and goes, 'pop, pop,' and the other person dies without blood. That's worse to me than realistic violence."

As Stone says this, it occurs to him that "Platoon," for all its pain and suffering, will probably drive some young men to want to seek out the experience first hand. He should know.

"Even if you tell the truth and show it as it is, certain people are going to be attracted by that, like moths to the light."

Reunion: Men of a Real Platoon

Jay Sharbutt

Source: *Los Angeles Times*, February 7, 1987

This week in Hollywood, it was glitz, glamour and talk that the three Golden Globe Awards for Oliver Stone's "Platoon" might presage more honors for his powerful Vietnam War drama at Oscar time.

It was a somewhat headier setting than last month, when five men, Stone among them, came to New York to meet in a large oak-paneled room at the stately old 7th Regiment Armory here. Their talk was of a far different world than Hollywood, a 15-years-ago world of things like bee-hive rounds, the NVA, 11-Bravos, lifers, LAAWs, leechers, Claymores, AKs, a place called Firebase Burt.

Vietnam Memories

It was hard for some of the men to talk about sad or tragic moments. One asked that the names of three dead men he mentioned not be used, lest it cause their families further pain.

All thought that Stone's "Platoon" would help Americans understand – at least to some degree – what the ordinary riflemen, the grunts, went through in the war.

They all laughed at John Rambo, winner of the Hollywood Medal of Honor.

"I hope this movie blows 'Rambo' right out of the water," said one of the real veterans. "Yeah," said another, "because Rambo was nothing but one hero that never went there."

"If we'd had two Rambos, we'd have won the war," he chuckled as two TV cameras recorded the reunion of Stone with four other ex-grunts – three of whom he'd served with in Vietnam. Those three: Ben Fitzgerald, 43, now a die-cast operator living in Humboldt, Tenn.; Crutcher Patterson, 39, co-owner of a used auto parts yard in Pulaski, Tenn., and Jim Pappert, 38, a production mechanic in St. Louis, Mo.

They were joined by a friend of Stone's from Los Angeles, Ruben Gomez, 45, who also was in Vietnam but not in their unit.

Their reunion was arranged by and taped for CBS' new "The Morning Program." ... It was an unusual, at times quietly emotional three-hour session. It was moderated by Stone, 40, who now lives in Brentwood.

His film, while generally acclaimed, hasn't been without controversy.

Some of the controversy comes from vets themselves, people like Jim Thomas, an Army medic at a battle called Hamburger Hill – which is both the name and basis of another Vietnam movie that recently completed filming.

Thomas, now a postal worker in Hayward, Calif., recently saw Stone's film. In a phone interview, he said he was outraged by parts of the movie, particularly one scene in a hamlet that "made me cower down in my chair and hope no one would think I was a Vietnam veteran."

In that scene, after a platoon member is killed, some – but by no means all – of the men in his platoon erupt in blind rage after uncovering North Vietnamese weapons and explosives hidden in the hamlet.

Thomas conceded that Vietnam was not the same war to every grunt who served there. The type of combat, a unit's discipline and compassion or the lack of either – all that could and did vary markedly in the war.

"I'm not saying things like that didn't happen," the ex-medic said of the brutal hamlet scene in Stone's film. "But it (the movie) wasn't a representation of all of us."

Although Stone recalled witnessing such moments when he was in Vietnam, none of the three with whom he served wanted to dwell on it, particularly Pappert, a short, bearded, soft-spoken man.

Interviewed during a pause in the CBS taping, he declined to be specific. But he told a reporter that "there were a lot of things in there (the movie) that I don't relate to."

More should have been shown about the ambiguous feelings of GIs toward the Vietnamese, he added: "Like when you first got there, you felt sorry for the people, the way they were being treated.

"But then it got to a point, after a period of time, that you didn't give a damn about them. You didn't care who they were or their feelings … you were just waiting for your day to get out."

The taping session had its lighter moments, the easy banter of friendships born in war – as when Stone kidded Patterson about turning him on to pot (which, all agreed, never was smoked in the field).

"I have been known to smoke a joint, yeah," drawled the burly Tennessean, a plain-spoken man who proved eloquent in his directness. He'd been a squad leader. He hadn't wanted the job, he said, but "the rest of them had either gone home or got wounded or killed."

The five covered a wide range of topics – the misery of life in the bush; racism toward the Vietnamese and among US troops; the closeness of the grunts, whether black, white or Latino; the music of the time, and homecomings and problems of adjustment.

At one point, Patterson grew impatient on a different subject – when Gomez spoke of the high suicide rates of veterans and reeled off statistics about homeless Vietnam veterans in Los Angeles. "Is it Vietnam's fault?" he demanded.

"No, no," Gomez said. "I think it was that America couldn't – didn't deal with the problem at the beginning ... it was just like, 'Get lost!'"

Patterson agreed. But he also made clear his pride and lack of self-pity as he softly added: "We've got to get over it sometime."

As the taping wore on, that attitude of putting the war behind them also seemed the underlying philosophy of Pappert and Fitzgerald, the latter the only black in the group, a man Stone affectionately called "Fitz."

At the end, Pappert, picking his words carefully and with difficulty, tried to sum up his thoughts about Vietnam.

"The best way to explain it is just this," he said, "I'd like to put it all in my past, and hope for a better future for this country. . . . History repeats itself, but we hope it doesn't this time."

That night, the visitors adjourned to the Lion's Head, a cheery Greenwich Village pub. They were later joined by Stone, retired Marine Capt. Dale Dye, who trained the actors in "Platoon" and played an Army captain in it, and Tom Cruise, the young "Top Gun" fighter pilot.

Beer and good talk flowed freely around their table.

During the CBS taping session, Fitzgerald had jokingly groused about all the guys he knew who didn't go to Vietnam but who, when he came back, wanted him to buy them a drink.

"And they've been sitting home, making all the money, and here you are over there fighting all this time," he marveled.

So that evening, someone who had been at the CBS taping and came away with a great deal of admiration for Stone's friends from Vietnam, bought the table a round of drinks.

He made sure that Fitz got two.

Readings and Screenings

For a brief overview of Vietnam War-era films, their politics, and their reworking of the past, see Pat Aufderheide, "Good Soldiers," in Mark Crispin Miller, ed., *Seeing Through the Movies* (New York: Pantheon Books, 1990), 81–11; also see, chapter 3, "Hollywood's Vietnam, 1961–1989," in Guy Westwell, *War Cinema: Hollywood on the Front Line* (London and New York: Wallflower Press, 2006). There are quite a few books that explore the subject in much greater depth. The best works include Robin Wood, *Hollywood From Vietnam to Reagan. . . and Beyond*, revised and expanded edition, (New York: Columbia University Press, 2003); Michael Anderegg, ed., *Inventing Vietnam: The War in Film and*

Television (Philadelphia, PN: Temple University Press, 1991); Linda Dittmarr and Gene Michaud, eds, *From Hanoi to Hollywood: The Vietnam War in American Film* (New Brunswick, Canada: Rutgers University Press, 1990); Albert Auster and Leonard Quart, *How the War Was Remembered: Hollywood and Vietnam* (New York: Praeger, 1988); Gilbert Adair, *Hollywood's Vietnam* (London: Heinemann, 1989). For a filmography of 600 features, TV movies, and short films made throughout the world between 1939 and 1992 dealing with Vietnam, see Jean-Jacques Malo and Tony Williams, eds, *Vietnam War Films* (Jefferson, NC and London: McFarland and Company, Inc., 1994). For other useful filmographies of Vietnam war films, see Michael Lee Lanning, *Vietnam at the Movies* (New York: Ballantine Books, 1994); Jeremy M. Devine, *Vietnam at 24 Frames a Second: A Critical and Thematic Analysis of Over 400 Films About the Vietnam War* (Jefferson, NC and London: McFarland and Company, Inc., 1995). The link between film, war, and gender during this era is perceptively examined in Susan Jeffords, *The Remasculinzation of America: Gender and the Vietnam War* (Bloomington, IN: Indiana University Press, 1989). For an entertaining look at the behind-the-scenes workings of filmmakers during this era, see Peter Biskind, *Easy Riders, Raging Bulls: How the Sex-Drugs-and Rock 'n' Roll Generation Saved Hollywood* (New York: Simon and Schuster, 1998).

The cinematic starting point for Vietnam films is *The Green Berets* (1968), which lays out the rationale for our participation in the war. The culture of militarism that helped propel and sustain the American war effort is described in the documentary *Hearts and Minds* (1975). Although Ryan and Kellner emphasize their conservative aspects, *The Deer Hunter* (1978) and *Apocalypse Now* (1979) were initially regarded by most viewers – including the editor of this collection – as anti-war films. Watch these two films and see what you think. For more explicit critiques of the war and the military, see *Go Tell the Spartans* (1978), *The Boys in Company C* (1978), *Platoon* (1986), and *Full Metal Jacket* (1987). There are several excellent films that describe the problems faced by returning veterans: *Coming Home* (1978), *Who'll Stop the Rain* (1978), *Cutter's Way* (1981), and *Born on the Fourth of July* (1989). The revisionist view of the military began innocently enough in early 1980s films such as *Private Benjamin* (1980) and *An Officer and a Gentleman* (1982). They were soon followed by a more stalwart defense of military actions in Vietnam and elsewhere. The most powerful of these films – *Missing in Action* (1984), *Missing in Action 2 – The Beginning* (1985), *Rambo: First Blood Part II* (1985), *Rambo III* (1988) – attributed our failure in Vietnam to a weakness of will and suggested that one truly tough man could have changed the course of the war.

11

Reagan's America:
The Backlash Against
Women and Men

Introduction to Article

Ideas about the family and the "proper" roles of men and women are not absolute truisms but social constructions that often change with the times. If the 1960s can be described as an era of sexual and gender liberation, then the 1980s might best be called an era of backlash – a backlash against earlier political, social, sexual, and cultural movements that challenged traditional roles and ideas. Films of the 1970s often showed men and women struggling to understand one another's desires and to see each other as "people" rather than as narrowly defined "men" or "women." The 1980s, however, proved a tough decade for strong-minded, independent women – on screen and off screen.

Susan Faludi reveals how the conservative political climate of the Reagan era manifested itself on screen in a spate of anti-feminist films. After making pro-feminist films in the 1970s, producers grew more cautious and turned out movies that called for a return to more traditional gender roles, for men as well as for women. In backlash films, Faludi argues, "women were set against women," their "anger at their social circumstances was depoliticized" and their lives were "framed as morality tales in which the 'good mother' wins and the independent woman gets punished." The ultimate message of these movies was that "American women were unhappy because they were too free; their liberation had

Movies and American Society, Second Edition. Edited by Steven J. Ross.
© 2014 John Wiley & Sons, Inc. Published 2014 by John Wiley & Sons, Inc.

denied them marriage and motherhood." The author also turns a critical eye at several Yuppie (young urban professional) films and explores the ways in which they reinforced conservative ideas about the interactions of class and gender. Taken collectively, the "You can't have it all" message that permeated 1980s films called for Americans to return to the more narrowly proscribed and allegedly happier gender roles and family life styles of the 1950s.

Discussion Points

How do films teach us what it means to be a man or a woman in our culture? How would movie plots and cinematic images of men and women change if we suddenly reversed traditional gender roles so that women became the primary breadwinners and men the primary child-care providers and homemakers?

Fatal and Fetal Visions: The Backlash in the Movies

Susan Faludi

Source: Susan Faludi, *Backlash: The Undeclared War Against American Women* (New York: Anchor Books, 1991), 112–39

"Punch the bitch's face in," a moviegoer shouts into the darkness of the Century 21 Theater, as if the screenbound hero might hear, and heed, his appeal. "Kick her ass," another male voice pleads from the shadows.

The theater in suburban San Jose, California, is stuffy and cramped, every seat taken, for this Monday night showing of *Fatal Attraction* in October 1987. The story of a single career woman who seduces and nearly destroys a happily married man has played to a full house here every night since its arrival six weeks earlier. "Punch the bitch's lights out! I'm not kidding," a man up front implores actor Michael Douglas. Emboldened by the chorus, a man in the back row cuts to the point: "Do it, Michael. Kill her already. Kill the bitch."

Outside in the theater's lobby, the teenage ushers sweep up candy wrappers and exchange furtive quizzical glances as their elders' bellows trickle through the padded doors. "I don't get it really," says Sabrina Hughes, a high school student who works the Coke machine and finds the adults' behavior "very weird," an anthropological event to be observed from a safe distance. "Sometimes I like to sneak into the theater in the last twenty minutes of the movie. All these men are screaming, 'Beat that bitch! Kill her off now!' The women, you never hear them say anything. They are all just sitting there, real quiet."

Hollywood joined the backlash a few years later than the media; movie production has a longer lead time. Consequently, the film industry had a chance to absorb the "trends" the eighties media flashed at independent women – and reflect them back at American moviegoers at twice their size. "I'm thirty-six years old!" Alex Forrest, the homicidal single career woman of *Fatal Attraction*, moans. "It may be my last chance to have a child!" ...

The escalating economic stakes in Hollywood in the eighties would make studio executives even more inclined to tailor their message to fit the trends. Rising financial insecurity, fueled by a string of corporate takeovers and the double threat of the cable-television and home-VCR invasions, fostered Hollywood's conformism and timidity. Just like the media's managers, moviemakers were relying more heavily on market research consultants, focus groups, and pop psychologists to determine content, guide production, and dictate the final cut. In such an environment, portrayals of strong or complex women that went against the media-trend grain were few and far between.

The backlash shaped much of Hollywood's portrayal of women in the eighties. In typical themes, women were set against women; women's anger at their social circumstances was depoliticized and displayed as personal depression instead; and women's lives were framed as morality tales in which the "good mother" wins and the independent woman gets punished. And Hollywood restated and reinforced the backlash thesis: American women were unhappy because they were too free; their liberation had denied them marriage and motherhood.

The movie industry was also in a position to drive these lessons home more forcefully than the media. Filmmakers weren't limited by the requirements of journalism. They could mold their fictional women as they pleased; they could make them obey. While editorial writers could only exhort "shrill" and "strident" independent women to keep quiet, the movie industry could actually muzzle its celluloid bad girls. And it was a public silencing ritual in which the audience might take part; in the anonymity of the dark theater, male moviegoers could slip into a dream state where it was permissible to express deep-seated resentments and fears about women.

"It's amazing what an audience-participation film it's turned out to be," *Fatal Attraction*'s director Adrian Lyne would remark that fall, as the film continued to attract record crowds, grossing more than $100 million in four months. "Everybody's yelling and shouting and really getting into it," Lyne said. "This is a film everyone can identify with. Everyone knows a girl like Alex." That women weren't "participating," that their voices were eerily absent from the yelling throngs, only underscored Lyne's film message; the silent and impassive female viewers were serving as exemplary models of the "feminine" women that the director most favored on screen.

Efforts to hush the female voice in American films have been a perennial feature of cinema in backlash periods. The words of one outspoken independent woman, Mae West, provoked the reactionary Production Code of Ethics in 1934. It was her caustic tongue, not her sexual behavior, that triggered these censorship regulations, which banned premarital sex and enforced marriage (but allowed rape scenes) on screen until the late 1950s. West infuriated the guardians of the nation's morals – publisher William Randolph Hearst called her "a menace to the sacred institution of the American family" – because she talked back to men in her films and, worse yet, in her own words; she wrote her dialogue. "Speak up for yourself, or you'll end up a rug," West tells the lion she tames in *I'm No Angel*, summing up her own philosophy. In the thirties, she herself would wind up as carpeting, along with the other overly independent female stars of the era: Marlene Dietrich, Katharine Hepburn, Greta Garbo, Joan Crawford and West were all officially declared "box office poison" in a list published by the president of Independent Theater Owners of America. West's words were deemed so offensive that she was even banned from radio.

Having stopped the mouth of the forty-year-old West and the other grown-up actresses, the thirties studios brought in the quiet good girls. The biggest Depression female star, Shirley Temple, was not yet school age – and got the highest ratings from adult men. When she played "Marlene Sweetrick" in *War Babies*, she was playing a version of the autonomous Dietrich, shrunk now to a compliant tot.

During World War II, in a brief burst of enthusiasm for strong and working women, a handful of Rosie-the-Riveter characters like Ann Sothern's aircraft worker in *Swing Shift Maisie* and Lucille Ball's *Meet the People* flexed muscles and talked a blue streak, and many female heroines were now professionals, politicians, even executives. Throughout the forties, some assertive women were able to make themselves heard: Katharine Hepburn's attorney defended women's rights in the courtroom in *Adam's Rib*, and Rosalind Russell's single reporter in *His Girl*

Friday huskily told a fiancé who wanted her to quit work and move to the country, "You've got to take me as I am, instead of trying to change me. I'm not a suburban bridge player; I'm a newspaperman."

But even in this decade, the other Hollywood vision of womanhood vied for screentime, and it began to gain ground as the backlash built. Another group of women on screen began to lose their voices and their health. A crop of films soon featured mute and deaf-mute heroines, and the movie women took to their beds, wasting away from brain tumors, spinal paralysis, mental illness, and slow poisons. As film historian Marjorie Rosen observes, "The list of forties female victims reads like a *Who's Who* hospital roster." The single career women on screen, a brittle, dried-up lot, were heading to the doctor's office, too, for psychiatric treatment. In movies like *Dark Mirror, Lady in the Dark*, and later *The Star*, they all received the same medical prescription: quit work and get married.

By the fifties the image of womanhood surrendered had won out, its emblem the knock-kneed and whispery-voiced Marilyn Monroe – a sort of post-lobotomized "Lady in the Dark," no longer fighting doctor's orders. Strong women were displaced by good girls like Debbie Reynolds and Sandra Dee. Women were finally silenced in fifties cinema by their absence from most of the era's biggest movies, from *High Noon* to *Shane* to *The Killing* to *Twelve Angry Men*. In the fifties, as film critic Molly Haskell wrote, "There were not only fewer films about emancipated women than in the thirties or forties, but there were fewer films about women." While women were relegated to mindless how-to-catch-a-husband movies, men escaped to womanless landscapes. Against the backdrop of war trenches and the American West, they triumphed at last – if not over their wives then at least over Indians and Nazis.

In late-eighties Hollywood, this pattern would repeat, as filmmakers once again became preoccupied with toning down independent women and drowning out their voices – sometimes quite literally. In *Overboard*, an unexceptional product of the period, Goldie Hawn's character, a rich city loudmouth (like *Fatal Attraction*'s antiheroine, also named Alex), plunges off a yacht and suffers a spell of amnesia. A rural carpenter she once tongue-lashed rescues her – and reduces her to his squeaky-voiced hausfrau: "Keep your mouth closed," orders the carpenter (played, curiously, by Hawn's real-life husband Kurt Russell), and she learns to like it. ...

Glenn Close's character in *Fatal Attraction* was not the only independent working woman whose mouth gets clamped shut in a Lyne production. In $9\frac{1}{2}$ *Weeks*, released a year before *Fatal Attraction*, a single career woman plays love slave to a stockbroker, who issues her this command: "Don't talk." ...

The plots of some of these films achieve this reverse metamorphosis, from self-willed adult woman to silent (or dead) girl, through coercion, others through the female character's own "choice." In any case, only for domestic reasons – for the sake of family and motherhood – can a woman shout and still come out a heroine in the late-eighties cinema. The few strong-minded, admirable women are rural farm mothers defending their broods from natural adversity (*Places in the Heart*, *The River*, and *Country*) and housewives guarding their families from predatory single women (*Tender Mercies*, *Moonstruck*, *Someone to Watch Over Me*, and *Terms of Endearment*). The tough-talking space engineer who saves an orphan child in *Aliens* is sympathetically portrayed, but her willfulness, too, is maternal; she is protecting the child – who calls her "Mommy" – from female monsters.

In Hollywood, 1987 was a scarlet-letter year for the backlash against women's independence. In all four of the top-grossing films released that year, women are divided into two groups – for reward or punishment. The good women are all subservient and bland housewives (*Fatal Attraction* and *The Untouchables*), babies or voiceless babes (*Three Men and a Baby* and *Beverly Hills Cop II*). The female villains are all women who fail to give up their independence, like the mannish and child-hating shrew in *Three Men and a Baby*, the hip-booted gunwoman in *Beverly Hills Cop II*, and the homicidal career woman in *Fatal Attraction*. All of these films were also produced by Paramount – ironically, the studio that had been saved from bankruptcy a half century earlier by Mae West.

Of all Paramount's offerings that year, *Fatal Attraction* was the one that most mesmerized the national media. Completing the feedback loop, the press even declared the movie's theme a trend and scrambled to find real live women to illustrate it. Story after story appeared on the "*Fatal Attraction* phenomenon," including seven-page cover stories in both *Time* and *People*. A headline in one supermarket tabloid even dubbed the film's single-woman character the MOST HATED WOMAN IN AMERICA. Magazine articles applauded the movie for starting a monogamy trend; the film was supposedly reinvigorating marriages, slowing the adultery rate, and encouraging more "responsible" behavior from singles. *People* promoted this trend with cautionary case studies of "Real Life Fatal Attractions" and warned, "It's not just a movie: All too often, 'casual' affairs end in rage, revenge, and shattered lives." Though in real life such assailants are overwhelmingly male – a fact surely available to the six reporters assigned this apparently important story – all but one of the five aggressors *People* chose as examples were women.

Fatal Attraction, Before and After

British director and screenwriter James Dearden first dreamed up the story that became *Fatal Attraction* one solitary weekend in London in the late seventies. He was battling writer's block; his wife was out of town – and he wondered to himself, "What if I picked up that little black address book and rang that girl who gave me her number at a party six months ago?" The original plot was simple. Dearden recalls it this way:

> A writer takes his wife to the station in the morning with their child and sees them off. Then he picks up the phone and rings a girl whose number he's got. He takes her out to dinner, takes her to bed. He thinks that's the end of it, but the phone rings the next day and it's her. So he goes over to see her and spends Sunday with her. And Sunday evening she freaks out completely and cuts her wrists. ... He stays the second night and gets home early in the morning. His wife gets back. The phone rings and it's the girl. He fobs her off and the phone rings again and the wife goes to pick up the phone and you know that's going to be it. She's going to find out about the affair. The wife picks up the phone and says hello, and the screen goes black.

Dearden says he intended the story to explore an individual's responsibility for a stranger's suffering: he wanted to examine how this man who inflicted pain, no matter how unintentionally, must eventually hold himself accountable. In 1979, Dearden turned his screenplay into a forty-five-minute film called *Diversion*, highly acclaimed at the Chicago Film Festival the following year.

In the early eighties, American producer Stanley Jaffe was in London looking for new talent, and he paid Dearden a call. The former president of Paramount had recently teamed up with Sherry Lansing, former president of production at 20th Century-Fox, to launch an independent movie production company that would be affiliated with Paramount. Lansing had left Fox in 1982, where she was the first woman ever to be put in charge of production at a major film studio, because she wanted more authority than Fox was willing to grant her. Jaffe returned from London with a stack of scripts for Lansing. "I kept coming back to *Diversion*," she recalls. It was the film's potential to deliver a feminist message that appealed to her most, she says:

> I always wanted to do a movie that says you are responsible for your actions. ... And what I liked in the short film was that the man is made responsible. That there are consequences for him. When I watched that short film, I was on the single woman's side. And that's what I wanted to convey in our film. I wanted the audience to feel great empathy for the woman.

Lansing invited Dearden to Los Angeles to expand the story into a feature film, a story from the woman's point of view with a turning-of-the-tables message: The Other Woman shouldn't be getting all the blame; let the adulterous man take the fall for a change.

But Paramount didn't want to make that kind of movie. "[Paramount president] Michael Eisner turned it down because he thought the man was unsympathetic," director Adrian Lyne recalls. When Eisner left Paramount in 1984, Lansing tried again, and this time the studio agreed to take the film. Almost immediately, however, the old objections were raised. "My short film was a moral tale about a man who transgresses and pays the penalty," Dearden says. "But it was felt, and it was a feeling I didn't particularly agree with, that the audiences would not be sympathetic to such a man because he was an adulterer. So some of the onus for the weekend was taken off his shoulders and placed on the girl's." With each rewrite, Dearden was pressured to alter the characters further; the husband became progressively more lovable, the single woman more venomous. Dearden finally did away with the man's little black address book and made the single career woman the initiator of the affair. "As we went along, Alex became much more extreme," Dearden says. "She ended up having a kind of predatory quality. It weakened her case and strengthened his."

"The intent was to soften the man," a studio executive who was involved in the development discussions explains. "Because if you saw him shtup a different woman every week, then people would see him as cold and deliberate, and obviously you had to feel for him." Apparently no one had to feel for the single woman. The feelings of another man were involved, too: Michael Douglas, who was cast early on to play the husband, made it clear to *Fatal Attraction*'s producers that he was not going to play "some weak unheroic character," Dearden recalls.

With Douglas on board, the next task was finding a director. Adrian Lyne was the producers' first choice – a peculiar one for a film that was supposed to empathize with women. Of course, they chose him not for his perspective on the opposite sex but for his record at the box office. In 1983, Lyne directed *Flashdance*, a hit MTV-style musical in which the dancing women's rumps received far more screen time than their faces.

Following *Flashdance*'s commercial success, Lyne had also directed $9\frac{1}{2}$ *Weeks*, which attracted media attention for its glossy depiction of sadomasochism and for a particularly graphic episode, ultimately excised from all but the video version, in which the masochistic woman is forced to grovel for money at her stockbroker boyfriend's feet. During the filming, the humiliation continued between takes. Kim Basinger, the actress who played the woman, was cringing not only before her character's lover but also from the ministrations of Lyne, who waged an intimidation campaign against the actress – on the theory that an "edge of terror" would "help" prepare her for the role. At one point, heeding Lyne's instructions that "Kim had to be broken down," co-star Mickey Rourke grabbed and slapped Basinger to get her in the mood. ...

"Where is the new Kim Basinger?" casting agent Billy Hopkins recalls Lyne demanding throughout the auditions for *Fatal Attraction*. "Get me the new Kim Basinger." The casting agents went after several name actresses, including Debra Winger and Jessica Lange, who turned them down. Meanwhile, they kept getting calls from Glenn Close's agent. Close was determined to have the role; she was even willing to come in for a screen test, an unheard-of gesture for a major star. Close was anxious to shed the good-girl image of her previous roles, from the nurse–mother in *The World According to Garp* to the lady in white in *The Natural*. And late-eighties Hollywood offered actresses only one option for breaking typecasts: trading one caricatured version of womanhood for another.

Once Close was hired, the casting agents turned their attention to the character of the wife. In the original script she was a side character, unimportant. But the producers and Lyne wanted her remade into an icon of good wifery. Producer Stanley Jaffe says, "I wanted her to be – and I think this is the way she turned out – a woman who is sensitive, loyal, and acts in a way that I would be proud to say, 'I would like to know that lady.'" Casting agent Risa Bramon recalls that she was told to find an actress who "projected incredible warmth and love and strength in keeping the family together." Meanwhile, Dearden was sent back to his desk to turn the two women into polar opposites – as he puts it, "the Dark Woman and the Light Woman." Originally the wife, Beth, had a job as a teacher that she was anxious to resume. But by the final version, all traces of a career were excised and Beth transformed into the complete Victorian hearth angel (à la the prototypical Victorian "Beth" of *Little Women*), sipping tea, caressing piano keys, and applying cosmetics with an almost spiritual ardor.

Concurrently, Lyne was pushing Close in the other direction, transforming her character, as he describes it, into "a raging beast underneath." It was his idea to dress her up in black leather and turn her apartment into a barren loft in New York's meat market district, ringed by oil drums that burned like witches' caldrons.

To inspire this modern vision of the Dark Woman, Lyne says he "researched" the single women of the publishing world. "I was mostly interested in their apartments," he says. He looked at Polaroids of dozens of single women's studios. His "research" didn't involve actually talking to any of the inhabitants of these apartments; he had already made up his mind about unmarried career women. "They are sort of overcompensating for not being men," he says. "It's sad, you know, because it kind of doesn't work." ...

In Lyne's analysis, the most unfeminine women are the ones clamoring for equal rights:

> You hear feminists talk, and the last ten, twenty years you hear women talking about fucking men rather than being fucked, to be crass about it. It's kind of unattractive, however liberated and emancipated it is. It kind of fights the whole wife role, the whole childbearing role. Sure you got your career and your success, but you are not fulfilled as a woman.

For his ideal of the "feminine" woman, he points to his wife:

> My wife has never worked. She's the least ambitious person I've ever met. She's a terrific wife. She hasn't the slightest interest in doing a career. She kind of lives this with me, and it's a terrific feeling. I come home and she's there.

Michael Douglas harbored similar ill will for feminism and its effects. He told a reporter:

> If you want to know, I'm really tired of feminists, sick of them. They've really dug themselves into their own grave. Any man would be a fool who didn't agree with equal rights and pay but some women, now, juggling with career, lover, children [childbirth], wifehood, have spread themselves too thin and are very unhappy. It's time they looked at *themselves* and stopped attacking men. Guys are going through a terrible crisis right now because of women's unreasonable demands. ...

Originally, *Fatal Attraction* was supposed to end with Alex in deep despair over her unrequited love, committing suicide by slitting her throat to the music of *Madame Butterfly*. But when Paramount showed this initial version to test audiences, the response was disappointing. "It was not cathartic," Dearden recalls. "They were all wound up to a pitch and then it all kind of went limp and there was no emotional payoff for them. They'd grown to hate this woman by this time, to the degree that they actually wanted him to have some retribution." Suicide, apparently, was insufficient punishment.

The film's creators immediately decided to redraft the ending with an audience-pleasing climax – a last-minute revision that would cost them $1.3 million. Alex's death would be a homicide, they decided – and the Light Woman would kill the Dark Woman. They set the climactic blowout in the home, "the final sanctum," as Dearden describes it. The evil Alex invades, clutching a meat cleaver, and Dan grabs her by the throat, tries to drown her in the tub. But it is up to the dutiful wife to deliver the fatal shot, in the heart. The film ends with a slow pan of a framed family portrait, the family restored – the Gallagher family anyway. (For all their domestic sentimentality, the filmmakers gave no thought to the fact that Alex was pregnant when Beth shot her.)

What of Lansing's original objective – to make a feminist film? Lansing concedes that by the end of the film, "Your allegiance is not with Alex. It's with the family." But she contends that the film is on Alex's side to a point. "I do sympathize with her up until she dumps the acid on the car," Lansing says. She realizes, though, that most male viewers don't share her feelings. In one scene in the movie, Alex sits on the floor in tears, compulsively switching a light on and off. "I just found that tragic," Lansing says. "But in the screenings that often gets laughter. That surprised me."

Still, Lansing maintains that this remains a story about "the moral consequences of a man's actions." For the straying husband, she says, "his whole life turns into a horrendous nightmare." That may be true, but it's a nightmare from which he wakes up – sobered, but unscathed. In the end, the attraction is fatal only for the single woman.

"I think the biggest mistake filmmakers can make is to say, okay, we're only going to show women who are together and stable and wonderful people," Lansing says. In late eighties Hollywood, however, there didn't seem much danger of that. Asked to come up with some examples of "together and stable and wonderful" single women in her films, Lansing says, "Oh, I've made plenty." Such as? "I'm sure I've shown characters like this," she repeats. Pressed once more to supply a specific example, she finally says, "Well, Bonnie Bedelia in *When the Time Comes* [an ABC television movie] was just this functioning, terrific Rock of Gibraltar." But then, Bedelia was playing a young woman dying of cancer – another Beth of *Little Women*. Lansing's example only underscores the point driven home in the final take of *Fatal Attraction*: The best single woman is a dead one.

The Seventies: Unmarried Women and Brilliant Careers

For a while in the seventies the film industry would have a brief infatuation with the feminist cause. Just as silent-era Hollywood gave the movement a short run – after a series of low-budget pro-suffrage films turned into big hits – movie studios in the late seventies finally woke up to the profit potential in the struggle for women's independence. In films like *Diary of a Mad Housewife, A Woman Under the Influence, An Unmarried Woman, Alice Doesn't Live Here Anymore, Up the Sandbox, Private Benjamin,* and *The Turning Point,* housewives leave home, temporarily or permanently, to find their own voice. At the time, the female audience seemed to be on a similar quest. In New York movie theaters in 1975, women were not sitting placidly in their seats. They were booing the final scene of the newly released *Sheila Levine Is Dead and Living in New York,* because the script rewrote the best-seller's ending to marry off the single woman – to a doctor, of course, who would presumably cure her of her singles' sickness.

Eventually, filmmakers came around to the boisterous audience's feminist point of view. The end of *Private Benjamin,* where the heroine rebuffs her domineering groom, is a case in point. "It was very important to me that she walk out of that church," recalls Nancy Meyers, who created the film with Charles Shyer. "It was important to write about women's identity, and how easily it could be lost in marriage. That sounds almost old-fashioned now, I guess. But I know it mattered to many, many women." After *Private Benjamin* came out, Meyers was inundated with letters from women "who saw themselves in her character." It was a liberating event for the film's leading actress, too: Goldie Hawn had been typed up until then as a blond bubblehead.

In *Private Benjamin,* Hawn plays the single Judy, whose "life's desire" – marriage – comes crashing down when her husband dies on their wedding night. "If I'm not going to be married, I don't know what I'm supposed to do with myself," she says. She winds up enlisting in the army, where basic training serves as a metaphorical crash course in emotional and economic independence. Over thirty but not panicked about her single status, Judy goes to work and lives on her own in Europe. Eventually she meets a French doctor and they are engaged, but when she discovers his philanderings, she calls a halt to the wedding in midceremony, flees the church, and flings her bridal crown to the heavens. The scene recalls the famous ending of the 1967 *The Graduate;* but in the feminist version of this escape-from-the-altar scenario, it was no longer necessary for a man to be on hand as the agent of liberation.

The women who go mad in the 1970s women's films are not over-thirty single women panicked by man shortages but suburban housewives driven batty by subordination, repression, drudgery, and neglect. In the most extreme statement of this theme, *The Stepford Wives,* the housewives are literally turned into robots created by their husbands. In *Diary of a Mad Housewife* and *A Woman Under the Influence,* the wives' pill-popping habits and nervous breakdowns are presented as not-so-unreasonable responses to their crippling domestic condition – madness as a sign of their underlying sanity. What the male characters label lunacy in these films usually turns out to be a form of feminist resistance.

Women in these seventies films do not turn to male "doctors" to cure them: in *Private Benjamin*, when her fiancé (who is, significantly, a gynecologist) offers to give Judy a shot to help her "calm down," she slaps his face. Instead, these heroines seek counsel from other women, who dispense the opposite advice of traditional male clinicians: take action and speak up, they urge. The housewife in Paul Mazursky's *An Unmarried Woman* seeks advice from an independent female therapist, who tells her to go out, enjoy sex, and "get into the stream of life." ...

The American marriage, not the woman, is the patient under analysis in the seventies women's films, and the dialogue probes the economic and social inequities of traditional wedlock. "A woman like me works twice as hard and for what?" Barbra Streisand, the housewife Margaret in *Up the Sandbox*, demands of her husband, a history professor. "Stretch marks and varicose veins, that's what. You've got one job; I've got ninety-seven. Maybe I should be on the cover of *Time*. Dust Mop of the Year! Queen of the Laundry Room! Expert on Tinker Toys!" Margaret's mother offers the most succinct summation of what, in the opinion of these films, lies at the core of marital distress: "Remember, marriage is a 75–25 proposition. The woman gives 75."

In these films, the heroines are struggling to break out of the supporting-actress status that traditional marriage conferred on them; they are asking to be allowed, for once, to play a leading role in their own lives. "This story is going to be all about me," announces Judy Davis's Sybilla, in the first line of Gillian Armstrong's *My Brilliant Career*, an Australian film that became a hit in the United States in the late seventies. The youthful heroine turns down a marriage proposal not because she doesn't care for her suitor, but because marriage would mean that her own story would never have a chance to develop. "Maybe I'm ambitious, selfish," she says apologetically. "But I can't lose myself in somebody else's life when I haven't lived my own yet."

Of course, according to the conventional eighties analysis, these seventies film heroines *were* selfish, their pursuit of self-discovery just a euphemism for self-involvement. But that reading misses a critical aspect of the female quest in these movies. The heroines did not withdraw into themselves; they struggled toward active engagement in affairs beyond the domestic circle. They raised their voices not simply for personal improvement but for humanitarian and political causes – human rights in *Julia*, workers' rights in *Norma Rae*, equal pay in *9 to 5*, and nuclear safety in *The China Syndrome*. They wished to transform not only themselves but the world around them. They were loud, belligerently loud, because speaking up was a social, as well as a private, responsibility. "Are you still as angry as you used to be?" Julia, the World War II resistance fighter, asked Lillian Hellman in the biographical *Julia*. "I like your anger. ... Don't you let anyone talk you out of it."

The Eighties: The Celluloid Woman's Surrender

If Vanessa Redgrave's Julia represented the kind of heroine that 1970s feminist cinema would single out for biographical study, then it fell to Redgrave's daughter, Natasha Richardson, to portray her counterpart for the late 1980s: Patty Hearst. As conceived in Paul Schrader's 1988 film, the bound and blindfolded heiress is all victim; her lack of identity is her leading personality trait. ...

The same might be said of the droves of passive and weary female characters filling the screen in the late 1980s. In so many of these movies, it is as if Hollywood has taken the feminist films and run the reels backward. The women now flee the office and hammer at the homestead door. Their new quest is to return to traditional marriage, not challenge its construction; they want to escape the workplace, not remake it. The female characters who do have professional lives take little pleasure from them. They find their careers taxing and tedious, "jobs" more than callings. While the liberated women of seventies films were writers, singers, performers, investigative reporters, and political activists who challenged the system, the women of the late eighties are management consultants, investment advisers, corporate lawyers, behind-the-scenes production and literary assistants. They are the system's support staff.

Most women in the real contemporary labor force are, of course, relegated to ancillary, unsatisfying or degrading work, but these films aren't meant to be critiques of sex discrimination on the job or indictments of a demoralizing marketplace. They simply propose that women had a better deal when they stayed home. The films stack the deck against working female characters: it's easier to rationalize a return to housekeeping when the job left behind is so lacking in rewards or meaning. It's hard to make the case that a woman misses out if she quits the typing pool – or that society suffers when an investment banker abandons Wall Street.

The career women of the late-eighties cinema are an unappealing lot. They rarely smile and their eyes are red-rimmed from overwork and exhaustion. ...

In *Surrender*, Sally Field's Daisy is an "artist." But her artistry is performed at an assembly-line factory, where she mass-produces landscape art for hotels. Her one stab at a personal statement is to brush a tiny female figure into one of the canvases; it is a picture of herself drowning. All she wants to do, understandably, is quit and devote her life to marriage and motherhood. "If I'm not married again by the time I'm forty-one," she moans, "there's a 27 percent chance I'll end up a lonely alcoholic." Her "biological clock" is practically a guest star in this film. She has a dream, she tells her enviably fertile friend, who is pregnant for the fourth time. "This dream has a husband and baby in it." The "bottom line," says Daisy, is, "I want a baby." Although she claims to aspire to a career as a painter, after five minutes in front of the easel she is side-tracked by her more important marital mission. She hums the wedding march as she chases her prospective husband, a prolific and successful novelist. . . .

The professional women on screen who resist these nesting "trends," who refuse to lower their expectations and their voices, pay a bitter price for their recalcitrance. In *Broadcast News*, Holly Hunter's Jane, a single network producer, fails to heed the cocooning call. She's not out there beating the bushes for a husband and she's passionate about her work. Her male co-worker, a single reporter, has the same traits; on him they are admirable, but on her they constitute neurosis. She is "a basket case" and "an obsessive," who dissolves into inexplicable racking sobs in the middle of the day and compulsively chatters directions. "Except for socially," a female colleague tells her, "you're my role model." While the two lead male characters wind up with brilliant careers and full private lives, Jane winds up alone. Her aggressiveness at work cancels out her chances for love. Her attempts to pull off a romantic encounter fail miserably every time. "I've passed some line someplace," she says. "I'm beginning to repel people I'm trying to seduce."

In these backlash films, only the woman who buries her intelligence under a baby-doll exterior is granted a measure of professional success without having to forsake companionship. In *Working Girl*, Melanie Griffith's Tess, an aspiring secretary with a child's voice, rises up the business ladder *and* gets the man – but she achieves both goals by playing the daffy and dependent girl. She succeeds in business only by combing the tabloid gossip columns for investment tips – and relying on far more powerful businessmen to make the key moves in her "career." She succeeds in love Sleeping Beauty-style, by passing out in a man's arms.

Tess is allowed to move up in the ranks of American business only by tearing another woman down; in the eighties cinema, as in America's real boardrooms, there's only room for one woman at a time. Female solidarity in this film is just a straw man to knock down. "She takes me seriously," the naive Tess confides to her boyfriend about her new boss,

Katharine. "It's because she's a woman. She wants to be my mentor." The rest of the narrative is devoted to disabusing Tess of that notion. Katharine, a cutthroat Harvard MBA with a Filofax where her heart should be (the film's ads called her "the boss from hell"), betrays Tess at the first opportunity. The film ends with a verbal cat fight between the Dark and Light Woman, a sort of comic version of *Fatal Attraction*'s final scene, in which Tess orders Katharine to get her "bony ass" out of the office. Not only does Katharine *not* get the man; she doesn't even get to keep her job.

The incompatibility of career and personal happiness is preached in another prototypical woman's film of the eighties, *Baby Boom*. Like *Fatal Attraction*, it was a movie that the media repeatedly invoked, as "evidence" that babies and business don't mix. ...

As was the case in *Working Girl*, the male boss's hands in *Baby Boom* are clean. A benign patriarch, he reminds J. C. Wiatt, an aspiring management consultant with a messianic complex to match her initials, that she must choose between the corner office and the cradle. He's not being nasty, just realistic. "Do you understand the sacrifices?" he asks as he offers her a chance to become one of the firm's partners. "A man can be a success. My wife is there for me whenever I need her. I'm lucky. I can have it all." *Baby Boom* was cowritten by Nancy Meyers, creator of *Private Benjamin*, so one might expect that the film would set out to challenge this unjust arrangement – and argue that the corporation must learn to accommodate women, not the other way around. But this is a very different Nancy Meyers from the one who championed Private Benjamin's liberation seven years ago.

In keeping with the decade's prevailing views, Meyers now envisions women as divided into two hostile camps. "There are certain women who are very aggressive and great at business but who know nothing about babies and are intimidated by the thought of having kids," she told the press now. "They want them but don't know how to go about settling down and having one out of fear of what it'll do to their careers. I feel bad for those women."

"I don't see women having it all and achieving great things," Meyers says later in an interview. She's sitting in her Studio City house with a baby in her arms. "I don't see them in the corporate world." Rather than protest the lack of progress, Meyers has made adjustments. She says she has chosen to take a back seat to her creative partner and common-law husband, director Charles Shyer, so she can look after their two young children. ...

In scaling back her female characters' expectations, Meyers got plenty of encouragement from the Hollywood studios. When she and Shyer wrote *Protocol*, they ran into heavy interference from the presiding studio, Warner Brothers. The story was supposed to be about a naive waitress, again played by Goldie Hawn, who has her consciousness raised and becomes a politically wise diplomat. The studio insisted the producers rewrite the female character's development, Shyer recalls, removing Hawn's political evolution from the script. In the final version, she winds up a scatterbrained national sweetheart, cheerleading for the American way. "They were very nervous about the content of the movie, that it not have a political point of view," Charles Shyer recalls. "It was the beginning of the Reagan administration and they didn't want anything that might be seen as an anti-Reagan movie." A woman who thinks for herself, apparently, could now be mistaken for a subversive.

By the time production rolled around for *Baby Boom* in the mid-eighties, Meyers and Shyer had internalized the studio's commands; no unseemly political outbursts sully Diane Keaton's performance. At the start of *Baby Boom*, J. C. Wiatt, the Tiger Lady of the boardroom, has "chosen" career over marriage and maternity and in the process scoured away any trace of womanhood – or humanity. Diane Keaton's Wiatt is an efficient machine; even her sexual encounters are confined to passionless four-minute couplings. When a baby is forced into her unwilling arms by the death of a distant relative, she tries to explain about the zero-sum game of "choice": "I can't have a baby," she says, "because I have a twelve-thirty lunch meeting." Because she has cast her lot in a man's world, she is also seemingly incapable of the simplest acts of child care. Diapering the baby becomes an impossible ordeal for this Ivy Leaguer. Eventually, in the female game of trade-offs, as her baby skills ascend, her career plummets. Devotion to the baby destroys her chances of a promotion; the partnership offer is retracted and she is demoted to the dog-food account.

It never occurs to the highly educated Tiger Lady that her treatment might constitute sex discrimination. Instead of proceeding to the courtroom, she quits and moves to the country. Ensconced in a bucolic estate, she soon softens up, learning to bake and redirecting her business skills to a more womanly vocation, making and marketing gourmet baby food. Ultimately, her truly feminine side is awakened by the local veterinarian "Cooper." Like Tess, she finds love the old-fashioned way – by fainting. The doctor revives her on his examining table, and she falls in love.

Baby Boom's values are muddled; the film takes a feeble swipe at the corporate system before backing off completely. It pretends to reject the eighties money ethic without ever leaving its orbit. The Tiger Lady retreats to the country, but to an obscenely expensive farmhouse that she can afford only because of her prior Wall Street paychecks. She turns up her nose at yuppie materialism, but supports herself by selling boutique applesauce baby food to yuppie mothers. When one of her old corporate accounts at the firm offers to buy her baby-food company for $3 million in cash, she marches into the boardroom to reject the deal. "Country Baby is not for sale," she says piously. Her speech might have been an opportunity to take the firm to task for expelling its most valuable employee simply because she had a child. She could have spoken up for the rights of working mothers. But instead, the former Tiger Lady's talk dribbles off into a dewy-eyed reverie about the joys of rural living. "And anyway, I really think I'd miss my sixty-two-acre estate," she explains. "Elizabeth [her baby] is so happy there and well, you see, there's this veterinarian I'm seeing. ... "The last shot shows her back at home in a rocking chair, baby in her arms, surrounded by curtain lace and floral upholstery.

Like *Fatal Attraction*'s creators, Meyers and Shyer defend the "you-can't-have-it-all" message of the film by explaining that they based it on "research." To their credit, they did go to the trouble of interviewing an actual career woman. They modeled the Tiger Lady on a management consultant with a Harvard MBA. "She was so torn by the whole thing," Meyers says. "It was so hard for her. She didn't know what to do." What their model, Nadine Bron, didn't do, however, was give up work. She managed to find love and marry, too, despite the career. She's not even particularly "torn," she says.

"Well, I know it's Hollywood and all," Bron says diplomatically when asked later for her view of *Baby Boom*, "but what bothered me is that the movie assumed that is the only way – to give it all up and move to the country." Bron's life does not fit the you-can't-have-it-all thesis: she has worked for a large consulting firm and now runs her own money-management business – without abandoning a personal life. Her marriage, she says, is stronger because both she and her husband have "full lives." She has no desire to become a country housewife. ...

"For some women," Bron says, "staying home is preferable, but I could never do it. For me, it's very important to work." The problem, as she sees it, is not women wanting to go home but the male business world refusing to admit the women on equal terms. "Society has not been willing to adapt to these new patterns of women," she says. "Society punishes you."

Bringing Up the Cinematic Baby

An unintentionally telling aspect of *Baby Boom* is its implication that working women must be strong-armed into motherhood. The film is not the first of its era to suggest that, at a time when "baby fever" was supposedly raging in female brains, intense pressure, scoldings or a deus ex machina (like the Tiger Lady's improbable inheritance of a stranger's baby) is necessary to turn these reluctant modern women into mothers. Like the media, these movies aren't really reflecting women's return to total motherhood; they are marketing it. ...

The backlash films struggle to make motherhood as alluring as possible. Cuddly babies in designer clothes displace older children on the eighties screen; the well-decorated infants function in these films more as collector's items than people. The children of a decade earlier were talkative, unpredictable kids with minds of their own – like the precocious, cussing eleven-year-old boy who gives his mother both delight and lip in *Alice Doesn't Live Here Anymore*, or the seventeen-year-old girl who offers her mother both comfort and criticism in *An Unmarried Woman*. In the late 1980s, by contrast, the babies hardly cry.

Once again, women get sorted into two camps: the humble women who procreate and their monied or careerist sisters who don't. *Overboard's* haughty heiress refuses to reproduce. But by the end of the film – after she is humiliated, forced to scrub floors and cook meals, and at last finds happiness as a housewife – she tells her tyrannical new husband of her greatest goal in life: having "his" baby. Women who resist baby fever, by controlling their fertility or postponing motherhood, are shamed and penalized. In *Immediate Family*, Glenn Close's career woman – an Ivy League-educated realtor – delays and her biological clock expires. After a grueling round of visits to the infertility doctors, she has to hire a teenage surrogate to have a baby for her.

In this sanctimonious climate, abortion becomes a moral litmus test to separate the good women from the bad. On the day the husband in *Parenthood* loses his job, his good wife announces she's pregnant with child number four; she recoils in horror from the mere mention of abortion. The options of her sister-in-law's pregnant teenage daughter are presented as similarly limited. She's just received her high SAT scores in the mail, but, of course, the movie assures, she'll give up her college plans to have the baby and marry her deadbeat boyfriend – an unemployed dragstrip racer. Abortion is denounced in *Listen to Me*, which is supposedly an even-handed debate on the issue, and demonized in *Criminal Law*, where the abortionist, Sybil, is a witchlike figure whose profession traumatizes her son and turns him into a psychopath. Even more intelligent films preach on this subject. In Woody Allen's *Another Woman*, the single scholar, a rigid unfeeling spinster, flashes back to a shameful youthful memory – her selfish decision to have an abortion. "All you care about is your career, your life of the mind," her lover charged at the time, and now she sees, too late, that he was right to castigate her.

Three Men and a Baby became the most popular of the pronatal films (later inspiring the sequel *Three Men and a Little Lady*) with its baby-girl heroine center stage and its career woman expelled from nursery heaven. The premise – a single woman with career ambitions dumps her off-spring at the doorstep of three bachelors – recalls the antisuffrage films seventy years earlier. ...

Three Men and a Cradle, the original French version of the film, was such a hit with American audiences that Paramount hastened to release its own version, and the revisions are illuminating. For the American story, Paramount inserted a new character, wretched Rebecca, a dour lawyer with perpetually pursed lips. The wet-blanket girlfriend of bachelor Peter, Rebecca recoils with disgust at their new bundle of joy. When the baby drools on Rebecca's fingers, she can barely suppress her nausea. Peter pleads, "Rebecca, please stay with me – help me take care of her," but callous Rebecca refuses. She has no maternal juices, nor any romantic ones either. ...

At first glance, *Three Men and a Baby* might seem like a film with feminist tendencies; after all, the men are taking care of the baby. But the movie does not propose that men take real responsibility for raising children. It derives all its humor from the reversal of what it deems the natural order: mom in charge of baby. Viewers are regaled with the myriad ways in which these carefree bachelors are not cut out for parenthood. The fact that one of them actually *is* the father is played for laughs. "How do I know it's mine?" he says blithely. "Boys Will Be Boys" is the song that plays incessantly throughout the film. Indeed, despite their upwardly mobile careers and advancing middle age, the three bachelors celebrate their arrested development inside a high-priced frat house. ...

Unlike the French version, the American film keeps anxiously bolstering its male characters' masculinity. As if terrified that having a baby around the house might lower the testosterone level, the guys are forever lifting weights, sweating it out on the playing fields and jogging to the newsstands for the latest issue of *Sports Illustrated* and *Popular Mechanics*. In the American remake, the straying mother will eventually learn to uphold the traditional "feminine" role, too. In the final frame, remorseful mom not only reshoulders her maternal responsibilities but agrees to live under the men's roof. The baby, one of the bachelors asserts, "needs a full-time mother" – and, one gets the impression, so do they.

The American film industry in the eighties was simply not very welcoming to movie projects that portrayed independent women as healthy, lusty people without punishing them for their pleasure. Producer Gwen Field's experience with *Patti Rocks*, released soon after *Fatal Attraction*, is one measure of Hollywood's hostility to such themes in the decade.

In Field's film, an opinionated single woman shuns marriage ("Marriage is fattening," she jokes), enjoys sex, chooses to have a child on her own and yet pays no price for her behavior. *Patti Rocks* received its share of good reviews from the critics, but generated nothing but animosity and rejection from the guardians of Hollywood. Field was turned away by one studio after another and always for the same reason; they told her the film's message was "irresponsible" because it showed a single woman indulging in sex with whomever she pleased. (This same moral concern never surfaced over *Three Men and a Baby*, where the randy bachelors randomly scatter their seed.) The industry's ratings board tried to assign the film an X rating, even though it featured no violence and no more sex than the average R movie. Field recalls that the board members disapproved not of the visual display but "the language" – the same offense that brought down Mae West a half century earlier. As Field observes, "It was very ironic that we had received an X rating for a film that is against what pronography depicts – the degradation of women." It took three formal appeals before the board members finally approved an R rating. Ultimately *Patti Rocks*'s chances for commercial success were slim anyway; as an independently produced film with out-of-the-mainstream content, it would get distributed to only a handful of theaters.

The Celluloid Man Takes Charge

"Who am I?" the single female psychiatrist asks her male mentor, a small-time gambler and con artist, in David Mamet's 1987 *House of Games*. Although she's the one with the medical degree, he's playing doctor. Her hair shorn, her face severe and unsmiling, she clutches the book she has written, *Driven: Obsession and Compulsion in Everyday Life*, but its contents have no answers for her. Those must come from him. The consultation that follows recalls a therapy session from the last backlash cinema, between the male psychoanalyst and the driven single magazine editor in *Lady in the Dark*. That earlier film's dialogue:

> HE: You've had to prove you were superior to all men: You had to dominate them.
> SHE: What's the answer?
> HE: Perhaps some man who will dominate you. After half a century of "progress," the diagnosis remains the same in *House of Games*:
> SHE: What do I want?
> HE: Somebody to come along. Somebody to possess you. Would you like that?
> SHE: Yes.

Offscreen, David Mamet was complaining bitterly about women in the entertainment business who apparently prefer to dominate and "won't compromise." In a 1988 essay on women entitled "Bewitched, Bothered and Bewildered," he asserted, "The coldest, cruelest, most arrogant behavior I have ever seen in my professional life has been – and *consistently* been – on the part of women producers in the movies and the theater." In Mamet's *House of Games*, the stepped-on confidence man slips the cold careerist woman back under his thumb through his sleights of hand. And who is the actress Mamet cast in the demeaning female role? Lindsay Crouse, his own wife.

The eighties backlash cinema embraces the Pygmalion tradition – men redefining women, men reclaiming women as their possessions and property. In the most explicit statement of this theme, the Wall Street tycoon in *Pretty Woman* remakes the loud, gumsmacking hooker into his soft-spoken and genteel appendage, fit for a Ralph Lauren ad. In film after film, men return to their roles of family potentate, provider, and protector of female virtue. In films from *Moonstruck* to *The Family*, the celluloid neopatriarchs preside over "old-fashioned" big ethnic families. ... In films like *Someone to Watch Over Me, Sea of Love*, or *Look Who's Talking*, the backlash heroes play Big Daddy guardians to helpless women and families threatened by stalkers. In the real world, blue-collar men might be losing economic and domestic authority, but in these movies the cops and cabbies were commanding respect from cowering affluent women.

For all the sentimental tributes to the return of the all-American household – "Nothing can take the place of the family!" the son toasts in *Moonstruck*, and "Nice to be married, huh?" the men tell each other in *The Untouchables* – the late-1980s pro-family films are larded with male anger over female demands and male anxiety over women's progress. ... In *Surrender*, the male protagonist, a twice-divorced author, suspects all women of malicious ulterior motives. "We're all just meat to them," he says of women, and vows to move to Kuwait "because women don't vote there." Standing in the lobby of his divorce lawyer's building, he faces a choice: entering one elevator with a leather-clad woman or another elevator with a snarling Doberman and street hood. He takes his chances with the canine-and-criminal duo.

The decade in family cinema ended not with a heartwarming salute to home's cozy comforts but with an explosion of hateful marital fireworks. The underbelly of the backlash finally surfaced on screen, as spouses lunged for each other's throats in films like *The War of the Roses, She-Devil, I Love You to Death*, and *Sleeping with the Enemy*. Usually hidden fears about strong women's powers are on bold display. In both *The War of the Roses* and *She-Devil*, the wives are virtual witches, controlling and conquering their husbands with a supernatural and deadly precision.

In the 1970s women's liberation films and 1940s wartime movies, men and women struggled endlessly with each other, too, but they argued with good intentions – to understand and enlighten each other, to close rather than widen the gender gap. When the dust clears after the shouting match between Ellen Burstyn and Kris Kristofferson in *Alice Doesn't Live Here Anymore*, each comes to see the other's point of view, and they walk away from the struggle with stronger empathy and love. In *Adam's Rib*, Spencer Tracy's lawyer stomps from the house demanding divorce after his wife (Katharine Hepburn) wins her feminist case in court. "I like two sexes," he shouts at her. "And another thing. All of a sudden I don't like being married to what is known as the New Woman." She calls after him, "You are not going to solve anything by running away," and in the end, he agrees; they reunite and work out their differences. In *The War of the Roses*, by contrast, there's no hope for reconciliation, truce, or even escape from the marital battle – both spouses wind up dead, their bodies smashed in the familial foyer.

In many of these late-eighties films, men and women not only have quit trying to hash things out, they don't even keep company on the same film reel. Like the fifties backlash cinema, independent women are finally silenced by pushing them off the screen. In the tough-guy films that proliferated at the end of the decade, male heroes head off to all-male war zones and the Wild West. In the escalating violence of an endless stream of war and action movies – *Predator*, *Die Hard*, *Die Harder*, *RoboCop*, *RoboCop 2*, *Lethal Weapon*, *Days of Thunder*, *Total Recall* – women are reduced to mute and incidental characters or banished altogether. In the man–boy body-swapping films that cropped up in the late eighties – *18 Again*, *Like Father, Like Son*, and, the most memorable, *Big* – men seek refuge in female-free boyhoods. And male characters in another whole set of films retreat even further, to hallucinatory all-male fantasies of paternal renewal. In such films as *Field of Dreams*, *Indiana Jones and the Last Crusade*, *Dad*, and *Star Trek V: The Final Frontier*, mother dies or disappears from the scene, leaving father (who is sometimes resurrected from the dead) and son to form a spiritually restorative bond.

Not surprisingly, when the Screen Actors Guild conducted a count of female roles in Hollywood in 1990, the organization discovered that women's numbers had sharply dropped in the last two years. Men, the guild reported, were now receiving more than twice as many roles as women.

While men were drifting off into hypermasculine dreamland, the female characters who weren't already dead were subject to ever more violent ordeals. In 1988, all but one of the women nominated for the

Academy Award's Best Actress played a victim. (The exception, fittingly, was Melanie Griffith's working "girl.") The award's winner that year, Jodie Foster, portrayed a rape victim in *The Accused*. The producer of that film was Sherry Lansing.

Lansing released *The Accused* a year after *Fatal Attraction*, and hoped that it would polish up her feminist credentials. The film told the story of a young working-class woman gang-raped at a local bar while a crowd of men stood by and let it happen – a tale based on a grisly real gang rape at Big Dan's tavern in New Bedford, Massachusetts. "If anyone thinks this movie is antifeminist, I give up," Lansing told the press. "Once you see this movie, I doubt that you will ever, ever think of rape the same way again. Those images will stick in your mind, and you will be more sympathetic the next time you hear of somebody being raped."

Did people really need to be reminded that rape victims deserve sympathy? Apparently Lansing did: "Until I saw this film, I didn't even know how horrible [rape] is," she announced. Apparently many young men watching this film needed the reminder, too: they hooted and cheered the film's rape scene. And clearly a society in which rape rates were skyrocketing could stand some reeducation on the subject.

Lansing said *The Accused* should be hailed as a breakthrough movie because it tells America a woman has the "right" not to be raped. But it seems more reasonable that it should be mourned as a depressing artifact of the times – because it tells us only how much ground women have already lost. By the end of the eighties, a film that simply opposed the mauling of a young woman could be passed off as a daring feminist statement.

Documents

Introduction to Documents

Throughout the twentieth century, and especially during its last four decades, Americans have hotly debated the question of what should be the role, rights, and responsibilities of women. The National Organization of Women (NOW), founded in 1966 with the goal of achieving equal rights for women in partnership with men, lobbied hard for a constitutional amendment that would end all forms of gender discrimination. The Equal Rights Amendment, our first document, was passed by Congress in 1972 and sent to the states for ratification; however, the measure died when it fell three states short of ratification. In our second document, Phyllis Schlafly, one of the leaders of the "STOP ERA" campaign, describes the limitations of women's liberation and the ways in which a Positive Woman can achieve a more productive and fulfilling life than her feminist counterpart. Observing that "lots of people look to the movies for role models," Richard Cohen, in our last document, analyzes how messages and gender stereotypes conveyed in *Fatal Attraction* (1987) conformed to or conflicted with off screen debates over the best way for men and women to find happiness.

Equal Rights Amendment, 1972

Section I

Equality of rights under the law shall not be denied or abridged by the United States or by any State on account of sex.

Section 2

The Congress shall have the power to enforce, by appropriate legislation, the provisions of this article.

Section 3

The amendment shall take effect two years after the date of ratification.

A Backlash Manifesto

Phyllis Schlafly

Source: Phyllis Schlafly, *The Power of Positive Women* (New Rochelle, NY: Arlington House Publishers, 1977), 9–21

The cry of "women's liberation" leaps out from the "lifestyle" sections of newspapers and the pages of slick magazines, from radio speakers and television screens. Cut loose from past patterns of behavior and expectations, women of all ages are searching for their identity – the college woman who has new alternatives thrust upon her via "women's studies" courses, the young woman whose routine is shattered by a chance encounter with a "consciousness-raising session," the woman in her middle years who suddenly finds herself in the "empty-nest syndrome," the woman of any age whose lover or lifetime partner departs for greener pastures (and a younger crop).

All of these women, thanks to the women's liberation movement, no longer see their predicament in terms of personal problems to be confronted and solved. They see their own difficulties as a little cog in the big machine of establishment restraints and stereotypical injustice in which they have lost their own equilibrium. Who am I? Why am I here? Why am I just another faceless victim of society's oppression, a nameless prisoner behind walls too high for me to climb alone? ...

For a woman to find her identity in the modern world, the path should be sought from the Positive Women who have found the road and possess the map, rather than from those who have not. In this spirit, I share with you the thoughts of one who loves life as a woman and lives love as a woman, whose credentials are from the school of practical experience, and who has learned that fulfillment as a woman is a journey, not a destination.

Like every human being born into this world, the Positive Woman has her share of sorrows and sufferings, of unfulfilled desires and bitter defeats. But she will never be crushed by life's disappointments, because her positive mental attitude has built her an inner security that the actions of other people can never fracture. To the Positive Woman, her particular set of problems is not a conspiracy against her, but a challenge to her character and her capabilities.

Understanding the Difference

The first requirement for the acquisition of power by the Positive Woman is to understand the differences between men and women. Your outlook on life, your faith, your behavior, your potential for fulfillment, all are determined by the parameters of your original premise. The Positive Woman starts with the assumption that the world is her oyster. She rejoices in the creative capability within her body and the power potential of her mind and spirit. She understands that men and women are different, and that those very differences provide the key to her success as a person and fulfillment as a woman.

The women's liberationist, on the other hand, is imprisoned by her own negative view of herself and of her place in the world around her. ...

Someone – it is not clear who, perhaps God, perhaps the "Establishment," perhaps a conspiracy of male chauvinist pigs – dealt women a foul blow by making them female. It becomes necessary, therefore, for women to agitate and demonstrate and hurl demands on society in order to wrest from an oppressive male-dominated social structure the status that has been wrongfully denied to women through the centuries.

By its very nature, therefore, the women's liberation movement precipitates a series of conflict situations – in the legislatures, in the courts, in the schools, in industry – with man targeted as the enemy. Confrontation replaces cooperation as the watchword of all relationships. Women and men become adversaries instead of partners.

The second dogma of the women's liberationists is that, of all the injustices perpetrated upon women through the centuries, the most oppressive is the cruel fact that women have babies and men do not. Within the confines of the women's liberationist ideology, therefore, the abolition of this overriding inequality of women becomes the primary goal. This goal must be achieved at any and all costs – to the woman herself, to the baby, to the family, and to society. Women must be made equal to men in their ability *not* to become pregnant and *not* to be expected to care for babies they may bring into the world. ...

The Positive Woman will never travel that dead-end road. It is self-evident to the Positive Woman that the female body with its baby-producing organs was not designed by a conspiracy of men but by the Divine Architect of the human race. ... The Positive Woman looks upon her femaleness and her fertility as part of her purpose, her potential, and her power. She rejoices that she has a capability for creativity that men can never have.

The third basic dogma of the women's liberation movement is that there is no difference between male and female except the sex organs, and that all those physical, cognitive, and emotional differences you *think* are there, are merely the result of centuries of restraints imposed by a male-dominated society and sex-stereotyped schooling. The role imposed on women is, by definition, inferior, according to the women's liberationists. ...

The women's liberationists and their dupes who try to tell each other that the sexual drive of men and women is really the same, and that it is only societal restraints that inhibit women from an equal desire, an equal enjoyment, and an equal freedom from the consequences, are doomed to frustration forever. It just isn't so, and pretending cannot make it so. The differences are not a woman's weakness but her strength. ...

The new generation can brag all it wants about the new liberation of the new morality, but it is still the woman who is hurt the most. The new morality isn't just a "fad" – it is a cheat and a thief. It robs the woman of her virtue, her youth, her beauty, and her love – for nothing, just nothing. It has produced a generation of young women searching for their identity, bored with sexual freedom, and despondent from the loneliness of living a life without commitment. They have abandoned the old commandments, but they can't find any new rules that work.

The Positive Woman recognizes the fact that, when it comes to sex, women are simply not the equal of men. The sexual drive of men is much stronger than that of women. That is how the human race was designed in order that it might perpetuate itself. The other side of the coin is that it is easier for women to control their sexual appetites. A Positive Woman cannot defeat a man in a wrestling or boxing match, but she can motivate him, inspire him, encourage him, teach him, restrain him, reward him, and have power over him that he can never achieve over her with all his muscle. How or whether a Positive Woman uses her power is determined solely by the way she alone defines her goals and develops her skills. ...

One of the strangest quirks of women's liberationists is their complaint that societal restraints prevent men from crying in public or showing their emotions, but permit women to do so, and that therefore we should "liberate" men to enable them, too, to cry in public. The public display of fear, sorrow, anger, and irritation reveals a lack of self-discipline that should be avoided by the Positive Woman just as much as by the Positive Man. Maternal love, however, is not a weakness but a manifestation of strength and service, and it should be nurtured by the Positive Woman. ...

Finally, women are different from men in dealing with the fundamentals of life itself. Men are philosophers, women are practical, and 'twas ever thus. Men may philosophize about how life began and where we are heading; women are concerned about feeding the kids today. No woman would ever, as Karl Marx did, spend years reading political philosophy in the British Museum while her child starved to death. Women don't take naturally to a search for the intangible and the abstract. The Positive Woman knows who she is and where she is going, and she will reach her goal because the longest journey starts with a very practical first step. ...

An effort to eliminate the differences by social engineering or legislative or constitutional tinkering cannot succeed, which is fortunate, but social relationships and spiritual values can be ruptured in the attempt. Thus the role reversals being forced upon high school students, under which guidance counselors urge reluctant girls to take "shop" and boys to take "home economics," further confuse a generation already unsure about its identity. They are as wrong as efforts to make a left-handed child right-handed.

A New Stereotype: The Crazy Career Woman

Richard Cohen

Source: *Washington Post*, October 6, 1987

A week after it was released, the movie "Fatal Attraction" became the nation's No. 1 box-office hit. Little wonder. The movie features Glenn Close and Michael Douglas, is redolent with sex, and scary enough to make women shriek in their seats and cause a friend of mine, a World War II combat veteran, to have a post-cinema nightmare. The film's ultimate nightmare, though, is for the women's movement.

That, I hasten to add, is not the way some women see it. The movie, after all, is about a married lawyer (Douglas) who has a brief but oh-so-passionate affair with a successful career woman (Close), a book editor – not to mention psychopath. For Douglas, a few hours of heaven becomes weeks of hell – the kind that hath no fury like a woman scorned. Here is the peril of the one-night stand, a morality tale for men as women would like to tell it.

For men, too, the picture has resonance. It suggests the old aphorism: Never eat at a place called Mom's, play poker with a man named Doc, or sleep with a woman crazier than you are. Many men have done the latter, although few with the complicating and tragic consequences that befall Douglas. At any rate, for a slick film, there is food for thought here for both sexes. Where AIDS cautions, "Fatal Attraction" screams "Stop!"

And yet the movie says something else. It totally reverses the stereotype of recent years. Instead of the career woman being the one who has it all (a terrific job, a sensational apartment and the freedom to sexually engage at whim), it is the non-working wife-cum-mother who is the paragon of mature womanhood. Played by Anne Archer, she exudes contentedness, serenity and, in the end, a formidable strength. She is complete unto herself.

A movie is just a movie and too much should not be made of it. It's doubtful that the makers of "Fatal Attraction" were attempting to make a statement about feminism. But in the same way that "Rambo" was in sync with the Tarzan ethic of the Reagan years, this movie seems to have struck a cultural chord. Its very premise – the fulfilled wife–mother, the unfulfilled and (therefore?) crazy career woman – might well have been rejected just a few years ago.

In fact, so acceptable is the stereotype of the successful-yet-whacko career woman that the audience has swallowed it as easily as popcorn.

Never mind that it's a contradiction in terms. After all, aside from running Bates Motel, could a psychopath actually become successful in business? Probably not. Conversely, could a bright, educated woman be totally fulfilled playing with a pre-schooler by day and accompanying her husband to cocktail parties by night? Again, probably not. This, though, is the way both women are portrayed.

The problem with the movie is, in a way, the problem with all movements and counter-movements. There is an absolutist quality to them – a kind of either-or mentality. In movies, this is understandable because a film script is usually too slight a vehicle to shoulder ambiguity. That's too bad because lots of people look to movies for role models. But in a movement, such simplicity can be even more disastrous since it exists to point the way. It asserts The Truth.

Just a short time ago women were told to follow the career path. A job, a title, a couple of dress-for-success suits and a stock broker's card on the Rolodex would add up to fulfillment. When that turned out to be not always the case, a counter-prescription was offered: Stay home, stay pregnant and, in the process, stay happy. This is the chirpy advice of anti-feminists.

Neither path is either right or wrong. What's right for one woman may be wrong for another and, just to make things more complicated, right at one age and wrong at another. But none is a panacea – a ticket to happiness. Yet, the reaction to the women's movement (some of it valid) has gone so far as to proclaim the status quo ante as a heaven that can be reclaimed. It makes no allowance for the increasingly higher educational levels of women, birth control and, of course, the well-documented misery of women who once had to follow the only path open to them: wife and mother.

For both men and women, the challenge is to re-invent the way we live, to grope for the proper mix, to live in the present while retaining an attentive respect for what worked in the past. But too much has changed and nostalgia, like "the other woman," is often an escape from reality. When it comes to proclaiming a path to happiness, it could be the most fatal attraction of them all.

Readings and Screenings

Susan Faludi's *Backlash: The Undeclared War Against Women* (New York: Anchor Books, 1991) is an insightful look into a wide variety of topics regarding women's role in American life during the 1970s and 1980s. Several books offer sweeping examinations of the political, social, and economic content of 1980s films and contain specific chapters on portrayals of women and gender roles: Michael Ryan and Douglas Kellner,

Camera Politica: The Politics and Ideology of Contemporary Hollywood Film (Bloomington, IN: Indiana University Press, 1988); William J. Palmer, *The Films of the Eighties: A Social History* (Carbondale and Edwardsville, IL: Southern Illinois University Press, 1993); Elizabeth Traube, *Dreaming Identities: Class, Gender and Generation in 1980s Hollywood Movies* (Boulder, CO: Westview Press, 1992); Alan Nadel, *Flatlining on the Field of Dreams: Cultural Narratives in the Films of President Reagan's America* (New Brunswick, Canada: Rutgers University Press, 1997). Depictions of gender in more recent Hollywood films are explored in Murray Pomerance, ed., *Ladies and Gentlemen, Boys and Girls: Gender in Film at the End of the Twentieth Century* (Albany, NY: State University of New York Press, 2001); Yvonne Tasker, *Working Girls: Gender and Sexuality in Popular Cinema* (London and New York: Routledge, 1998); Suzanne Ferriss and Mallory Young, eds, *Chick Flicks: Contemporary Women at the Movies* (London: Routledge, 2007). For a more general overview of film during the Reagan era, see Chris Jordan, *Movies and the Reagan Presidency: Success and Ethic* (Westport, CN and London: Praeger: 2003). For cinematic portrayals of gender during an earlier era, see Jeanine Basinger, *A Woman's View: How Hollywood Spoke to Women, 1930–1960* (Middletown, CN: Wesleyan University Press, 1995).

Those interested in a closer look at images of masculinity during the 1980s should read Susan Jeffords, *Hard Bodies: Hollywood Masculinity in the Reagan Era* (New Brunswick, Canada: Rutgers University Press, 1994). For images of men in other eras, see Dennis Bingham, *Acting Male: Masculinities in the Films of James Stewart, Jack Nicholson, and Clint Eastwood* (New Brunswick, Canada: Rutgers University Press, 1994); Steven Cohan, Ina Rae Hark, eds., *Screening the Male: Exploring Masculinities in Hollywood Cinema* (New York: Routledge, 1993); David Greven, *Manhood in Hollywood from Bush to Bush* (Austin, TX: University of Texas Press, 2009); Susanne Kord and Elisabeth Krimmer, *Contemporary Hollywood Masculinities: Gender, Genre, and Politics* (New York: Palgrave Macmillan, 2011). Two older but highly readable works that survey cinematic images of women during the twentieth century are Marjorie Rosen, *Popcorn Venus: Women, Movies, and the American Dream* (New York: McCann & Georhegan, 1973) and Molly Haskell, *From Reverence to Rape: The Treatment of Women in the Movies* (Chicago, IL: University of Chicago Press, 1973).

Given the amount of space Faludi devotes to it, *Fatal Attraction* (1987) is a good starting point for looking at controversial images of "good" and "bad" men and women. Those interested in contrasting films of the 1970s with their more conservative counterparts of the 1980s might watch *Up the Sandbox* (1972), *Alice Doesn't Live Here Anymore* (1974), *Julia* (1977), *The Turning Point* (1977), *An Unmarried Woman* (1978), *Norma Rae* (1979), and *The China Syndrome* (1979). As for the 1980s, *Working Girl* (1987) is an entertaining and perceptive examination of the interplay of class and gender. Students love it. Other films about love, career, family, and gender roles worth looking at are *Tootsie* (1982), *Baby Boom* (1987), *3 Men and a Baby* (1987), *Surrender* (1987), *Broadcast News* (1987), *Overboard* (1987), *Crossing Delancy* (1988), *Parenthood* (1989), and *The War of the Roses* (1989). Two contrasting images of women in early 1990s films can be seen in *Pretty Woman* (1990) and *Thelma and Louise* (1991). Jane Fonda's *Coming Home* (1978) shows how political activism can help women overcome traditional gender roles and discover a greater sense of who they are. Likewise, *Nine to Five* (1980) is a humorous fantasy of how three competent women rise up against their incompetent boss and transform gender and class relations at the workplace. At the other end of the political spectrum, *Conan the Barbarian* (1982) and *The Terminator* (1984), both starring Arnold Schwarzenegger, offer visions of masculinity in tune with the Reagan era.

12

American Film in the Age of Terror: The Wars in Afghanistan and Iraq

Introduction to Article

Over the course of the twentieth and twenty-first centuries, the United States has engaged in a number of "good" wars and "not so good" wars. Part of the distinction between the two derives from the ways in which the war was portrayed and understood by a mass public. For most Americans, the events of September 11, 2001 wiped away the bad memories of Vietnam and led to widespread support for military retaliation against Osama bin Laden and al-Qaeda forces hidden away in the hills of Afghanistan. Likewise, most citizens initially supported the joint American and United Kingdom-led invasion of Iraq begun on March 20, 2003 – a war justified in part by President George W. Bush's insistence that Iraqi dictator Saddam Hussein possessed "weapons of mass destruction" (WMD) that he planned to use against domestic and foreign enemies. As the war dragged on and no such weapons were found, American attitudes toward war grew more complex. Various groups and media outlets slowly began voicing their opposition to the war, while at the same time praising the valiant efforts of our troops. This would not be a repeat of Vietnam when public opinion turned against both the war and the warriors.

Visual representations of the wars in Afghanistan and Iraq differed from previous wars in one crucial respect: this was the first time soldiers (using cell phones and digital cameras) sent back their own unfiltered

Movies and American Society, Second Edition. Edited by Steven J. Ross.
© 2014 John Wiley & Sons, Inc. Published 2014 by John Wiley & Sons, Inc.

on-the-ground images of war. Indeed, never before has a war-in-progress been so completely documented and from so many points of view. Susan L. Carruthers' sweeping essay surveys the content and politics of several types of filmic representations of war: those taken by combat soldiers, those produced by documentarians, and feature films made by commercial studios. Unlike Vietnam, Hollywood did not wait until the end of hostilities, but turned out feature films during the early years of war. And unlike Vietnam, many filmmakers focused on what happened to often traumatized soldiers when they returned home. Despite the plethora of productions, Carruthers argues "the war in Iraq has produced few great films – arguably none at all."

Discussion Points

What do you think should be the purpose of wartime films: should it be to educate the public? To evoke patriotism? Or, to question our war aims? How have filmmakers explained – or failed to explain – the origins, course, and consequences of war? Which of these three types of films – features, documentaries, or those shot by soldiers – is most powerful? Why? Why do you think audiences grew quickly bored by films about the war in Iraq?

Limited Engagement: The Iraq War on Film

Susan L. Carruthers

Source: Cynthia Lucia, Roy Grundmann, and Art Simon, eds, *The Wiley-Blackwell History of American Film*, vol. IV (Malden, MA and Oxford: Wiley-Blackwell, 2012), 472–94

Imagine a landscape of desolate streets strewn with vast mounds of garbage and burnt out vehicles. Buildings – an indistinguishable jumble of shops and homes, punctuated by golden-domed mosques and filigreed minarets – are pock-marked by artillery rounds where they haven't been pulverized into rubble. Everything chokes with dust. And everyone is armed – armed with a camera if not also with more lethal weapons. Cell phones serve both to detonate improvised explosive devices and to document the carnage. While "jihadis" film beheadings and suicide bombers record their last messages before martyrdom, American troops engage in their own obsessive digital self-documentation. Flurrying shutters click to produce a grue-some montage of grins, grimaces, tears, blood, corpses, and severed body parts.

Or so it would seem as a distant conflict comes into blurry focus from the welter of photographs, video-clips, and feature-length films that collectively constitute "Iraq" as American viewers apprehend it. Indeed, it has become something of a truism that never before in history has a conflict-in-progress been subject to such relentless imagistic documentation. In whatever other ways Iraq's intractability may or may not resemble the quagmire of Vietnam, cultural critics have pointed to one striking discrepancy. Vietnam – the first "television war" – was avoided by the film industry until it was over, Hollywood studio executives reluctant to tackle a war that was both too divisive and too visible. Iraq, by contrast, having been largely abandoned by network news after the first flush of "mission accomplished" euphoria, has attracted an unprecedented number of filmmakers eager to fill the void. . . .

To date, at least 40 [documentaries] have appeared, together with a smaller number of narrative Films distributed by major studios.

Here, I will chart the key thematic preoccupations of American filmmakers as they have engaged the war's origins, course, and consequences. How far have their political concerns, emotional investments, and aesthetic strategies shifted over time? To what end has Iraq been the most heavily "documentaried" war to date? If everyone is making pictures, who has actually been looking, and what have they seen?

The Soldier as Cinematographer

Given the daunting number of war-related films, I propose to begin by taking a close look at one that condenses many key features of Iraq war cinema more broadly. After its premier at the 2006 Tribeca Film Festival, Deborah Scranton's *The War Tapes* garnered widespread critical acclaim and an Oscar nomination for best documentary film (lost to Al Gore's *An Inconvenient Truth*). Like other films that preceded it such as Michael Tucker and Petra Epperlein's *Gunner Palace* (2005) and Garrett Scott and Ian Old's *Occupation: Dreamland* (2005), *The War Tapes* sets out to document a year-long tour of duty in Iraq, in this case by members of C Company of the New Hampshire National Guard.

Unlike those earlier productions, however, the "war tapes" in Scranton's film are supplied by men on active duty, providing this documentary with a distinctive promotional hook: the first war film to be shot by soldiers themselves. Having declined an offer to embed with the National Guard, Scranton instead sought permission to give cameras to the guardsmen themselves. Ten volunteers received a one-chip Sony MiniDV camera, tripod, microphones, an array of lenses, and a stack of blank tape.[1] Some sent Scranton only raw footage, while others maintained regular contact via email and instant messaging. Edited into final form, *The War Tapes* foregrounds the camerawork and reflections of three men in particular. Specialist Mike Moriarty, Sergeant Steve Pink, and Sergeant Zack Bazzi offer a compelling study in contrasts: Moriarty, a "substantially patriotic" father of two, laid off from his fork-lift-driving job and struggling to shore up his imperiled masculinity; Pink, a cynical 24-year-old carpenter with writerly inclinations, hoping to eliminate debts accrued as a college English major; and the laconic, *Nation*-reading, Arabic-speaking Bazzi, the apple of his Lebanese mother's teary eyes.

This biographical mise-en-scène, introducing Moriarty's wife, Pink's girlfriend, and Bazzi's mother, occupies *The War Tapes'* first 15 minutes. From the outset, then, it is clear that the relationship between "over here" and "over there" – between domesticity and military service, between men and women, family and country – is central to Scranton's mission of establishing "the possibility of empathy in the middle of war." A film about the first-hand experience of soldiers, *The War Tapes* also reflects the experience of the women who wait and worry at home: a portrait of relationships strained by prolonged absence, and under threat of fatal termination, that can't be readily resumed "as normal" by men who return home altered, angry, and estranged. This looming alienation is foreshadowed at the outset when, on the eve of his deployment, Moriarty films his four-year-old son running across a parking lot to greet him. Seen through night-vision lenses, he is an eerily luminescent little figure – tinged in green, not quite of this world – who interrupts filming by jumping up for a hug.

Then, with little orientation (it is November 2004 in the turbulent city of Fallujah), *The War Tapes* plunges viewers into the maelstrom. Since no single narrator lends overall coherence to the video collage, we are left to make our own sense of the disorienting experience of soldiering in Iraq. Chaos reigns. Firefights erupt from nowhere and end just as suddenly: a blizzard of bullets; a din of expletives, commands, and yells; a confusion of injuries; vehicles on fire; blood on the road; the camera upended. If it is impossible to tell who is firing at whom, it is also hard not to question the wisdom of soldiers doing double duty as cinematographers, when their sights might more appropriately be trained elsewhere.

Throughout *The War Tapes*, Iraq is mainly viewed through the windscreen or turret of an armored personnel carrier: a blasted wasteland of arid countryside and cratered streetscapes moved through at speed. At rest, the soldiers of C Company face daily mortar and rocket attacks on their flimsy encampment near Bilal. But while they are in constant danger, they also present a lethal menace to the civilian population of Iraq. Barreling down single-gauge highways at 50 miles per hour, the armored convoys stop for no one. Iraqi drivers who move too slowly are bulldozed aside, their cars furiously bumped off the road like fairground dodgems. Heedless pedestrians face a more lethal fate. In one of *The War Tapes'* most disturbing sequences, also rendered in night-vision's ominous green, Moriarty's vehicle plows into a young Iraqi woman who had dashed out to cross the road. By the time they lurch to a halt, her body lies in pieces, dimly captured on video as several guards struggle to drag her remains off the road before more trucks hurtle past. Troubled by the indignity of her death, one soldier remarks on the crumbled remains of cookies she'd been carrying – a badge of her innocence and their culpability. "The Iraqi people are who we're here to help, and we just killed one of them," a guardsman notes. Revolted by the sight of "pieces of her head," which he urges another soldier not to look at, he is instantly aware that such a scene is never forgotten. And it isn't. On return to New Hampshire, this vision of wasted life haunts Moriarty in post-traumatic flashback. ...

Together the protagonists of *The War Tapes* provide candid insights into the operation of untrammeled greed in what one of them dubs the "war for cheese." They are well placed to do so, for the primary mission of C Company is providing armed protection for convoys of trucks operated by Kellogg, Brown and Root (KBR, a Halliburton subsidiary) as they deliver supplies to military bases across Iraq. As Pink explains, desperate TNRs (third country nationals) receive a pittance to drive unroadworthy vehicles through hostile territory while hapless "rear echelon motherfuckers," who had never expected to see combat, ride in the most vulnerable position – poised to fire at insurgents who might ambush them en route. KBR, meanwhile, profits handsomely: empowered to do so by a monopolistic deal that lets it run everything from laundries, to canteens, to PXs and barbershops, egregiously bilking the Pentagon for services the military hitherto undertook itself. Even those soldiers who robustly champion America's right to profit through the exploitation of others draw the line at KBR's inequitable divvying of the spoils. That the US Vice President also happened to serve as CEO of the war's biggest beneficiary hardly passes them unnoticed. ...

Critics applauded *The War Tapes*, in part precisely because of its ideological understatement. According to film scholar Charles Musser, the strident populism of Michael Moore's loved-and-loathed *Fahrenheit 9/11* (2004) had left audiences (or at least critics) fatigued by such full frontal polemicism (2007, 12–13). Reviewers duly commended Scranton's film as a nonpartisan offering that would elicit viewers' sympathy irrespective of their attitudes toward the war – views that had become thoroughly polarized by the time of its release in mid-2006. If critics of the war detected a kindred spirit in Scranton, supporters could hardly charge her with being disrespectful of "the troops" since soldiers had shot and narrated much of the film themselves. *The War Tapes*, in other words, was sufficiently open a text that it could be read as supportive of various incompatible viewpoints. What looked like an exposé of corporate war profiteering to some struck Michael Atkinson of the *Village Voice* as "a worthless ration of war propaganda – ethnocentric, redneck, and enabling" (2006).

This kind of indeterminacy typifies numerous films about the Iraq War. While few espouse an enthusiastically supportive stance, many filmmakers have also avoided an explicit antiwar politics, preferring a skepticism – or more direct hostility – aimed primarily at Bush rather the particularities of the war itself. ... Devoting its final 20 minutes to C Company's New Hampshire homecoming, *The War Tapes* anticipates a series of films – fictional narratives like *Home of the Brave* (2006), *The Valley of Elah* (2007), and *Stop-Loss*, and documentaries such as *The Ground Truth* (2006), *Lioness* (2008), and *Body of War* (2007) – devoted to the tribulations of soldiers returning to a tuned-out America. As this focus on service personnel suggests, the overriding preoccupation of US filmmakers has been with the war as an *American* experience: an experience all too vivid for those who serve and all too invisible to those who choose to avert their gaze. Very few filmmakers have situated themselves among Iraqis to observe the occupation and its consequences as a wrenching chapter of Iraqi history. In this regard, *The War Tapes* is also typical. Iraqis, always male, appear infrequently and fleetingly – generally as comic relief, from the young boys hawking ornamental swords and enquiring of Bazzi whether he owns a donkey back in Amerikah to the trainee Iraqi police whose inept marksmanship elicits derision from the guardsmen.

Opening Shots: American Cinema's
First Cycle of Violence

For many, the terms "war film" and "combat movie" surely appear synonymous. (What else would a war film be about than men – more specifically, *our* men – in battle?) Predictably, then, the first theatrically exhibited documentary to deal with the war in Iraq made American soldiers its subject. Released in March 2005, two years after the launch of Operation Iraqi Freedom and 22 months after Bush had declared a victorious end to "major combat operations," *Gunner Palace* enjoyed the widest release of any nonfiction Iraq War film to date. Critics enthusiastically greeted its portrayal of the 2/3 Field Artillery as they go about the daily business of pacifying Baghdad, headquartered in a bombed-out palace formerly inhabited by Uday Hussein.

Pitched squarely at the MTV generation and its You Tube siblings, *Gunner Palace* deploys a familiar cultural motif: the surrealism of war. Of the various contradictions it exposes, none glares more garishly than the palace itself. Crammed with oversize chandeliers, swags of satin, circular beds, and plastered in gold leaf, it symbolizes the corruption, bombast, and megalomania of the deposed regime – a monument to kleptocratic excess. Yet the palace is hardly a five-star residence. Partially demolished, it is in a precarious condition, as is its plumbing. It is, then, an unlikely place for soldiers to call home. The toilets don't flush, but the swimming pool seems to work just fine, and when the unpleasant work of raiding Iraqi homes is done, poolside partying is the order of the day.

The meta-contradiction, however, is the war itself. This paradox persistently marks films on Iraq: How do we understand – and what do we call – a war that was long since declared over, in which the enemy remains largely invisible yet seemingly ubiquitous? For the makers of *Gunner Palace* and their protagonists the answer seems to be a mess. Asked by the unseen director what they make of their mission, the gunners' responses darken over time, as frustration and rage deepen that the Iraqis are so wretchedly ungrateful for being "helped," and that the hajjis won't fight fair. Pissed off about being tasked with the impossible, their anger runs on both adrenalin and vengeance, so while war may be hell, retribution has its rewards. ...

With its ambiguous anti-Bush, pro-military sensibility, *Gunner Palace* set the tone for much of what would follow, positioning soldiers as the sole objects of viewers' attention and empathy – fundamentally decent guys assigned a lousy mission by a mendacious president abetted by a sycophantic press. ...

A handful of American documentaries belonging to this first wave (2005–2006) did place Iraqis at the center of the frame, however James Longley's *Iraq in Fragments*, Laura Poitras's *My Country, My Country* (both Oscar nominees in January 2007), and Andrew Berends' *The Blood of My Brother* (2006) all eschew the use of authorial voiceover in favor of a more quietly observational style, though their tone and mood differ considerably. ...

A few months earlier, critics had hailed the gritty immediacy of *Gunner Palace*, which claimed the novelty of being the first Iraq war film to reach US movie theaters. Yet despite high profile advertising and favorable notices, it didn't linger. When *Occupation: Dreamland* – a more traditional vérité style treatment of the experiences of the 82nd Airborne's Alpha Company 1/501 – opened in September 2006, it struggled considerably harder to find an audience. The pattern was set, with filmmakers battling first to secure distributors and second to fill theaters. Like Moriarty's coworkers in *The War Tapes*, American civilians appeared singularly uninterested in looking at pictures of Iraq. Fox Television pulled its Iraq War series *Over There* after just one season. And when Hollywood released its first Iraq-related feature, Irwin Winkler's *Home of the Brave* in December 2006, it lasted just one week in New York City before sinking ignominiously under the weight of hostile reviews and audience indifference – this despite the lure of big name stars like Samuel L. Jackson, Jessica Biel and, in his first acting role, Curtis Jackson (better known as rapper 50 Cent).

As the war progressed, the "occupation documentary" became ever less visible, though not altogether extinct. Whether deterred by rising casualty rates in Iraq or escalating civilian displeasure with the war in America, professional documentary filmmakers largely surrendered this terrain to soldier amateurs, who continued to produce video records of their tours that continued to fare badly at home.[2]

The Soldier as Perpetrator – and Victim

If few civilians appeared interested in pictures of counterinsurgency soldiering, and even fewer in portraits of Iraqi life, there were nevertheless some pictures that every media-sentient American had seen – whether or not he or she cared to scrutinize what these images depicted. These were the infamous pictures of naked Iraqi prisoners stacked in human pyramids; men forced to masturbate for their camera-wielding American guards; inmates chained in crucifixion postures with women's panties over their heads; a hooded figure with arms outstretched and wires dangling from his fingers; a female MP (military police) ghoulishly posing by a corpse, grinning and giving the thumbs-up. In short, Abu Ghraib.

By the time HBO broadcast Rory Kennedy's prize-winning documentary *Ghosts of Abu Ghraib* in February 2007, the furor that first erupted in April 2004 had long since dimmed. President Bush had apologized, or at least attempted to explain to outraged foreigners that Americans did not *do* torture, and that when wayward soldiers did misbehave, democratic states ordered transparent investigations. Numerous investigations, of varying degrees of opacity, were duly conducted. As a result, Brigadier General Janis Karpinski was dishonorably discharged, and a "few bad apples," as Donald Rumsfeld memorably termed the miscreant MPs in the notorious photographs, were sent to prison. Seemingly defused, at least on the home front, the crisis had passed. One American poll conducted in 2006 found that a majority of those questioned could not identify "Abu Ghraib." . . .

Kennedy's was the first of a series of films dedicated to disinterring the "ghosts of Abu Ghraib." It was soon followed by Alex Gibney's *Taxi to the Dark Side* (2007), Michael Tucker and Petra Epperlein's *The Prisoner, Or How I Tried to Kill Tony Blair* (2007) and Errol Morris's *Standard Operating Procedure* (2008), all of which contributed to a larger Anglo-American cycle of films tackling atrocities in Iraq and the "war on terror" more broadly: Michael Winterbottom's *The Road to Guantánamo* (2006), Nick Broomfield's *The Battle of Haditha* (2008), in addition to *The Situation* and *Redacted*. . . .

Operation Homecoming: The Veteran as Cipher

The returning warrior is a favored figure of classical literature and classical Hollywood alike. Not for nothing is the amputee protagonist of William Wyler's *The Best Years of Our Lives* (1946) named Homer. But while homecoming lends itself to sentimentality, narratives of return have commonly assumed darker shadings. Since war is neither easily left behind by soldiers nor readily comprehended by civilians, friction ensues: the brief bliss or reunion giving way to protracted struggles to readjust, recuperate, and achieve equilibrium if not the status quo ante. As Wyler showed, and as others like John Huston and Fred Zinnemann documented more unflinchingly in films like *Let There Be Light* (1946) and *The Men* (1950), the "good war" did bad things to those who fought it. And if this was true of World War II, the less popular wars that followed it produced increasingly conflicted on-screen characterizations of the veteran. After the Korean War, the combat veteran seemed to fall from cinematic fashion altogether, supplanted by the former prisoner-of-war – a hapless or more malign victim of communist "brainwashing" like Laurence Harvey in *The Manchurian Candidate* (1962). As for Hollywood's Vietnam veteran, he was as apt to be plagued by what he had done to Vietnamese civilians as by what the VC had done to him.

Given American cinema's extensive repertoire of veteran types – from garlanded hero to pent-up psycho, paraplegic demon-lover to brainwashed assassin – can we discern novel patterns in the filmic representation of soldiers returning from Iraq? Two striking phenomena immediately stand out. First, we might note the extraordinary number of films (documentary and narrative features alike) that foreground the veteran, and second, at how early a date this concentration became evident. Almost as soon as there were films about the war in Iraq, there were films about soldiers returning home, bearing the physical and psychological scars of service. If *The War Tapes* blazed this particular trail, it did not take others long to follow Scranton's lead. The veteran is thus no longer an artifact of *post*war – as we might have hitherto imagined – but rather a disruptive reminder of what many civilians appear apt to forget: that the war in Iraq is still going on. How, after all, would one know?

A unifying motif of homecoming films is thus the immovable indifference of civilian America to an ongoing war that's over neither in reality nor in the consciousness of those who fought it. That the war constitutes unfinished business is underscored by the fact that many veterans remain on active duty, whether by personal choice or military fiat thanks to the policy of "stop loss" that gives Kimberley Peirce's film its name. Remobilization looms. This theme, first explored in Irwin Winkler's *Home of the Brave*, which ends with one of the distressed returnees reenlisting, unable to slide back into the oblivion of civilian life, would resurface in Kathryn Bigelow's *The Hurt Locker* (2008), whose protagonist is similarly incapable of swapping the adrenalin highs of bomb disposal for the steady thrum of domesticity.

A distinct subgenre, these films raise a variety of issues: the rehabilitation of gravely wounded men and women (*Home Front*, 2005; *Fighting for Life*, 2008); grief and mourning (*Jerabek*, 2007; *Operation Homecoming*, 2007; *Grace is Gone*, 2007); the pernicious effects of post-traumatic stress disorder (PTSD) (*Home of the Brave*; *The Ground Truth*, 2006; and, to varying degrees, almost all these films); the veteran as antiwar activist (*Body of War*); conscientious objection (*Stop-Loss*; *Breaking Ranks*, 2007); the novel phenomenon of women in combat, and the particular problems of readjustment faced by female soldiers when their front-line service is obfuscated by a military that does not formally permit such a thing (*Lioness*).

Where front-line documentaries tended to fly-on-the-wall understatement, many of these films adopt a more strident mode of address. If their purpose is illustrative, the visceral confrontation of viewers with uncomfortable evidence of damage also serves to rebuke. Emotional in their appeal to viewers' sympathies, these filmmakers press insistent claims on behalf of soldiers suffering a deficit of military care and civilian attention. The traumatized veteran thus provides a powerful vehicle for oppositional critique – an emblem of the war's wastefulness suggestive of the larger blows "Iraq" has dealt the American body politic. Where Vietnam era documentaries such as *Winter Soldier* (1972) and *Hearts and Minds* (1974) enlisted the veteran to attest US war crimes perpetrated against the Vietnamese, the Iraq War veteran serves more as testament to self-inflicted injury. This time, the wounded soldier isn't the war criminal but evidence of a war crime, victimized by a reprehensible war of choice. Nowhere is this message more forcefully driven home than in Phil Donahue and Ellen Spiro's *Body of War*, which centers on paraplegic veteran and antiwar activist Tomas Young, whose severely incapacitated body, paralyzed from the chest down, is presented as an unanswerable interrogative: The war was worth *this*?. . . .

Finally, we might note that Hollywood has been far more attentive to the home front than to Iraq in its few war-related features to date. With the exception of Brian De Palma's Mahmoudiya atrocity reconstruction, *Redacted*, other studio releases – *Home of the Brave*, *The Valley of Elah*, and *Stop-Loss* – are homecoming dramas that cast the traumatized veteran as a source of murderous danger to himself and others, or the dead soldier as a source of unspeakable grief (as in James C. Strouse's *Grace in Gone*).

Of these, *The Valley of Elah* merits particular attention. The work of Oscar-winning director Paul Haggis, it occasioned more excited anticipation than most Iraq-related films on release in September 2007. Tommy Lee Jones soon claimed an Oscar nomination for his performance as a bereaved father who attempts to fathom his returned soldier-son's murder by tracing clues in corrupted digital images retrieved from the boy's cell phone. But while these markers of critical esteem distinguish Haggis's film, *The Valley of Elah* is also a perfect distillation of Hollywood's prevailing mood: one that has taken the war primarily as an occasion for patriotic lamentation. Where conservative critics interpreted the offerings of Haggis, Winkler, and Peirce as the predictably jaundiced output of a liberal institution, it would be truer to say that these directors are not so much *anti*war as war-*averse*. Iraq itself occupies little if any space in their work. . . . In *The Valley of Elah*, Iraq is rendered solely in the form of indecipherable pictures and footage: images that prove impossible to read without contextual clarification. The problem confronting

Tommy Lee Jones's character – how to make sense of entirely murky events – stands as an overburdened metaphor for the filmmakers' own predicament. How to render intelligible a war that so thoroughly resists representation?

Most have turned away from this daunting task, seemingly less interested in the war per se than in what this debacle might reveal of a country in grave trouble. If the military (or its upper echelons) appear in an unflattering light, civilian America looks even worse – bloated, complaisant, distracted. ...

In the hands of Haggis, Winkler, and Peirce, "Iraq" is less shorthand for a ruinous war than a marker of precipitous national decline. Their jeremiads strain with yearning for America to be "good again" – as patriotic in their own way as more conventional, flag-waving war movies. Indeed, Haggis's moral in *Elah* is underscored by the prominence it attaches to the flag. When we first see the stars and stripes, it is fluttering upside down outside a school in New Mexico, where Tommy Lee Jones's character has gone to investigate his son's disappearance from Fort Rudd. Appalled, he stops to tell the El Salvadoran janitor responsible for this lapse that the flag must *never* fly upside down: that the inverted flag is an international distress signal, denoting the need for assistance in dire peril. In the final scene, he returns to the school to hoist aloft the flag his son has left behind. This time, he inverts the flag himself. If the janitor's initial action was inadvertent, it turns out not in fact to have been a mistake. Disturbed by his son's death and the military's attempt to cover up fellow soldiers' responsibility, the father has lost faith in war's nobility, in martial justice, in national virtue. America requires rescue.

An Audience of One

By common critical consent, the war in Iraq has produced few great films – arguably none at all. By unanimous accord, it has produced a glut of mediocre treatments and several execrable failures, particularly among Hollywood's offerings such as De Palma's *Redacted* and Strouse's "grief porn," *Grace is Gone*, about a man so far gone in denial when his wife dies in Iraq that he cannot break the news to his two daughters, taking them instead on a road trip to a Florida amusement park. It is also clear that American audiences have populated theatrical screenings of these films in inverse proportion to the latter's profusion. In other words, the Iraq War has proven to be a very poor box office draw indeed. ...

The patterns are clear enough: many films produced with a limited repertoire of themes that few Americans are watching. But how do we account for the peculiarities of Iraq War cinema and its critical and popular rejection? Most of the standard answers do not withstand closer scrutiny. Some cultural commentators propose that it is simply *too soon* for this war to have been transmuted into cinematic art, pointing out that many of the most enduring films of World War II appeared in the 1950s, just as Hollywood's definitive treatments of Vietnam appeared at the tail end of the 1970s and in the 1980s. Others contend that there are simply *too many* films, leaving audiences fatigued by the surfeit of war-related offerings. Or alternatively, that it is precisely because most Iraq-related films are not great cinematic art that they have failed to lure audiences, the up-close immediacy of several early Iraq documentaries having made it hard for Hollywood's narrative features to convince viewers of their own verisimilitude. Why pay to see B-list actors – with trainer-honed physiques and radiant dentition – playing soldiers from unglamorous red states where teenage recruits most assuredly do not resemble these perfect-skinned imposters? Despite their claims to facticity (and *Redacted*, *Stop-Loss*, and *Elah* all loudly touted their real-life referents), these films did not seem as "authentic" as those made by people who had visited, or indeed served in, Iraq. ...

But these propositions do not add up to a coherent explanation. Great films *do* emerge from the midst of war, generally from the very thick of it. (Think, for example, of John Huston's *Battle of San Pietro*, 1945, or Gillo Pontecorvo's *Battle of Algiers*, 1966.) Similarly, three of the most acclaimed recent films – Oscar-nominated documentaries *The War Tapes*, *Iraq in Fragments* and *My Country, My Country* – are vérité style treatments made about and in Iraq at war. Yet they did not achieve strikingly greater box office success than several later productions that were panned, and this at a conjuncture when popular/populist documentary filmmaking had become a resurgent commercial force in US cinema.[3] ...

Alternative explanations are thus required, and we might begin by inverting one of the familiar hypotheses. Perhaps Americans' resistance to war-related material is not a function of the proximity of these events but rather of their own distance? In other words, potential viewers have shied away from films about the war less because these productions are insufficiently compelling or excessively numerous but rather because most Americans were already detached and disinclined to view. The real task, then, is to fathom how and why "Iraq" is at once broadly yet shallowly unpopular in the United States – for the same forces productive of public aversion to certain forms of inquiry also structure filmmakers' limited engagement with the war.

To say that Americans are, by and large, tuned out from the war in Iraq is hardly to venture a controversial assertion. Yellow ribbon decals aside, there's little discernible evidence in broad swathes of the country that US troops are fighting in both Afghanistan and Iraq. This is not wartime as normal. Yet if there is no surge of patriotic fervor among a population increasingly attenuated from a downsized and outsourced military, nor is there much sign of widespread disaffection either: few protests, few placards, no broad-based social movement rallying opposition. Unlike its predecessor in Vietnam, this unpopular war has given rise to no "war at home." Antiwar sentiment, if we can call it that, exhibits far greater national self-absorption than transnational solidarity.

As evidenced by the films surveyed here, the affective response aroused by the war ranges from vague skepticism to splenetic apoplexy. Very few filmmakers have proffered outright support. But if most have no trouble in saying – or at least insinuating – that the war is wrong, *why* it is wrong has generated much confusion, and no consensus.[4]

Choked with inchoate rage, filmmakers have frequently struggled to articulate their precise animus against the war – other than that it is *Bush's war* and as such, the apotheosis of everything stupid, misguided, and mendacious about his presidency. Viewed through the prism of liberal nationalism, the war is thus wrong because it has squandered America's patrimony and prestige; because it has generated profits only for its corporate beneficiaries and architects; because consent was fraudulently mustered; because it has turned ordinary decent Americans into torturers and war criminals; because the victory proclaimed prematurely has proven so elusive; because the war was badly planned or simply because Iraq is a huge confounded mess, and there's "no end in sight." ...

But what remains most telling about these films, a handful of notable exceptions aside, is their treatment of – or rather their refusal to inspect – Iraq itself: a charge also applicable to Bigelow's multiple Oscar-winning *The Hurt Locker*, which generates suspense from improvised explosive devices (IEDs) without exploring the politics of those planting the bombs, an inquiry deferred by the urgency of disposal. The reasons for this are complex, and my interpretation is necessarily speculative. In part, however, this aversion would seem to spring from a profound ambiguity about America's purposes in Iraq. It is worth recalling that many liberals (filmmakers included) were initially supportive of Operation Iraqi Freedom. Far from seeing it as an egregious violation of international law, a violent rending of Iraqi sovereignty, they endorsed "preemption" as a way to depose a noxious dictator. That the war did not *go* wrong but *was* wrong is a viewpoint that finds only muted expression in the whole roster of films concerned with Iraq. For many liberal critics, a central objection is that the Bush administration failed to instantiate democracy, one of its core stated objectives, and that the other aims – ridding Iraq of weapons of mass destruction and severing the alleged nexus between al-Qaeda and Baghdad – proved bogus: the products of faulty intelligence, if one accepted the official line, or outright fabrications if one did not.

Dissecting these operational failures and uncovering administration falsehoods has not been difficult, and several filmmakers have duly documented lapses and lies that were hardly well hidden.[5] Much harder, however, is the task of explaining Iraq's unraveling and doing so with some empathy – for Iraqis rather than simply for the US military. Other than Steve Connors and Molly Bingham's *Meeting Resistance* (2007), the war's filmic record offers remarkably little guidance as to precisely who contested the occupation and, more broadly, who is fighting whom in Iraq and why. Do filmmakers believe that US audiences simply aren't interested in, or capable of grasping, such complexity? Or are they themselves too uninterested, too impatient, or too irked by Iraqi intransigence to chart the contours of Iraq's crisscrossing vectors of conflict?

Near the end of Philip Haas's Sunni triangle-set love triangle, *The Situation* (2006), the journalist (played by Connie Neilson) turns to her CIA officer boyfriend for assistance in charting Iraq's sectarian landscape. His answer, though less than helpful, speaks volumes: "It's just the situation, Anna. It's just *Iraq*." If Sunni and Shia have been killing each other since, like, forever, what's really to be explained? And what else is to be expected except an endless cycle of bloodletting? At only slight risk of exaggeration, one might propose that a similar compound of intellectual laziness tinged with anti-Muslim disdain saturates much American filmmaking about the war in Iraq and explains why so few films have examined Iraq: as though hands have been collectively thrown up in the face of confounding, sometimes infuriating, complexity – and *ingratitude*. For filmmakers are surely not all immune from antipathy toward people who, dammit, ought to have been more thankful for their liberation, stepping up boldly to freedom's gilded plate. Yet the Iraqis failed to do so. Instead, they turned on their liberators before turning on one another. So, if their wretched country is now fouled up beyond all recognition, is that not essentially their own fault?. ....

If contemporary antiwar sentiment is striking in its singular lack of emotional affiliation with suffering Iraqis, this may seem entirely predictable. Necessarily at least a two-sided business, war is often rendered one-dimensional by commercial media that sequester sympathy for "our side" alone. When Randall Wallace's *We Were Soldiers* appeared in 2002, critics were quick to remark that it was the first American production to render a North Vietnamese officer sympathetically – 30 years after America's withdrawal. But in pointing this out, such commentators often replicated the same oversight at work in claims that *The Green Berets* was the only Vietnam War film made before it ended. Equating film with narrative features alone, they neglected the documentaries that emerged during the war. One distinctive facet of the latter was their willingness to engage the war from multiple perspectives, including those of Vietnamese peasants and guerrillas. ...

It remains to be seen when and how this war will end, how it will be inscribed in US popular memory, and what role film will play in shaping that consciousness. It also remains to be seen how future scholars and critics will make sense of the films discussed in this essay. If Barack Obama, having repudiated Iraq as not *his* war, succeeds in affirming Americans' desire to feel virtuous once again, it is possible that these works will be conceived less as "Iraq War films" than as cinema of the late Bush era – when good Americans were bamboozled into a bad war by their least popular president. After all, they offer a far more comprehensive index of American dissatisfactions than of Iraq's destruction. Just as Salon.com's Andrew O'Hehir observed of *Taxi to the Dark Side* that it was "not about America at war in Iraq or in Afghanistan but America at war with itself" (quoted in Filasteen 2007), so the same might be said of a whole series of films that have domesticized the war without ever bringing it home.

Notes

This essay draws on three contributions the author made to *Cineaste*: "Say Cheese! Operation Iraqi Freedom on Film," 22.1 (Winter 2006), 30–36; "Question Time: The Iraq War Revisited," 22.4 (Fall 2007), 12–17; "Bodies of Evidence: New Documentaries on Iraq War Veterans," 34.1 (Winter 2008), 26–31.

1   See http://www.thewartapes.com/2006/03/living_journalism.shtml (accessed March 2011).
2   See, for example, John Laurence's *I Am an American Soldier* (2007) and Jeremy Zerechak's *Land of Confusion* (2008). Meanwhile, the war in Afghanistan – for long far less visible than that in Iraq – received its first full-scale documentary treatment with Sebastian Junger and Tim Hetherington's *Restrepo* in 2010.
3   It is also instructive to note that *The Hurt Locker*, which would subsequently garner six Oscars in 2010, grossed just $145,352 during its opening weekend in US theaters in June 2009.

4   Explicitly pro-administration films are few and far between, but would include the supposedly nonpartisan film made "by the Iraqi people" (with US government money), *Voices of Iraq* (2004).

5   The administration's rationalizations are treated with outright disbelief in Greenwald's films, as also in Eugene Jarecki's *Why We Fight* (2005), Danny Schechter's *WMD: Weapons of Mass Deception* (2004), and David Wald's *Buried in the Sand: The Deception of America* (2004).

References

Atkinson, Michael. (2006). "Casualties of War." May 23, at http://www.villa-gevoice.com/2006-05-23/film/casualties-of-war/ (accessed March 2011).

Aufderheide, Patricia. (2007). "Your Country, My Country: How Films about the Iraq War Construct Publics." *Framework*, 48.2, 56–65.

Dittmar, Linda, & Michaud, Gene. (eds) (1990). *From Hanoi to Hollywood: The Vietnam War in American Film*. New Brunswick: Rutgers University Press.

Filasteen. (2007). "*Taxi to the Dark Side*." December 2, at http://filasteen.word-press.com/2007/12/02/taxi-to-the-dark-side/ (accessed March 2011).

Gaines, Jane M. (2007). "The Production of Outrage: The Iraq War and the Radical Documentary Tradition." *Framework*, 48.2, 36–55.

Grajeda, Tony. (2007). "The Winning and Losing of Hearts and Minds: Vietnam, Iraq, and the Claims of War Documentary." *Jump Cut*, Spring, 49, at http://www.ejumpcut.org/archive/jc49.2007/Grajeda/index.html (accessed March 2011).

Musser, Charles. (2007). "War, Documentary and Iraq Dossier: Film Truth in the Age of George Bush." *Framework*, 48.2, 9–35.

Documents

Introduction to Documents

As in most past wars, the initial forays into Afghanistan and Iraq were greeted with more patriotic cheers than questions. Yet within a short time, the public seemed to grow tired of the war and even more tired of war films and documentaries. In the first document, journalist Tom Streithorst offers a compelling explanation as to why Iraq war films fared so poorly at the box office. Our second document provides figures regarding production costs and box-office returns for twenty-six Afghanistan and Iraq-themed documentaries and feature films.

Why Iraq War Films Fail

Tom Streithorst

Source: *Prospect*, March 17, 2010; www.prospectmagazine.co.
uk/magazine/why-iraq-war-films-fail/ (last accessed July 2013)

A US army private based deep in the Sunni "triangle of death" south of
Baghdad put it piquantly to me in May 2007: "We're a reality show everybody's bored of." The soldiers know that nobody cares. According to
minute-by-minute television ratings, viewers switch off as soon as an Iraq
story hits air. When Siegfried Sassoon wrote his poems, and when Erich
Remarque wrote *All Quiet on the Western Front*, much of their audience
had lived through the same hell. During both the world wars, the entire
nation was involved, and the experience of the soldiers was an intrinsic
part of the national psyche. Not any more. I've met dozens of soldiers
who, since the invasion, have served three or more tours in the warzone,
spent more time with their platoons than with their families – and yet
they realise that, back home, nobody knows or is interested in what they
have been through.

Hollywood also recognises that the Iraq war is bad box office. Even
winning the Oscar didn't goose *The Hurt Locker's* ticket sales much. In
mid March it barely beat *Tooth Fairy* on the earnings list in America. On
the same three days as Tim Burton's critically panned *Alice in Wonderland*
grossed $62m, *The Hurt Locker* only took in $800,000. The big-budget
Green Zone also opened to disappointing numbers. And yet, thankfully,
some film and documentary makers still feel compelled to explore the
topic. More than 30 movies have been made about the Iraq war.
Considering how little the average person knows – or cares – about the
conflict, we urgently need these films to tell us what is going on. Do they
succeed?

Kathryn Bigelow's Oscar-triumphing *Hurt Locker* brilliantly evokes
the look and texture of Iraq, with shaky handheld camera shots of
armoured Humvees travelling through dusty boulevards. It also succeeds in showing the intense relationships men forge with their comrades by working together in war, and how the adrenaline rush of
risking your life can make the ordinary world a little bland. Yet its
story, of a "cowboy" bomb disposal specialist habitually putting his

team and himself in grave danger, is naïve and inaccurate. In Iraq, "force protection" is emphasised above all else. Putting your men in unnecessary danger is utterly unacceptable; not at all part of the corporate culture. "Cowboys" in the real American military, unlike the ones in the film, are not reckless with their own or their comrades' lives, but with the lives of non-Americans. So while one could argue that *The Hurt Locker* is a great war film, it is certainly not a great Iraq war film. Iraq is just the landscape for a tale that could be set in any random conflict.

Other films are based on actual stories from Iraq. Brian DePalma's *Redacted* (2007) is the fictionalised retelling of the brutal rape and murder of a young Iraqi girl in Mahmudiyah, and the response of the jihadis, who captured American soldiers from the same company and beheaded them on camera. Meanwhile Nick Broomfield's *Battle for Haditha* shows the massacre of innocent Iraqi civilians by a US Marine platoon in frenzied revenge after one of their own had been killed by a roadside bomb. Using documentary style and improvised ensemble acting, both films look realistic enough, but most of the characters, unfortunately, are two-dimensional. We know Specialist Rush is a redneck nutter because De Palma shoots him sprawling under a Confederate flag, while Broomfield's villagers are a textbook loving family turned into innocent victims.

Perhaps more importantly, by focusing exclusively on these terrible war crimes, the films give a misleading impression of the US army in Iraq. In my experience, the military is extremely well disciplined and obeys the rules of war. Yes, thousands of innocent Iraqis have been killed by the Americans, but the great majority of them have been killed by mistake: because of misunderstandings and mutual incomprehension rather than through deliberate brutality. The classic example is the family ordered in shouted English to slow down at a checkpoint and when, for whatever reason they don't, a nervous soldier opens fire, killing mom and dad, leaving screaming children covered in blood in the backseat. In a way, this much too typical accident is just as reprehensible, if less cinematic than the much rarer deliberate murder.

A whole slew of other films don't even attempt to show Iraq, other than in hallucinogenic flashback. *In the Valley of Elah* (2007), for example, tells the story of a father whose son has been murdered within days of his return from war. Our sympathies here are with the normal Americans back home. The soldiers are seen as damaged, alien. Their experience has more to do with the clichés of war films than the actual day-to-day life of soldiers serving in Iraq.

Heavy Metal in Baghdad, by contrast, offers a unique and refreshing perspective. In 2003, *Vice* magazine published an article about an Iraqi heavy metal band and then returned to Iraq in 2006 (right in the middle of the Shia-sunni civil war) to make a documentary about these four Iraqi musicians. Unlike most Iraq war films, Americans play a minor role and the documentary fluently demonstrates the hell that Iraq became a few years after the invasion. Our sympathies are with the Iraqis, in part because they share an obsession with a western subculture – something tangible that audiences can relate to.

However, the newly-released *Green Zone* (which could have been titled "The Bourne Conspiracy Goes to Iraq") is probably my favourite. It is big-budget Hollywood, fun to watch; its hero an incredibly dedi-cated soldier who doesn't think twice about disobeying his superiors (something soldiers don't do), but it does try to answer a big question: why did the Americans dismantle the Iraqi army, when it was their only chance to hold the country together? While the film is utterly inaccurate in its particulars, it is, I believe, truthful about the bigger picture. America failed in Iraq in large part because the men running the war were more interested in perceptions back home than the reality on the ground.

On and off, I have spent several years in Iraq and if there is one thing that strikes me it is the remarkable separation between the occupiers and the occupied. The Americans live on base or in forti-fied compounds. They meet few Iraqis that have not been vetted. Almost no Americans speak Arabic. Incomprehension is endemic. I'm sure more than a few soldiers have gone through their year-long tour and not had a conversation with a single Iraqi. This is unprece-dented. In Vietnam, American soldiers had Vietnamese girlfriends, sometimes rented apartments, mixed often with the general popula-tion. So did the Germans in Paris, and the Russians in Berlin. The film I would like to see is one about this apartheid and how it led to disaster. The Iraq war was forged in a bubble, and fought in a bubble. It is a tragedy that deserves its Tolstoy. It still awaits its Francis Ford Coppola.

Total Receipts and Production Costs for Films About Afghanistan and Iraq

John Markert

Source: John Markert, *Post-9/11 Cinema: Through a Lens Darkly* (Latham, MD: Scarecrow Press, 2011), 212

Film	Total receipts* (in millions)	Production budget** (in millions)
Day Zero	$.088	$8
Cavite	$.378	$.007
Bottle for Haditha	$.620	$1.5
Redacted	$1.1	$5
War, Inc.	$2.1	$10
The Lucky Ones	$2.7	$14
Grace Is Gone	$5	$4.1
Home of the Brave	$5.7	$12
Southland Tales	$6.6	$17
Stop-Loss	$15.9	$25
Rendition	$26.4	$27.5
Valley of Elah	$27.7	$23
Traitor	$41.1	$22
Brothers (USA)	$43.3^	$25
Harold and Kumer Escape from Guantanamo	$67.2	$12
Hurt Locker	$68.6	$15
Lions for Lambs	$72.4	$35
Kite Runner	$73.2	$20
The Kingdom	$120.5	$72.5
Body of Lies	$130.1	$67.5
The Insurgents	$.023†	$8
The Messenger	$4.6	$6.5
Dear John	$137.8^	$25
Home of the Brave	$5.2	$12
The Green Zone	$107.3	$100^
Restrepo	$2.9•	$1

* Domestic and foreign theatrical gross plus domestic DVD sales through 2010. International DVD sales tend to be in the same range as domestic DVD sales, plus/minus 10 percent.

** Hard production costs. Does not include ad and print costs. Figures are rounded.

† No box office receipts; film went straight to DVD.

• DVD sales not calculated since did not go to DVD until late 2010.

^ These three films are worth special note because of the generous gross from television and ancillary rights. *Brothers* added $10.2M from these sources; *Dear John*, $23M; and *Green Zone*, $20.1M.

Source: Nash Information Services, www.the-numbers.com.

Readings and Screenings

There is no shortage of books that examine Hollywood's depictions of war. Readers wishing to gain a broad overview wartime and postwar cinema would do well to start with Peter Rollins and John O'Connor, eds, *Why We Fought: America's Wars in Film and History* (Lexington, KT: University Press of Kentucky, 2008); J. David Slocum, ed., *Hollywood and War: The Film Reader* (London: Routledge, 2006); Robert Eberwein, *The Hollywood War Film* (Malden, MA and Oxford: Wiley-Blackwell, 2010); Lawrence H. Suid, *Guts and Glory: The Making of the American Military Image in Film* (Lexington, KT: University Press of Kentucky, revised edition, 2002); Steven Jay Rubin, *Combat Films: American Realism 1945–2010* (Jefferson, NC: McFarland, 2nd edition, 2011); Yvonne Tasker, *Soldiers' Stories: Military Women in Cinema and Television since World War II* (Durham, NC: Duke University Press, 2011). Media depictions of the first Gulf War are explored in Susan Jeffords and Lauren Rabinovitz, eds, *Seeing Through The Media: The Persian Gulf War* (New Brunswick, NJ: Rutgers University Press, 1994); Paul Virilio, trans. Michael Degener, *Desert Screen: War at the Speed of Light* (New York: Continuum, 2002).

Many recent books have dealt with filmic depictions of the wars in Iraq and Afghanistan, including images shot by soldiers as well as documentarians and Hollywood studios. The following books offer detailed synopses and/or analyses of the films made by all three groups. Douglas Kellner, *Cinema Wars: Hollywood Film and Politics in the Bush-Cheney Era* (Malden, MA and Oxford: Wiley-Blackwell, 2009); Martin Barker, *A "Toxic Genre": The Iraq War Films* (London: Pluto Press, 2011); Guy Westwell, *War Cinema: Hollywood on the Front Line* (London and New York: Wallflower Press, 2006); Stephen Prince, *Firestorm: American Films in the Age of Terrorism* (New York: Columbia University Press, 2009); John Markert, *Post 9/11 Cinema: Through a Lens Darkly* (Lanham, MD: Scarecrow Press, 2011); Carl Boggs and Tom Pollard, *The Hollywood War Machine: US Militarism and Popular Culture* (Boulder, CO: Paradigm Publishers, 2006). For the government's recent role in shaping the way Hollywood depicts war, see David L. Robb, *Operation Hollywood: How the Pentagon Shapes and Censors the Movies* (Amherst, NY: Prometheus Books, 2004).

Documentary productions dominated early filmic representations of war. The most acclaimed of these include *Gunner Palace* (2005), *The War Tapes* (2006), *My Country, My Country* (2006), *Iraq in Fragments* (2006) and *Land of Confusion* (2008); for events Afghanistan, see *Restrepo* (2010).

The shocking events at Abu Ghraib and other wartime horrors are explored in *The Road to Guantámamo* (2006), *Taxi to the Dark Side* (2007), *Standard Operating Procedure* (2008), and *The Battle of Haditha* (2008). Examining a different aspect of war, *The Ground Truth* (2006), *Operation Homecoming: Writing the Wartime Experience* (2007) and *Body of War* (2007) offer compelling portraits of the problems faced by returning soldiers. *The Lioness* (2008) tells the story of the first group of women soldiers in US history to be sent into direct ground combat. For polemical documentaries on the left, see *Fahrenheit 9/11* (2004), *Iraq for Sale: The War Profiteers* (2006), *Rethink Afghanistan* (2009); for a conservative view, see *Voices of Iraq* (2004).

Despite the critical acclaim received by several productions, feature films fared poorly at the box-office. Here, in chronological order, are a number of films worth screening in class or at home: *Home of the Brave* (2006), *The Valley of Elah* (2007), *Lions for Lambs* (2007), *Redacted* (2007), *Stop-Loss* (2008), and *The Hurt Locker* (2008). *Green Zone* (2010), one of the few feature films explicitly critical of the Bush administration, presents its politics in the form of an action film starring Matt Damon as a patriotic Chief Warrant Officer who soon realizes that his men are needlessly being put at risk – and dying – for political rather than military reasons.

13

Hollywood Goes Global: The Internationalization of American Cinema

Introduction to Article

What constitutes a Hollywood film in the twenty-first century? To what extent do American movies still reflect American values? Who are the audiences that today's filmmakers are aiming to please? In 2001, US revenues were the predominant source of box office for the US Top 100 films. In 2011, international box office accounted for 58.4 percent of revenues for the Top 100 films produced in the United States. This growing reliance on foreign markets has changed the content, form, financing, and number of American films. Producers are increasingly inclined to put out blockbuster action films that contain little dialogue and can be easily understood by non-English speaking audiences throughout the world. As producers poured more money into fewer potential blockbusters, the total number of major studio films declined from an average of 190 a year between 2000 and 2007 to 168 in 2008 and 158 in 2009.

In answering the question "Why Hollywood Rules the World and Whether We Should Care," Tyler Cowen explains why so much international filmmaking clusters around Hollywood and why European movies in particular have failed to penetrate global markets. In the mid-1960s, American films accounted for 35 percent of European box office revenues; by the end of the century, the figure ranged between

Movies and American Society, Second Edition. Edited by Steven J. Ross.
© 2014 John Wiley & Sons, Inc. Published 2014 by John Wiley & Sons, Inc.

80 and 90 percent. Hollywood filmmakers have fared better in the current international marketplace, Cowen argues, because unlike their heavily government subsidized European counterparts the only way they can make substantial profits is by appealing to global rather than national audiences. To that end, Hollywood films – albeit it increasingly transnational in their personnel and financing – succeed in part because they sell American glamour and ideology as much as they do sheer entertainment.

Discussion Points

Is an American-made film that is shot in a foreign country, features a foreign-born star, a foreign-born director, and is heavily financed by a foreign company still an "American" film? What makes a Hollywood film distinctly American?

Why Hollywood Rules the World, and Whether We Should Care

Tyler Cowen

Source: Tyler Cowen, *Creative Destruction: How Globalization is Changing the World's Cultures* (Princeton, NJ: Princeton University Press, 2004), 73–101

Cinema is one of the hard cases for globalization. When we look at world music, the visual arts, or literature, it is readily apparent how trade has brought a more diverse menu of choice *and* helped many regions develop cultural identities. In each of these cultural sectors, the market has room for many producers, in large part because the costs of production are relatively low.

But what about film? In no other cultural area is America's export prowess so strong. Movies are very expensive to make, and in a given year there are far fewer films released than books, CDs, or paintings. These conditions appear to favor dominant producers at the expense of niche markets. So if cross-cultural exchange will look bad anywhere, it is in the realm of cinema.

Moviemaking also is prone to geographic clustering. Many cultural innovations and breakthroughs are spatially concentrated. If a good Italian Renaissance painter was not born in Florence, Venice, or Rome, he usually found it worthwhile to move to one of those locales. An analogous claim is true for Hollywood, which attracts cinematic talent from around the world, strengthening its market position.[1]

The degree of clustering has reached a sufficient extreme, and Hollywood movies have become so publicly visible, as to occasion charges of American cultural imperialism. European movies, in particular, have failed to penetrate global markets and also have lost ground at home. Many individuals claim that when it comes to cinema, global culture is a threat rather than a promise.

What lies behind these charges? To what extent is movie production clustered in Hollywood, and why has such clustering taken place? Why is European cinema so economically moribund? Have other national cinemas fared badly as well? Is cinematic clustering inimical to diversity, and if so, could it be reversed? Most generally, has cross-cultural exchange damaged diversity in the realm of cinema?

Why Clustering in Hollywood?

The current malaise in European cinema is driven by a concatenation of unfavorable forces, involving television, excess subsidies, demographics, language, the size of the American market, and Hollywood's more entrepreneurial environment. While some negative charges can be pinned on globalization, we will see that cross-cultural exchange is not the primary culprit in the story.

The United States has at least one natural advantage in moviemaking – it has the largest single home-market for cinema in dollar terms (although total attendance is higher in India). The countries that specialize in moviemaking will tend to be those countries where movies are most popular, in this case America and India. Hong Kong has been an exception to this principle, but a large domestic market does give a natural advantage. Home audiences often (though not always) prefer native products, if only for reasons of language and cultural context, and this encourages production to shift to that market.

Aggregate market-size nonetheless remains only a single factor in determining who becomes a market leader. The United States, for instance, has been a large country for a long time, but only recently have European movies held such a low share of their home markets. In the mid-1960s, American films accounted for 35 percent of box office revenues in continental Europe; today the figure ranges between 80 to 90 percent. The greater population of the United States, and the greater American interest in moviegoing, do not themselves account for these changes.[2]

Furthermore, only certain kinds of cinema cluster in Hollywood. In a typical year the Western European nations make more movies than America does. In numeric terms most of the world's movies come from Asia, not from the United States. It is not unusual for India to release between 800 and 900 commercial films a year, compared to about 250 from the United States.[3]

The Hollywood advantage is concentrated in one very particular kind of moviemaking: films that are entertaining, highly visible, and have broad global appeal. The typical European film has about 1 percent of the audience of the typical Hollywood film, and this differential has been growing. American movies have become increasingly popular in international markets, while European movies have become less so.[4]

Not surprisingly, the Europeans invest less money in each film than do Hollywood producers. One estimate from the early 1990s placed the average European film budget at $3 million and the average American budget at $11 million. The average film budget for a major Hollywood studio (as opposed to an independent studio) has been estimated at $34 million. These numbers omit marketing and audience research budgets, the area where American moviemakers outspend their European counterparts most. For an average Hollywood movie, domestic and foreign marketing expenditures might run at least $30 million. European estimates are hard to find, in part because the numbers are so small and not susceptible to easy measurement.[5] The question is not why Hollywood makes more movies than Europe, because it does not. The question is why Hollywood movies have more global export success, while European movies are aimed at small but guaranteed local audiences. ...

...

The turning point in this dynamic appears to have started in the 1970s. Before the 1970s, most national European cinemas still experienced a significant degree of export success, whatever problems the industry as a whole had. Since that time, European moviemakers have seen their export markets collapse. In essence, Hollywood is now competing with the native European producers in each individual country, rather than with cross-European exports.

The popularization of television, and the timing of this popularization, damaged European cinema. As television became widespread throughout Europe, movie audiences dwindled. In Germany, 800 million movie tickets were bought in 1956, but only 180 million were bought in 1962.

At the same time, the number of television sets rose from 700,000 to 7.2 million. In the U.K., cinematic attendance fell from 292 million in 1967 to 73 million in 1986. In France, movie attendance dropped from 450 million in 1956 to 122 million in 1988. In Japan, the number of movie tickets sold in 1985 was only a sixth of what it had been twenty-five years earlier. The cataclysmic nature of these shocks should not be underestimated.[6]

...

American moviemakers had experienced a similar audience crisis, but much earlier, due to the more rapid spread of television in the United States. Television became common in the United States ten or more years before it did in Europe. The U.S. film audience declined by 50 percent, but this happened over the 1946–1956 period rather than later, as in Europe. By 1955, two-thirds of all American households already had television sets.[7]

Hollywood responded actively to this challenge. Starting as early as the 1950s, American moviemakers responded to television by making high-stakes, risky investments in marketing, glamour, and special effects. In the 1960s American directors found greater latitude to experiment with sex and violence; this trend was formalized with the abandonment of the Hays Code in 1966. By the 1970s, Hollywood movies had become significantly more exciting to mass audiences than they had been a decade before. *Jaws* and *Star Wars* were emblematic of this new era. Hollywood was ready to move in with innovative products, expressly designed to compete with television. At exactly the same time, the European moviemakers found themselves unable to compete with television, and reeling from this very strong negative shock. For Hollywood it turned out to be a blessing in disguise that television hit the American market first. ...

...

A self-reinforcing dynamic has since expanded Hollywood's export advantage. American success has led to easier finance and greater marketing expenditures, which in turn has led to greater export potential. Hollywood films have become successively more global, while European films target small but guaranteed revenue sources, such as state subsidies, or television rights, sold to government-regulated stations. A vicious circle has been created: the more European producers fail in global markets, the more they rely on television revenue and subsidies. The more they rely on television and subsidies, the more they fail in global markets.

...

The roles of television and subsidies are closely linked. Most west European nations have television stations that are owned, controlled, or strictly regulated by their respective governments, which use them to promote a national cultural agenda. Typically the stations face domestic-content restrictions, must spend a certain percentage of revenue on domestic films, must operate a film production subsidiary, or they willfully overpay for films for political reasons. The end result is overpayment for broadcast rights – the most important subsidy that many European moviemakers receive. Audience levels are typically no more than one or two million at the television level, even in the larger countries such as France – too small to justify the sums paid to moviemakers for television rights on economic grounds.[8]

European films receive many other forms of subsidy. In France, for instance, direct subsidies are available from the national government, regional governments, European subsidy bodies (such as Eur-images) and coproduction subsidies through other national governments. Often French producers need only put up 15 percent of the budget of their films to receive subsidies. ...

Martin Dale, a cinema industry analyst, has estimated that the state provides at least *70 percent* of the funding for the average continental film, taking all subsidies into account. This figure is speculative rather than exact, if only because the wide variety of subsidy schemes, and their complex nature, makes their final impact difficult to trace. ...

Subsidies encourage producers to serve domestic demand and the wishes of politicians and cinematic bureaucrats, rather than produce movies for international export. Many films will be made, even when they have little chance of turning a profit in stand-alone terms. The film industries will not develop specialized talents in demand forecasting and marketing, as Hollywood has done. ...

...

The two non Hollywood cinemas that have enjoyed the most export success – India and Hong Kong – are run on an explicitly commercial basis. Some segments of the Indian film industry receive government subsidies, but the overwhelming majority of new releases do not. They are commercial productions made for profit and frequently exported abroad, usually to other underdeveloped nations but often to the United Kingdom as well. By numerous measures, such as attendance or number of films released, the Indian movie industry is the largest and the most successful in the world. Indian movies are frequently criticized for their generic nature or sappy plots, but in terms of music, cinematography, and use of color, they are often quite beautiful and even pathbreaking compared to Western productions.

The Hong Kong film industry has experienced export success from the 1970s onward, mostly throughout Southeast Asia. At its peak it released more films per year than any Western country, and as an exporter it was second only to the United States. Furthermore, Hong Kong cinema arose in a market that was dominated by Hollywood up through the late 1960s. In the 1970s and 1980s, however, Hollywood sometimes failed to capture even 30 percent of the domestic Hong Kong market. Only since 1997, when Hong Kong returned to China, did Hollywood movies take in more than half of the total local box office.[9]

At first Hong Kong movies focused on the martial arts, but they subsequently branched out to include police movies, romance, comedy, horror, and ghost stories, among other genres. The best of these movies, such as John Woo's *The Killer*, or *Hardboiled*, are acclaimed as high art and have had considerable influence on directors around the world. David Bordwell, in his recent *Planet Hong Kong*, claimed, "Since the 1970s it has been arguably the world's most energetic, imaginative popular cinema." Hong Kong movies are made on a commercial basis and have received no government assistance. In recent times, however, the industry has been damaged by the Chinese takeover of Hong Kong and by fears of censorship.[10]

Many of the complaints about American cultural imperialism have an excessively Eurocentric slant. Today's mainstream European cinema does appear less creative and less vital than its 1950–1970 heyday. But by most common critical standards, cinematic creativity has risen in Taiwan, China, Iran, South Korea, the Philippines, Latin America, and many parts of Africa, among other locales. Even within Europe, the creative decline is restricted to a few of the larger nations, such as France and Italy. Danish cinema is more influential and more successful today than in times past, and arguably the same is true for Spanish cinema as well. Mexican and Argentinean filmmakers are enjoying a resurgence. While these producers all struggle against Hollywood competition, creative world-filmmaking is not on a downward trajectory.

The English Language, and the Move from Silents to Talkies

The English language, combined with America's role as world leader, has strengthened Hollywood exports. Cinematic clustering, and the current crisis of European cinema, is rooted partially in the transition from silent film to talkies.

Counterintuitively, the onset of the sound era increased Hollywood's share of world cinematic revenue. At the time of the transition, equipping the theaters with sound and making movies with sound were costly.

To recoup these costs, theaters sought out high-quality, high-expenditure productions for large audiences. The small, cheap, quick film became less profitable, given the suddenly higher fixed costs of production and presentation. This shift in emphasis favored Hollywood moviemakers over their foreign competitors.[11]

More generally, the higher the fixed costs of production, the greater the importance of drawing a large audience and the greater the importance of demand forecasting and marketing. Today costly special effects and expensive celebrity stars drive the push for block-busters in similar fashion, and favor Hollywood production as well.

The talkies, by introducing issues of translation, boosted the dominant world language of English and thus benefited Hollywood. Given the growing importance of English as a world language, and the focal importance of the United States, European countries would sooner import films from Hollywood than from each other. . . .

. . .

Once America, and the English language, became established as a world standard, this proved self-reinforcing. American audiences, the world's largest moviegoing audience at the time, became accustomed to seeing films in their native language. Dubbed or subtitled movies have a difficult time in the United States to this day whereas most other audiences accept them with few complaints. . . .

. . .

The move to sound, and the rise of English as an export standard, provided a strong boost to the movie exports of Great Britain. While the U.K. has never seriously rivaled Hollywood as a moviemaking power, many U.K. releases have succeeded on a global scale, essentially by mimicking the Hollywood style. The James Bond movies and David Lean's *Lawrence of Arabia* or *Bridge over River Kwai* are some of the best-known British successes.[12]

Today the United Kingdom is the leading European exporter of movies to other European nations. In 1991, the U.K. put out 36 movies, 56 percent of which were exported to France. In the same year, France put out 140 movies, only 14 percent of which were exported to the U.K. Italy, Spain, and Germany have export performances that are far worse than the French record. Not surprisingly, U.K. moviemakers spend more per film than anywhere else in Europe and rely less on subsidies than their continental counterparts. U.K. producers also have been geared to export for a long time. Given how much of their home market is captured by Hollywood, U.K. features must reap export revenue to turn a profit.[13] . . .

. . .

The Drive Towards Clustering

In part, movie production clusters in particular geographic areas simply because there is no reason *not* to have clustering. When the cost of shipping the relevant goods and services are low, clustering makes economic sense.

Consider a more general economic analogy. There is more trade and mobility across the United States of America than across the disparate countries of Western Europe. This trade causes the economic profiles of the American states to diverge.

In economic terms, the countries of Western Europe are more likely to resemble each other than are the American states. Most of the American states have no steel industry, no automobile industry, and no wheat industry; instead they buy the products of these industries from other states or countries. But typically a nation of western Europe has its own steel, automobile, dairy, and agriculture sectors, largely because of subsidies and protectionism. Free trade within the United States allows states and regions to specialize to a high degree and causes their economic profiles to diverge; in a freer economic environment, the economies of western Europe would take the same path.[14] ....

...

It is not always the case that movies can be *filmed* more cheaply in Hollywood than elsewhere. In fact, Hollywood studio hands are worried about how many movies are being outsourced to Canada, Australia, and other non-U.S. locales, to lower production costs. Rather, clustering eases the finding, lining up, and evaluating of the movie's critical assets, such as stars, directors, and screenplays. These tasks are still done in Hollywood rather than in Vancouver or Sydney, regardless of where the movie is filmed.

The Hollywood cluster has a superior ability to evaluate cinematic projects and, in particular, to forecast and meet consumer demand. Hollywood is the geographic center for these kinds of talent. Ironically, it is easier to get a film made in Europe than America. In Hollywood, studios scrutinize projects intensely and refuse to finance projects that do not have a good chance of commercial success. Most European moviemakers do not apply similar filters. Hollywood is a cluster, in part, for the same reasons that New York and London are clustered banking centers. In both cases talents for large-scale project evaluation gravitate towards a single geographic area.[15]

Moviemaking has become more expensive over the last thirty years, due largely to special effects, rising celebrity salaries, and marketing expenditures. All of these features have increased the natural advantage of talents for demand forecasting and project evaluation. They have increased the natural advantage of Hollywood.

Initial clusters often generate snowball effects, attracting yet more talent to the commercial center. When European directors want to make popular movies, they now go to Hollywood, as we have seen with Ridley Scott, Paul Verhoeven, Bernardo Bertolucci, and Jean-Jacques Annaud, among many others. Initial differences thus become self-cumulating rather than self-reversing.

For this reason, one "turnaround" event can shift a cluster from one local to another. In the case of cinema, the French lost their dominant market position only with the First World War, which caused the major combatants to virtually cease film production for four years. Hollywood stepped into the vacuum and first penetrated world markets on a large scale in the 1920s. The snowball effect shifted the direction of its momentum, and the United States rapidly surpassed the French as the world's largest movie exporter in only a few year's time after the First World War.[16]

Clustering Myths

A common myth is that America dominates world cinematic markets because of its monopoly power. Yet all the primary distributors in Europe are owned by European media groups and regulated by European governments. When the Cineplex Odeon movie theater chain in the United States was Canadian-owned, and for a while jointly Canadian- and British-owned, it made little difference on the screen.

A second myth is that Hollywood dominates because it can sell its movies so cheaply abroad, having recovered their costs in the home market. The claim is that the movie can be dumped abroad, since "it has already been paid for."

This argument does not provide the fundamental reason for America's market share. At most it explains why Hollywood films are booked by cinemas, not why they are so popular with audiences. When European consumers choose whether to see an American or an indigenous production, typically the ticket prices are the same or roughly the same (if anything the American movie might be more costly, all things considered, given time spent waiting in line). The American dominance arises because at equal admission prices, European consumers prefer to see American movies. ...

...

The argument that Hollywood movies have "already been paid for" has another logical flaw. Movies from all countries have already been paid for, once they are made. The fundamental issue is what gets made in the first place, and what then gets shown abroad, and that depends on consumer demand. So many Hollywood movies are made, and with such high levels of funding and marketing, because they can draw large audiences.[17]. ...

...

The correct version of the argument notes that suppliers with a large home or captive market often can afford to make better products. Given their larger built-in audience, they can invest more money in quality, and earn the investment back on ticket sales more easily. Films from Burkina Faso do not have expensive special effects. This argument, however, leads us back to the conclusion that the more expensive movies are better movies, at least in the eyes of the audience, if not always in more objective aesthetic terms. ...

...

American Cultural Imperialism?

When Hollywood penetrates global markets, to what extent is *American* culture being exported? Or is a new global culture being created, above and beyond its specifically American origins? There is no simple answer to this question.

Critics of cultural imperialism make two separate and partially contradictory charges. Some are unhappy with the global spread of the American ethos of commercialism and individualism. Other complaints focus on the strong global-market position of a relatively universal cultural product, rather than local products based on national or particularist inspirations. There is some truth to each complaint, although they point in opposite directions.

If we look at the national identities of the major individuals involved, Hollywood is highly cosmopolitan. Many of the leading Hollywood directors are non-Americans by birth, including Ridley Scott (British) and James Cameron (Canadian), who were among the hottest Hollywood directors circa 2001. Arnold Schwarzenegger, Charlie Chaplin, and Jim Carrey have been among the leading non-American U.S. stars. Most of the major studios are now foreign owned. A typical production will have Sony, a Japanese company, hire a European director to shoot a picture in Canada and then sell the product for global export. Of the world's major entertainment corporations, only Time-Warner is predominantly American in ownership.

For better or worse, Hollywood strives to present the universal to global audiences. As Hollywood markets its films to more non-English speakers, those films become more general. Action films are favored over movies with subtle dialogue. Comedy revolves around slapstick rather than verbal puns. The larger the audience, of course, the more universal the product or celebrity must be. There is relatively little that the world as a whole, or even a select group of fifty million global consumers, can agree on. Greater universality means that the movies are relevant to general features of the human condition, but it also can bring blandness and formulaic treatment. Critics allege that American culture is driving the world, but in reality the two are determined simultaneously, and by the same set of forces.

Non-American movies, when they pursue foreign markets, must strive for universality as well. The Jackie Chan Hong Kong movie *Rumble in the Bronx* was marketed in the United States with success. The producers, however, cut parts of the movie to appeal to American audiences. All of the action sequences were kept, but the relationship of Chan with the co-star was diminished, in part because the woman (Anita Mui) was a star in Asia but not in the United States, and in part because the relationship was based on the "Chinese" values of obligation and loyalty, rather than on a Western sense of erotic romance.[18]. ...

...

Despite these powerful universalist forces, the American and national component to Hollywood moviemaking cannot be ignored. Hollywood has always drawn on the national ethos of the United States for cinematic inspiration. The American values of heroism, individualism, and romantic self-fulfillment are well suited for the large screen and for global audiences. It is true that Hollywood will make whatever will sell abroad. ...

...

For this reason, dominant cultures, such as the United States, have an advantage in exporting their values and shaping the preferences of other nations. Consider food markets. Many Third World citizens like to eat at McDonald's, not just because the food tastes good to them, but also because McDonald's is a visible symbol of the West and the United States. When they walk through the doors of a McDonald's, they are entering a different world. The McDonald's corporation, knowing this, designs its Third World interiors to reflect the glamour of Western commerce, much as a shopping mall would. McDonald's shapes its product to meet global demands, but builds on the American roots of the core concept. The McDonald's image and product lines have been refined in the American domestic market and draw heavily on American notions of the relation between food and social life.

The promulgated American ethos will, of course, successfully meld both national and cosmopolitan influences, and will not be purely

American in any narrow sense. American cinema, like American cuisine, has been a synthetic, polyglot product from the beginning. Hollywood was developed largely by foreigners – Jewish immigrants from Eastern Europe – and was geared towards entertaining American urban audiences, which were drawn from around the world.

Furthermore, Hollywood's universality has, in part, *become* a central part of American national culture. Commercial forces have led America to adopt "that which can be globally sold" as part of its national culture. Americans have decided to emphasize their international triumphs and their ethnic diversity as part of their national self-image. In doing so, Americans have, to some extent, traded away particularist strands of their culture for success in global markets.

In this regard Hollywood's global-market position is a Faustian bargain. Achieving global dominance requires a sacrifice of a culture's initial perspective to the demands of world consumers. American culture is being exported, but for the most part it is not Amish quilts and Herman Melville. *Jurassic Park*, a movie about dinosaurs, was a huge hit abroad, but *Forrest Gump*, which makes constant reference to American history and national culture, made most of its money at home.

The Virtues of Living at the Margins

Hollywood's export success shapes the cinematic market. First and most prominently, it finances spectacular, blockbuster productions. While many of these productions are aesthetically mediocre, others are excellent, though few critics agree on which are the good ones. Clearly, to the extent we use audience preferences as the relevant standard of value, Hollywood succeeds.

In addition to these blockbusters, the financial success of the industry supports diversity. Not all Hollywood products fit the "least common denominator" model. Hollywood puts out a wide range of independent releases, creative comedies, and films that do not fit any easily identifiable category. The late 1990s have in particular were renowned for the wide variety of high quality, non-mainstream fare coming out of Hollywood.

"Microbudget" films are far more common in the United States than in Europe. A microbudget film is one made by a previously amateur director on a minuscule budget, typically less than $100,000. Among the best-known microfilms are Spike Lee's *She's Gotta Have It*, the Coen brothers' *Blood Simple*, and *The Blair Witch Project*. All of these innovative projects have been made under director control and liberated from the constraints of studio production.

It is no accident that Hollywood has both the largest studio apparatus and the greatest number of microbudget films. Building a film industry of any kind requires a regular supply of popular product. A healthy commercial base is needed to support an infrastructure of theaters, production companies, film schools, and marketing institutions. Independent or innovative filmmakers benefit from this infrastructure just as the major studios do.

The major studios typically seek to buy out and "corrupt" the independent filmmakers, and in this sense the two cinematic worlds are always at war with each other. But in a larger sense they are complements. The mainstream desire to commercialize the independents helps finance their existence. Directors invest their money in microbudget films in part because they have a chance of receiving a subsequent contract from a major studio. Such contracts bring both money and the resources to film their larger visions. In addition to the Coen brothers and Spike Lee, Francis Coppola, Peter Bogdanovich, Martin Scorsese, Jonathan Demme, David Lynch, Sam Raimi, John Sayles, and Jim Jarmusch all first made their names with micro-budget films. The directors of *The Blair Witch Project* were courted for a Hollywood sequel, which earned them millions, despite its low quality. Hollywood studios, whatever their conservatism and their flaws, are always looking for the "next hot thing." If they can find a microbudget production that is marketable, they will seek to co-opt it, but in the meantime they are providing the "prizes" that drive the independent market.

European studios, in contrast, never expect high returns from projects, and thus they adopt a more conservative attitude. Notable European directors such as Godard, Bertolucci, Truffaut, Besson, and Pasolini found their start with microbudget films, but the overall commercial weakness of European cinema is making those kinds of opportunities harder to find and exploit.[19]

It is not altogether bad that European cinema lacks the export promise of Hollywood. While commercial improvement would undoubtedly benefit European cinema, diversity would not be served by a fully "level playing field" in the industry. The dirty little secret of today's cinematic world is the following: the very features of the film industry behind American export dominance also have supported diversity of style around the globe.

The global prowess of Hollywood means that European moviemakers pursue different markets and produce different kinds of creativity. Many of the interesting qualities of European movies come precisely from their *inability* to reach world markets on a large scale. Shut out of world markets, European movies have been able to focus on nuances of language and culture. They typically do not have happy but superficial endings, opting, rather, for something more interesting. The non-Hollywood productions that have success abroad, such as *Four Weddings and a Funeral* or *Like Water for Chocolate*, often have many of the flaws that plague mainstream Hollywood releases: saccharine, cliched characters or an unrealistically happy ending. ...

...

Similarly, the creativity of Hong Kong moviemaking in the 1980s would not have been possible had those pictures been geared to export to American and Europe, rather than the smaller and more specialized Southeast Asian market. The Hong Kong movie *Dr. Lamb* was a success in the Hong Kong market of the 1990s. The movie was explicitly patterned after *Silence of the Lambs*, a U.S. and global hit in 1992, but the two movies could not be more different in tone. *Silence of the Lambs* plays up its two celebrities, Jodie Foster and Anthony Hopkins, and gives them a strong, caricatured presence in the movie. They engage in witty repartee and are made into glamorous figures. The last segment of the movie plays the viewer for mechanical suspense, as Jodie Foster chases down another serial killer. *Dr. Lamb* is a far scarier entry. It never plays the viewer for suspense but, instead, reveals its denouement at the beginning. The killer is a sullen and nasty figure, rather than the charismatic and articulate Anthony Hopkins playing Hannibal Lecter. We see the killer dismembering his victims, indulging his perverse fetishes, and having brutal arguments with his family. There is no feeling of resolution offered at the end; rather, the viewer is left feeling uneasy. Not surprisingly, *Dr. Lamb* has never been released in the U.S. market.

The Future of Global Cinema

It remains an open question whether Hollywood will gain or lose relative market position over the next few years. European cinema does show some encouraging signs. In the year 2000, for instance, French films captured 60 percent of their domestic market, the most in twenty years, largely because of a few hit comedies. More generally, most of the major Western European countries are relying less on subsidies to support their culture. None have cut their movie industries loose, but the long-run trend appears to lie in this direction.[20]

European governments are understandably reluctant to remove cinematic subsidies. Once the dynamic of Hollywood export superiority is in place, most European productions, as we know them, cannot survive without governmental assistance. In the short run, laissez-faire would likely lead to a greater Hollywood presence in European cinema. But in the long run, European moviemakers would be induced to make a more commercially appealing product, and not necessarily at the expense of artistic quality. The natural European advantage is in making art-house films, not blockbusters or special-effects spectaculars.

Hollywood holds a potentially vulnerable market position, given how much it spends on celebrity salaries and marketing. While these expenses give Hollywood movies a huge global boost, they also mean that American moviemakers have lost their ability to control their costs, often a sign of forthcoming commercial weakness. Witness the history of the once-dominant American auto industry. Digital technology also promises to open up moviemaking to outsiders, by lowering the costs of production.

The history of cinema shows many times over that a truly great movie can be made for very small sums of money. Films of this kind may not outdraw *Titanic* at the box office, but they could resuscitate cinema in the countries where it is currently floundering. Of course it remains an open question whether European moviemakers will fill this market niche, or whether Asia has already beaten them to it.

Nonetheless it is possible for Europeans to reverse unfavorable trends, as they have in the past. In 1973, Hollywood held only 23 percent of the Italian market, and large numbers of high-quality Italian movies were commercially viable. Hollywood had dominated the Italian market after the Second World War, but Italian moviemakers fought back, in part using the techniques they learned from studying Hollywood releases.[21]

Ideally, European governments would like to return to something like the 1930–1970 period. These years show that the strong presence of Hollywood in world markets does not mean an end to European movie-making.

After the Second World War, European movies typically did receive subsidies, but of a much smaller magnitude than today. Martin Dale estimates that in 1960 subsidies accounted for only 20 percent of the average European film, compared to his current estimate of 70 percent. The notable movies of Truffaut, Fellini, Visconti, Bergman, and others were fundamentally money-making endeavors, aimed at the competitive marketplace, despite the involvement of government at various levels.[22]

Going back earlier, the 1930s in particular were a "golden age" for French cinema; the best-known French films of this era include *L'Atalante* (Jean Vigo), *Le Jour se lève* (Marcel Carné), *La Chienne, The Grand Illusion*, and *The Rules of the Game* (all by Jean Renoir). Over thirteen hundred

French feature films were issued, covering a wide range of genres. During this period, French cinema received no government subsidies. The legal restrictions on American films were insignificant and did not keep Hollywood productions out of the French market.[23]

In the early silent era, France dominated world cinema markets. Before the First World War, French movies accounted for up to seventy percent of the American market, and even more in Latin America. In a reversal of contemporary trends, American filmmakers charged the French with cultural imperialism and asked Washington for trade protection. It was commonly charged that European movies encouraged lax morals and corrupted American culture. The French responded by noting the openness of their cinematic markets and asking America to compete on equal terms. Like Hollywood today, the French market dominance was achieved without significant subsidies from the French government.[24]

Global cinema is in any case flourishing today, most of all in Asia. As for European cinema, its best hope is to rediscover an economic and cultural dynamic that combines both commercialism and creativity. Such a dynamic will require reliance on international markets and global capital, and is unlikely to flourish in a narrowly protectionist setting. The marketplace never guarantees a favorable result, but excessive insulation from competitive pressures can virtually guarantee an unfavorable result, whether economically or aesthetically.

Notes

1 On cultural clustering generally, see Kroeber (1969); Porter (1990) and Hall (1998) provide a more modern treatment. The phenomenon was first noted by the Roman writer Velleius Paterculus (1967 [A.D. 30]).
2 On the increase of American revenue in Europe, see Puttnam (1998, p. 266).
3 On western Europe, see Ilott (1996, p. 14).
4 On the growing differential, see Dale (1997, p. 119).
5 See Ilott (1996, p. 27), and Dale (1997, p. 31).
6 See Kaes (1997, p. 614), Dunnett (1990, p. 43), Noam (1991, p. 59), and Dissanayake (1988, p. 16).
7 See Rifkin (2000, p. 25) on the timing of the decline in America. On the 1955 statistic, see Caves (2000, p. 94).
8 For details on European television regulations, see Grantham (2000, chap. 4), Dale (1997, p. 119), and Noam (1991, pp. 107, 112).
9 On Hong Kong cinema, see Bordwell (2000, pp. 1, 34, passim).
10 See Bordwell (2000, p. 1).

11   Segrave (1997, p. 74; Usabel 1982, pp. 80–82).

12   See, for instance, Puttnam (1998, p. 113) on how sound boosted the English export sectors in its early years.

13   Ilott (1996, pp. 14, 28).

14   Note that clustering will tend to maintain distinct regional ethoses as well, by giving each area a different economic and thus social flavor.

15   The above analysis draws on Ilott (1996).

16   See Krugman (1979, 1980) on the operation of snowball effects.

17   We do find some times when American films are plentiful in a country but do not draw so many viewers. Germany in the 1950s provides one example (Garncarz 1994, p. 101), but this case is an exception to the general state of affairs. For other criticisms of this explanation for Hollywood domination, see Noam (1991, pp. 12–20).

18   See Fore (1997, p. 250).

19   See Dale (1997, p. 243).

20   On the recent French success, see A. James (2001).

21   See Muscio (2000, p. 127).

22   See Dale (1997, p. 123).

23   See Crisp (1993, p. 12), Andrew (1983, p. 57), Hayes (1930, pp. 194–95), and Sklar (1975, p. 222). Quotas limited American films to seven-eighths of the market, which was more than the American share had ever been. Gomery (1985, p. 31) argues that French quotas, which were enforced in a changing and complex manner, had some effects on American exports, but even in his account the effect is a small one, limiting Hollywood exports by no more than 15 percent.

24   On early French dominance, see Abel (1999), Pearson (1997, p. 23), Roud (1993, p. 7), Armes (1985, pp. 19–23), and Abel (1984, p. 6; 1994). On the plea for government assistance, see Puttnam (1998, p. 41).

Documents

Introduction to Documents

As Hollywood permeated more and more of the world media market, foreign governments moved to limit what they saw as the negative effect of American culture – American cultural imperialism as some called it – by imposing quotas on the import of American films and television shows. In our first document, several prominent movie industry leaders testify to Congress about the globalization of entertainment and the impact of American film on European culture. Our second document features a summary of global box-office statistics for 2011 that were released by the Motion Picture Association of America.

Testimony Before Congressional Hearings on Television Broadcasting and the European Community

Source: Hearing Before the Subcommittee on Telecomunications and Finance of the Committee on Energy and Commerce, House of Representatives, July 26, 1989

Testimony of Jack Valenti, President and Chief Executive Officer, Motion Picture Association of America

Why this quota? Its defenders, those who would build the siege walls, claim that "Our culture is at stake." Can this really be true? Is the culture of a nation to wither with 80 percent, 50 percent, or 15 percent of American programming? Is there a line to be drawn wherein a national culture is safe from intrusion by non-Europeans? Has the culture of any European country collapsed or eroded over the last fifteen or so years? Is the culture of any European country so flimsily anchored, so tenuously rooted, that European consumers and viewers must be caged and blinded else their links with their historic and distinguished past suddenly vanish, like an exploding star in the heavens?

Statement of Robert Maxwell, Chairman, Maxwell Communications

No nation should tolerate its culture being subjugated by a foreign one. This is an extremely sensitive issue with European nations. This cannot be put into the category with beef and automotive products. This issue speaks to the hearts of cultural integrity. European citizens will not sit in the parlors watching their cultures being replaced by Hollywood, Mexico City, or Tokyo.

Statement of Richard Frank, President, Walt Disney Studios

The good news is that 1992 will mark the end of national barriers in Western Europe. The bad news is that 1992 will mark the end of national barriers in Western Europe. At Disney we've had firsthand experience with this schizophrenic view of the recent evolution of the European community. ...

The television without frontiers directive is only the latest wall of protection that's been proposed in an apparent effort to turn Europe into an economic fortress. ... Let me give you just a few examples. Stations in France are prohibited from airing more than 192 movies a year, and only 40 of these can be produced in non-EC nations. In other words, every station in France, including the largest, TF-1, is limited to broadcasting a maximum of just 76 American films a year.

Compare this to the smallest station in Italy, RAI-3, which last year had a total of 409 films, 232 of which were American. A full 57 percent. This is all the more remarkable because RAI-3 is controlled by the Communist Party. The number of films shown on Italy's six stations last year totaled 3,645. In Germany, over 3,000 movies were broadcast. In both these nations American films consistently rank among the top 10 weekly shows. This is what happens when markets are allowed to be free and open with decisions being based on what people want to see and not what some self-appointed guardians of culture think they should see. ...

If television with frontiers is adopted, you can be certain cinema without frontiers, and home video without frontiers will soon follow. Of course, the stated rationale for these quotas is to stave off American cultural imperialism. All we want is a fair shot at selling our product in a free and open marketplace. The flip side of the cultural imperialism argument is the argument that quotas are needed to protect the local culture. This, too, is a sham. ...

We should not focus exclusively on matters of economics. This issue involves not just entertainment, but also ideas. American films and TV shows are just that, American. They show our country and what it stands for, from our highest ideals to our gravest challenges. The power of film cannot be underestimated. I won't be so bold as to say that American movies are responsible for the popular uprising in China. But I am willing to bet that for more than a few Chinese citizens our films served as an inspiration to strike for something better.

Statement of William A. Shields, Chairman, American Film Marketing Association

Our basic tenet is that quotas artificially imposed will destroy freedom of choice and inhibit the open exchange of ideas. They are anathema to the tradition of democracy – a fundamental value Western Europe shares with us. ... The impending globalization of the entertainment industry – fewer and bigger companies – along with quotas, will limit the ability of the smaller independent companies to survive and compete. .... If this globalization and the problem quotas prevail, there is no doubt that movies such as "Platoon," "The Last Emperor," the "Rambos" and "The Name of the Rose," to mention just a few, would never have been made. These scripts were rejected by the majors but were financed by bold and daring independent entrepreneurs who believed the public – in various countries around the world – would respond to their vision.

American culture, including motion pictures and television, have become international. Whether it's Coca-Cola or blue jeans, "Platoon" or "Dallas," people not governments should be given the right to accept or reject whatever product – filmed or otherwise – to which they are exposed. The box office is the best barometer for acceptance or rejection. If the audience doesn't want it, they'll tell us. That's the way it is and that's the way it should be.

Global Box Office Climb Continues in 2011

Source: Motion Picture Association of America, Inc. report released March 22, 2012, www.mpaa.org/resources/9308dcf8-c857-4fbe-89e0-0255d193488b.pdf (last accessed August 2013)

WASHINGTON – The Motion Picture Association of America, Inc. (MPAA) today released its annual Theatrical Market Statistics Report for 2011. The report shows that global box office receipts for all films released around the world reached $32.6 billion, an increase of 3% over 2010, due to ongoing growth of box office in international markets. Each international region experienced box office growth in 2011. Chinese box office grew by 35% in 2011 alone, by far the largest growth in major markets.

"These numbers underscore the impact of movies on the global economy and the vitality of the film-watching experience around the world," said Senator Chris Dodd, Chairman and CEO of the MPAA. "The bottom line is clear: people in all countries still go to the movies and a trip to the local cinema remains one of the most affordable entertainment options for consumers."

"The figures on box office reflect only one indicator of an extremely complex, and evolving movie industry," Dodd said. "We're working harder and smarter to keep moviegoers coming back for more, whether at the cinema, at home or on the go." The U.S./Canada box office market finished at $10.2 billion, down 4% compared to last year, but up 6% from 5 years ago. 3D box office was down $400 million in 2011 in comparison to 2010, which is not surprising given that 2010 included Avatar's record-breaking 3D box office performance. 2D box office remained consistent from 2010 to 2011.

Cinema ticket sales continue to be fueled by repeated visits by frequent moviegoers – those who go to the movies once a month or more. Frequent moviegoers represent only 10% of the population but purchased half of all tickets sold in 2011.

Globally, cinema screens increased by 3% in 2011. Digital cinema continues its rapid growth so that just over half of the world's screens are now digital. The number of digital screens in the U.S. nearly doubled in 2011, now comprising 65% of all U.S. screens.

"Global box office continues to grow nicely as new markets develop," said John Fithian, President of the National Association of Theatre Owners (NATO). "In mature markets such as the United States the business can be more cyclical in the short term, driven by product supply and distribution patterns. In the long term, however, domestic receipts continue to grow. Though 2011 U.S. box office was down 4%, 2012 looks to be another growth year. Box office is up nearly 14% year-to-date so far in 2012, with a strong slate of summer movies coming."

"Innovation and technology continue to be a driving force for our business," Dodd said. "People are driven to fill theater seats by the promise of great films and a great, technologically enhanced movie going experience. But online content theft continues to threaten the economic success of our industry – an industry that employs millions of Americans and brings money into the U.S. economy from around the world. We should protect that success, not undermine it by stealing products and cutting the revenue it puts into the U.S. economy."

Readings and Screenings

The starting points for those interested in learning more about the early globalization of Hollywood are Ruth Vasey, *The World According to Hollywood, 1918–1939* (Madison: University of Wisconsin Press, 1997); Kristin Thompson, *Exporting Entertainment: America in the World Film Market 1907–1934* (London: BFI Press, 1985); Ian Jarvie, *Hollywood's Overseas Campaign: The North Atlantic Movie Trade, 1920–1950*

(Cambridge, UK: Cambridge University Press, 1992); John Trumpbour, *Selling Hollywood to the World: U.S. and European Struggles for Mastery of the Global Film Industry* (Cambridge, UK: Cambridge University Press, 2007). For a brief overview of Euro-American relations, see Chapter 3, "The Star System: How Hollywood Turned Cinema Culture into Entertainment Value," in Victoria de Grazia, *Irresistible Empire: America's Advance Through Twentieth-Century Europe* (Cambridge, MA: Harvard University Press, 2005). The multi-faceted nature of globalization is discussed in Frank J. Lechner and John Boll, eds, *The Globalization Reader*, 4th edition, (Malden, MA: Wiley-Blackwell, 2011). There is now a spate of books dealings with the globalization of American cinema. The most accessible works include Paul McDonald and Janet Wasko, eds, *The Contemporary Hollywood Film Industry* (Malden, MA: Wiley-Blackwell, 2008); Wheeler Dixon, *21st Century Hollywood* (New Brunswick, NJ: Rutgers University Press, 2011); Toby Miller, Nitin Govil, John McMurria, Ting Wang, and Richard Maxwell, *Global Hollywood: No. 2* (London: British Film Institute, 2nd edition, 2008); Geoffrey Nowell-Smith and Steven Ricci, eds., *Hollywood and Europe: Economics, Culture, National Identity, 1945–95* (London: BFI Publishing, 1998); Steve Neale and Murray Smith, eds, *Contemporary Hollywood Cinema* (London and New York: Routledge, 1998); Peter Lev, *The Euro-American Cinema* (Austin, TX: University of Texas Press, 1993); Ann Cvetkovich and Douglas Kellner, eds., *Articulating the Global and the Local: Globalization and Cultural Studies* (Boulder, CO: Westview Press, 1997). The reception of Hollywood films by non-American audiences is surveyed in Melvyn Stokes and Richard Maltby, eds, *Hollywood Abroad: Audiences and Cultural Exchange* (London: British Film Institute, 2008); for blockbusters that appeal to worldwide audiences, see Geoff King, *Spectacular Narratives: Hollywood in the Age of the Blockbuster* (London: I. B. Tauris, 2001).

Although there are no films about the globalization of Hollywood per se, there are a number of productions that fit into the category of transnational films, either because of their financing, director, writer, stars, or marketing strategy. For prominent examples of such hybrid productions see *Independence Day* (1996), *Starship Troopers* (1997), *Face/Off* (1997), *Kung Fu Hustle* (2004), and *Babel* (2006). For a comprehensive list of feature films and documentaries that deal with various aspect of the globalized world, see Tom Zaniello, *The Cinema of Globalization: A Guide to Films About the New Economic Order* (Ithaca, NY: Cornell University Press, 2007).

Index

Movies and American Society, Second Edition. Edited by Steven J. Ross.
© 2014 John Wiley & Sons, Inc. Published 2014 by John Wiley & Sons, Inc.